P9-DMC-458

DATE DUE

JUN 1 0 1967

THE TRYING-OUT OF
MOBY-DICK

Property of Arkansas Library Commission
506½ Center Street
Little Rock, Arkansas

Cutting-in and Trying-out

Trying-out is the process of boiling oil from the blubber.

THE
TRYING-OUT
OF
MOBY-DICK

Howard P. Vincent

SOUTHERN ILLINOIS UNIVERSITY PRESS

CARBONDALE AND EDWARDSVILLE

Copyright © 1949 by HOWARD P. VINCENT
Reprinted by special arrangement with Howard P. Vincent
All rights reserved
Arcturus Books® edition, October 1965
Library of Congress Catalog Card Number 65–12397
This edition manufactured by offset lithography
in the United States of America

To Mary, Judith, and John

Acknowledgments

> "And certainly there were many others . . .
> from whom I had assimilated a word, a
> glance, but of whom as individual beings I
> remembered nothing; a book is a great
> cemetery in which, for the most part, the
> names upon the tombs are effaced."
>
> MARCEL PROUST, *Time Regained*

A STUDY extending over five years of research and writing, *The Trying-Out of Moby-Dick* has been written in several libraries and in correspondence and conversation with many friends. To all who have helped me I express my gratitude. Specifically and especially, however, the libraries of Illinois Institute of Technology, George Williams College, American Museum of Natural History, Chicago Natural History Museum, Newberry Library of Chicago, University of Chicago, John Crerar Library of Chicago, Boston Public Library, Library of Congress, and Harvard College have patiently and promptly met my many requests for services.

The unselfish help and advice of John Birss, Harriet Hale, Leon Howard, Henry Murray, Egbert Oliver, Gordon Roper, and Merton Sealts have made my work far better than it would otherwise have been. Mr. Perc Brown of Montclair, New Jersey, generously allowed me to examine Melville's copies of Beale's *Natural History of the Sperm Whale* and Chase's *Narrative of the Sinking of the Whaleship Essex,* two of many treasures in his library. My debt to Harrison Hayford of Northwestern University is enormous; by reading my manuscript he has helped me to avoid many errors of fact as well as of interpretation, especially in the chapter "The Breaching of Moby-Dick." And climactically, it is no scholarly cliché but a matter of record that my first, last, and deepest debt is to my wife; without her continual assistance and encouragement this book would not have been tried-out.

HOWARD P. VINCENT

Chicago, 1949.

Author's Note

PRACTICALLY ALL the footnotes in this volume are informational in intent, not referential. Since there was no acceptable scholarly edition of *Moby-Dick* available at the time that this book was written, and since the first American edition, from which I quote, is to be found in the major libraries only, referential footnotes for all quotations from *Moby-Dick* would have been of no real help. But since all chapter numbers have been indicated in the text — at that point where the chapter is the main theme — it is a comparatively simple matter to find the quotation from any unabridged edition of *Moby-Dick*, most of the chapters being extremely short. Furthermore, there is in preparation at the present moment an edition of *Moby-Dick* as part of the *Collected Works of Herman Melville,* and that volume will contain elaborate footnotes in which the original sources will be cited *in extenso* so that the scholar need not possess copies of Scoresby, Beale, Bennett, etc., to have the precise paginal information and citation. Reference notes for general quotations are not necessary since the quotations are either familiar (as those from Eliot and James) or the source of them is of secondary importance — their meaning being what matters. The chapter on "The Cetological Center" considers succinctly the necessary bibliographical details concerning Melville's chief sources.

The use of the hyphen in all references to *Moby-Dick* the book, and the omission of the hyphen in all references to the whale, are in accordance with Melville's own example.

Contents

I.

Loomings

IN 1841 A DISTRICT SCHOOLMASTER near Albany, having no money in his purse and nothing particular to interest him on shore, decided that the best way to drive the November drizzle from his soul was to "sail about a little and see the watery part of the world." As an ordinary sailor he explored the mysterious paradises of the South Seas and searched the Pacific Ocean for spermaceti whales. Nine years later the same man, a Berkshire farmer and well-known author, ventured those seas again, this time traveling by mind and this time searching for one sperm whale in particular. *The Trying-Out of Moby-Dick* is a study of Herman Melville's transformation of the *Acushnet* Melville into the *Pequod* Ishmael, the transformation of actuality into truth which produced the whaling classic, *Moby-Dick*. "A strange process too, this," said Emerson, "by which experience is converted into thought, as a mulberry leaf is converted into satin. The manufacture goes on at all hours."

At the time when *Moby-Dick* was launched, in 1851, few Americans attended the ceremony; and they were not lavish in their praise nor very intelligent in their criticism. Generally, those who saw *Moby-Dick* sail into the sea of books contented themselves with disapproving comments as to her unseaworthiness.[1] Not long after, they forgot her. Melville

[1] *Moby-Dick*, however, did not meet with neglect, like *The Confidence-Man*, nor with contempt, like *Pierre*. At least two reviewers showed real understanding of the meaning and the merit of the book (cf. *Harper's New Monthly Magazine*, IV (December, 1851), 137; and *Bentley's Miscellany*, XXXI (January, 1852), 104–105. But the general misunderstanding and the numerous critical qualifications compared strangely with the hosannas which, in general, had greeted *Typee, Omoo, Redburn,* and *White-Jacket*. See H. W. Hetherington, *The Reputation of Herman Melville in America* (University of Michigan Ph.D. thesis, 1933), and David Potter, "Reviews of *Moby-Dick*," *Journal of Rutgers University Library*, III (June, 1940), 62–85 (who concludes that *Moby-Dick* had a moderate success).

stoically accepted the verdict of his contemporaries, and, after a few more attempts to win back his public, retired into the depths of his own brooding mind, while the last thirty years of his life wore away in the obscurity of New York City. As a writer he had early discovered what Henry Adams later discerned, that "America has always taken tragedy lightly." At the close of his life, indulging in a humorously grim commentary upon his fate, Melville addressed a short poem to his early writings, his "Children of my earlier prime," proudly and ironically reminding them that since they had not been delivered up to mediocrity, their integrity determined that they must lie peacefully "snugged in the arms of eternal night."

Posterity, however, refused the consignment to oblivion. Throughout sixty years of general neglect in America, discerning readers in England read the novels and enthusiastically praised them. In shameful contrast confirming the adage about a prophet's lack of honor in his own country, Melville's fellow Americans failed for many years to recognize their compatriot's genius. In England, Viola Meynell could write in 1920: "Herman Melville satisfies not only every judgment but every inmost preference; so that it seems as if no greatness that has ever been surpasses his greatness" — perceptive, bold words which at that time found no echo in America. Not until publication of Raymond Weaver's pioneer biography, *Herman Melville: Mariner and Mystic* (1921), was there a large public response to the name and the novels of Melville. Since then, however, general reader interest has snowballed to tremendous proportions. Today the students of American letters pursue the mysteries of Melville's life and of his writings. Learned and literary quarterlies now devote a high percentage of space to Melville studies; the bibliography of Melville is now a good-sized volume in itself.[2] First editions of *Moby-Dick* which thirty years ago sold from fifty cents to two dollars now bring anywhere from a hundred dollars up. Even Hollywood has

---

[2] Dr. John Birss of New York University is preparing this much needed work.

profitably pawed two of the novels, and the rugged, scarred face of Ahab has appeared on the screen in the romantic profile of John Barrymore. In short, readers everywhere have discovered Melville, or at least *Moby-Dick*. Serious critics, recognizing his greatness, name him as the single American author worthy of a place among the great world writers, one of the few American writers whose genius transcends national boundaries. Melville is unquestionably the phoenix of American letters.

Even among the enthusiasts, however, it has not long been the fashion to regard Melville as a great artist. For too many decades the critics, applying their precise rules, decreed that Melville was a *lusus naturae,* an artless teller of tales who wrote as instinctively as the whale spouted. According to these oracles, *Moby-Dick* and *White-Jacket* were unforgettable stories of sea life, but woefully defective in structure and style. Conceding that *Moby-Dick* was a masterpiece, the critics nevertheless felt that it was a blunder into greatness: the narrative sprawled, the characters were unreal or abnormal, the whaling details overloaded the story, and the metaphysical and symbolical ambiguities were Gothic excess. They felt that a book so full of faults could not be great — and yet, they had to admit greatness for *Moby-Dick* despite their rules.

Melville, a master ironist, would have appreciated this crowning irony — his book called both great and inartistic. For if anything is obvious, it is the fact that a work of art — a sonnet, a novel, a play, a song, a painting — can be great only in fulfillment of the fundamental requirements, dynamic as well as static, of a work of art. The syllogism covering the situation is valid and is built on sound premises: A great novel is *ipso facto* a work of art; *Moby-Dick* is a great novel; therefore, *Moby-Dick* must be a work of art. *Quod erat demonstrandum.*

The critical confusion probably lay in the inflexible application of irrelevant canons, of critical standards suitable to the delicate miniatures of *Pride and Prejudice* but not applicable to the great canvas of *Moby-Dick*. Form follows function. If judicious, one does not apply identical standards to the quatrain and the ode, to the Gothic cathedral and the Greek temple, to *Moby-Dick* and *Omoo*.

First of the serious studies to treat Melville's compositional procedures was Charles R. Anderson's *Melville in the South Seas* (1939), a detailed study of the materials which Melville consulted in writing *Typee, Omoo*, and *White-Jacket*.[3] Massing the evidence, Anderson showed how carefully and how deftly Melville adapted many details from travel books to insure accuracy and authenticity for his own narratives of travel. Always, as Anderson pointed out, Melville transformed his borrowings with such skill that the charge of plagiarism is inadmissible. Melville's "artless" tales turn out to be patterned travel narrative, instead of the spontaneous outpourings of a flooded memory.

Anderson also showed that Melville's consciousness of craft increased from novel to novel. For example, the alterations of source material discernible in *Typee* are fewer and more superficial than those to be noted in *White-Jacket*, which was written four years later. As Melville's mind matured so did his technique. *Typee* is a Burton Holmes travelogue in technicolor, delightfully simple, vernally fresh. *White-Jacket* is also a documentary film (not unlike *Fighting Lady*), telling with hard, straightforward detail the life on board an American naval vessel. Moreover, woven into *White-Jacket*, and giving it complexity and depth not seen before in Melville, are two important themes: man's inhumanity to man, and the dignity and worth of each and every individual man. Such a complex book was consciously designed and deftly executed.[4] As Melville himself changed from "the idle singer of an empty day" into an artist of deep compassion and savage indignation, his growth as a man was

[3] The excellent spadework of R. S. Forsythe should not be overlooked: "Herman Melville in Honolulu," *New England Quarterly*, VIII (March, 1935), 99–105; "Herman Melville in the Marquesas," *Philological Quarterly*, XV (January, 1936), 1–15; and "Herman Melville in Tahiti," *Philological Quarterly*, XVI (October, 1937), 344–357.

[4] In classifying *Typee, Omoo, Redburn*, and *White-Jacket* as reportage, and then in alluding to the new depth of *White-Jacket* there is no fundamental inconsistency. Of course Melville's work deepened with the passing years; only, the *conscious* attempt in those novels, as he says in more than one place, was to do journeyman work. *Moby-Dick* and *Mardi* are deliberate attempts to work in another mode.

accompanied by an equivalent and necessary growth as a literary artist.

Other scholars have more briefly studied the sources of Melville's writing, but all have carefully left *Moby-Dick* alone. Why this shyness? Source hunters are usually bold. Have they felt that Melville's frankness in acknowledging indebtedness to "my numerous fish documents" was sufficient? Or have they neglected *Moby-Dick* because of its vastness, the complexity with which many strands are woven into the pattern? Whatever their reasons, they have neglected *Moby-Dick*, resting content with criticism and interpretation,[5] so that no one has yet tried-out the sources of Melville's masterpiece.

The Trying-Out of Moby-Dick, therefore, combines a study of the whaling sources of *Moby-Dick* with an account of its composition, and suggestions concerning interpretation and meaning.

In dealing with the whaling sources an attempt has been made to discover the materials, literary and biographical, from which Melville tryed-out his whaling epic. Unfortunately, no man has yet devised a technique of analysis and comparison delicate enough to determine decisively in what proportion a work of art has been created from life experience or from a literary document, or how far native imagination has amended and expanded experience. A work of art is built out of incidents and events from anywhere in the entire life of the artist. No one writes from a *tabula rasa* mind; even when most "original" one creates esthetic and moral truth from the flotsam and jetsam of the past — either his own lived past, or the record and report of another's. As Goethe told Eckermann, "There is through all art a filiation. If you see a great master, you will always find that he used what was good in his predecessors, and that it was this which made him great."

The study of source materials is but the beginning for

---

5 Probably the finest and most detailed criticism of *Moby-Dick* is that by William Ellery Sedgwick, *Herman Melville: The Tragedy of Mind* (Cambridge, Mass., 1944), and F. O. Matthiessen, *American Renaissance* (New York, etc., 1941).

criticism. "Scholars," said Thoreau perceptively, "are wont to sell their birthright for a mess of learning." Sources are of secondary importance; the text itself must be primary in our attention. The fundamental meanings of a work of art may be learned by direct study of the work itself. Therefore, *The Trying-Out* does more than list source materials; it attempts to show Melville's artistic enrichment of mundane fact; and it moves on further to suggest the universal meanings of *Moby-Dick*. *The Trying-Out*, then, interprets the novel in its parts and in its entirety. It moves from the safe shore of source-hunting through the shoals of interpretation.[6] But the tender-minded need not fear for *Moby-Dick*, remembering Amiel's words: "A work of art withstands all interpretations; it is adequate to them and it survives them; rich and complex like the idea which it is."

Moby-Dick is rich and complex above any other novel in American literature. With a boldness of plan and a breadth of scope unequaled since the Renaissance, with a wealth of unusual experience in the worlds of the familiar and the unfamiliar, with a penetrating understanding of the significance inherent in the varied phenomena of its age, and with a vigor of animal spirits which sweeps all before it, *Moby-Dick* brings into magnificent focus the emergent forces of the western world. *Moby-Dick*, so complex as to be many things to many men, has been interpreted as a satire of nineteenth-century finance capitalism, as a vast nature myth like *Beowulf*, as an allegory of Man's search for Paradise — or simply as a narrative of the sea and nothing more. To these and other interpretations it may be further added that *Moby-Dick* is a satire of New England Transcendentalism, a criticism of American social and ethical thought, a condemnation of brutalizing materialism, and an affirmation of the dignity and nobility of Man. *Moby-Dick* is all of these, but none exclusively, for in stressing any one part we neglect others — such the penalty of partial analysis. A psychological penetration into the American spirit, *Moby-Dick* is at once

---

[6] And even touches on the artist himself, despite Freud's warning: "Unfortunately, before the problem of the creative artist, analysis must lay down its arms."

the expression of all the thoughts and feelings of 1851 America [7] put into a vigorous, sweeping style well fitted to the subject and the time: violent, exaggerated, and, if at times bathetic, more often soaring into a lyric loveliness and passion previously, and since, unknown in American prose.

Such a book is not easy to grasp; it is the study of a lifetime. But there comes a time when the student must make a report, even as he knows it to be incomplete. To Ishmael's words, "I try all things; I achieve what I can," may be added the statement of Socrates: "What I have understood is good; and so, I think, is also what I have not understood; only the book requires a Delian diver to get at the meaning of it." Melville once wrote Duyckinck: "I love all men who *dive*."

[7] Cp. Emerson's "Art": "As far as the spiritual character of the period overpowers the artist and finds expression in his work, so far it will retain a certain grandeur, and will represent to future beholders the Unknown, the Inevitable, the Divine."

II.

The Breaching of *Moby-Dick*

"Breach – the leap of a whale out of water"

1

"I had no development at all"

HERMAN MELVILLE'S ADVENTURES as whaleman, beachcomber, and sailor ended in October, 1844, upon the arrival of his ship, the *United States,* in Boston harbor. Not long after this Melville turned his attention to writing and to his travels in the South Seas as the materials from which books might be shaped. The first fruit of his writing was the immensely successful *Typee* (1846). Five more novels followed within the next five years, culminating in 1851 with *Moby-Dick.* Whaling life aboard the *Acushnet* had waited several years before receiving treatment. Consideration of this delay throws light on Melville's self-realization of his powers, his instinctive artistic wisdom.

Typee necessarily had to be the first of Melville's novels. Among all of his novels the chronicle of life in the Marquesan valley cried out first and most imperatively for translation from life into art. Melville's adventures among savages and South Seas sirens had the nice proportion of terror and erotic suggestiveness appealing to the public taste, and with their picturesque, idyllic setting lent themselves more readily to literature than the gurry and grime of whaling. Furthermore, supporting *Typee* was an established tradition, but one not yet exhausted. Through their crude, vigorous chronicles the many voyagers to the South Seas had familiarized the western world with the mystery and charm of unexplored Oceania. Anson, Dampier, Byron, Colnett, Krusenstern, Kotzebue, Porter, Stewart, Wilkes, and above all, Captain Cook had firmly fixed the Paradise-savage fantasy in men's imaginations. Excitingly the myths suggested by the voyagers seemed to verify the popular interpretations of Rousseau's theory of the goodness of Nature and of the Noble Savage — theories which had ravished the romantic imagination of Europe. Ideologically and factually the way

13

was prepared for a writer who could report with literary charm and grace; who could bring into artistic focus the well-established tradition of Primitivism. England and America were rotten-ripe for a book like *Typee*. On the other hand, there was no such ready market for *Moby-Dick*. Shrewdly capitalizing on a literary trend, Melville, at the urging of his relatives who had delighted in his sailor yarns, wrote *Typee* and *Omoo*. For the whaling book he waited several years until he felt the time was ready and until he felt that he could cope in words with the clumsy gambols of the sperm whale. *Typee* and *Omoo* were a South Sea diptych, framing experiences which required but little embellishment from Melville's imagination. Even the straightforward reportorial fact was edged with mystery and delight; the everyday life of the Marquesan was mysterious and wonderful to the decadent and weary West. It was sound instinct when Melville chose simple travel narrative for his artistic debut, for the early novels called for less technical skill, a slighter craftsmanship, than did the later narratives of intellectual and spiritual adventure.

Not that Melville began unskillfully; he was completely the master of his journalistic materials. *Typee* is a captivating story — fresh, direct, glowing with the rich colors of a Marquesan valley; it is verbalized Gauguin. But *Typee* is trivial, although the adjective is comparative. In comparison with the travel writing and, indeed, with the fiction in America from 1819 to 1844 (the first twenty-five years of Melville's life), *Typee* is not trivial, for it has an unpretentiousness and simple integrity of style lacking in the writing of Cooper, Irving, or Simms. *Typee* is trivial only when compared with its author's later and greater works: *White-Jacket*, *Moby-Dick*, "Benito Cereno," or *Billy Budd*. The judgment is relative. Shakespeare's *Love's Labor's Lost* is slight only when compared with *Hamlet*; not when set against Lyly's "Campaspe," or Peele's *Old Wives' Tale*. *Typee* is a book from Melville's literary youth; *Moby-Dick* from his maturity. *Typee* is vivid experience recollected in immediacy, but *Moby-Dick* is a powerful emotion recollected in tranquillity, after an intense and intelligent genius had brooded over the meaning of those experiences for which the earlier novels were, in part, but as a journal. If it is true that it requires a deed to complete a thought, it is also true that it requires thought to complete a deed. Consciousness must be subjugated to form.

Every reader of *Moby-Dick* who enjoys its grotesqueness and its complexity — its infinite variety — may be grateful that circumstances and Melville's instinctive good sense first led him to employ for fiction the more tractable and sensational episodes from his career, that the artist first restricted his palette to the rich and bold colors.

Moby-Dick was six years maturing. It was not until a signally successful reputation had been established that Melville was ready, as he put it, to "turn blubber into poetry." His was a literary and spiritual growth as profound, if not so precocious, as that experienced by John Keats between the naïve, enthusiastic *Poems* of 1817 and the shadowed richness of the six great odes which flowered at Hampstead in the spring of 1820. During six years Melville "unfolded" as an artist. Looking back over these years, Melville himself understood something of what had happened to him, for he wrote to Hawthorne, in a passage now famous:

> Until I was twenty-five, I had no development at all. From my twenty-fifth year I date my life. Three weeks have scarcely passed, at any time between then and now, that I have not unfolded within myself.

The unfolding included an equivalent growth in craftsmanship, in technical dexterity, and a movement from the reportorial and surface adventures to the psychological and philosophical, from competent reportage to true creative art. The growth was, like all true growth, organic.

2

"Give ear to Mr. J. Ross Browne, and hearken"

Moby-Dick was begun 1 August, 1819, in a house at six
Pearl Street, New York City, for on that day Herman
Melville was born. Such a statement about literary origins
is true, however, only when one assumes the point of view
of Virginia Woolf:

> Books are the flowers or fruit stuck here and there on
> a tree which has its roots deep down in the earth of our
> earliest life, of our first experiences. But . . . to tell the
> reader anything that his own imagination and insight have
> not already discovered would need not a page or two of pre-
> face but a volume or two of autobiography. . . .

A statement not far from Thoreau's observation, "A man's
whole life is taxed for the least thing well done. It is a net
result. Every sentence is the result of a long probation." [1]
But while it is unquestionably true that a work of art is the
summation of a life up to the time of the artistic creation,
it also follows that a full understanding of the work may be
acquired only by an equally full comprehension of the biological, historical, sociological, and psychological back-
grounds of the artist. "Man is explicable by nothing less
than all his history," said Emerson. Nevertheless, such a
study completely pursued would be a complex and lengthy
biography, not a critical study. Space and critical principles
require that the literary geneticist leave such devious and
far-flung origins to others, himself to seek elsewhere for the

[1] Fauré has made the same point in reference to the plastic artist: " . . .
there must pass into each stroke of the sculptor's chisel the whole of his
past and present life: the intoxication of his senses before the freshness of
water and verdure, the thirst of his senses for blood — or their aversion to it,
his anxiety in the presence of women, his bitterness at being despised and
his joy at being understood, his revolt against the yoke, the blinders, and
the rod, his refusal or his consent that society, the country, and the world
should be what they are, down to the very influence of the air he breathes
and the food he digests upon his health, his waking and sleeping, his cheerful
or sullen humor."

beginnings of *Moby-Dick*. We must trace the more immediate, not the hidden, beginnings of the novel. We must start with the external initiatory act.

Precisely when *Moby-Dick* began to take definite shape within Melville's mind is indeed difficult to determine. Our records are few. Custom suggests that we accept the spring of 1850, but like Ahab himself, we might well toss aside the quadrant of traditional knowledge to find the time when the very *idea* of writing a whaling book first became part of Melville's program.

On 6 March, 1847, the *Literary World,* then America's most influential literary review, edited by Melville's good friends, George and Evert Duyckinck, published Melville's unsigned review of J. Ross Browne's *Etchings of a Whaling Cruise, with Notes of a Sojourn on the Island of Zanzibar. To which is Appended a Brief History of the Whale Fishery: Its Past and Present Condition* (New York, 1846).[2] As the Duyckincks well knew, no man in America was better qualified as a writer and as a veteran whaleman to review Browne's book. Melville's essay-review is a clouded mirror wherein we discern the stirrings within Melville himself. Melville's review was written with the relish which one might expect from a man who had himself undergone the dangers detailed in the unadorned prose of *Etchings.* Spotting only "one or two curious errors," Melville praised Browne's writing for its rough realism: "The scenes presented are always graphically and truthfully sketched . . . as true, unreserved descriptions, they are in no way faulty." Obviously carried back in memory to the months he had endured aboard the *Acushnet,* Melville in several places spoke out not as a reviewer but as a witness, to give his own "true, unreserved" picture. Clearly the following passage is from recollected experience:

> Then the whaling part of the business. — My young friends, just fancy yourselves, for the first time, in an open boat (so slight that three men might walk off with it), some twelve

2 In a letter Evert Duyckinck received 3 February, 1847, Melville wrote: "I have procured the book you spoke of from the Harper's & shall find much pleasure in making it the basis of an article for your paper."

or fifteen miles from your ship, and about a hundred times as far from the nearest land, giving chase to one of the oleaginous monsters. "Pull, pull, you lubberly *hay makers!*" cries the boat-header, jumping up and down in the sternsheets in a frenzy of professional excitement, while the gasping admirers of Captain Marryat and the sea, tug with might and main at the buckling oars — "Pull, pull, I say; break your lazy backs!" Presently the whale is within "darting distance," and you hear the roar of the waters in his wake. How palpitating the hearts of the frightened oarsmen at this interesting juncture! My young friends, just turn round and snatch a look at that whale. There he goes, surging through the brine which ripples about his vast head, as if it were the bow of a ship. Believe me, it's quite as terrible as going into battle, to a raw recruit.

This quotation is only part of Melville's levy on personal knowledge for purposes of his review. It is of sufficient length, however, to show that Browne's book had revived within him some of the original excitement of the whale chase. But Melville's passage also shows that he was not yet ready to write *Moby-Dick*. The style of this paragraph, for instance, is neither bad nor meritorious, but it is far from Melville's ability two years later. Even a year later he would not have included the awkward phrase "gasping admirers of Captain Marryat," nor the cumbersome expression "oleaginous monsters." But this passage is a five-finger exercise which helped him in creating one of the better passages in *Moby-Dick*. Describing a similar situation, Melville wrote:

It was a sight full of quick wonder and awe! The vast swells of the omnipotent sea; the surging, hollow roar they made, as they rolled along the eight gunwales, like gigantic bowls in a boundless bowling-green; the brief suspended agony of the boat, as it would tip for an instant on the knife-like edge of the sharper waves, that almost seemed threatening to cut it in two; the sudden profound dip into the watery glens and hollows; the keen spurrings and goadings to gain the top of the opposite hill; the headlong, sled-like slide down its other side; — all these, with the cries of the headsmen and harpooneers, and the shuddering gasps of the oarsmen, with the wondrous sight of the ivory Pequod bearing down upon her boats with outstretched sails, like a wild hen after her screaming brood; — all this was thrilling. Not the raw recruit, marching from the bosom of his wife into the fever heat of his first battle; not the dead man's ghost encountering the first unknown phantom in the other world; — neither of these can feel stranger and stronger emotions than that man does, who for the first time finds himself pulling into the charmed, churned circle of the hunted sperm whale.

This passage from *Moby-Dick* had its strange origin in the review of Browne's *Etchings*. In both pieces we have the gasps of the oarsmen, the comparison of the whaleman to the raw recruit in battle, but only in the great novel do we have the rolling rhythms, wavelike in effect, and the concentration of images. The later superiority is one of more skillful prosody and technique: in the rise and descent of the long sentences, in the use of onomatopoeia ("sled-like slide"), or in the sharpness of the alliteration ("stranger and stronger" and "charmed, churned circle"). But the later passage is discernible in the early one, just as surely as the theme of the slow movement in Beethoven's *Eroica Symphony* may be seen in the groping jottings of the composer's notebook.

Etchings roused memories within Melville which later led him to *Moby-Dick*. His blood was stirred to start a whale and not a fantasy. But writing his review, Melville's appreciation distorted his judgment, making him write, "Indeed, what Mr. Dana has so admirably done in describing the vicissitudes of the merchant-sailor's life, Mr. Browne has very creditably achieved with respect to that of the hardy whaleman's." It is true that Browne showed the roughness of life aboard a whaleship, but he scarcely did so with the vigor of Dana's writing. *Etchings* has merit, but it is not in the same literary class with *Two Years Before the Mast*. It was Melville who was destined to write the whaling equal of Dana's masterpiece — but at least it was *Etchings* which set his mind voyaging in seas from which *Moby-Dick* might be captured.

The effect of *Etchings* upon Melville's mind is apparent in his next book, *Mardi*. *Mardi* teems with allusions to whaling life, indicating that Melville had already begun a reading program, possibly haphazard at first, which might eventually gather into a whaling book. It would seem that Melville had already become the "Sub-sub-librarian" collecting "Extracts" later prefixed to *Moby-Dick*.[3] Early in *Mardi* Melville refers to "this horrid and indecent Right whaling, I say, compared to a spirited hunt for the gentlemanly Cachalot in southern and more genial seas, is as the butchery of white bears upon blank Greenland icebergs to zebra-hunting in Caffraria, where the lively quarry bounds before you through leafy glades." A similar antithesis is made much of in *Moby-Dick*, where Melville carefully and wittily rings the changes on the elegance of the South Sea sperm-whale fishery as contrasted with the barbaric butchery of the Greenland whale hunters. A minor theme in *Moby-Dick* was first enunciated in *Mardi*.

Another germinal whaling idea appears soon after the *Etchings* review, in *Mardi*. Melville mentions a fight between a Right Whale and a Killer Whale, suggesting the pictorial possibilities of the scene to the painter:

> . . . Had old Wouvermans, who once painted a bull-bait, been along with us, a rare chance, that, for his pencil. And Gudin or Isabey might have thrown the blue rolling sea into the picture. Lastly, one of Claude's setting summer suns would have glorified the whole. Oh, believe me, God's creatures fighting, fin for fin, a thousand miles from land, and with the round horizon for an area, is no ignoble subject for a masterpiece.

From this passage in *Mardi*, and from another in a whaling book, Melville later developed in *Moby-Dick* his four remarkable chapters on the iconography of the whale and whaling. Increasingly, it would seem that Melville wasted none of his early notes.

[3] It would be useful could one trace Melville's procedure in gathering these whaling quotations in "Extracts." I am of the opinion that most of them came from secondary sources, but until we have a fairly complete collection of the books consulted by Melville before 1851, we can never be certain of this.

A third illustration of how surely and effectively the whale had seized Melville's imagination and enlivened his style is seen in another passage from *Mardi*, potent with the very spirit and rhythms later found in *Moby-Dick*:

> Suddenly, as we gazed, there shot high into the air a bushy jet of flashes, accompanied by the unmistakable deep breathing sound of a sperm whale. Soon, the sea all round us spouted in fountains of fire; and vast forms, emitting a glare from their flanks, and ever and ever anon raising their heads above water, and shaking off the sparkles, showed where an immense shoal of Cachalots had risen from below to sport in these phosphorescent billows. The vapor jetted forth was far more radiant than any portion of the sea; ascribable perhaps to the originally luminous fluid contracting still more brilliancy from its passage through the spouting canal of the whales.

Redburn, which followed *Mardi,* continued the list of whale allusions. Even though the setting of *Redburn* was the Atlantic Ocean — waters not generally associated with the sperm whale — Melville mentioned "the enormous head of the sperm whale, and vast masses of unctuous blubber," and he also described Wellingborough Redburn's wide-eyed excitement on first hearing the cry of "*whales* alongside!" Melville also referred in *Redburn* to the commonly held opinion that whaling was a "low" occupation and whalers "low" people, a theme worked out at some length in *Moby-Dick.* And finally, there are several allusions of a humorous nature to whaling in *White-Jacket,* a novel whose subject matter (the American Navy) did not allow much scope for whaling lore. But the allusions could not be kept out entirely. Slowly, deep within himself, Melville had steadily been moving towards his whaling masterpiece.

During the years of preparation, Melville was an active man. As a writer he composed *Mardi, Redburn,* and *White-Jacket,* and wrote reviews for the *Literary World.* In 1847 he married Elizabeth Shaw, and in 1849 his first child was born. And he read widely and intently: Browne, Carlyle, Bayle, Plato, the Bible, and Shakespeare. All the time, his insight grew more penetrating, his point of view broadened and became less parochial even as it also deepened. His craft gained in skill, in expressiveness, and in the capacity to undertake the complex statement required by the half-awakened tragic vision. Finally, after three years, having learned how to adapt his large aims to his powers, Melville was ready again — *Mardi* the precedent — to ignore public demand and to deal with the arcana of cetology and the mist of metaphysics.

3

"About the 'whaling voyage'"

ON 2 FEBRUARY, 1850, Melville landed in New York City after a short and successful visit to London, where he had sold the proof sheets of *White-Jacket*. It is unlikely that *Moby-Dick* was begun before this time. No evidence exists for an earlier date, and all the circumstances argue against one. Certainly he had no time after *White-Jacket* to compose, for he took ship almost immediately, and his journal of his trip contains not a reference to writing of any sort. The long shipboard discussions with Taylor and Adler on metaphysical matters reveal directions of thought pointing to *Moby-Dick*, but they argue convincingly against any actual writing. *Moby-Dick* was not begun until after Melville's return from Europe, for not until then could he find the "grass-growing mood" so necessary, he said, to artistic creation.

Ironically, Melville began to write a book which in no way stretched his powers and which by no means met his deepest wish. *Moby-Dick* was first intended to be a whaling story pure and simple, much as *White-Jacket* had been a naval yarn with plot secondary to the description of shipboard life. Not until at least six months after he began to write about whaling did Melville suddenly alter his design to attempt a book of the fullness of *Moby-Dick*. *Moby-Dick* was begun as a whaling document; it was not until later that it exploded into a tragic drama of Aeschylean proportions.

The modestly planned book occupied Melville between February and August of 1850. The great *Moby-Dick* was written between November, 1850, and August, 1851. What is the justification for seeing *Moby-Dick* in two such contrasting stages of development?

For one thing, the speed with which Melville progressed in his writing after his arrival in New York argues the beginning of a simple work, not a difficult one — or not too difficult. By 1 May, 1850, Melville was well into his work, as he told Dana:

About the "whaling voyage" — I am half way in the work, and am very glad that your suggestion so jumps with mine. It will be a strange sort of book, tho', I fear; blubber is blubber you know; tho' you may get oil out of it, the poetry runs as hard as sap from a frozen maple tree; — and to work the thing up, one must needs throw in a little fancy, which from the nature of the thing, must be as ungainly as the gambols of the whales themselves. Yet I mean to give the truth of the thing, spite of this.

From these words it is possible to imagine Melville halfway through a book of slight scope, but never, in three months, halfway through the seven hundred pages of *Moby-Dick* as we now have it.

Melville's letter to Dana raises several questions. What did he mean by "the truth of the thing," or by "blubber is blubber"? And what was Dana's suggestion which so "jumped" with Melville's purpose? A clue to Melville's meaning is suggested by the withdrawal on 29 April of William Scoresby's *An Account of the Arctic Regions*, one of the most important books on whaling ever published.[4] Another clue is the receipt on 10 July — over two months

4 Melville's father-in-law, Chief Justice Lemuel Shaw, drew Scoresby's book from the Boston Athenaeum on 30 December 1850 and returned it 16 January 1851. Was Herman Melville visiting him at this time? — most probably.

later — of his copy of Thomas Beale's *Natural History of the Sperm Whale*, procured for him from London by Putnam's in New York. To get such a book would have required about two months from the time of writing to Putnam's to the time of delivery, transatlantic communications being what they were, so that Melville's order for Beale apparently went in just about the same time (late April) as his borrowing from the New York Society Library of Scoresby's two volumes. What he apparently meant, then, in saying that he had just arrived at the same idea as that suggested by Dana, and that achieving that idea would be difficult ("blubber is blubber") was that he had decided to incorporate into his "whaling voyage" a large mass of cetological and whaling data (blubber), but that to do so would be difficult. To force expository data into a story already well developed would certainly not be easy. One may suggest that between 29 April and 18 July Melville was, among other matters, writing those parts of *Moby-Dick* which involve Scoresby and his book, and that beginning on 10 July he began to incorporate the details from Beale into his "voyage." And although "blubber is blubber" — detailed information in a sea yarn is refractory — few acquainted with Melville's facility in composition would doubt that he had proceeded far with his work in Beale when all plans were upset by the arrival of *Mosses from an Old Manse*. It should be noted that Melville quoted Dana's description of his book as a "whaling voyage"; the narrative structure came first, but probably not the narrative pattern which we now have.

From May to July Melville's pen moved with the same facility and speed as during the first three months of composition, for by 27 June he had so nearly finished his assignment that he dared to write to Bentley in London offering him for £200 the publication rights of "a romance of adventure, founded upon certain wild legends in the Southern Sperm Whale Fisheries," and he assured Bentley that the book would be ready by early autumn. Placing early autumn at 1 October, one may estimate almost three months allowed for the inclusion of the Beale cetological data. A month later, 7 August, Evert Duyckinck, visiting in the Berkshires, wrote to his brother George, "Melville has a new book mostly done — a romantic, fanciful and literal and most enjoyable presentment of the Whale Fishery — something quite new." Duyckinck's description contains no hint of the philosophical depths abounding in *Moby-Dick* as we know it; his words apply to a "whaling voyage" ballasted by whaling facts and touched up with what Melville called "a little fancy."

The conclusion is clear: Melville's "whaling voyage" was almost ready for publication by late summer of 1850. But *Moby-Dick* was not published until October 1851, almost a year and two months later. It was not Melville's practice to let his manuscripts gather dust. Upon looking over what he had done he either sent it to the publishers or set to work at revisions radical in character. The latter course was the one followed in *Mardi* and *Billy Budd* — and *Moby-Dick*. Only the hypothesis of an important revision can adequately account for the year's delay. Such an hypothesis fits the facts gleaned from the letters to Duyckinck and Hawthorne, and such a theory explains the revolution within Melville's mind which led him to his genius. That revolution may be seen in two parts: first as the result of forces long gathering within Melville as he brooded on life and read Shakespeare; second, as the sudden and magnificent release of those Shakespearean forces when Melville met Nathaniel Hawthorne.

We pass from the shadow of Dana to the haunted mind of Hawthorne; from a good book by Melville to a masterpiece by Melville.

4

*"What I feel most moved to write, that is banned,
— it will not pay"*

AHAB, doomed by his dark destiny to hunt for the great White Whale, is an unusual but felicitous emblem of Melville and his hunt for the meaning of life in the seas of art. *Moby-Dick* was created by a compulsive necessity as great, but saner, as that which kept Ahab on his unswerving course. *Moby-Dick* was revised — rewritten would be the more judicious word — because of an artistic and spiritual upheaval within Melville, and not because he feared for the success of his "whaling voyage." *White-Jacket* and *Redburn* predicted the success. In fact, as Melville knew, the simpler story with which he had begun would have pleased his public to a much greater extent than did, eventually, *Moby-Dick*. The "whaling voyage," almost completed by August, 1850, was undoubtedly a competent and attractive work. Duyckinck, for instance, expressed his approval of the manuscript, and his opinion was professional and reliable. Nevertheless, Melville deliberately turned his back on the temptations of an easy success, to venture into the literary unknown.

In considering the intellectual and spiritual compulsion which led Melville to revise *Moby-Dick* so completely, we must first consider the dilemma of the sincere artist forced by circumstances into distasteful artistic compromise. "Dollars damn me," Melville complained, a disintegrating fact known to many artists in history: Ryder, Franck, Faulkner — the list would stretch far. Melville met the dilemma head-on.

Typee, Omoo, Redburn, and *White-Jacket* had described with sharpness and simplicity (but each novel goes deeper than its predecessor) the surface of Melville's South Seas experiences. But to the artist of integrity, intelligence, and hard-won vision there comes a moment in his absorption of objective experience when a mere recounting is unsatisfying. Primarily to report without understanding is to remain a Meissonier, never to become a Rembrandt. At the moment of discontent with description and report, the artist requires not more experience, but an intellectual, emotional, and spiritual comprehension of those adventures he has met in his terrestrial and intellectual wanderings. One must come home again. By the summer of 1850, writing the first draft of *Moby-Dick,* Melville was compelled to explore the *significance* of the bewilderingly rich life he had lived. If one has perceived, as Melville later wrote in *Pierre,* that Life increasingly "unfolds mysteries interpierced with mysteries, and mysteries eluding mysteries; and [begins] to see the mere imaginariness of the so-supposed solidest principle of human association," he will not, if he is honest, continue to report an unambiguous world.

Melville's mounting discontent with mere report had early broken forth in *Mardi,* wherein, no longer penning a literature of diversion, he attempted to make his novel a criticism of life. Thereupon, as he later wrote Bentley, *Mardi* confused and displeased the public which had come to expect only entertainment from him. Experiments like *Mardi* are costly; the needs of a growing family and the public distaste for allegorical satire frightened Melville back to the reportage which had established his wide reputation. Atoning for *Mardi,* Melville wrote *Redburn* and *White-Jacket* and thus whistled his public again to heel. What Melville felt about these books is frankly stated in a letter to his father-in-law, Chief Justice Lemuel Shaw:

> But no reputation that is gratifying to me, can possibly be achieved by either of these books. They are two jobs, which I have done for money — being forced to it as other men are to sawing wood. And while I have felt obliged to refrain from writing the kind of books I would wish to; yet in writing these two books, I have not repressed myself much — so far as *they* are concerned; but have spoken pretty much as I feel. — Being books, then, written in this way, my only desire for their "success" (as it is called) springs from my pocket, & not from my heart so far as I am individually concerned, & independent of my pocket, it is my earnest desire to write those sort of books which are said to "fail."

To Duyckinck Melville expressed a similar distaste for what he termed literary carpentry. Expressing surprise at the favorable reception of *Redburn,* he said (14 December, 1849):

> I am glad of it — for it puts money into an empty purse. But I hope I shall never write such a book again — tho' when a poor devil writes with duns all round him, & looking over the back of his chair — & perching on his pen & diving in his inkstand — like the devils about St: Anthony — what can you

expect of that poor devil? — What but a beggarly "Redburn!" And when he attempts anything higher — God help & save him! for it is not with a hollow purse as with a hollow balloon — for a hollow purse makes the poet *sink* — witness "Mardi." But we that write & print have all our books predestinated — & for me, I shall write such things as the Great Publisher of Mankind ordained.

Two years later, in *Pierre,* Melville alluded again to the *Redburn* sort of writing. Like Melville, Pierre had found it folly to compose for public demand or

by the hard constraint of some social necessity. Equally paltry and despicable to them, are the works thus composed; born of unwillingness and the bill of the baker; the rickety off-spring of a parent, careless of life herself, and reckless of the germ-life she contains.

Divided in mind, Melville returned to America (having sold Bentley the English rights to *White-Jacket*) to begin work on a new book, a "whaling voyage" this time, for the fear of failure and of bills kept him from attempting "anything higher." But such a statement as "I shall write such things as the Great Publisher of Mankind ordained" displays the seed of spiritual revolution soon to burst forth in a passionate declaration, and into an even greater act, of independence.

But making a resolution and acting on it are two different steps. Frequently the intention must be stated long before it becomes an act. Melville was whistling bravely when he wrote to Duyckinck in December, 1849; eight months later he put his words into action when he began the revision of the "whaling voyage."

Melville was right to insist that he be true to the "germ-life" within him. Spender said recently, "In order to be true to external nature a poet must first of all be true to his own nature. He must write about what really interests him, be it fashionable or unfashionable, great or small, virtuous or venal." Melville's course was difficult to follow, however, for it threw the author back into himself. Individual independence always involves the danger of cutting oneself off

from the social group. Too great a self-reliance may result in
Ahab's pursuit. Melville might now try to reveal the tragic
vision of life which had come to him over the years, or,
tempted by popular rewards, he might sidestep the problem
of Evil, blandly ignoring the desperate and demonic depths
of life, recording only the surface scenes and events which so
titillated the sensibilities of English and American readers.
To stay on the surface or to dive deep — this was Melville's
difficult choice, demanding courage and integrity, qualities
with which life had well endowed Melville. Rather than be
a spiritual renegade, untrue to himself and the necessities of
his being, Melville deliberately turned his back on the easy
way of certain public approval. In running counter to the
reading tastes of his own generation, Melville chose immediate neglect, but also insured a larger and far less fickle public — the readers of the future, the readers of the world.

Moby-Dick grew as Melville composed it — grew in that
mysterious and fetal way in which works of art develop
within the minds of their creators, in a way not unlike
Prokofieff's experience in musical composition:

> "Do you hear the sounds that you make before you sit
> down to music paper, or do you discover them as you work
> along?" "Both," replied Prokofieff. "One starts to develop a
> definite, if incomplete musical conception. The rest follows,
> according to one's mental force and creative ability, and the
> 'logic' of the idea."

Prokofieff's testimony brings up the question of the inherent "logic" of any artistic material. While it is true that
the nature of his medium — stone, paint, words, sounds —
imposes certain inevitable restrictions upon the artist, it is
also true that the "logic" of the material depends in equal
part upon the kind of mind which seeks to find that "logic."
This is to say that no two artists will treat identical subjects
in the same way; the logic of the idea changes with the artist.
Whaling life, for instance, offered rich materials for literary
exploitation in the first half of the nineteenth century, but
during that time only a few men had attempted any report
of those materials, and what they saw differed according to

their training and their temperaments. Beale and Bennett had seen whaling as a scientific phenomenon to be recorded objectively; Browne had reported bitterly on the brutality of whaling life; Hart had created a strange novel of fatality in the sperm-whale fishery. Artists, and the rest of us as well, are like the six blind men describing the elephant. Each bears witness to the limitations of his own vision.

On the face of it, nothing seems much more grotesque than the idea that a great tragic drama, or epic, could be shaped out of the brutal and unseductive details of the American sperm-whale fishery, or that a tragic hero worthy to be placed in the company of Orestes, Hamlet, Macbeth, Lear, and Don Quixote might be found on the sandy little island of Nantucket, a few miles off the New England coast.

Significance, like beauty, lies in the eye of the beholder. With the artist the most insignificant events come together within his mind to form significant and living patterns. Melville's memory of calloused hands, of raging storms, blistering calms, of breaching and flurried whales, of cockroaches and human vermin, blended with his reading in the Bible, in Shakespeare, in Bayle, and in Hawthorne, to form a new unity. T. S. Eliot described the process:

> When a poet's mind is perfectly equipped for its work, it is constantly amalgamating disparate experiences; the ordinary man's experience is chaotic, irregular, fragmentary. The latter falls in love or reads Spinoza, and these two experiences have nothing to do with each other, or with the noises of the typewriter or the smell of cooking; in the mind of the poet these experiences are always forming new wholes.

In other words the artistic and esthetic quality which is present in all normal experience is made use of only by the attending mind of the artist.

To seize on the essential quality of a fact is not so simple as it sounds. First of all, as Rilke has pointed out, that fact must have been truly seen. The first problem of the artist, therefore, is to see the object completely, to behold a chair as Van Gogh saw one in Arles, to look at an old woman with the penetration of Epstein, to turn one's eyes on one's self with the sad wisdom of the aged Rembrandt. The discipline is severe, but Melville had learned it in his graphic apprentice novels. The one occasion when he had not "looked" at his subject had resulted in failure; as Hawthorne wisely said: " 'Mardi' is a rich book, with depths here and there that compel a man to swim for his life. It is so good that one scarcely pardons the writer for not having brooded long over it, so as to make it a great deal better." By the time he wrote *Moby-Dick*, Herman Melville had learned the lesson of looking; to gather his emotions around concrete objects, "not merely to see a thing, not merely to describe a thing (but to *become* the thing, not merely to hover about it like an atmosphere), or, rather, to create from the thing and from his contemplation of it a third and independent thing, a work of art." [5] Between 1846 and 1850 Melville the reporter had become Melville the artist, no longer satisfied to examine the surface of experience, but eager to grapple with its basic reality in the hope of baring the meaning of life.

Hebbel's first law of art, that "the infinite shall be made visible in the concrete and the particular," has been universally recognized by the great artists. With this insight, the artist is distinguished from the poetaster and the talented juggler. To behold a world in a grain of sand, infinity in an hour, inevitably leads to the tragic vision: for the eye which has looked piercingly on harpoons and savages and sharks, looks upon hate and hypocrisy as well as upon unselfishness and heroism, upon man's pettiness and upon his spiritual magnitude. He sees Thersites as well as Hector; the Yahoos as well as the Houyhnhnms; Claggart as well as Billy Budd. He sees man's small realization and his great potentiality. The tragic vision, to put it in a capsule, is discerned disenchantment.

The vision which beholds multiple meanings in a single fact, is a profound and disturbing possession shared by the greatest artists: Giotto, Michelangelo, Rembrandt, and Daumier; William Byrd, Handel, Beethoven, and Bloch; Homer, Vergil, Dante, and Milton. And Melville. The pos-

---

[5] Rainer Maria Rilke, *Requiem and Other Poems*, translated with introduction notes by J. B. Leishman (London, 1935), p. 50.

sessor of this vision will never see life steadily nor will he see it whole, for life seen whole cannot be seen steadily, while life seen steadily is life seen dully or partially.

The tragic vision, involving as it does both the heart and the head, the total man, was what Melville had grown to by 1850. But, to repeat, *Moby-Dick* was first written from the more limited approach of the author of *Redburn* or *White-Jacket,* only to demand a complete reshaping as a result of Melville's new self-consciousness. It was as though he had begun to construct a whaleboat, only to find that what he was compelled to create was a three-masted whaling ship.

If, as in Amiel's journal, "All semination is a mysterious thing, whether the seed falls into the earth or into souls," it is also true that the subsequent growth in embryo is almost as mysterious and equally interesting. Nowhere has the development of the artistic idea within the depths of the unconscious, creating mind been better described than in William James's *Varieties of Religious Experience:*

> A man's conscious wit and will are aiming at something only dimly and inaccurately imagined. Yet all the while the forces of mere organic ripening within him are going on to their own prefigured result, and his conscious strainings are letting loose subconscious allies behind the scenes which in their way work toward rearrangement, and the rearrangement toward which all these deeper forces tend is pretty surely definite, and definitely different from what he consciously conceives and determines. It may consequently be actually interfered with (*jammed* as it were) by his voluntary efforts slanting toward true direction.

Melville himself,[6] a year after writing *Moby-Dick*, similarly

[6] It is appropriate to consider briefly the demonic possession of Melville's creating mind as he revised his novel. Melville himself was aware of it; his letters to Hawthorne imply the excited state of mind driving him through his manuscript. "Demonic possession" is of course merely another way of saying "inspiration." That Melville was inspired when he wrote *Moby-Dick* admits of no doubt. But one who believes that only artists are inspired and that non-artists, "practical men," are not inspired, makes the mistake of placing the artist in a non-human group. The artist is not distinguished from his fellow men by a special gift from the gods, peculiar to him, like a third arm or an extra pair of eyes in the back of his head. When he paints or carves or composes, the artist simply uses the same life gifts possessed by

described in *Pierre* the rearrangement of creative work caused by the emergence of hidden, deeper forces:

> For when unfathomably stirred, the subtler elements of man do not always reveal themselves in the concocting act; but, as with all other potencies, show themselves chiefly in their ultimate resolvings and results. Strange wild work, and awfully symmetrical and reciprocal, was that now going on within the self-apparently chaotic breast of Pierre.

These words describe the "wild work" within Melville's mind in rewriting *Moby-Dick*. In a later passage in *Pierre,* Melville varied the idea: "that which now absorbs the time and life of Pierre, is not the book, but the primitive elementalising of the strange stuff, which in the act of attempting that book, had upheaved and upgushed in his soul. Two books are being writ."

The "deeper forces," not revealed in the "concocting act," which had "upheaved and upgushed in his soul" were Melville's matured vision of the ambiguity of appearances and his bitter awareness of man's tragic fate. These emergent forces interfered (*"jammed* as it were") with his initial narrative, the "whaling voyage," until they finally took the pen from his hand and wrote a new, and ampler, book — *Moby-Dick*.

Stimulated by reading and writing about J. Ross Browne's *Etchings of a Whaling Cruise,* Melville's thoughts had returned to his life from 1841 to 1844. But between 1844 and 1850, Melville had lived a different life, one of the mind, immersed in great books, so that muscular memories of tar buckets and oars, of whalemen and savages, mingled strangely with the philosophical and metaphysical reflections of Fate and Free Will, on the changing face of Truth, on the ulti-

---

all men, only in him these gifts, or functions, have an alertness, a sensitivity, and an efficiency of performance beyond "normality." According to laboratory testing, the athlete has a much faster muscular reflex than you or I, but we have the same but slower reflex. As Wordsworth wisely put it, a poet (artist) is a man speaking to men, but a man endowed with a higher organic sensibility, with an imaginative skill in combining his perceptions (Coleridge called it the "esemplastic power"), and a verbal skill in projecting these shapes of the mind. John Milton and John Doe differ mainly in skill and awareness, not in basic gift — although one is tempted to term that difference a special gift. Demonic possession occurs when the dissonance of unconscious forces and conscious intention are being resolved into harmony.

mate problem of the One and the Many. In his "whaling voyage" Melville had not planned to include the intellectual voyage. As he began the task of conquering the large and untractable materials of whaling life and of whaling literature, there came the clash of whaling lore with the larger truth. To bring them together Melville had to revise his book from the very beginning. *Moby-Dick* may be explained "as partly due to explicitly conscious processes of thought and will, but as due largely also to the subconscious incubation and maturing of motives deposited by the experiences of life."

A word of qualification is needed here. *Moby-Dick* must not be considered as the immediate record, pleasing to external biography, of Melville's life aboard the *Acushnet,* any more than *Hamlet* is Shakespeare's report of a personal attempt on his part to kill his uncle or to jilt Ophelia. But we can surely insist that *Moby-Dick* grew out of Melville's deepest interests in himself and in his world, and that Melville's spiritual biography can be known only by comprehension of his writings. "Shakespeare," Keats told his brother, "led a life of Allegory: his works are the comments on it . . ." *Moby-Dick* is not the agitated report of a mind in disruptive spiritual conflict, for, as Amiel wrote, "In order to sing an affliction, one must be already, if not healed of the affliction, at least in convalescence." The mastery of materials discerned in *Moby-Dick* argues spiritual health — a health lacking, one would say, a year later, as Melville's distressed explorations into ambiguity provoked the disintegrated power of *Pierre*. In *Moby-Dick,* Melville did not transcribe old experiences; he *utilized* them.

What Melville had fumblingly tried to say in *Mardi* was now said in *Moby-Dick* through mastered symbol and boldness of expression. "It is hard to be finite upon an infinite subject," Melville wrote in his review of *Mosses,* adding significantly, "and all subjects are infinite." Including whaling. The "whaling voyage," a nearly completed manuscript, must now treat of the universal as well as the particular. Characters must be altered, enlarged; the *Pequod's* captain must be magnified; his crew described in new terms, now to carry the same high load of tragic import which ancient writers had put upon the shoulders of kings and princes. The growth from *Typee* simplicity to *Moby-Dick* complexity may be noticed by comparing Kory-Kory with his later counterpart, Queequeg. A simple savage soul has in the change of name gathered unto himself a world of meaning. No longer is a savage by a river's brim merely a savage — he is a way of life, a symbol of ethical truths. Equally radical and rich changes in plot were needed to make the "whaling voyage" into *Moby-Dick*.

But first of all something had to happen to bring into activity the latent powers, the hidden intentions of Melville.

5

"This, surely, is the place to write of Hawthorne"

BY THE MIDDLE of July, 1850, Melville's "whaling voyage" was in sight of port when, on the eighteenth, a tempest arose which drove Melville out into the broad ocean. An aunt of his gave him a copy of Nathaniel Hawthorne's *Mosses from an Old Manse*. Seldom has such an unassuming gift had such epic consequences. Reclining comfortably on a Pittsfield haymow, Melville raced through Hawthorne's two volumes, jotting in the margins such phrases as "The moral here is wonderfully fine," "exquisite," and "What a revelation," and making checkmarks beside the many passages which struck his fancy. But the real revelation of how deeply Melville had been stirred by Hawthorne's stories is the essay-review which he wrote for publication in Evert Duyckinck's *Literary World,* 17 and 24 August, 1850. In other words, within a month after reading *Mosses*, Melville's article on the book was published — suggesting a speed well in keeping with the violent and generous enthusiasm of the tribute itself.[7]

---

[7] Harrison Hayford, "Melville and Hawthorne," unpublished Yale Ph.D. dissertation, has gathered the evidence about the relationship between the two writers. The excellence of his report and the cogency of his arguments makes for a study which should be made available to many readers.

Recognizing that it is rash to select a specific moment for Melville's conscious awareness of his proper artistic role, and that such a selection runs counter to Melville's warning in *Pierre*: "Nor will any thoroughly sincere man, who is an author, ever be rash in precisely defining the period, when he has completely ridded himself of his rubbish, and come to the latent gold in his mind," nevertheless I feel that it is safe to designate 18 July, 1850, as the time when Melville "ridded himself of his rubbish." Melville's spiritual response to *Mosses* and his review for the *Literary World* were unquestionably responsible for the birth of the great Melville in the revised and great *Moby-Dick*.

Mosses from an Old Manse stirred Melville to the depths of his being, much as he had been moved by his discovery of Shakespeare the year before.[8] Shakespeare had led to profound self-realization; Hawthorne led to Melville's expression of his Shakespearean insight. It is revealing to read how Melville's review intertwines the names of Hawthorne and Shakespeare in lavish praise. "Shakespeare," he said audaciously, "has been approached. There are minds that have gone as far as Shakespeare into the universe. And hardly a mortal man, who, at some time or other, has not felt as great thoughts in him as any you will find in *Hamlet*." Nathaniel Hawthorne, he implied, was the first American mind to penetrate into the meaning of the universe as had Shakespeare; Hawthorne was an augury of greatness in American letters. Hawthorne, he went on to say, had a "great, deep intellect, which drops down into the universe like a plummet"; he

8 Professor F. O. Matthiessen, *American Renaissance* (New York and London, 1941), pp. 412–417, 423–431, 431–435, and 449–451, is the first to study intelligently the effect of Shakespeare upon Melville's mind and art. Matthiessen based some of his study on an article by Charles Olson, whose book *Call Me Ishmael* (New York, 1947), stresses the Shakespearean side of Melville's genius. But Leon Howard in "Melville's Struggle with the Angel," *Modern Language Quarterly*, I (June, 1940), 195–206, was the first to suggest that *Moby-Dick* had been written in two distinct stages, the second inspired by Melville's reading of Coleridge's lecture on *Hamlet* in which had been pointed out that "one of Shakespeare's modes of creating characters is to conceive any one intellectual or moral faculty in *morbid* excess, and then to place himself . . . thus mutilated or diseased, under given circumstances" — a quotation which with others in the lecture suggests the shaping of tragic Ahab.

had, furthermore, an understanding of Evil: " . . . now, it is that blackness in Hawthorne, of which I have spoken, that so fixes and fascinates me." Hawthorne, he publicly testified, "has dropped germinous seeds into my soul. He expands and deepens down, the more I contemplate him; and further, shoots his strong New England roots in the hot soil of my southern soul." These and many more jubilant sentences reveal Melville even more than they criticize Hawthorne, for as he read *Mosses* Melville was in reality staring into a mirror to behold the reflection of his own self.

Despite the fact that *Mosses* compelled Melville to rewrite almost in entirety his "whaling voyage," nevertheless, the task was undertaken with little or no regret and weariness. There is, on the contrary, a feeling of exultation, as if Melville were writing from powers at last realized and released. Hawthorne had showed Melville that one American was expressively aware of the evil at the core of life, a perception toward which Melville had been groping for seven years of authorship and of self-scrutiny, but which he had not completely realized nor dared to disclose. Exploded into self-realization by Hawthorne's words, Melville was now released to speak the truth previously withheld, or badly expressed in *Mardi*. Specific encouragement came to Melville from *Mosses*:

> Thus it is that ideas, which grow up within the imagination and appear so lively to it and of a value beyond whatever men call valuable, are exposed to be shattered and annihilated by contact with the practical. It is requisite for the ideal artist to possess a force of character that seems hardly compatible with its delicacy; he must keep his faith in himself while the incredulous world assails him with its utter disbelief; he must stand up against mankind and be his own sole disciple, both as respects his genius and the objects to which it is directed.

Mosses gave Melville the strength to realize his genius in such a way that he might give to his private experience the universal, representative values implicit in them. From *Mosses* he learned to be artistically self-reliant. "It is better to fail in originality than to succeed in imitation," Melville wrote, not so much as a commentary on *Mosses,* although that was his intention, but as a condition of his own novel then in preparation. Melville needed no longer to bottle up his deepest thought while he labored away at "sweat art" like *Redburn*; he could now speak out and create — *Moby-Dick.*

Within three weeks of reading *Mosses,* Melville discovered its author living but a few miles from him in the Berkshires. On 5 August, 1850, Melville and Hawthorne met for the first time at a picnic excursion, now famous, engineered by David Dudley Field.[9] Dating after this meeting we have the superb letters from Melville to Hawthorne, letters even surpassing those he wrote to Duyckinck, for in Hawthorne Melville had found a kindred spirit to whom he might talk on subjects beyond the understanding of the more limited Duyckinck. Nowhere outside the novels do we come closer to the mind of Melville than by studying these documents. It is a tragedy that Hawthorne's letters in reply have probably been destroyed. Melville and Hawthorne struck up an immediate friendship. During the year which followed the men exchanged letters and visits;[10] in both they tried to settle the problems of the universe. One evening, for instance, they argued long of "time and eternity, things of this world and

[9] Harrison Hayford, in "Melville and Hawthorne," has presented the evidence by which we may date the beginning of the writing of Melville's review. He argues cogently that Melville did not write it until after he had met Hawthorne on 5 August, and that the whole essay was written and printed between then and 17 August when the first part of it appeared in the *Literary World.* Despite the temptation to cling to the ironic picture of Melville's meeting with Hawthorne when in the middle of his review, one must incline to Hayford's argument. He recently reminded me of the passage from *Pierre*: "A man will be given a book, and when the donor's back is turned, will carelessly drop it in the first corner; he is not over-anxious to be bothered with the book. But now personally point out to him the author, and ten to one he goes back to the corner, picks up the book, dusts the cover, and very carefully reads that invaluable work. One does not vitally believe in a man till one's own two eyes have beheld him." If this remark applies to Melville personally, maybe the *Mosses* review came after Melville's enthusiasm had been stirred by meeting Hawthorne 5 August and *then* by reading through *Mosses.*

[10] Hayford lists at least nine known meetings. I must resist the temptation to take up the details of this friendship — it is an attractive subject — but the student in the East may come close to it by visiting the Harvard Library to see the books which Hawthorne gave to Melville during this time.

the next . . . and all possible and impossible matters." Much of the talk about moral and metaphysical matters undoubtedly found its way, directly or symbolically, into the pages of *Moby-Dick*. Unfortunately we have only Melville's side of the story and some students have the idea that in the friendship Melville was the active agent and Hawthorne the passive. It is true that Hawthorne was shy, but he was an attentive listener, and whenever he did speak it was to the point. To him Melville could "talk out" his ideas at length, knowing that he had a responsive auditor. But Hawthorne was of course much more than an intellectual scratching post for Melville. Only we do not know exactly what his contributions were. He probably furnished many a fact (e.g. about the Transcendentalists at Brook Farm and in Concord) and many a reflection (e.g. on the problem of Evil) which helped to mold the metaphysics of *Moby-Dick*. The friendship of Hawthorne and Melville was the sort of companionship described in Emerson's sentence, "For when they shall meet as they ought, each a benefactor, a shower of stars, clothed with thoughts, with deeds, with accomplishments, it should be the festival which all things announce." This particular festival resulted in the revised *Moby-Dick*. It is one of the great tragedies of American letters that circumstances soon separated the two men. It is almost as if Fate played a deliberate rôle, for no sooner had *Moby-Dick* been published than Hawthorne, just as if his work were done, left the Berkshires to return to Concord. With his departure Melville was turned back on himself, to find his bearings alone. Though "Benito Cereno" shows that Melville found those bearings even in the heart of darkness; nevertheless, the strange, tortured tackings of *Pierre* might not have occurred had Hawthorne been at hand to discuss with its author the problems raised in that wild, and yet wonderful, book.

The godfather of *Moby-Dick* was guaranteed additional fame when Melville gratefully dedicated his whaling epic to Hawthorne "In Token of my Admiration for his Genius."

6

"Taking a book off the brain"

EARLY IN AUGUST, 1850, the first *Moby-Dick* was "mostly done," and then came the meeting with *Mosses* and with Hawthorne. Just when did Melville decide that he must recast his "whaling voyage"? No answer is forthcoming, but he probably did not actually begin work on this revision until well into November. In September, for instance, he bought a farm near Pittsfield — the now famous "Arrowhead" — and a week or so later he was in New York, lunching with Bayard Taylor and Sir Edward Belcher. Early in October, back again in Pittsfield, Melville was hard at work preparing his new home for residence. "For a month to come," he wrote Duyckinck, "I expect to be in the open air all day, except when assisting in lifting a bedstead or bureau." It was not until November that he had the time to attack his whaling book seriously.

By 12 December, however, he was in full swing at his revision; his letter to Duyckinck reveals concentrated literary activity. He was so engrossed by his book that he cared little for idle gossip to his friend and, fortunately for us, elected instead to discuss his composition. *Moby-Dick* was spinning in his mind so that when he described the view from his window he automatically employed voyaging imagery:

> I have a sort of sea-feeling here in the country, now that the ground is all covered with snow. I look out of my window in the morning when I rise as I would out of a port-hole of a ship in the Atlantic. My room seems as a ship's cabin; & at night when I wake up & hear the wind shrieking, I almost fancy there is too much sail on the house, & had better go on the roof & rig in the chimney.

This shows that Melville's retirement in his Berkshire quarters was symbolically in key with his spiritual retirement into himself for the creation of *Moby-Dick*, illustrating Thoreau's words:

The poet too is, in one sense, a sort of dormouse gone into winter quarters of deep and serene thoughts, insensible to surrounding circumstances; his words are the relation of his oldest and finest memory, a wisdom drawn from his remotest experience. Other men [like Duyckinck] lead a starved existence, meanwhile, like hawks, that would fain keep on the wing, and trust to pick up a sparrow now and then.

Just how deeply engrossed Melville was with his manuscript appears in a thumbnail sketch of his daily routine:

> Do you want to know how I pass my time? — I rise at eight —thereabouts — & go to my barn — say good-morning to the horse, & give him his breakfast. (It goes to my heart to give him a cold one, but it can't be helped) Then, pay a visit to my cow — cut up a pumpkin or two for her, & stand by to see her eat it — for its a pleasant sight to see a cow move her jaws — she does it so mildly & with such sanctity. — My own breakfast over, I go to my work-room & light my fire — then spread my M.S.S. on the table — take one business squint at it, & fall to with a will. At 2½ P.M. I hear a preconcerted knock at my door, which (by request) continues till I rise & go to the door, which serves to wean me effectively from my writing, however interested I may be.

So then, in the middle of winter, four months after the "whaling voyage" was "mostly done," Melville was working on his manuscript from five to six hours a day, a schedule now habitual for some time and to grow more so in the future.[11] His words to Duyckinck carry not the slightest suggestion that he was nearing a goal; on the contrary, they place him in midstream. Now *Moby-Dick* is growing.

Melville's words suggest that this revision was provoked by much deeper feelings than those mentioned in the May, 1850, letter to Dana, which had inspired the first draft. Melville was now writing from depths of mind and heart not tapped before in the first account of whaling. This December letter is full of the jubilation of a man passing through an aroused and glorious period of his artistic life. Melville's mind was overflowing; his heart was full of futurity. So con-

[11] Mrs. Melville wrote in her diary that Herman "would sit at his desk all day not eating anything till four or five o'clock."

cerned was he to glean his teeming brain that he begged
Duyckinck to send him "fifty fast-writing youths, with an
easy style, & not averse to polishing their labors? If you can,
I wish you would, because since I have been here I have
planned about that number of future works." Such a sentence reveals the excitement of the artist at full tide, as, for
instance, John Keats, writing to Woodhouse, 27 October,
1818: "The faint conceptions of Poems to come bring the
blood frequently into my forehead." Melville's words to
Duyckinck are those of a man at the height of powers as wide-
ranging and unquenchable as old Ahab's. They are words
which lead us to *Moby-Dick* in a way that the letters to Dana
fail to do.

Interestingly, Melville's request suggests that he had run
into difficulty in recording precisely what he wanted to say,
that the "easy style" and the "polishing" he required of
amanuenses were somewhat painful to him. The new wine
required new bottle manufacture.

How deeply Melville had plunged into himself in this new
direction of *Moby-Dick* is shown by the next words to
Duyckinck: "Taking a book off the brain is akin to the
ticklish & dangerous business of taking an old painting off
a panel — you have to scrape off the whole brain in order to
get at it with due safety." Melville had found that looking
into one's heart and writing therefrom was not easy.

The December letter to Duyckinck should go far in correcting the romantic notion long held of Melville as a Prometheus chained to a Berkshire rock while the vulture-critics
pecked at his vitals, or ignored him while a callous nation
slowly thickened to empire, more concerned with its manifest destiny than with the fate of its artists. Melville's letters
to Duyckinck and Hawthorne are highly charged, it is true,
but charged and radiant with potent, not with defeated or
defiant, spirits. Ahab was defiant, but not Ishmael or Melville. From the letters we see that Melville had at last found
the "grass-growing mood" which he felt so necessary for creative work — that relaxation of his energies (Keats' "Ode to
Indolence") in which hidden attitudes and buried perceptions might find release, soon to coalesce, at the will of the

artist, into a work of art. This does not mean that *Moby-Dick* was equivalent to automatic writing. It is more like the experience known to T. S. Eliot:

> To me it seems that at those moments, which are characterised by the sudden lifting of the burden of anxiety and fear which presses upon our daily life so steadily that we are unaware of it, what happens is something *negative*: that is to say, not "inspiration" as we commonly think of it, but the breaking down of strong habitual barriers — which tend to re-form very quickly. Some obstruction is momentarily whisked away. The accompanying feeling is less like what we know as positive pleasure, than like a sudden relief from an intolerable burden.

This is what Melville said when he wrote to Hawthorne after the publication of *Moby-Dick*: "I have written a wicked book, and feel as innocent as the lamb." [12] It is true, as Yeats said, that "only an aching heart / Conceives a changeless work of art," but a changeless work of art comes only when the ache is in the past and when the mind and sensibility of the artist have understood the meaning of his experience. *Moby-Dick* was the result of trained craftsmanship working with maximum skill upon the deepest thoughts of Melville. *Moby-Dick* represents Melville "in his wholeness, wholly attending."

Exactly two months later Melville wrote again to Duyckinck, 12 February, 1851, evading a request of his friend's by replying: " 'A dash of salt spray'! — where am I to get salt spray in inland Pittsfield? I shall have to import it from foreign parts." The "salt spray" was undoubtedly a metaphor for a specimen section [13] of *Moby-Dick* which

---

[12] A reaction exemplifying Henry James's observation: "It appears to me that no one can ever have made a seriously artistic attempt without becoming conscious of an immense increase — a kind of revelation — of freedom."

[13] "What a quenchless feud hath Time with the sons of men," Melville wrote in *Pierre*. One of her victories has been the destruction of the *Moby-Dick* manuscript — perhaps in the Harper Brothers fire in 1856. But anyone who is familiar with Melville's habits of writing may guess what his manuscript must have been like. The state of a Melville manuscript is an index to the author's state of mind as he wrote. For instance, the drafts of two highly different poems, "The Scout toward Aldie" and "Art," show clearly the

Duyckinck wished to read. Melville at that moment was in no mood for outside criticism, especially from the conservative editor, so that his tactful-facetious refusal is a recognition that the piety of Duyckinck would have been offended by his "wicked book."

Melville also refused a second request from his friend. Since he was just taking over a new periodical, Holden's *Dollar Magazine*, Evert Duyckinck had asked Melville to contribute to the venture. Melville's reply was revealing: "I am not in the humor to write the kind of thing you need — and I am not in the humor to write for Holden's Magazine." Of course it was not in Melville's humor at that moment. A man who is trying to concentrate the problems of the universe within the slippery framework of a novel could scarcely be interested in dashing off reviews of trivial books for a popular magazine. Now, at least, Melville would not let dollars damn his whaling book. The writing of book reviews for Duyckinck required a different set of sail from the composition of a tragic epic. Book reviews could only weaken Melville's struggle with the angel — art. The artistic act demands a total possession of the artist in his work.

So scanty is the evidence for following the growth of Melville's composition through the winter of 1850–1851 that we must seize upon every clue, develop every hint to fill out the story. Perhaps the most significant suggestion is found in a letter from Melville to Hawthorne, March, 1851. In this letter, the greatest he ever wrote, Melville referred to the "man who, like Russia or the British Empire, declares himself a sovereign nature (in himself) amid the powers of heaven, hell, and earth. He may perish; but so long as he exists he insists upon treating with all the Powers upon an equal basis." These words might well be applied to Ahab

---

ease or difficulty with which he composed, depending on his subject matter. The eleven lines of "Art," in which Melville distilled his theory of artistic creation, caused him far more trouble than the hundreds of lines of "The Scout toward Aldie," a long narrative poem dealing with straightforward adventure. It is safe to assume that in the *Moby-Dick* manuscript these chapters composed at Arrowhead during the winter of 1850–1851 would, at least in the first draft, be tortuously revised, almost illegible with corrections and cancellations.

defiant of the thunder, lightning, and the White Whale.
Like Russia and the British Empire, Ahab asserts his self-
sovereignty with defiant and heroic boldness — in a manner incompatible with the hero of a mere "whaling voyage."
Clearly the old Nantucket whaling captain is, in March,
1850, being remodeled to meet the new artistic concept; an
old whaleman is being changed into a tragic hero. Melville's
words to Hawthorne are probably simultaneous in time and
certainly similar in thought to the closing words of Father
Mapple's sermon in *Moby-Dick*:

> Delight is to him — a far, far upward, and inward delight
> — who against the proud gods and commodores of this earth,
> ever stands forth his own inexorable self. Delight is to him
> whose strong arms yet support him, when the ship of this base
> treacherous world has gone down beneath him. Delight is to
> him, who gives no quarter in the truth, and kills, burns, and
> destroys all sin though he pluck it out from under the robes
> of Senators and Judges.

Within these soaring sentences we find one of the central
themes of *Moby-Dick*; it is no coincidence that Melville expressed similar sentiments to Hawthorne in a letter written
during the revision of the novel. The theme of the individual and his selfhood was much in the minds of Melville
and Hawthorne during this winter in the Berkshires — as
their writings show.

The rewriting of *Moby-Dick* required that sentences, paragraphs, and even chapters of the old "whaling voyage" be
fused with the new and larger artistic dream. Fundamental
alterations were demanded: the plot must be changed, or a
new one found which might better carry the various levels
of communication now to be attempted; old themes had to
be deepened and new ones added to communicate Melville's
awakened intellectual penetration into life.

If the plot of *Moby-Dick* was added after September,
1850, what was the original narrative structure of the "whaling voyage"? The final answer to this question must remain
a mystery, but here a suggestion by way of tentative answer
may not be amiss. It is possible that the original "whaling

voyage" plot was that of a conflict between two men, an officer and a common sailor. This plot pattern was almost habitual with Melville, even as early as 1849. *Redburn* portrays the minor opposition between young Redburn and the tyrannical, malevolent Jackson. *White-Jacket* placed the brutal officers of the quarter-deck in irreconcilable difference against the ordinary seaman, pointing up the drama by several striking instances. In *Moby-Dick*, the original or first plot was quite possibly the "Town-Ho's Story," included in the fifty-fourth chapter as a digressive yarn. "The Town-Ho's Story" deals with the conflict between natural man, Steelkilt, the strong, admired leader among the men in the forecastle, and the mate Radney, representative of officer brutality. Radney is a portrait of motiveless malignity just as was Jackson in *Redburn* or, later, Claggart in *Billy Budd*. Steelkilt's cousins are Jack Chase of *White-Jacket* and Billy Budd himself. But the weakness of such a plot was that it focussed the attention of the reader on the human conflict, away from the documentary, whaling materials. The reader's attention shuttled back and forth from the whaling exposition to the dramatic conflict; the narrative was split into two distinct and poorly connected parts. Melville, then, saw that he could unify his story by depicting a conflict between man and whale by making the whale itself one of the chief actors in the story. Man against whale would have the appeal of surprise and novelty and would link closely the narrative and expository threads of the novel. Plot and exposition would reinforce each other. Furthermore, though the struggle between man and man is absorbing, the struggle of man against the forces of nature is epic and epochal; it is universal and cosmic. Melville's hero would become the prototype of all men struggling against the malevolent, implacable hostility of nature. Ahab against Whale would place him with Beowulf against Grendel, Prometheus against Zeus, and Lucifer against God. The equation of the White Whale with Zeus or with Nature was a grotesque development, but one of grim humor and bold imagination. Therefore, "The Town-Ho's Story" was concentrated into a single chapter, becoming a short story, and connected, at least superficially, with the story of Moby Dick, and the story of the White Whale superseded it. Ahab, whatever his original name was we cannot know, was enlarged so that despite an artificial leg he strides the decks of the *Pequod* like a true Homeric hero. Between August, 1850, and August, 1851, we may conclude that *Moby-Dick* was transformed from adventure story to *mythos*.

Having the Homeric struggle of man against nature as the pattern, we may wonder when the White Whale himself swam into Melville's manuscript. Probably in March or April, 1851. In March Nathaniel Hawthorne had given his friend the four volumes of *The Mariner's Chronicle* containing stories of tragedy at sea. The gift suggests that Melville had discussed his plot problems with his friend and that Hawthorne had given his old volumes (they had been given him by his uncle years before) in a helping spirit. In them, Melville found no plot for his purpose. But in reviewing the famous tragedies at sea his mind recalled the *Essex* disaster, in which a whaleship had been sunk when rammed by a gigantic sperm whale in the Pacific Ocean. Melville had known the story for a long time and had talked with a relative of one of the few survivors. As he said in *Moby-Dick*, "I have seen Owen Chace [*sic*], who was chief mate of the *Essex* at the time of the tragedy; I have read his plain and faithful narrative; I have conversed with his son; and all within a few miles of the scene of the catastrophe." The effect of this meeting on Melville's mind was great, as he himself testified in his copy of Chase's pamphlet:

> I questioned him concerning his father's adventure; and when I left his ship to return again the next morning (for the two vessels were to sail in company for a few days) he went to his chest & handed me a complete copy (same edition as this one) of the Narrative. This was the first printed account of it I had ever seen, & the only one copy of Chase's Narrative (regular & authentic) except the present one. The reading of this wondrous story upon the landless sea, & close to the very latitude of the shipwreck had a surprising effect upon me.

When Melville was writing during 1850 he did not have, one gathers, any copy of Owen Chase's *Narrative of the most extraordinary and distressing shipwreck of the Whale-Ship Essex, of Nantucket; which was attacked and finally destroyed by a large spermaceti-whale, in the Pacific Ocean.* That he soon acquired a copy [14] suggests that he deliberately set out to find one in order to refresh his memory with precise details of the great whaling disaster. Unable to find one himself, he probably sought the help of his distinguished father-in-law, Chief Justice Lemuel Shaw of Massachusetts. But certainly, even if Melville did not approach Shaw, the Judge was aware that Herman was working on a whaling story and that he would not mind having Chase's pamphlet. The fact that Shaw procured his copy from Thomas Macy [15] of Nantucket, however, suggests that he made a special effort as the result of a special request on his son-in-law's part. Shaw sent Chase's *Narrative* in April, 1851, and Melville devoured the book, marking it up with his pencil and adding eighteen pages of commentary on its authorship, its significance, and his own feeling and connection with the characters of the tragedy. The destructive whale, then, became part of *Moby-Dick* before April, but not long before, since Melville would not work on such an important subject without consulting the main source, already known to him in the strange way he tells. The seed of the *Essex* plot was dropped into Melville's mind in 1841 or 1842 when he was a sailor on the *Acushmet*. Ten years later it burst into bloom as Melville saw its possibilities in revising the "whaling voyage."

The monstrous fish which rammed the *Essex* was not white. The albino fish of *Moby-Dick*, as will later appear, came from whaling history and tradition, to be fused with the *Essex's* villain. But by the spring of 1851 the White Whale was the deuteragonist of the story, and Hawthorne in July wrote in *A Wonder Book*: "On the hither side of Pitts-

---

[14] This bibliographical treasure is one of many owned by Mr. Perc Brown of Montclair, New Jersey, who generously allowed me to study it at his home. Included with the *Narrative* are eighteen pages of Melville's notes discussing the tragedy, the characters, and his own interest in the famous episode. It has a place on Mr. Brown's shelf with Melville's annotated copy of Thomas Beale's *Natural History of the Sperm Whale* — the narrative and expository sources of *Moby-Dick* side by side!

[15] Thomas Macy's letter to Shaw, 4 March, 1851, is inserted in Melville's copy of Chase's *Narrative*.

field sits Herman Melville, shaping out the gigantic conception of his 'White Whale' while the gigantic shape of Grey-
lock looms upon him from his study-window."

By June of 1851 *Moby-Dick,* in its second and revised
form, was almost finished, for Melville told Hawthorne:

> In a week or so, I go to New York, to bury myself in a
> third-story room, and work and slave on my "Whale" — while
> it is driving through the press. *That* is the only way I can
> finish it now, — I am so pulled hither and thither by circum-
> stances.

Another reference later in the letter indicates that he was
slaving on last details:

> But I was talking about the "Whale." As the fishermen say,
> "he's in his flurry" when I left him some three weeks ago. I'm
> going to take him by his jaw, however, before long, and finish
> him up in some fashion or other.

In whaling parlance, a whale went into a "flurry," violently
thrashing about in the water, shortly before death at the
hands of his hunters.

"Disgusted with the heat and dust and Babylonish brick-
kiln of New York," as he said, Melville returned to the
cooler climate of Pittsfield "to feel the grass, and end the
book reclining on it." He fulfilled his resolve to finish off
his book, so long in preparation, and by 13 September arranged with Bentley, his English publisher, for an advance
of £150 on a half-profits arrangement, so that on 18 October
The Whale, in three octavo volumes, was published in England. A month later — probably on 14 November — with a
new title which Allan Melville said was more attractive as
well as more appropriate to the "hero of the volume," *Moby-
Dick* rolled from the presses of Harper's in New York City.
At last *Moby-Dick* had breached into view.

7

"You understood the prevailing thought that impelled the book"

THE ARGUMENT of this chapter may be summed up briefly. With the completion of *White-Jacket* in the fall of 1849, Melville cast about for a new subject on which to write a novel. Instinctively he looked, as he had done before, into his own personal past, to find that one important segment of his experiences still remained for literary revelation: his whaling life. Furthermore, he had been preparing himself to write such a book by much reading and long meditation about whaling — and about life. An intelligent man, he probably recognized that since he was one of the few ex-whalemen sufficiently literate and literary to write a popular book on the sperm-whale fishery, the field was wide open to him. The authority of hard experience, the research of the conscientious student, and the technique of literary art combined uniquely in him for the creation of a whaling story. Above all, he possessed the creative imagination to transfigure fact into truth.

Early in February, 1850, if not shortly before, he began to write a "whaling voyage," intending to spice the expository facts about life in the sperm-whale fishery with a narrative to hold the reader's interest. As he had done in his two novels of the previous year, he probably shaped a story involving a struggle between a tyrannical officer and a noble young man. But as he moved into his book, Melville discerned that such a plot split rather than unified his book. Accordingly, much later, he hit upon the idea of using for his narrative structure the celebrated *Essex* story, thereby making the whale a prominent actor, the dramatic center of the novel.

In the meantime, however, Melville was exploded into the fullest development of powers hitherto unrevealed, by his new friendship with Nathaniel Hawthorne, the one writer in America who had expressed the tragic point of view, which was deeply felt, but not hitherto declared, by Melville himself. Hawthorne was the catalyst speeding Melville's accumulated reflections into expression. As Fauré said, "A revolution occurs when the depths are ready." And Hawthorne stirred depths within Melville which had been created by Shakespeare. Almost completed by August, 1850, *Moby-Dick* was entirely rewritten throughout the succeeding year, not being finished until mid-summer of 1851. *Moby-Dick* was the result of a long incubation.

"Art," Emerson said, "is nature passed through the alembic of a man." *Moby-Dick* grew from a "whaling voyage" into a great tragic epic because Melville had pursued the sperm whale along the line and had read and thought much about man's destiny. From 1841 to 1844 Melville had been "a messmate of the elements" and had known "daedal life in boats and tents": from 1845 to 1850 Melville had explored "Plato's theme." The richness of his wandering past fused with the reflective wisdom of the thoughtful present. *Moby-Dick* apprehends two worlds and two sets of experiences: material and immaterial, physical and metaphysical. The mature apprehension of both sets of experiences, both within themselves and also in their relationship to each other, makes *Moby-Dick* the full, many-leveled, and inexhaustible book that it is. Such a large apprehension could not have been achieved by chance, and its revelation in winged words was no accident. While it may have been chance that Melville began only a whaling handbook, and chance again that the whaling lore entangled with the universal questions which Melville's mind was seeking to master, it was artistry and not chance that when the two levels of being came together, Melville knew how to combine, in a net of words, Free Will and Fate with a ball of yarn, a manila monkey rope with the social nexus whence each derives his fundamental humanity, or a tattooed Polynesian with Instinctual Man. Such an artistry and such a sense of relationships had grown from the experiments, at first confusing, of *Mardi,* and the photographic sharpness of *Redburn* and *White-Jacket. Moby-Dick* was composed of fire *and* ice.

Begun as a simple book, *Moby-Dick* grew into rich complexity. It is coagulate of strange stuff. It audaciously encircles at least five worlds to federate them in one vast universe: the sensuous and stormy seas of Oceania; the American sperm-whale fishery; the zoology of whales; the intellectual tides of Melville's America; and the uncharted currents of tragic truth as old as Aeschylus and as young as America of 1851. Travel, economics, zoology, intellectual history, metaphysics, and the mystery of the avenging dream — in more than one sense *Moby-Dick* is a casement opening on the seas of faery lands forlorn.

III.

The Narrative Beginnings

1

"I am quick to perceive a horror"

"CALL ME ISHMAEL." Arrestingly, dramatically, as though a mysterious dissonance had been plucked by the massed strings, Melville's great whaling symphony begins. The three opening words are as hauntingly suggestive, and as symbolic, as the snapped well rope in Chekhov's *Cherry Orchard*. Few sentences in fiction condense more thought, emotion, and criticism than Melville's lean, sinewy line. In its wide allusiveness and in its subtle ambiguity, the opening sentence of *Moby-Dick* is an appropriate opening for the complex art to follow.

"Call me Ishmael." Each reader, even in our un-Biblical age, swiftly discerns the reference to the Ishmael of the Old Testament.[1] Having established the allusion, the intelligent reader senses that Melville's initial sentence states the central theme of *Moby-Dick*, that it is the opened door through which one may enter into the vast and turbulent world of the novel. We are told that we are about to set out on an adventure into the wide wastes of life, and that since Ishmael is the familiar symbol of the lonely wanderer we may expect *Moby-Dick* to be a study of Odyssean faring. *Moby-Dick* unfolds before us as a story of the whale hunt, and it becomes at the same time the quest of the human heart for its spiritual and psychological home.

"Call me Ishmael." Concentrating on Ahab, as most readers do, we forget the narrator of the story: quiet Ishmael.

[1] Nathalia Wright says in "Biblical Allusion in Melville's Prose," *American Literature*, XII (July, 1940), 198: "Biblical allusion in Melville's pages appears as his chief method of creating an extensive background for his narratives. It magnifies his characters and themes . . . so that they appear larger and more significant than life. It suggests the existence of a world beyond the world of sense, which exerts influence upon this world, and in which ultimate truth resides. Above all, it helps establish a background of antiquity for his sequence of events, thus investing them with a certain timeless quality."

With his lonely journey to New Bedford the adventure begins; with his lonely survival from the ship's sinking, the tragic drama closes. Ishmael is narrator, but he is also prologue and epilogue. "An individual," said Emerson, "is an encloser" — such is Ishmael's dramatic function. Ishmael is the chorus character whose commentary elucidates and whose person enfolds the entire work. No less than Horatio in *Hamlet,* Ishmael is the author's surrogate among the *Pequod* crew.

Ishmael is Everyman. Ishmael is Melville; Ishmael is any man, anywhere, confronted with the flux of circumstance and with the chaos of his own being. But Everyman comprehends the particular natures of all men, and since each of us contains, potentially, the good and evil of all men, each of us may be Everyman, or Ishmael, but each of us is nothing more than our special, idiosyncratic self. Everyman defies quick analysis, just as the mythical Average Man eludes statistical tables. To analyze the whole, however, we must analyze the constituent parts; consequently, Melville has atomized the various selves of Everyman-Ishmael, projecting each of them in a separate character within the novel. Ishmael, like Richard II, might say: "Thus play I in one person many people." [2] Ahab, Starbuck, Queequeg, Fedallah, Flask, and Pip are phases of Ishmael's total self — they are selves personified and elaborated for special examination. The sobriety and good sense of Starbuck, the animal grace and undivided mind of Queequeg, the frivolity of Flask, the self-assertiveness of Ahab — all add up together with the other characters to total Ishmael. Significantly, no concrete details concerning Ishmael (the color of his eyes and hair, his size, his address, his parents, etc.) have been written into *Moby-Dick.* Ishmael remains nebulous and neutral as, in

[2] This ability of Man to identify with his fellows is described by Amiel (9 November, 1861): "Everyone thus possesses in himself analogues of everything, the rudiments of everything, of all beings and all the forms of life. Whoever can detect the minute beginnings, the germs and the symptoms, can find in himself the mechanism of the universe. . . . A subtle and powerful mind can pass through all potentialities and draw forth in a flash at every point the monad, the world that it contains. This is to achieve consciousness and possession of the general life and to pass once more into the divine sanctuary of contemplation."

the work of art, Everyman must. Ishmael is the monistic self; Ahab and his crew are the pluralistic selves. Stemming from Ishmael, *Moby-Dick* is a study of both single and multiple personality; it is concerned with the psychological phase of the problem of the One and the Many.

This technique of character portrayal in which we are first presented with the unitary character, soon broken up into the component selves, was not new to Melville, nor did he hesitate to use it later in his career. Two years before, in *Mardi,* Melville had employed the principle of character fragmentation. The central figure, Taji, is generalized, and is not to be remembered for his features nor for his special personality. He is seen chiefly as symbol — the symbol of the seeker; he seeks the blond Yillah as unswervingly as Ahab searches for the White Whale, or as Ishmael seeks peace of spirit. Once Taji's pursuit of Yillah is well under way, he fades from the foreground just as Ishmael does in *Moby-Dick* once the *Pequod* is in the open seas. To replace Taji, Melville brings forward four characters: Media, the average man (as his name suggests) ; Babbalanja, the metaphysician and philosopher; Mohi, the historian; and Yoomy, the poet. Clearly these figures are phases of Taji himself, but Taji himself becomes prominent again at the end of the book, even as Ishmael dominates the scene in the Epilogue of *Moby-Dick.*

Melville repeated this pattern of character portrayal in *Clarel,* a two-volume narrative poem published twenty-five years later. Clarel, the titular figure, never clearly described, stays in the reader's mind not as graphic fact but mainly as the symbol of the seeker. Once Clarel's search for faith is begun, and the pilgrims have set out on their tour of the Holy Land, he moves out of the foreground while others in the pilgrimage band are successively brought into focus. The similarity in structure to *Mardi* and to *Moby-Dick* is striking; the pilgrimage group is isolated for purposes of particular study even as the group in Media's war canoe, or the hell-bound crew on the *Pequod.*

Before modulating into Ahab, Queequeg, and the others, Ishmael is first seen as almost pure symbol. Allusively, as has been pointed out, he is the wanderer in the desert, except that the Ishmael of *Moby-Dick* differs from his Old Testament namesake in being, at first, completely alone, with no Hagar to accompany him. Perhaps the quick appearance of Queequeg on the scene supplies an equivalent to the Biblical Hagar, but if so, it is indeed a strangely humorous one! The Ishmael-wanderer image was impressed indelibly on Melville's mind. In *Redburn* (1849) he had written: "So that at last I found myself a sort of Ishmael in the ship, without a single friend or companion; and I began to feel a hatred growing up in me against the whole crew." A year later he mentioned it in *Pierre:* "Fain, then, for one moment, would he have recalled the thousand sweet illusions of Life; though purchased at the price of Life's Truth; so that once more he might not feel himself driven out an infant Ishmael into the desert, with no maternal Hagar to accompany and comfort him." The Ishmael of *Moby-Dick* is a profound symbol of the shelterless person in the face of almost absolute nothingness, when the supports and solaces of family, education, and habit have been suddenly removed, and the world has been revealed in its instability and unreliability. "Solidity is but a crust," Melville wrote in one of his later poems, and Ishmael has seen beneath the crust. Ishmael is the man to whom the problem of the One has become the problem of the Many.

Throughout *Moby-Dick* Melville progressively develops the theme of the isolated individual.[3] Unequivocally, he calls the *Pequod* whalemen "isolatoes." The theme, the problem, the fact of isolation haunted the most sensitive minds of Melville's century, from Coleridge to Arnold, and from Emerson to Emily Dickinson, and it still hovers above the twentieth century, a restless and unlaid ghost. In *Moby-Dick* the theme moves like a corposant from Ishmael to Ahab, from Father Mapple to Queequeg; it is found perched on the masthead of the *Pequod* as Ishmael gazes across the deceitful

---

[3] Cp. D. H. Lawrence's remark: "He records also, almost beyond pain or pleasure, the extreme transitions of the isolated, far-driven soul, the soul which is now alone, without any real human contact." For Ishmael, however, the human contact is Queequeg.

serenity of the sea, and it is discernible in the unctuous spermaceti dipped from the sperm whale's case; it moves to the massive and awful head of the White Whale himself; and, finally, back again to Ishmael, lonely survivor afloat in the coffin life-buoy. It is a theme worked out with remarkable variations, as skillfully and as subtly as the closing movement of Beethoven's *Sonata for Pianoforte,* Opus 111, which, probably, treats the identical problem. Melville's initial statement of his universal theme is distilled in the opening words, "Call me Ishmael."

To see *Moby-Dick* as a study of aloneness and isolation is to place the book directly in the main cultural current of modern times.

The psychological history of man has been his struggle to realize himself — to comprehend the fact of, and finally to accept, his own Ego. Stephen Spender observes that for all men "there are only two realities: all the things which are outside himself — the universe, other people, the whole accumulation of human experience handed down from the past — and himself," but it is only recently in human history that the idea has been so clearly realized and made explicit. From one point of view the emergence of the Ego concept may be regarded as a primary criterion of human progress. Primitive man, we have been told frequently,[4] was unable to distinguish clearly between Ego and non-Ego. Only in modern history has man dichotomized his universe, achieved this schismatic realization. To be sure, a few people, caught in the web of tragic circumstance, perceived the individual in opposition to a non-personal world, and only a few of those perceiving it gave expression to the fact of man's es-

[4] E.g. "One difference between primitive human society and civilized human society is that in primitive human society the individual self is much more completely determined, with regard to his thinking and behavior, by the general pattern of the organized social activity carried on by the particular group to which he belongs, than he is in civilized human society. In other words, primitive human society offers much less scope for individuality — for original, unique, or creative thinking . . . and indeed the evolution of civilized human society from primitive human society, has largely depended upon or resulted from a progressive social liberation of the individual self and his conduct." George Mead, *Mind, Self, and Society* (Chicago, c. 1934), p. 221.

sential loneliness. Though two of the world's greatest stories depict man's separateness — Buddha's lonely wanderings across India, and the crucifixion of Jesus, especially when he cried out that even God had forsaken him — it is not until the end of the Middle Ages that we find the separateness of the Ego stated in art. Man's loneliness is the theme of the noblest of all morality plays, *Everyman*. Not long after it was the dominant theme of *Hamlet*. With the Renaissance the concept emerges; the split between the individual and his society — and the urgent necessity for their union — becomes increasingly apparent.

The history of the concept of aloneness — not to mention its cognate, individualism — is too complex to be worked out in a few paragraphs, but one or two points should be made to indicate the immediate conceptual background from which Ishmael came, points which *Moby-Dick* pregnantly criticizes.

In recent history the idea of man alone is connected with the "natural man" created for Europe by Jean Jacques Rousseau, whose lively imagination had concocted attractive paradoxes from ideas traceable to John Locke and the Earl of Shaftesbury. Man, Rousseau said, is naturally good; man is evil only as his institutions have made him so; and could man return to a state of nature he might recapture the state of goodness which he had enjoyed before the expulsion from Eden. His ideas were of course antipodal to the Calvinistic glooms. Although the flaws in his argument are so obvious, and well known, that they need not to be taken up here, nevertheless Europe — weary of sterile rationalism — was seduced by his half-truths. Critics have gone so far as to attribute to Rousseau the political and social revolutions in France and America, and to argue, not without reason, that the shadow of Rousseau still falls across the theories of our thinkers, the parleyings of our politicians, and the dreams of workers chained to the machines of man's invention.

Rousseau, it has been said, was a prime force in the Romantic movement. It is difficult to define Romanticism briefly, but certainly one of its important characteristics was its reaction to materialism. Alarmed at the growth of the machine, men feared the mechanization of the most vital forces of life — the instinctive. And the growth of the factory system brought megalopolis — populations massed together in stone and steel canyons rather than dispersed among green fields (a state of nature). The psalmist had found his strength from looking to the hills, but the tenement dweller in London and New York found little spiritual restoration in paved streets. Ironically, only as man's inventive ingenuity threatened to destroy him did man become conscious of his fundamental needs. Paradoxically, only as the pressures of large societies threatened individuality did men analyze and objectify that individuality. The concepts of Ego and non-Ego, objective and subjective, are a development of the last one hundred and fifty years. Only recently have we developed "psychology."

With the spread of industrialism throughout the western world, there has been an accompanying consciousness of the theory of individualism. Literature and art burgeon with the cry of man facing his own self, isolated from the society about him. As Friedell says, "What are tone-sequences and orders of battles, skirts and regulations, vases and meters, dogmas and the shapes of roofs, but the outpoured philosophy of an age?" Most vividly does the isolation theme appear in the *Rime of the Ancient Mariner* when, "Alone on a wide sea," the mariner cries out that "Even God scarce seemed there to be." Aloneness is the theme of "La Belle Dame Sans Merci," and it is the dramatic center of Keats' greatest letters. Aloneness looms large in the lyrics of Matthew Arnold and in the better poetry of Tennyson. It is found spread over the black rocks of Eliot's waste land, and so frequently has it been voiced in modern poetry that Louis MacNeice complains: "These are the times at which / Aloneness is too ripe." Aloneness is painted into the canvases of Blakelock and Ryder, of Chirico and Feininger. It sounds in the harmonic and contrapuntal patterns of Beethoven and Vaughan Williams. It is carved into the durable stone of St. Gaudens's masterpiece, the Adams Memorial in Rock Creek Park, Washington. James, Royce, and Dewey have discussed its philosophical aspects; Freud, the psychological. Only a long doctoral dissertation could even list the contemporary treatments of the many phases of aloneness: as nationalism in politics, as *laissez-faire* in economics, as Protestantism in Religion, as individualism in ethics. The words of the concept — such as "egoism," "individualism," "collectivism," "socialism," etc. — are not even two hundred years old in general usage.

At the time *Moby-Dick* was written, the question of the individual and his unique personal rights was nowhere more alive than in America. The newly formed United States was the symbol to the world of an individual freedom — in Europe both threatened and throttled. The American government had been founded on the libertarian philosophy of Locke and the French Encyclopedists. More eloquently than any other document in political history, the Declaration of Independence had unequivocally stated the rights of every individual to life, liberty, and the pursuit of happiness. Furthermore, America possessed a proud, if somewhat narrow, Puritan tradition which had long emphasized the separateness and integrity of each individual soul, its right to independent judgment and authority. American democracy predicated individual freedom under social protection — in essence, the right of every human being to self-realization. Philosophically and politically America was and is Protestant. Said a discerning critic in 1833: "In most operations of mind, each American appeals only to the individual effort of his own understanding. . . . Every one shuts himself up in his own breast, and affects from that point to judge the world."

Moby-Dick was composed during a period of rampant individualism. "Another sign of the times," Emerson wrote in 1837, "is the new importance given to the single person." The frontier with its limitless opportunities for personal escape and advancement made for ferment. According to one historian:

> The generation of the thirties and forties . . . saw the acme of a particular development of individualism which had for some time been gaining ground and from which there was to be a rapid change to a more rigid system of community

control. It presents one of the outstanding instances in history of the working of individuals trammeled by a minimum of law and convention. Its accomplishments were almost unprecedentedly the work of individuals, for leaders had little to enforce their leadership; they were the result of the independent work of more individuals than had ever before been free to work by and for themselves, at what they chose, and how they pleased.[5]

Within this social framework, and part of it, *Moby-Dick* is a thoroughly American book: in themes, in style, and in subject matter. Written in the generation immediately following the upsurge of Jacksonian democracy, *Moby-Dick* inevitably mirrored American direction. No work of art can avoid the stain of its times. Emerson wisely put it:

> No man can quite exclude this element of Necessity from his labor. No man can quite emancipate himself from his age and country, or produce a model in which the education, the religion, the politics, usages and arts of his times shall have no share. Though he were never so original, never so wilful and fantastic, he cannot wipe out of his work every trace of the thoughts amidst which it grew.

Out of America's new experiment in human freedom, in individualistic enterprise, has arisen a large literature of that struggle: the Declaration of Independence, the Monroe Doctrine, the Emancipation Proclamation, *Walden, Leaves of Grass*, Emerson's *Essays*. No less American, *Moby-Dick* sprang from the same national, cultural, and philosophical matrix. In no lesser degree, *Moby-Dick* is both revelation and criticism of the American pattern of life. This wealth of entertainment and instruction is opened up to us through the three words, "Call me Ishmael."

5 Carl Fish, *The Rise of the Common Man, 1830–1850* (New York, 1941), pp. 337–338. (Vol. VI, *A History of American Life*.)

2

"I duly arrived in New Bedford"

TEN of the early chapters of *Moby-Dick* are set in New Bedford, Massachusetts, center of American whaling. Every one of the chapters leans heavily on recollection of sights and events recorded ten years earlier in Melville's impressionable mind, when he sailed with the *Acushnet* from Fairhaven. This is not to imply that the ten chapters reproduce Melville's early experiences journalistically. *Moby-Dick* is dramatic, not autobiographical. Behind every work of art, however, is a memory; and behind every memory is an experience which the literary geneticist must find before he considers how personal history has become artistic account, how recollection has grown into revelation.

It is possible in dealing with the New Bedford and Nantucket scenes in *Moby-Dick* to distinguish between effects produced from Melville's personal experiences, and writing founded on literary sources only. But be his source life or letters, Melville's imagination transformed it to suit his narrative needs. New Bedford was part of his past, so that the chapters placed there contain such precise, physical detail that the scenes are powerfully etched on the reader's mind. Nantucket, which he knew from reading and hearsay, is described in general terms devoid of concrete, distinguishing detail. To cover his lack of sharp particularity Melville here resorted to rhetoric and to lyrical celebration. Knowing Melville's methods of composition, one is not rash in suggesting that had Melville sailed from Nantucket instead of from Fairhaven — just across the Acushnet River from New Bedford — or had he visited Nantucket at any time before writing *Moby-Dick,* he would have produced an incisive sketch of the gray, sandy island, a pen landscape graphically supporting his prose poem to Nantucket the symbol.[6]

[6] Melville did not visit Nantucket until shortly *after* the publication of *Moby-Dick,* going there in 1852 in the company of his distinguished father-in-law, Chief Justice Lemuel Shaw. It was at this time that he saw (as described in *Clarel*) the retired Captain Pollard of *Essex* fame.

The New Bedford scenes in *Moby-Dick* remind us forcibly that whenever Melville felt that anything was to be gained by fidelity to historical fact, faithful he then remained. Never, it should be hastily added, is this fidelity an infidelity to "creative art," nor does he avoid the obligation imposed on every artist to understand his materials. Melville records New Bedford with reportorial skill, but every fact in some way contributes to the grand total effect of his book. To visit the Seaman's Bethel on Johnny Cake Hill, for instance, is to see an illustration of Melville's closeness to guidebook fact. With Melville, however, faithful recollection was not sentimental; from physical fact he moved on to create imaginatively for that chapter, out of the person of its minister, the immortal figure of Father Mapple preaching the greatest of all Jonah sermons. A New Bedford chapel, its minister, and a book from the Old Testament — two personal recollections and one literary — fused into one great episode which provides the intellectual and spiritual groundwork upon which *Moby-Dick* is built. Only a pedestrian mind could mistake Father Mapple's sermon to Ishmael as a transcript of Father Mudge's to Melville. On the other hand, only the narrow esthete would be uninterested in the fact that Melville had once probably heard a sermon in a setting similar to that within the novel, and that Melville had stored the memory to good purpose. The sermon stands alone as a work of art, that is true, but it is not less effective in its setting of everyday geographical and antiquarian fact. And of Melville's life.

The features of New Bedford which Melville evoked from memory were those relevant to a whaling story. *Moby-Dick* is no guidebook to the city which young Melville had seen.

Radically different today from what it was one hundred years ago — for now it is an industrial city — New Bedford of the past may be reconstructed only from old prints and books. Nevertheless, the spirit of that old seaport is captured better in *Moby-Dick*, albeit briefly, than in any other document. Although he did not write a directory of New Bedford — selecting sights with a single purpose in mind — Melville more than any other single man has bestowed immortality on her. If ever Melville owed New Bedford a debt — for a night's lodging, for a job — he has repaid it hundredfold.

Several events in *Moby-Dick* suggest remembered experience. Ishmael seeks lodgings his first night in New Bedford, but it is late and he gropes through the "very dark and dismal night" looking for an inn. The second door he opens brings him an unexpected sight:

> It seemed the great Black Parliament sitting in Tophet. A hundred black faces turned round in their rows to peer; and beyond, a black Angel of Doom was beating a book in a pulpit. It was a negro church; and the preacher's text was about the blackness of darkness, and the weeping and wailing and teeth-gnashing there. Ha, Ishmael, muttered I, backing out, Wretched entertainment at the sign of "The Trap!"

It is a slight and humorous incident, but it has the ring of reality. And when one finds that New Bedford had two Negro churches at the time of Melville's visit to the city, one is inclined to think that he is speaking from personal experience. It is possible, however, that Melville had once blundered into the Negro Church in Pittsfield, and that he had used the incident for Ishmael in New Bedford.[7]

As described in *Moby-Dick*, the Seaman's Bethel with its memorial tablets, its strange pulpit, and its unusual minister have the remarkable combination of hard realism and hovering strangeness which is characteristic of almost every scene in the novel. The Seaman's Bethel of *Moby-Dick* is anchored firmly to recorded fact. The building erected in 1830 was the church attended by Melville. Despite a severe fire which in 1866 gutted the structure and consumed the tower, the church was restored to its original form and still serves as a house of worship, to be seen by the Melville tourist. Appropriately, it is just across the street from the Jonathan Bourne Whaling Museum, so that the New Bedford Melville associations are briefly encompassed. In his description of the earlier building Melville made one important and sig-

---

[7] Dr. Egbert Oliver has pointed out to me that the Second Congregational Church of Pittsfield, consisting entirely of Negroes, was formed in 1846.

nificant alteration from memory, incorporating in the chapel a prow pulpit (some people read it as a masthead pulpit) into which Father Mapple clambers by means of a rope ladder. The fantastic pulpit is Melville's vivid addition to actuality, felicitously and humorously reinforcing the nautical-whaling character of the book, and pointing up the loneliness-isolation theme. Professor Anderson had suggested the possibility of a literary inspiration for the novelty.[8] But even while labeling Father Mapple's pulpit as a figment of Melville's mind, one must entertain the possibility that in *Moby-Dick* we have report and not fiction. In recent years the Reverend Charles Thurber, present incumbent of the Seaman's Bethel, wished to install a pulpit similar to that in *Moby-Dick*.[9] When the workmen were digging to prepare the supports, they found signs of old cement work still remaining on the bedrock underlying the building. The cement remains suggest that possibly a former support for a previous and similar pulpit had been thrust down and cemented in place. If so, this unusual pulpit probably burned in the fire of 1866.

It is almost certain that Father Mapple, the whalemanminister in *Moby-Dick*, was drawn from life. Scholars have been almost unanimous in identifying him with the famous Father Edward Taylor, the Boston minister whose vivid, metaphorical style had attracted wide attention, and the written admiration of Harriet Martineau, Charles Dickens, and Ralph Waldo Emerson.[10] Unfortunately the identifica-

8 Charles R. Anderson, *Melville in the South Seas* (New York, 1939), pp. 24–25. The passage he cited is from Joseph C. Hart's *Miriam Coffin; or, The Whale Fisherman* (New York and London, 1834), I, XXVII: "Every inch of room was economized, and how sleeping chambers were scaled by perpendicular step-ladders, like those used to descend to the pent-up cabin of a fishing-smack, or to clamber up the sides of a merchantman; — and how the best and most spacious room in the house is finished like the cabin of a ship, with projecting beams, whose corners are beaded and ornamented with rude carving."

9 Mr. Thurber tells me that the pulpit which he had put up was soon removed by the order of a displeased church committee. Apparently they felt that it distracted from rather than added to the divine worship.

10 The best brief account of Father Edward Taylor is R. E. Watters's "Boston's Salt-Water Preacher," *South Atlantic Quarterly*, XLV (July, 1946), 350–361.

tion has been made on slight grounds. It is true that Melville may well have heard Father Taylor preach and it is equally true that there are resemblances between Father Taylor's dramatic style and the figurative rhetoric of Father Mapple, but no evidence has turned up to admit a positive identity. It rests on an attractive idea and nothing else.

It seems much more probable that Father Enoch Mudge was the man from whom Melville took the character of Father Mapple. For one thing, the similarity of the initial letters of their last names is noteworthy. Then, too, Father Enoch Mudge was the actual minister of the New Bedford Seaman's Bethel at the time Melville had visited there, and it is almost certain that Melville attended worship under Father Mudge shortly before sailing for the Pacific. Father Mudge had held his office from the time of its creation in 1832, and he was a venerable old man due to retire within three years — 1844.[11] Although no samples of his sermons survive to place beside Father Mapple's for comparison, Father Mudge left a reputation for activity in his gospel duties and for zeal in searching out the sinners at the waterside and drawing them to the Seaman's Bethel for worship. It is reasonable to assume that a man of Father Mudge's energy, required as he was to hold the attention of an unlettered audience, would have been skilled in making vivid the gospel story; through long experience as well as by instinct addressing the old salts of his sailor audience in their own terms. A New Bedford man, his imagery would have been that of his locality — the New Bedford of the sea and of whaling.[12]

It is too much to expect that the sermon which Father Enoch Mudge preached when Melville attended his church was on the Jonah story; but had it been so, nothing of

[11] *History of the Churches of New England* (New Bedford, 1869), pp. 106–108.

[12] It seems to me that the most effective argument for Father Taylor is the similarity between the painting at the back of his pulpit (see Gilbert Haven and Thomas Russell, *Father Taylor, the Sailor Preacher* [Boston, 1872], pp. 356–357) and the one behind Father Mapple. It is of course quite likely that both Father Taylor and Father Mudge contributed to the portrait of Father Mapple in *Moby-Dick*, and that both their churches went into the making of Melville's fictional church.

Mudge's could equal the driving, impassioned words flowing from the lips of Father Mapple in *Moby-Dick*. For in Father Mapple's sermon we are transported from the actuality of New Bedford into the timeless world of spiritual truth.

Melville's description of New Bedford justifies Ishmael's conclusion that it was a "queer place." Pulpit, parson, and sermon are all strange — or they are everyday reality seen through the eyes of a wise man. And the city itself wears a garb of strangeness. It was, said Ishmael, entirely a whaling town, so concentrated on the pursuit of the sperm whale, that he dared the metaphor that New Bedford's fine houses and beautiful gardens must have "been harpooned and dragged up hither from the sea. Can Herr Alexander perform a feat like that?" And as Ishmael and Queequeg, sailing out to Nantucket, look back towards shore, they see the city of New Bedford glistening in the winter air, much as Melville himself had seen it from the deck of the *Acushnet* ten years before:

> On one side, New Bedford rose in terraces of streets, their ice-covered trees all glittering in the clear, cold air. Huge hills and mountains of casks on casks were piled upon her wharves, and side by side the world-wandering whale ships lay silent and safely moored at last; while from others came a sound of carpenters and coopers, with blended noises of fires and forges to melt the pitch, all betokening that new cruises were on the start; that one most perilous and long voyage ended, only begins a second; and a second ended, only begins a third, and so on, for ever and for aye. Such is the endlessness, yea, the intolerableness of all earthly effort.

But such a paragraph is much more than mere memory; it is both picture and idea, in the manner of Prospero's description of the vanished masque and masquers "like a dream." Melville's ten-year-old sight of the New Bedford panorama has joined with recent philosophical reflection. *Vanitas vanitatum.* Writing to Hawthorne, Melville had recently expressed his sense of the unending pressures of life:

> Would that a man could do something & then say — It is finished — not that one thing only, but all others — that he

has reached his uttermost, & can never exceed it. But live and push — tho' we put one leg before forward ten miles — its no reason the other must lag behind — no, *that* must again distance the other — & so we go till we get the cramp & die.

And for a third time in one year he expressed the thought again, when having written *Moby-Dick*, he asked Hawthorne with humorous despair: "Lord, when shall we be done growing? As long as we have anything more to do, we have done nothing. . . . Lord, when shall we be done changing?"

3

"The preacher slowly turned over the leaves of the Bible"

THE SERMON preached by Father Mapple from the prow pulpit of the Seaman's Bethel has been frequently praised, but never, so far as I know, has it been analyzed for its meaning; nor has it been seen in relationship to *Moby-Dick* as a whole.

Melville undoubtedly intended that Father Mapple's sermon should be the vehicle for the central theme of *Moby-Dick*. The year before, he had followed a similar practice in *White-Jacket* — a novel which is to be understood through comprehension of the sermon chapter with which it closes. Similarly, *Pierre* emerges from its ambiguities only when one has victoriously wrestled with "Chronometricals and Horologicals," the pamphlet-essay thrust into Pierre's pocket by the mysterious Plotinus Plinlimmon. Philosophically, *Moby-Dick* remains closed to us until we understand Father Mapple's sermon on Jonah and the Whale. With this key Melville unlocked his novel.

The sermon is a skillful adaptation of the Old Testament book of Jonah, especially that part dealing with Jonah's nautical adventures. The sonorous Biblical rhythms may be distinctly heard in Mapple's words. Diction and imagery

suit well the old whaleman-preacher and a whaling audience.
The setting of the sermon strengthens its message: the central theme first foreshadowed by the physical isolation of the
minister from his flock:

> No, thought I, there must be some sober reason for this
> thing; furthermore, it must symbolize something unseen. Can
> it be, then, that by that act of physical isolation, he signifies his
> spiritual withdrawal for the time, from all outward worldly
> ties and connexions? Yes, for replenished with the meat and
> wine of the word, to the faithful man of God, this pulpit, I
> see, is a self-containing stronghold — a lofty Ehrenbreitstein,
> with a perennial well of water within the walls.

Melville explains that Father Mapple's climb up the rope
ladder to his pulpit is not a "trick of the stage." The reader
sees it as a symbolical act similar in vein to the symbolical
gestures and motions of Nathaniel Hawthorne's characters
— for instance, in "The Minister's Black Veil." Part of the
nautical atmosphere of *Moby-Dick*, the isolating prow pulpit
symbolizes the fundamental isolation of all men — a point
underscored in the account of the waiting audience: "Each
silent worshipper seemed purposely sitting apart from the
other, as if each silent grief were insular and incommunicable." Everyman is an island — an isolato, Melville
later says — and in nothing is he more alone than in his relation to his God. Such is Melville's implication.

No less than John Milton, Father Mapple seeks in his sermon to justify the ways of God to man. The relationship of
the individual soul to God is difficult to determine and demands a consideration of the nature of "self" and selfhood.
And as has been argued in discussing the opening line, "Call
me Ishmael," *Moby-Dick* is concerned with the problem of
self-realization. Melville attempts in Father Mapple's sermon to establish the profoundest meaning of the concept of
"self." Self is made up of many selves; what we call self is a
unification of various selves, as the political, the economic,
the biological, the professional, the racial. Like all other
phenomena, Selfhood resolves itself into the eternal dialectic
of the One and the Many. Father Mapple's sermon is a

device, a touchstone for testing the revelations of selfhood made in Ahab, Queequeg, or Starbuck — all variously inadequate or superficial when compared with the wisdom of Mapple's definition. The individualism of Father Mapple is Christian, insisting that the personal will must submit to the will of God, personal self must be submerged in the Divine self. Father Mapple's sermon is built on the theme most memorably stated by Dante: "In His will is our peace." Father Mapple establishes in whaling language and through a whaling story the Christian paradox that the fullest selfhood may be won only by the annihilation of self.

Father Mapple tells his audience that the story of Jonah is a "two-stranded" lesson: the first strand a story of sin, punishment, and repentance; the second strand the account of Jonah's deliberate defiance of God's will. Mapple drives his point home: "And if we obey God we must disobey ourselves; and it is in this disobeying ourselves, wherein the hardness of obeying God consists." As the story of *Moby-Dick* unfolds, we realize the relevance, thematically as well as wittily, of the sermon on Jonah, for soon Jonah's fugue is repeated in the flight of Ahab. Ahab will set out on his vengeful voyage, determined to assert his might against the White Whale, and in defiance of the desires of his crew. But whereas Jonah at last heeded the will of God in time to save the ship and to still the storm, Ahab, unrepentant, imposes his will upon his men so that both he and the *Pequod* crew are destroyed. Ahab's defiance of the storm in "The Candles" (119), is in ironic contrast to Jonah's repentance; in Father Mapple's sermon we behold a man saved by a whale, but in Ahab's act we see a man destroyed by one. Humility and submission are the sign of Father Mapple's "self"; pride and arrogant confidence the sign of Ahab's.

Melville, in Father Mapple's message, does not neglect the meaning of the three days Jonah spent within the whale's belly, singing his canticle to Jehovah. Though the words of Jesus,"Even as Jonah descended into the belly of the whale for three days and three nights, even so shall the Son of God descend into the tomb and rise again," are not quoted, it is clear from the language of the sermon that Melville had seen

Jonah's experience as a form of resurrection.[13] The correlation is rather clear:

> As we have seen, God came upon him in the whale, and swallowed him down to living gulfs of doom, and with swift slantings tore him along "into the midst of the seas," where the eddying depths sucked him ten thousand fathoms down, and "the weeds were wrapped about his head," and all the watery world of woe bowled over him. Yet even then beyond the reach of any plummet — "out of the belly of hell" — when the whale grounded upon the ocean's utmost bones, even then, God heard the engulphed, repenting prophet when he cried. The God spake unto the fish; and from the shuddering cold and blackness of the sea, the whale came breaching up towards the warm and pleasant sun, and all the delights of air and earth; and "vomited out Jonah upon the dry land"; when the word of the Lord came a second time; and Jonah, bruised and beaten — his ears, like two sea-shells, still multitudinously murmuring of the ocean — Jonah did the Almighty's bidding. And what was that, shipmates? To preach the Truth to the face of Falsehood! That was it!

The graphic and poetic power of such phrases as "the ocean's utmost bones," or the delicate, yet strong, manipulation of antitheses such as "shuddering blackness of the sea" and "the warm and pleasant sun"; the skillful planting of the word "delight" which will be picked up again in the closing words of the sermon; and the melodic felicity of "still multitudinously murmuring of the sea" or "the engulphed, repenting prophet" — all this should not distract us from examining the symbolical significance of Father Mapple's paragraph. Its meaning recalls the famous passage towards the close of *White-Jacket* when the hero, just fallen from the yardarm into the depths of the sea, breaches to the surface, and rising, hears two sounds in his ears, the one a "soft moaning, as of low waves on the beach; the other wild and heartlessly jubi-

13 Another American has interpreted the Jonah story in much the same way: Carl Sandburg in "Losers" (from *Smoke and Steel*, by Carl Sandburg, copyright, 1920, by Harcourt, Brace, and Company, Inc.):

> If I should pass the tomb of Jonah
> I would stop there and sit for awhile;
> Because I was swallowed one time deep in the dark
> And came out alive after all.

lant, as of the sea in the height of a tempest. Oh soul! thou then heardest life and death." Reminiscent of the sweet sing- ing which reached the Mariner's ears when the albatross dropped from his neck, Melville's passages in *White-Jacket* and *Moby-Dick* set forth symbols of death and rebirth. To be born again, psychologically and religiously, is to renounce an old self so as to assume a new self, a new and deeper prin- ciple of life. Keats described the process as "dying into life." Stated most profoundly, as by Melville through Father Mapple, it is to renounce personal desire, and to accept the will of God.

Father Mapple closes his sermon with an unambiguous declaration of his point: to be reborn one must forget self in the service of God — thus, and only thus, may happiness (Delight) be found, the truest selfhood attained:

> Delight is to him — a far, far upward, and inward delight — who against the proud gods and commodores of this earth, ever stands forth his own inexorable self. Delight is to him whose strong arms yet support him, when the ship of this base treacherous world has gone down beneath him. Delight is to him, who gives no quarter in the truth, and kills, burns, and destroys all sin though he pluck it out from under the robes of Senators and Judges. Delight, — top-gallant delight is to him, who acknowledges no law or lord, but the Lord his God, and is only a patriot to heaven. Delight is to him, whom all the waves of the billows of the seas of the boisterous mob can never shake from this sure Keel of the Ages. And eternal delight and deliciousness will be his, who coming to lay him down, can say with his final breath — O Father! — chiefly known to me by Thy rod — mortal or immortal, here I die. I have striven to be Thine, more than to be this world's, or mine own. Yet this is nothing; I leave eternity to Thee; for what is man that he should live out the lifetime of his God? [14]

[14] Compare the following passage, of similar meaning, from Thomas à Kempis, *Imitation of Christ*: "Lord, thou knowest what is best; let this or that be according as thou wilt. Give what thou wilt, so much as thou wilt when thou wilt. Do with me as thou knowest best, and as shall be most to thine honour. Place me where thou wilt, and freely work thy will with me in all things. . . . When could it be evil when thou wert near? I had rather be poor for thy sake than rich without thee. I choose rather to be a pilgrim upon the earth with thee, than without thee to possess heaven. Where thou art, there is heaven; and where thou art not, behold there death and hell."

Delight is to him who reads Father Mapple's peroration. English prose is nowhere superior. The upward thrust of these climactic sentences through the relentless repetition of "delight," [15] the bold use of alliteration in the stabbing dentals, and the unexpectedness and perfection of the adjective "eternal" placed before the final "delight" — these and other effects (allusion, cadences) are the exercise of one both craftsman and artist.

No less powerful is the passage in its statement of spiritual truth, or in its enunciation of the dominant theme of *Moby-Dick*. In its recognition of the place of regeneration in spiritual maturation, and in its understanding of the deepest meaning of selfhood, Father Mapple's sermon is a far cry from the talk of selfhood heard from other Americans of Melville's day: Emerson or Whitman. The young Emerson who lay on his bed dreaming pleasantly of the harmony of God's world is not in the same church with Melville, whose appreciation of the terror and evil of life (learned on the pulses and not from texts) seems much more consonant with the harsh facts of common human experience.

From his eloquent and passionate affirmation the rest of *Moby-Dick* unfolds. Ahab no less than Father Mapple is in search of an Absolute, be its name God or Moby Dick, but unlike the whaleman-preacher, Ahab acknowledges no law but his own; his search will be carried on in self-assertion, not in self-submission. In the early, unrepentant Jonah, Ahab has been prefigured. Ahab defies God; his *hybris* is the antithesis of Jonah's submission. Great as Ahab is, he is not, to borrow a phrase from Keats, "magnanimous enough to annihilate self." Striving to be God himself, or in worshiping false gods (even as the Ahab of the Old Testament worshiped Baal), Ahab will never know delight. "Delight," Father Mapple states significantly and memorably, "can only be to him who has striven to be God's." Not to him who strives to be God. Ahab should have been one of the silent worshipers at the Seaman's Bethel.

15 Effectively and delicately contrasting in mood with the earlier repetition of "woe."

4

"A man like Queequeg you don't see every day"

FROM THE TORTUOUS SOUL-SEARCHING of Father Mapple, the
story of Moby-Dick moves immediately in vivid, even an-
tithetical, contrast, to the serenity of Queequeg, the pagan
harpooner. By all odds the most attractive character in the
novel, Queequeg is first discovered in a New Bedford water-
front lodging which was doubtless dredged from the less
pleasant depths of Melville's memory. Since Ishmael assures
us that Queequeg was quite a person and that "he and his
ways were well worth unusual regarding," we should take
the hint and consider for a moment Queequeg's dramatic
and symbolic function in *Moby-Dick*. For thematically,
Queequeg is a counterpoint to Father Mapple; it is no accident that Melville moved directly from the man of God to
the savage idolator, from the Christian to the Pagan.

Queequeg was a native of the island of Rokovoko — "not
down on any map; true places never are" — whence he had
been shanghaied by whalemen and carried against his will to
the shores of New England. Queequeg is a representation of
a form of selfhood antipodal to that described in Father
Mapple's sermon. Where Father Mapple was the extreme
intensity of spiritual consciousness, Queequeg is, on the other
hand, the instinctual and unconscious self. If we see *Moby-
Dick* as an account of Ishmael's attempt to find himself, his
inner harmony, and if we regard Ahab, Starbuck, Pip, and
the others as various of Ishmael's selves, real or potential,
Queequeg becomes no less alive as idea than he does as part
of the narrative.

There is but little, if any, ambiguity in Melville's portrait
of Queequeg as the Unconscious (in the sense of spontaneous) — man possessing the instinctual poise lost to
sophisticated man. Through all his experiences on shore
and on the *Pequod,* Queequeg maintains his magnificent
aplomb: "he seemed entirely at his ease; preserving the
utmost serenity; content with his own companionship;

always equal to himself." Clearly this tattooed Polynesian may be related to the Noble Savage of literary and sentimental tradition. In *Moby-Dick*, however, he is unsentimentally portrayed, for Melville had known such men well in the Typee Valley. Queequeg's poise is implicitly a criticism of the neurotic divagations of "civilized men." Queequeg never needed to think; he acted with instinctive good sense. "We mortals," said Ishmael, "should not be conscious of so living or so striving"; we should take Queequeg as model. Queequeg, we are told, "looked like a man who had never cringed and never had a creditor." Despite the hideous markings tattooed on his face, "his countenance yet had something in it which was by no means disagreeable. You cannot hide the soul." Only once is Queequeg thrown off balance or made ridiculous, and that, significantly, is when, affected by the modesties of civilization, he crawls beneath the bed in the Spouter Inn to put on — his boots! Thus, obliquely, Melville says that only in making concessions to the western conventions could the Polynesian lose his native dignity. Melville himself had seen the Tahitians, beautiful children of nature, dressed at the missionaries' insistence in Mother Hubbards or in cast-off shirts and trousers. This "civilizing" influence is satirized in Queequeg's aberration of modesty. But except for this one slip, Queequeg is always master of himself, and so of every situation in which he plays a part. When he rescues the man, his erstwhile tormentor, who falls from the Nantucket packet into the ocean, he makes nothing of his unselfish, heroic act, merely asking politely for some water with which to wash off the brine. "Was there," Ishmael admiringly and enviously asks, "ever such unconsciousness?" With the passage of time, this wholeness of mind, or spiritual health, served as an anodyne to Ishmael: "No more my splintered heart and maddened hand were turned against the wolfish world. This soothing savage had redeemed it. There he sat, his very indifference speaking a nature in which there lurked no civilized hypocrisies and bland deceits." The sunlight of Polynesia drove the November drizzle of New England Calvinism from his soul.

Thinking back, we recognize in Queequeg the most important themes of *Typee,* Melville's first novel. Neither Queequeg nor *Typee* is a sentimental, Pierre Loti flight from reality, although some writers have hastily and mistakenly charged Melville with Rousseauism. Melville was too realistic to perpetuate in fiction the myth of the goodness of natural man; he had seen mankind in its baseness, primitive and civilized, in two hemispheres. In the South Seas he had come close to cannibalism, and he had seen the selfish and senseless rapacity of the white traders, the lustful depravity of the sailors. He had also noted the white man's disregard for human dignity and decency, his strange urge to impose his own ways upon alien peoples. Furthermore, Melville had seen, as in a series of "before" and "after" pictures, the pedigree of Polynesian degradation. Among the Typee savages he had known the Noble Savage as fact. In Tahiti he had seen the same savage beauty in a state of decay. Finally, in the Sandwich Islands he had been sickened by the physical and psychological destruction wreaked by his fellow Westerners upon the primitive peoples. Melville's finest memory was that of the Marquesans, and he had lovingly described them in *Typee,* with an occasional pungent criticism upon their European opposites. Now in *Moby-Dick,* a book concerned primarily with European culture, Melville allowed Queequeg to serve implicatively as the critic of that culture. The Garden of Eden condemns us all.

In Queequeg, we have sharp proof that the seven years of writing and reading following Melville's return from the Pacific had resulted in maturity of mind and in depth of insight. The observation which so charmed in *Typee* is now reinforced by reflection. The seductive events of *Typee* are obliquely recalled in *Moby-Dick;* they are seen as a subordinate part of a much larger book; hence the crystallization of the themes of brotherhood, religious tolerance, the beauty of the instinctive, in the character of Queequeg. Resembling the friendship of Tom and Kory-Kory in *Typee,* the friendship between Ishmael and Queequeg is deepened and subtilized in the creation of Queequeg, who symbolizes more richly and ambiguously the values which Melville had earlier seen and earlier set forth. Queequeg is not only the entire

Typee Valley; he is Polynesia; he is Emerson's naked New Zealander "whose property is a club, a spear, a mat, and an undivided shed to sleep under. But compare the two men, and you shall see that the white man has lost his aboriginal strength." [16] Emerson's explicit statement is implicit in every scene involving Queequeg.

Through Ishmael and Queequeg, Melville continues his earlier attack on religious intolerance. This time his attack is oblique, subtle, humorous. In "The Ramadan" chapter, Ishmael returns to the Spouter Inn to find Queequeg fasting in honor of the Ramadan. It is curious, and perhaps puzzling, that Melville has described his South Sea Islander as observing a Mohammedan form of holy day for the worship of a Polynesian idol. The blend of two diverse religions must have been deliberate, for Melville had read widely enough to know what the Ramadan signified and that Mohammedanism was a non-idolatrous religion. When the Ramadan is over, Ishmael lectures Queequeg on the folly of his religious forms, and with amusing intolerance, tries to show him the error of his ways. Taking first a smugly liberal stand, Ishmael wrote:

> Now, as I before hinted, I have no objection to any person's religion, be it what it may, so long as that person does not kill or insult any other person, because that other person don't believe it also. But when a man's religion becomes really frantic; when it is a positive torment to him; and, in fine, makes this earth of ours an uncomfortable inn to lodge in; then I think it high time to take that individual aside and argue the point with him. . . . I then went on, beginning with the rise and progress of the primitive religions, and coming

16 "Self-Reliance." The South Sea savage was, of course, a popular nineteenth-century symbol. Compare Goethe's words to Eckermann, 12 March, 1828: "There is something more or less wrong among us old Europeans; our relations are far too artificial and complicated, our nutriment and mode of life are without their proper nature, and our social intercourse is without proper love and good will. Every one is polished and courteous; but no one has the courage to be hearty and true, so that an honest man, with natural views and feelings, stands in a very bad position. Often one cannot help wishing that one had been born upon one of the South Sea Islands, a so-called savage, so as to have thoroughly enjoyed human existence in all its purity."

down to the various religions of the present time, during which
time I labored to show Queequeg that all these Lents, Rama-
dans, and prolonged ham-squattings in cold, cheerless rooms
were stark nonsense; bad for the health; useless for the soul;
opposed, in short, to the obvious laws of Hygiene and common sense.

Ishmael's efforts to persuade Queequeg are of course a parody
of the activities of the missionaries in Polynesia, who pre-
tended tolerance, but tried to impose their ways on the
natives, only with incongruous and lamentable results — as
Omoo fully showed. And then suddenly, Ishmael becomes
Melville, student of comparative religions, and the most
tolerant of men:

> After all, I do not think that my remarks about religion
> made much impression upon Quequeg. Because, in the first
> place, he somehow seemed dull of hearing on that important
> subject, unless considered from his own point of view; and, in
> the second place, he did not more than one third understand
> me, couch my ideas simply as I would; and, finally, he no
> doubt thought he knew a good deal more about the true re-
> ligion than I did.

When, in *Typee* and *Omoo,* Melville had frankly aired his
views concerning the missionaries to Polynesia and the disastrous effects they had had upon the lives of the natives, he
had been attacked so severely by several reviews sympathetic
to the missionary interests that his publishers were forced to
mitigate Melville's anti-missionary zeal in later editions. But
in *Moby-Dick,* Melville again attacks religious bigotry,
though obliquely, with the scene between Ishmael and
Queequeg, a parody of the missionary failure. So subtle was
his satire that only one reviewer of the period discerned dis-
respectful irreverence in the Ramadan episode. Interestingly
enough that reviewer was Melville's close friend, Evert
Duyckinck. Duyckinck felt that Ishmael's kneeling in com-
radeship with Queequeg before the black idol, Yojo, "violated the most sacred associations of life."

5

"Where else but from Nantucket?"

TRAVELING on the little packet steamer *Moss,* Queequeg and Ishmael arrived at Nantucket, hoping to find there a whaleship suitable to their intention and desire. But why was Ishmael's mind "made up to sail in no other than a Nantucket craft" when Melville himself had never been in Nantucket and had instead sailed for the South Seas from the mainland port of Fairhaven? The answer to this question reveals the care Melville took with the smallest details of his story, his sense of artistic propriety.

In 1850, when Melville began to write *Moby-Dick,* New Bedford was the whaling center of the world, having years before wrested the leadership from little Nantucket. When Melville had shipped out, in 1841, New Bedford already boasted a whaling fleet almost twice the size of Nantucket's, and even though the island port clung securely to second place in whaling importance, New Bedford could claim the eminence. In 1847, for example, New Bedford had sent out 254 ships as against Nantucket's 75, and New London's 70. Why didn't Melville send Ishmael from New Bedford? The answer is simple. Melville was not writing his own journal in *Moby-Dick,* nor was he allowing statistical tables to dictate his story. He disregarded economic truth in order that symbolic truth might be served. Both determined for Melville that Ishmael should ship out — "Where else but from Nantucket?"

For Nantucket was and has remained the symbol of American whaling genius. She represented and represents the antiquity and the aristocracy of one of America's most romantic industries. New Bedford was the intrusive, albeit successful, newcomer. But although New Bedford had developed a devotion to whaling almost that of her rival's, the fact still remained that the *total* energies of Nantucket had been engrossed in the pursuit of whales from the very days of her founding; she had known little else but blubber and oil;

the energies, the interest, and the fortunes of every citizen, man, woman, and child were somehow tied up with spermaceti and whalebone. Nantucket prospered or drooped in exact ratio to the whale catch of the year and to the price of whale oil. So it had been for generations. Melville is explicit:

> . . . there was a fine, boisterous something about everything connected with that famous old island, which amazingly pleased me. Besides, though New Bedford has of late been gradually monopolizing the business of whaling, and though in this matter poor old Nantucket is now much behind her, yet Nantucket was her great original — the Tyre of this Carthage; — the place where the first dead American whale was stranded. Where else but from Nantucket did those aboriginal whalemen, the Red-Men, first sally out in canoes to give chase to the Leviathan? And where but from Nantucket, too, did that adventurous little sloop put forth, partly laden with imported cobble-stones — so goes the story — to throw at the whales, in order to discover when they were nigh enough to risk a harpoon from the bowsprit?

Nantucket *had* begun her whaling early. In 1672 a Right Whale entered her harbor to spout there for several days. Accepting this open challenge, the Nantucketers shaped a harpoon and set out to capture the fish. This was the blubbered spout from which grew Ahabs, even as Athena sprang full panoplied from the unblubbered head of Zeus. At first, the Nantucketers erected a tall pole with ladder cleats to serve as a lookout for whales. When a whale was sighted the boats would set out in pursuit. The first sperm whale captured by an American whaleship was that caught by Christopher Hussey, whose boat had blown out to sea, and who had become fast to a sperm whale. From this accident Nantucketers conceived the idea of going into the open ocean for their catch instead of waiting on shore for the whales to come to them. Soon whaling sloops of thirty tons were built to venture beyond soundings. Rapidly the ships increased in size and the voyages grew longer, stretching out in time and into strange places: to the Davis Straits in 1732, then to the Bahamas, the Gulf of Mexico, the Azores, and to the Coast of Africa. Finally, in 1791 American whalemen in one New Bedford and four Nantucket ships rounded Cape Horn to burst into that silent sea. Although they had followed by four years the epoch-making exploration of Samuel Enderby's *Amelia,* the Americans made up for lost time by the daring and vigor of their hunt so that it was not long before they were the masters of the Pacific whaling grounds. Such they remained throughout the next one hundred years. Their magnificent accomplishments were no less daring nor less interesting than the voyages of the Elizabethan sea-dogs, but where the English had sailed forth to plunder and kill their Spanish cousins, the Nantucket Quakers sought only to gather the oil and bone of the whale. They illustrated de Tocqueville's observation that

> In the United States, martial valor is but little prized; the courage which is best known and most esteemed is that which emboldens men to brave the dangers of the ocean, in order to arrive earlier in port, — to support the privations of the wilderness without complaint, and solitude more cruel than privations — the courage which renders them almost insensible to the loss of fortune laboriously acquired, and instantly prompts them to fresh exertions to make another. Courage of this kind is peculiarly necessary to the maintenance and prosperity of the American communities, and it is held by them in peculiar honor and estimation; to betray a want of it is to incur certain disgrace.

This was the quality, most vividly and admirably exemplified in the American whaling fishery, which Melville celebrated in *Moby-Dick*; and the *fons et origo* of American whaling was Nantucket. Melville honored the great, but then uncelebrated, tradition by sending Ishmael and Queequeg out to the South Seas on a Nantucket ship, made with artistic propriety an emblem of all American whaleships.

Although Melville had been able to draw upon personal recollections in creating the New Bedford background of his book, he was forced to rely upon the experiences and reports of others in setting up the Nantucket scenes. Therefore, he is not geo-graphic, but geo-fanciful. His main source was Obed Macy's little volume, *History of Nantucket,* supported, perhaps, by general atmosphere supplied in J. C. Hart's *Miriam Coffin*. Certainly the chapter on "Nantucket" is under the heaviest debt to Macy — "worthy Obed," as Melville termed him. With natural pride, with simple dignity, and with the authority one could expect from a descendant of Nantucket's founders, Obed Macy had set down the history of his little island. Since one does not discuss *Hamlet* without considering the titular character, Macy had incorporated in his book a short but valuable survey of the whaling industry. In various places in *Moby-Dick* Melville reworked suggestions from Macy's book, but one transformation is epochal. Here is Macy's tribute to the Nantucket whale hunters:

> The whaling business is peculiarly an ocean life. The sea, to mariners generally, is but a highway over which they travel to foreign markets; but to the whaler it is his field of labor, it is the home of his business. The Nantucket whaleman, when with his family, is but a visiter [*sic*] there. He touches at foreign ports merely to procure recruits to enable him to prosecute his voyage; he touches at home merely long enough to prepare for a new voyage. He is in the bosom of his family weeks, on the bosom of the ocean years. His youth and strength, and best manhood, are all devoted to a life of tedious labor and great peril. His boyhood anticipates such a life, and aspires after its highest responsibilities; his age delights in recounting its incidents. We read, and sometimes, perhaps, dwell with delight on the daring exploits of those whom the world calls heroes; and in proportion to the victims sacrificed on the altar of ambition, we attribute glory and honor to the visitor. Alas! what is bloodshed but murder . . .

Momentarily passing by the pacifist-Quaker slant of Macy's words, Melville transformed the passage by careful alliteration ("resides and riots") , expressive metaphor and simile ("prairie cocks in the prairie"), and rising periods which bespeak profound familiarity with the rhythms of the King James Bible. And then, probably recalling a passage from *Ribs and Trucks* (Boston, 1842):

> 'Tis your whaler alone, who goes down *to* the sea, in ships; other mariners hurry across it. He alone does business *upon*

the great waters; and, more emphatically than other 'sea-farers,' makes the ocean his home. With his top-sail-yard 'sharp up,' and his helm 'four spokes a-lee,' he rides out the storm, month in and month out — nestling like a sea-bird, in the trough, and feeling himself, as it were, in harbor; while other ships rise on the horizon and scud by, and lessen and reel out of sight, with blind celerity, on their respective courses.

Melville extracted shimmering gold from Macy's and "W.A.G.'s" ore:

And thus have these naked Nantucketers, these sea hermits, issuing from their ant-hill in the sea, overrun and conquered the watery world like so many Alexanders; parcelling out among them the Atlantic, Pacific, and Indian Oceans, as the three pirate powers did Poland. Let America add Mexico to Texas, and pile Cuba upon Canada; let the English over-swarm all India, and hang out their blazing banner from the sun; two thirds of this terraqueous globe are the Nantucketer's. For the sea is his; he owns it, as Emperors own empires; other seamen having but a right of way through it. Merchant ships are but extension bridges; armed ones but floating forts; even pirates and privateers, though following the sea as highway-men the road, they but plunder other ships, other fragments of the land like themselves, without seeking to draw their living from the bottomless deep itself. The Nantucketer, he alone resides and riots on the sea; he alone, in Bible language, goes down to it in ships; to and fro ploughing it as his own special plantation. *There* is his home; *there* lies his business, which a Noah's flood would not interrupt, though it over-whelmed all the millions in China. He lives on the sea, as prairie cocks in the prairie; he hides among the waves, he climbs them as chamois hunters climb the Alps For years he knows not the land; so that when he comes to it at last, it smells like another world, more strangely than the moon would to an Earthsman. With the landless gull, that at sunset folds her wings and is rocked to sleep between billows; so at nightfall, the Nantucketer, out of sight of land, furls his sails, and lays him to rest, while under his very pillow rush herds of walruses and whales.[17]

[17] Perhaps the first part of Melville's prose lyric incorporated an idea from Burke's famous peroration on the whaleman, quoted by Beale, p. 142, and

When Herman Melville's one hundred and twenty-fifth birthday anniversary was honored in Nantucket, 19 August, 1944, this passage, transcribed and broadcast to our troops overseas, was the only excerpt used from any of Melville's writings, a Melville gem in a radio setting. Rich as Melville's chapter "Nantucket" may be, it remains rhetoric, not the description it might have been had Melville visited Nantucket himself. The first three paragraphs, leading up to the passage just quoted, do not describe, they generalize, they jest about Nantucket's sandiness:

> Look at it [on a map] — a mere hillock, and elbow of sand; all beach, without a background. There is more sand there than you would use in twenty years as a substitute for blotting paper. Some gamesome wights will tell you that they have to plant weeds there, they don't grow naturally; that they import Canada thistles; that they have to send beyond seas for a spile to stop a leak in an oil cask; that pieces of wood in Nantucket are carried about like bits of the true cross in Rome; that people there plant toadstools before their houses, to get under the shade in summer time; that one blade of grass makes an oasis, three blades in a day's walk a prairie; that they wear quicksand shoes, something like Laplander snow-shoes. . . .

A study of Melville's habits of composition shows that when he indulged in this sort of verbal exercise he was letting

marked by Melville in his copy of Beale: "And pray, sir, what in the world is equal to it? Pass by the other parts, and look at the manner in which the New England people carry on the whale fishery. While we follow them among the trembling mountains of ice, and behold them penetrating into the deepest frozen recesses of Hudson's and Davis's Straits, while we are looking for them beneath the arctic circle, we hear that they have pierced into the opposite region of polar cold — that they are at the antipodes, and engaged under the frozen serpent of the south. Falkland Island, which seems too remote for the grasp of national ambition, is but a stage and resting place for their victorious industry. Nor is the equinoctial heat more discouraging to them than the accumulated winter of both poles. We learn, that while some of them draw the line or strike the harpoon on the coast of Africa, others run the longitude, and pursue their gigantic game along the coast of Brazil. No sea, but what is vexed with their fisheries — no climate that is not witness of their toils. Neither the perseverance of Holland, nor the activity of France, nor the dexterous and firm sagacity of English enterprise, ever carried this perilous mode of hardy industry to the extent to which it has been pursued by this recent people, — a people who are still in the gristle, and not hardened into manhood."

imagination canter in a direction already pointed out by someone else. Here Melville was probably expatiating on these passages in Joseph C. Hart's *Miriam Coffin*: [18]

. . . the little sandy island of Nantucket peeps forth from the Atlantic ocean. Isolated and alone amidst a wide waste of waters, it presents to the stranger, at first view, a dreary and unpromising appearance. The scrapings of the great African Desert, were they poured into the sea, would not emerge above its level with an aspect of more unqualified aridity than does this American island. . . . But few trees, and those, it is averred, not the natural growth of the soil, relieve the monotonous surface of the island . . . were it not for the moving things upon it that have life and activity, the island to most eyes would wear the face of utter desolation.

Hart's words may have helped Melville to portray the sandiness and treelessness of Nantucket.

It is interesting that Melville's other jest about the island touched on the natives' fondness for clams. In at least two places in *Miriam Coffin,* Joseph Hart mentions this with such emphasis that Melville, reading the novel, may have seized on the hints and built up his "Chowder" (15) chapter therefrom, making Ishmael complain: "Chowder for breakfast, and chowder for dinner, and chowder for supper, till you begin to look for fishbones coming through your clothes."

The characters which Ishmael discovered on Nantucket and described with particularity — the owners of the *Pequod,* Captains Bildad and Peleg, and Aunt Charity — are either pure imaginative reconstructions on Melville's part, or they are developments from the slightest and most general of hints in Hart or Obed Macy. Obed Macy, for instance, had stressed the universal Quakerishness of the island, a characteristic so pervasive, appearing in clothes and speech, that even Ishmael was affected by it:

[18] 3 vols. (New York, 1834). Leon Howard first pointed out the interesting similarities — other than those I have mentioned — between *Miriam Coffin* and *Moby-Dick* in "A Predecessor of Moby-Dick," *Modern Language Notes,* XLIX (May, 1934), 310–311. In *Miriam Coffin* a ship is dramatically sunk by a whale, and there is a prophecy of future tragedy, both slightly resembling features of Melville's novel.

"He says he's our man, Bildad," said Peleg, "he wants to ship."

"Dost thee?" said Bildad, in a hollow tone, and turning round to me.

"I dost," said I unconsciously, he was so intense a Quaker.

Macy referred so frequently to the Quaker principle of non-violence that Melville, amusedly noting the contrast of the Nantucketer's whaling violence and his pacifistic principles, ironically attributed the paradox to economic opportunism:

> Still, for all this immutableness [in religion], was there some lack of common consistency about worthy Captain Peleg. Though refusing, from conscientious scruples, to bear arms against land invaders, yet himself had illimitably invaded the Atlantic and Pacific; and though a sworn foe to human bloodshed, yet had he, in his straight-bodied coat, spilled tuns upon tuns of leviathan gore. How now in the contemplative evening of his days, the pious Bildad reconciled these things in the reminiscence, I do not know; but it did not seem to concern him much, and very probably he had long since come to the sage and sensible conclusion that a man's religion is one thing, and this practical world quite another. This world pays dividends.

Macy's reconciliation of economics and principles, which Melville so engagingly mocks, is a light-hearted treatment of a theme central to Melville's next novel, *Pierre.* Bildad's conclusion "that a man's religion is one thing, and this practical world quite another" is the subject discussed in "Chronometricals and Horologicals" and which is exemplified throughout the entire plot of *Pierre.*

Ishmael and Queequeg sign for the voyage. All the details of presailing activity come not so much from Macy's book as from Melville's memory and from general descriptions in the other whaling books. The exact location of sources for these materials is impossible to determine. But in total, whether from memory or from book, or both, they are placed in a dramatic, narrative, and humorous setting which animates them and lodges them in the pleasure of the reader. As for the ship itself, the immortal *Pequod,* that is a matter requiring special study.

6

"A noble craft, but somehow a most melancholy"

AMONG THE SHIPS at harbor at Nantucket, Ishmael and
Queequeg selected the *Pequod*. In a sense, the ship had been
selected for them by Queequeg's little black idol, but since
Yojo had not specified the ship's name, Ishmael sauntered
out to fulfill the ambiguous prophecy of the Yojo. Thus Melville humorously suggested a haphazard choice. And so it
was for Ishmael, but not for Melville, who carefully constructed the *Pequod* out of his mind, from fantasy working
on remembered experience. The *Pequod* is indeed an unusual sight, even among whaleships, but then *Moby-Dick*
abounds in exceptional sights and therefore the *Pequod* is
in keeping with her surroundings.

Melville's description of the *Pequod* reveals again his
sense of artistic propriety. For had not the artist in Melville
been at work, the reporter in Melville would have constructed a ship quite different from the *Pequod*. To repeat,
with Melville, as with any true artist, memory was but the
beginning of artistic creation. Nowhere in *Moby-Dick* may
we say: "This is what Herman Melville did on such a day."
Rather we recognize: "Ishmael does this, either because Melville had once known such experiences, or because he had
read about such matters as a corollary to his own personal
knowledge." The *Pequod* and her voyage has its logbook,
which is *Moby-Dick,* but it is not the same as the logbook
kept aboard the *Acushnet* by Captain Pease and his mates.
But only the knowledge that comes from experience could
have furnished Melville with the "feel" of the whaleship
life; such gives authority to *Moby-Dick.* Melville knew all
of this when he referred in *Pierre* to "the visible world of
experience being that procreative thing which impregnates
the muses."

Even as Melville refused, for artistic reasons, to ship
Ishmael from any port but Nantucket, so a similar nicety of
plot propriety made him create a ship like the *Pequod* for
Ishmael's whaling voyage. From the imagination of Melville,

the *Pequod* differed strikingly from the ship of Melville's memory, the *Acushnet*. Describing the *Pequod,* Melville becomes richly allusive, through various similes suggesting the barbaric and civilized forces of her making, from Ethiopia to Norway, from England to Japan:

You may have seen many a quaint craft in your day, for aught I know; — square-toed luggers; mountainous Japanese junks; butter-box galliots, and what not; but take my word for it, you never saw such a rare old craft as this same rare old Pequod. She was a ship of the old school, rather small if anything; with an old-fashioned claw-footed look about her. Long seasoned and weather-stained in the typhoons and calms of all four oceans, her old hull's complexion was darkened like a French grenadier's, who has alike fought in Egypt and Siberia. Her venerable bows looked bearded. Her masts — cut somewhere on the coast of Japan, where her original ones were lost overboard in a gale — her masts stood stiffly up like the spines of the three old kings of Cologne. Her ancient decks were worn and wrinkled, like the pilgrim-worshipped flagstone in Canterbury Cathedral where Beckett bled. But to all these her old antiquities, were added new and marvellous features, pertaining to the wild business that for more than half a century she had followed. . . . [Peleg] had built upon her original grotesqueness, and inlaid it, all over, with a quaintness both of material and device, unmatched by anything except it be Thorkill-Hake's carved buckler or bedstead. She was apparelled like any barbaric Ethiopian emperor, his neck heavy with pendants of polished ivory. She was a thing of trophies. A cannibal of a craft, tricking herself forth in the chased bones of her enemies. All round, her unpanelled, open bulwarks were garnished like one continuous jaw, with the long sharp teeth of the sperm whale, inserted there for pins, to fasten her old hempen thews and tendons to. Those thews ran not through base blocks of land wood, but deftly travelled over sheaves of sea-ivory. Scorning a turnstile wheel at her reverend helm, she sported there a tiller; and that tiller was in one mass, curiously carved from the long narrow lower jaw of her hereditary foe. The helmsman who steered by that tiller in a tempest, felt like the Tartar, when he holds back his fiery steed by clutching its jaw. A noble craft, but somehow a most melancholy! All noble things are touched with that.

The *Pequod* is appropriate in her grotesque picturesqueness to the fantastic adventures for which she is fated. First, however, she is a Nantucket ship, commanded and officered by Nantucketers. By extension she becomes the symbol of all American whaling ships, the representative of an old and honorable tradition of forthfaring to the ends of the earth. Further, the Pequod is, in an odd Melvillean way, a felicitous image of the weary world, both savage and civilized. She is the proper ship for the polyglot crew which mans her: "An Anacharsis Clootz deputation from all the isles of the sea, and all the ends of the earth," a savage but unforgettable congregation of heroes emblematic of the nations and races of mankind. It was Herman Melville's bold imagination which translated the finite *Acushnet* into the infinite *Pequod,* a statistical ship into the symbol of a universal fact, to stand as the emblem of the voyaging earth herself. The *Pequod* is at once nautical craft and microcosm.

Melville's description of the *Pequod* is in striking contrast to the *Acushnet.* Captain Pease's proud command was no fit symbol for the tired old world. In *Moby-Dick* Melville discarded actual fact for imaginative truth; when Melville first saw her the *Acushnet* was virgin, completely innocent of whale's blood, untried in the trough of the seas. Built at Rochester, Massachusetts, in 1840, and completed on December 30 of that year, the *Acushnet* was a three-masted, two-decked ship of 358 tons,[19] built on the snug, squat lines of her sister whaleships — disrespectfully said to be built by the mile, the individual craft chopped off the line, like sausages, as needed. Our pencil sketch of the *Acushnet* made upon her logbook of 1845 has sentimental value, but it is much easier to imagine the *Acushnet's* (and so, the *Pequod's*) appearance after study of old whaling prints and whaleship designs; [20] or following an inspection of the half-scale ship

[19] Owned by Bradford, Fuller & Co. It returned from its maiden voyage on May 13, 1845, minus Herman Melville but with 850 barrels of sperm oil, 1350 barrels of whale oil, and 13,500 pounds of whalebone.

[20] See Joseph Higgins, *The Whale Ship Book* (New York, 1927) ; Albert Church, *Whale Ships and Whaling* (New York, 1938) ; Dow, Ashley, *The Yankee Whaler* (New York, 1942); and Colton Waugh's hand-colored lithograph picture (12¾" x 14¾") published in 1928 by the Buffalo Consolidated Map Company.

model in the Jonathan Bourne Whaling Museum at New Bedford; or, best of all, after a tour of inspection of the *Charles W. Morgan*,[21] sole surviving old-time whaleship, now resting, a museum piece, at Mystic, Connecticut. Because the years have had their way with the *Charles W. Morgan* she more closely resembles the *Pequod* than did the *Acushnet,* but the *Charles W. Morgan* lacks, since Melville did not decorate her, the barbaric *vertu* which gave the *Pequod* her fittingly strange adornment.[22] In envisioning the *Pequod* from models and prints and even from the *Charles W. Morgan,* imagination, at Melville's direction, must amend eyesight.

With Ishmael and Queequeg's selection of their ship, Melville is well along. The old sea captains sadly leave their ship (their whaling days over), dropping advice behind them as they fumble their way to the boat to take them back to shore. And then the *Pequod* "blindly plunged like fate into the lone Atlantic." The adverb is heavily weighted, and so is the adjective. Even more significant, however, is the

---

[21] See G. Warren Hirshson, *The Whale Ship Charles W. Morgan* (New Bedford, Mass., 2d ed., 1926), and, more entertaining, Richard A. Shafter, "The Last of the Old-Time Whalers," *Travel,* LXXVIII (February, 1942), 4–[9], 40.

[22] In *The Illustrated London News,* 118 (January 12, 1946), 42–43, there is a two-page picture of a floating whale factory; an artist's sketch showing the plan of "Empire Victory," a sight which would have made Melville rub his eyes: "The ship shown is 535 ft. in length and 74 ft. in breadth, with a tonnage of 20,000, and her machinery can handle blue-nosed whales, of an average length of 85 ft., and weighing 200 tons or more, at the rate of one an hour. Attached to the factory ship are ten catcher vessels of the trawler type with a harpoon gun mounted on the raised forecastle, which two haul their prey to the mother-ship. The process from this point onwards begins with the whale being drawn by powerful winches up an inclined skidway at the stern and on to the flensing deck, where it is expertly cut up. From here, the cut-up slabs are conveyed through hatches to the pressure boilers, which cook bone and meat at a pressure of 60 lb. per square inch, the oil extracted being fed down pipes to the receiving tanks. Other whales products go into the Kvaerner boilers and rotary digestors, the extracted oil passing through separators to the tanks. The meat is dealt with by special machinery capable of handling 600 tons of raw meat and 35 tons of raw liver per day. The final products will be used for the making of edible fats, soap, cattle food, fertilizers, and various industrial purposes. An interesting modern feature of this floating factory is its radar installation, which not only helps to locate whales but gives warning of icebergs and makes possible safe navigation in fog." The old order changes, yielding place to the new.

simile. Melville did not write "like a desperate animal" nor did he use any other physical comparison flowing too easily from the pen. He said "like fate," equating ship with idea so that physical object acquires a margin of mystery and idea gains body. It is the poet's way of writing.

The voyage begins. Like so many of the great books of the world, *Moby-Dick* is a book of travel. Precisely why is it that so many of the world's literary masterpieces have been studies of travel: the *Odyssey*, the *Aeneid*, *Faerie Queene*, *Don Quixote*, *Pilgrim's Progress*, *Gulliver's Travels*, *Tom Jones*, and *Huckleberry Finn?* The answer lies in the nature of the basic metaphor, common to all of them, of the voyage as a symbol of spiritual forthfaring; that even as the physical self seeks new sights in strange places so the human soul in its necessary process of growth goes out into the sea of life "blindly like fate" — as the *Pequod*. Physical fact and spiritual idea join in a marriage which custom has not been able to stale nor familiarity make tiresome.

7

"The injustice hereby done to the hunters of whales"

THE LOW SOCIAL POSITION of whalemen was a minor problem that occupied Melville's attention for several years before he wrote his whaling book. As early as *Redburn* (1849) he touched on it, and again in *White-Jacket* (1850) the theme appears briefly and humorously in the gawky Downeaster, Dobbs, an ex-whaleman, and in some words from Jack Chase. But not until the twenty-fourth chapter of *Moby-Dick* does Melville really attack the question. Assuming the rôle of a barrister, Melville presents evidence to support the dignity of the whaleman and of his calling.

At first reading, "The Advocate" seems digressive, but when it is seen to be the general introduction to an important section of the novel — the presentation of the *dramatis personae* — then it falls into place. Since he is approaching tragic themes, and the great tragic character, Melville must justify whaling as a fit theme for tragedy:

> As Queequeg and I are now fairly embarked in this busi-
> ness of whaling; and as this business of whaling has somehow
> come to be regarded among landsmen as a rather unpoetical
> and disreputable pursuit; therefore, I am all anxiety to con-
> vince ye, ye landsmen, of the injustice hereby done to us hunters
> of whales.

Melville first turns to the widespread classification of whalemen as "low," attacking the position with humor:

> In the first place, it may be deemed almost superfluous to
> establish the fact, that among people at large, the business of
> whaling is not accounted on a level with what are called the
> liberal professions. If a stranger were introduced into any
> miscellaneous metropolitan society, it would but slightly ad-
> vance the general opinion of his merits, were he presented to
> the company as a harpooneer, say; and if in emulation of the
> naval officers he should append the initials S. W. F. (Sperm
> Whale Fishery) to his visiting card, such a procedure would
> be deemed pre-eminently presuming and ridiculous.

If whalemen were "low," then Melville himself was tarred
with the same brush. The son of the Gansevoorts and Mel-
villes must have recognized ironically the shock that some
of his experiences as whaleman and wanderer had been to
more conservative relatives. But how extensive had been
Melville's whaling experiences?

He had served on the *Acushnet* from 3 January, 1841, to
early July, 1842, as well as another six months or so on the
Julia, after leaving Eimeo (Moorea), before arriving in
Honolulu in the summer of 1843. Writing to Bentley in an
attempt to sell him the manuscript of *Moby-Dick*, Melville
alluded to some two years personal experience as a "harpooneer," a title which he had held, probably, for only part
of that time. Compared with the Nantucket and New Bedford veterans, Melville's service had been brief. But compared with the knowledge of the rest of us it had been extensive, of sufficient duration to have acquainted Melville with
the experiential facts of the whale fishery, and to have im-

pressed on him the subtleties of knowledge which make intelligent firsthand experience far superior to secondhand reports from books. While he was a whaleman and while he was in the South Seas Melville kept no journal; at the time he had not been sufficiently alert to the literary possibilities of his adventures to jot down notes outside of his memory. When eight years later he began to describe whaling he had recourse to what he called "my numerous fish documents" to refresh his fading memories of the precise facts. But for the "feel" of what he was describing, Melville could depend on memory. Although his personal experiences in the whaling industry had been curtailed when he deserted the *Acushnet,* refusing to be brutalized by the tyrannous Captain Pease; and although he could not speak with the encyclopedic authority of a Captain Scoresby, Melville had endured whaling sufficiently to have it in his bones, if not the minute details in his head. So he dipped into his well of memories for the life of the book; for the physical facts he dipped into literary record. It was a happy combination. Melville is an eloquent advocate of the unacknowledged heroism of whaling and the unrecognized worth of its practitioners.

In "The Advocate" Melville next presents a cluster of historical facts illustrating the importance, the size, and the economic reaches of the American whaling industry. He cogently concludes: "How comes all this, if there be not something puissant in whaling?" Whence Melville gathered his historical and economic facts is not certain. He had read them in at least two books: Scoresby's *An Account of the Arctic Regions* and Beale's *Natural History of the Sperm Whale,* both of which were open before him as he wrote *Moby-Dick.* Since the clearly traced borrowings are from Beale, it can be assumed that the *Natural History* contributed most of Melville's information.[23]

As a good advocate, Melville argued his case in sonorous periods which seem original enough, but the germinal ideas

[23] Francis Allyn Olmsted, *Incidents of a Whaling Voyage* (New York, 1841), pp. 126–128, has an encomium on the whaleman and his adventurous courage which Melville had undoubtedly read, but there is no *clear* sign of borrowing on his part.

came from a long passage out of Beale who himself quoted it from a nameless author: [24]

> The importance of the southern whale fishery [says a gentleman who is deeply conversant with the whole subject], has never been duly appreciated; it is not generally known [says he], that it is to this important branch of trade, and nursery for seamen, that we owe the opening of commerce with South America, and which even caused the separation of the Spanish colonies in the Pacific Ocean from the parent state. So meanly jealous was Spain of the interference of foreigners with the trade of her American colonies, that it was with the greatest difficulty, on the opening of the sperm whale fishery in the Pacific, that we could obtain permission for our ships to cruise within a hundred Italian miles of their coasts — and it was only through a few of our ships at first claiming the right of wooding and watering in a friendly port that a trade was first established, which spread in all directions the moment the great mutual advantages were felt. The enterprise of the ship-owners [he continues], engaged in the whale fishery knew no bounds. They sent ships to all parts of the world — to places at which no merchant vessel would have had cause to venture, so that lands were visited upon which important colonies have been formed: — what merchant vessel would have visited Van Diemen's Land, or even Australia? Having no object or prospect of gain, and lying as they both did, out of the track of our merchantmen, it is not to be believed that they could have been much visited by them. But our whaling vessels, cruising for whales, examined their shores and brought home information respecting their value, and what was still more important, they carried out people to reside upon them, and established a regular communication between them and our own country — by which the wants of the primitive settlers could be supplied and their persons protected, and which could not have been done by other ships except at a frightful expense — at a time too, when the settlement of the above now valuable and flourishing colonies was a mere experiment, with many sneering at the project as an ignis fatuus; — *evidence* inclines us to believe that these colonies would never have existed had it not been for whaling vessels approaching their

[24] Melville made a marginal line, now erased, beside this entire passage in his own copy of Beale.

shores. It is a fact, that the original settlers at Botany Bay
were more than once saved from *starvation* by the timely arrival of some whaling vessels.

But if our commerce has received benefit from our southern
whaling expeditions, our intimate knowledge of the Polynesian
islanders has also risen from the same means; and if missionaries have gone to reside among these people with the view
of spreading among them a belief in the Christian faith, these
messengers have been preceded by the whaler, who has opened
a barter with the savage, and brought about a friendly regard
towards us, by which he has secured a ready welcome to the
missionaries; and they are doing so at the present hour at New
Guinea, New Ireland, New Britain, and at hundreds of
islands in the south Pacific; New Zealand has been succeeded
with in the same way, and if it was not for these preliminary
meetings, not a missionary would dare to step upon their
shores.

What Melville did to give Beale's quotation vividness and
power is seen in the transformed passage in *Moby-Dick*:

I freely assert, that the cosmopolite philosopher cannot, for
his life, point out one single peaceful influence, which within
the last sixty years has operated more potentially upon the
whole broad world, taken in one aggregate, than the high and
mighty business of whaling. One way and another, it has be-
gotten events so remarkable in themselves, and so continuously momentous in their sequential issues, that whaling may
well be regarded as that Egyptian mother, who bore offspring
themselves pregnant from her womb. It would be a hopeless,
endless task to catalogue all these things. Let a handful suffice.
For many years past the whale-ship has been the pioneer in
ferreting out the remotest and least known parts of the earth.
She has explored seas and archipelagoes which had no chart,[25]
where no Cook or Vancouver had ever sailed. If American
and European men-of-war now ride peacefully in once savage

[25] The history of the whalemen's discoveries of Pacific islands has never
been satisfactorily investigated. Such being the character of the whalemen
— their disinclination to keep records — it is probable that research on the
problem would yield barren results. The only authoritative statement of
which I know is that by J. N. Reynolds, "Report on Islands Discovered by
Whalers in the Pacific," *House Executive Documents* 23rd Congress, 2d Ses-
sion, vol. III, Doc. 105, pp. 1–28, which is an 1835 report of an investigation
completed by 1828, and which was drawn up from conversations with
whaling captains.

harbors, let them fire salutes to the honor and the glory of the whale-ship, which originally showed them the way, and first interpreted between them and the savages. They may celebrate as they will the heroes of Exploring Expeditions, your Cookes, your Krusensterns; but I say that scores of anonymous Captains have sailed out of Nantucket, that were as great, and greater, than your Cooke and your Krusenstern. For in their succorless empty-handedness, they, in the heathenish sharked waters, and by the beaches of unrecorded, javelin islands, battled with virgin wonders and terrors that Cooke with all his marines and muskets would not willingly have dared. All that is made such a flourish of in the old South Sea Voyages, those things were but the life-time commonplaces of our heroic Nantucketers. Often, adventures which Vancouver dedicates three chapters to, these men accounted unworthy of being set down in the ship's common log. Ah, the world! Oh, the world!

Until the whale fishery rounded Cape Horn, no commerce but colonial, scarcely any intercourse but colonial, was carried on between Europe and the long line of the opulent Spanish provinces on the Pacific coast. It was the whaleman who first broke through the jealous policy of the Spanish crown, touching these colonies; and, if space permitted, it might be distinctly shown how from those whalemen at last eventuated the liberation of Peru, Chili, and Bolivia from the yoke of Old Spain, and the establishment of the eternal democracy in those parts.

That great America on the other side of the sphere, Australia, was given to the enlightened world by the whaleman. After its first blunder-born discovery by a Dutchman, all other ships long shunned those shores as pestiferously barbarous; but the whale-ship touched there. The whale-ship is the true mother of that now mighty colony. Moreover, in the infancy of the first Australian settlement, the emigrants were several times saved from starvation by the benevolent biscuit of the whale-ship luckily dropping an anchor in their waters. The uncounted isles of all Polynesia confess the same truth, and do commercial homage to the whale-ship, that cleared the way for the missionary and the merchant, and in many cases carried the primitive missionaries to their first destinations. If that double-bolted land, Japan, is ever to become hospitable, it is the whale-ship alone to whom the credit will be due; for already she is on the threshold.

The chief criticism of whaling, apparently, was that it was a brutal and bloody business. Melville met this attack with an apt comparison of whaling to the profession of the soldier:

> Butchers we are, that is true. But butchers, also, and butchers of the bloodiest badge have been all Martial Commanders whom the world invariably delights to honor. And as for the matter of the alleged uncleanliness of our business, ye shall soon be initiated into certain facts hitherto pretty generally unknown, and which, upon the whole, will triumphantly plant the sperm whale-ship at least among the cleanliest things of this tidy earth. But even granting the charge in question to be true; what disordered slippery decks of a whale-ship are comparable to the unspeakable carrion of those battle-fields from which so many soldiers return to drink in all ladies' plaudits? And if the idea of peril so much enhances the popular conceit of the soldier's profession; let me assure ye that many a veteran who has freely marched up to a battery, would quickly recoil at the apparition of the sperm whale's vast tail, fanning into eddies the air over his head. For what are the comprehensible terrors of man compared with the interlinked terrors and wonders of God!

This ringing defense was a rhetorical expansion of points made by Obed Macy in *The History of Nantucket*:

> Alas! what is bloodshed but murder; what are the pretences of war but words; what its dire effects but cold-blooded, purchased butchery. For deeds of true valor, done without brutal excitement, but in the honest and lawful pursuit of the means of livelihood, we may safely point to the life of a whaleman, and dare the whole world to produce a parallel.

Whether or not Melville's assessment of the whaleman's exploring achievements is a just one — it seems to be — it should carry the jury among his readers. For Melville is speaking not only as a whaleman, but also as an American proud of the magnificent accomplishments of his countrymen, mariners much less celebrated but no less glorious, in their plunge into the unknown, than the Viking navigators.

After the eloquent peroration on the greatness and daring of whalemen, Melville with judicial skill and humor winds up his case with a series of sharp questions, each followed by quick answers of fact. *"The whale no famous author, and whaling no famous chronicler?"* he asks, and cites Job, Alfred the Great, and Edmund Burke — about whom Melville would have known from his fund of general information, but about which he might have read, and probably did, in Scoresby's hundred-page historical account of whale fisheries, in Browne's *Etchings of a Whaling Cruise,* and in Beale's *Natural History of the Sperm Whale.* Melville answers his next question: *"No good blood in their veins?"* by citing Mary Morrel Folger, the Nantucket lady, at least married to whaling, who was the grandmother of Benjamin Franklin, — a piece of information which he possibly snatched from Joseph Hart's novel *Miriam Coffin.* Scoresby's account of the Act of Edward II (1315), in which the whale was declared a "royal fish," gave Melville the answer to his next question: *"Whaling not respectable?"* This was followed immediately by the query, *"The whale never figured in any grand imposing way?"* the answer citing the honored presence of a whale skeleton, transported from Syria, in one of the great Roman triumphs. Melville might have read this in Pliny's *Natural History*; it is more likely that he came across it in John Kitto's *Cyclopedia of Biblical Literature* under the heading "Whale." The final question: *"No dignity in whaling?"* is answered by illusion to the constellation Cetus, which Melville would have had from his sailor's knowledge of astronomy. Like a good lawyer, Melville wrote "The Advocate" from all the precedents he could collect.

Melville winds up his whaling apologetics with a personal reference, one quoted repeatedly by critics for its self-revelation and understanding. His own institutional training limited to the Albany Academy,[26] Melville forthrightly credits the whaling experiences as having been the chief source of his education:

> And, as for me, if, by any possibility, there be any as yet undiscovered prime thing in me; if I shall ever deserve any

[26] Teachers of writing and of Freshman Composition may well feel discouraged on knowing that Melville did not finish high school. As Emerson said: "The people, and not the college, is the writer's home."

real repute in that small but high hushed world which I
might not be unreasonably ambitious of; if hereafter I shall do
anything that, upon the whole, a man might rather have done
than to have left undone; if, at my death, my executors, or
more properly my creditors, find any precious MSS. in my
desk, then here I prospectively ascribe all the honor and the
glory to whaling; for a whale-ship was my Yale College and
my Harvard.

Let us not be deceived: The "ifs" of Melville's passage may
not conceal the profound conviction and understanding possessing him that he *had* deserved a "real repute in that small
but high hushed world" of great accomplishment. No man
of intelligence, having poured as much of his experience and
insight into the mold of words as Melville had done in *Moby-
Dick* but must have discerned that he had created well. Without the arrogance, Melville had as much confidence in his
achievements as did the egotistical Milton. If anything seems
to have issued directly from Melville's unassisted mind, without factual source or literary connection, his tribute to the
educational power of the whaleship certainly does. However, even here one may suggest that Melville shrewdly cap-
italized upon a paragraph from an obscure little book by
another whaleman, Nathaniel Ames, *A Mariner's Sketches*
(1830).[27] Writing in a retrospective mood, Ames said:

> Still I can look back to certain periods of my life with
> pleasure, and I continue to regard, as the happiest part of my
> existence, the three years passed at Harvard University, and
> the three and a half spent on board a man of war, two sem-
> inaries at which I had the honour to receive my polite educa-
> tion, and of which, in point of morality, I am inclined to
> prefer the latter.

Melville, unlike Ames, had not been to Harvard; he had
instead matriculated in the sperm-whale fishery, and, therefore, honored whaling more than formal education. Doing
so, he may have intended a pleasant and oblique satirical

[27] It was from this book that Melville took the climactic scene in *White-
Jacket*, the fall of the hero from the yardarm into the profound of the sea.
Anderson, who discovered Melville's act of transformation, discusses it in
Melville in the South Seas, pp. 415–417.

thrust against his learned father-in-law, Chief Justice Shaw, an extremely loyal Harvard man in frequent attendance at alumni functions, ever full of the old-school-tie spirit. Or the satire may have been more general in intent.

If a whaleship was Melville's "Yale College and my Harvard," one should bring the record up to date and say that the whaling books (his fish documents) were then his graduate school, and *Moby-Dick* the doctoral dissertation — which itself a hundred years later would provoke dissertations.

8

"Knights and Squires"

As WE HAVE SEEN, "The Advocate" was a general defense of whaling. Continuing his case through several chapters, Melville moves to the introductory sketches of Ahab and his mates. Having argued in serio-comic tones the nobility of whalemen, Melville now faces the necessity of presenting characters who would be convincing not only in their rough reality but also in their inherent greatness. In bold, ironic metaphors Melville sketches his leading characters.

Immediately following "The Advocate" in a very short chapter, fittingly called "Postscript" (25), Melville argues in proof of the "kingliness" of whaling that the English monarchs were always anointed at their coronations — "What then can it possibly be, but the sperm oil in its un-manufactured, unpolluted state, the sweetest of all oils?" The implied enthymeme which carries us into the next three chapters runs something as follows: Kings are crowned with oil; kings must use sperm oil; those who use sperm oil, or hunt it, must be kingly; or, rather, Ahab is a king, and his mates the knights and squires of his court. By outrageous and sardonic logic Melville passes to the metaphorical truth of "Knights and Squires" (26 and 27), and "Ahab" (28). The factual support of his syllogism — that sperm oil was used at British coronations — is nowhere in Melville's sources, and may have been a fanciful invention for the sake of his case.

In "Knights and Squires" (27) Melville begins with Starbuck, first mate of the *Pequod*. The description is no sooner completed than Melville comes into the open with the key point of his advocate's chapters: Kingliness and royalty as legal terms are barren; seen as metaphors of man himself, of what men potentially are, kingliness and royalty are worthy, vital concepts. As metaphors they may well be employed in an American democracy. Egalitarian enthusiasm may use the terms figuratively, and profit by their meanings. Ten years before *Moby-Dick* Emerson wrote in "Self-Reliance" (1841):

> The world has been instructed by its kings, who have so magnetized the eyes of nations. It has been taught by this colossal symbol the mutual reverence that is due from man to man. The joyful loyalty with which men have everywhere suffered the king, or the noble, or the great proprietor to walk among them by a law of his own, make his own scale of men and things, and reverse theirs, pay for benefits not with money but with honor, and represent the law in his own person, was the hieroglyphic by which they obscurely signified their consciousness of their own right and comeliness, the right of every man.

And three years later Emerson made the point again: "We must have kings, and we must have nobles. Nature provides such in every society, — only let us have the real instead of the titular." Speaking from the same belief as Emerson's, one inherent in the American experiment, proclaimed in the opening lines of the Declaration of Independence, Melville reaffirms it in two passionate paragraphs in *Moby-Dick*:

> But were the coming narrative to reveal, in any instance, the complete abasement of poor Starbuck's fortitude, scarce might I have the heart to write it; but it is a thing most sorrowful, nay shocking, to expose the fall of valor in the soul. Men may seem detestable as joint stock-companies and nations; knaves, fools, and murderers there may be; men may have mean and meagre faces; but man, in the ideal, is so noble

and so sparkling, such a grand and glowing creature, that over any ignominious blemish in him all his fellows should run to throw their costliest robes. That immaculate manliness we feel within ourselves, so far within us, that it remains intact though all the outer character seem gone; bleeds with keenest anguish at the undraped spectacle of a valor-ruined man. Nor can piety itself, at such a shameful sight, completely stifle her upbraidings against the permitting stars. But this august dignity I treat of, is not the dignity of kings and robes, but that abounding dignity which has no robed investiture. Thou shalt see it shining in the arm that wields a pick or drives a spike; that democratic dignity which, on all hands, radiates without end from God; Himself! The great God absolute! The centre and circumference of all democracy! His omnipresence, our divine equality!

If, then, to meanest mariners, and renegades and castaways, I shall hereafter ascribe high qualities, though dark; weave around them tragic graces; if even the most mournful, perchance the most abased, among them all, shall at times lift himself to the exalted mounts; if I shall touch that workman's arm with some ethereal light; if I shall spread a rainbow over his disastrous set of sun; then against all mortal critics bear me out in it, thou just Spirit of Equality, which hast spread one royal mantle of humanity over all my kind! Bear me out in it, thou great democratic God! who didst not refuse to the swart convict, Bunyan, the pale, poetic pearl; Thou who didst clothe with doubly hammered leaves of finest gold, the stumped and paupered arm of old Cervantes; Thou who didst pick up Andrew Jackson from the pebbles; who didst hurl him upon a war-horse! who didst thunder him higher than a throne! Thou who, in all Thy mighty, earthly marchings, ever cullest Thy selectest champions from the kingly commons; bear me out in it, O God!

Melville's words [28] give support to Theodore Sedgwick, Jr.'s statement, written in 1835, that the struggles of Jacksonian

[28] Melville's friend Hawthorne held the same view contemporaneously when he wrote in *A Wonder Book* (July, 1851): " 'When men do not feel towards the humblest stranger as if he were a brother,' said the traveller . . . 'they are unworthy to exist on earth, which was created as the abode of a great human brotherhood.' " Melville's eloquent statement of the unidealized heroic life around him is echoed in William James's realization years later of the same phenomenon. See *Talks for Teachers* (New York, 1899), especially pp. 274–275.

democracy had "urged forward the whole American mind." Not an active party man himself, nevertheless, in principle, Melville, in *Moby-Dick* especially, lined himself up with Jacksonian principles as the hope for true democracy in the future — an alignment common to most of the young writers then in America: to Hawthorne, Whitman, Cooper, Bryant, and Bancroft. Melville's words are not merely the rip tide of rhetoric. They are deep belief. But the profound and stirring democratic faith within Melville's sentences is not easy to hold at any time, nor was it the easier for Melville when slavery, for instance, was a hideous legal fact. Such a faith calls for a full appreciation of human worth beyond human weakness and failure. It requires the recognition of Whitman's truth that "the least developed person on earth is just as important and sacred to himself or herself, as the most developed person is to himself or herself." It demands that Pip and Queequeg and Daggoo and Flask be respected as well as the heroic (but scarred, also) Ahab. To have achieved a faith like Melville's while fully conscious, as he was, of man's misery, his meanness, his fallen estate, betokens not a bland, superficial optimism, but a profound love of life — what Keats called the "love of good and ill." It is the tragic vision.

Following his description of Starbuck, and the passionate statement of his own social credo, Melville proceeds with sketches of Stubb, Flask, Queequeg (the Polynesian), Tashtego (the American Indian), and Daggoo (the black giant). The significance of the latter two savages is made clear by Ahab's description of them as "Pagan leopards — the unrecking and unworshipping things, that live; and seek, and give no reasons for the torrid life they feel." The mates and harpooneers are the knights and squires attendant on kingly Ahab. They are barbaric and savage; they are rough and ragged, but each of them is a human soul, to be respected in its individuality; each of them is therefore a type of Self. They are presented as isolated monoliths, in variations repeating the loneliness theme of *Moby-Dick*. Melville insures that we see them in their separateness, calling them Isolatoes:

They were nearly all Islanders in the Pequod. *Isolatoes* too, I call such, not acknowledging the common continent of men, but each *Isolato* living on a separate continent of his own. Yet now, federated along one keel, what a set these Isolatoes were! An Anacharsis Clootz deputation from all the isles of the sea, and all the ends of the earth, accompanying Old Ahab in the Pequod to lay the world's grievances before that bar from which not very many of them ever come back.

The series of character portraits closes with a brief reference to "Black little Pip," the cabin boy from Alabama, soon to lose his selfhood in madness. Significantly, Pip loses his mind when the boat crew temporarily abandons him in the immensity of the Pacific. The vast spaces of the sea and the horror of his aloneness prove more than he can bear, and he loses his rational mind. Such, we see, is the danger of isolation; such is the precariousness of the Self without the social support. Little Pip has an important thematic part to play in *Moby-Dick*. Like the Fool in *Lear*, Pip is the low character serving as the foil to the noble one; Pip's madness is a companion piece to Ahab's derangement. Pip's is the lack of self-identity; Ahab's is the excess of selfhood. Nothing so much resembles a hollow as a swelling.

Suggested in the series of portraits made throughout these five chapters is the possibility that Starbuck, Flask, and the others are various phases of self. Melville never explicitly states such an intention, but the variety of personalities revealed ranges from the admirable down to the superficial. The self may be a Starbuck: practical, social, sensible, loyal — life lived with merit, if not exaltedly. The self may be Stubb: courageous because uncaring, cheerful, stubby of soul — life pursued Philistinely. The self may be also a Flask: fearless, foolhardy, frivolous; and the self may be Queequeg, Tashtego, or Daggoo: animal, instinctive, primeval. The self, finally, may even be Pip: its identity lost in the desperate failure to face its fundamental insularity. Yes, Ishmael has many selves. He may even be doomed Ahab, life endured on the tragic level, in the blind helplessness of man's fate, and in man's heroic suffering of dark destiny.

In the sequence of characters, Melville has at last reached

his hero, Captain Ahab of Nantucket, lord of the Knights and Squires of the *Pequod*. Only one way may we know Ahab and that is by reading *Moby-Dick*; to describe him and to interpret him is so difficult that one sympathizes with the *Bentley's Miscellany* critic who wrote in 1852: "Who in a few sentences can supply such a summary of the mental and physical qualities of Captain Ahab, as shall distinctly present to the mind's eye of the reader that extraordinary character? . . . who is to tell in a score or two of lines?" And years ago Viola Meynell warned us: "It is better to leave Ahab almost unhinted at; you cannot enter fleetingly into that over-whelming world of his spirit."

There are readers of *Moby-Dick* who assume that Captain Ahab of the *Pequod* was Herman Melville's fictionized portrait of Captain Valentine Pease [29] of the *Acushnet*. It may be so. It would be unrealistic to say that Pease was not in the back of Melville's mind when he wrote *Moby-Dick*. He was, undoubtedly, during the early stages of composition when *Moby-Dick* was a "whaling voyage," and not a tragic epic. But to assert identity is to be ignorant of the biographical facts, and to misunderstand Melville's conception of the heroic Captain Ahab.

Melville and Toby Greene deserted the *Acushnet* in the Marquesas Islands because of the tyranny of their captain — such is the story as read in *Typee*. But perhaps that story was an alteration of actual facts for artistic or dramatic effect. Maybe Melville and Greene really deserted for the sake of adventure, or because they were tired of the necessary restrictions of ship life, or of the monotony of a cruise already eighteen months long and threatening to continue long into the future.[30] Accepting, however, the *Typee* version as

[29] In the Harvard Library is a clipping from the *Vineyard Gazette*, 2 July, 1929, by Henry Beetle Hough, on Valentine Pease. He was born on the island of Chappaquiddick, near Martha's Vineyard, on 22 November, 1797, the son of Valentine Pease and Love Daggett Pease. In 1823 he married Prudence Ripley, and on 26 July, 1846, he was married a second time, to Mrs. Angeline Worth Bunting. After the second *Acushnet* voyage he took up the small coal business. Hough rightly says: "But for the fact that Herman Melville shipped on the *Acushnet* in 1841, Valentine Pease would have disappeared into . . . anonymity."

[30] Writing to Lemuel Shaw, 22 July, 1843, Gansevoort Melville said: "I am

reality, it is only Melville's side of the story. Captain Valentine Pease may not have been so brutal as the captain in the novel. His relatives were of the opinion that he must have been a harsh, violent man, because they had a low regard for a whaling captain who could not maintain discipline. The relatives' testimony as to Pease's harshness then is based on the doubtful premise that to maintain discipline a whaling captain had to be brutal. One fact we do know about Pease's character is that he was God-fearing but "terribly profane." The equation of the *Typee* captain with Valentine Pease is quite possible, but not proved. Assuming brutality and tyranny, the equation of Valentine Pease with Ahab is impossible, resting as it does on a complete misunderstanding of the character of Ahab. Ahab is not brutal; in *Moby-Dick* there are no floggings, no beatings, scarcely any physical violence except from the whale himself. The crew does not mutinously murmur in *Moby-Dick,* save for Starbuck, the symbolical opposition to the captain, and their pursuit of the White Whale is with the crew's consent. Ahab wins spiritually, not physically. Brutality is petty and unheroic. Conversely, Ahab has heroic grandeur. To have described him in terms of Pease would have been to reduce him to common size, just as a news photographer's pictures of Hector and Achilles would diminish them to unheroic proportions. Ahab does not need profanity [31] (there is *no* profanity whatsoever in *Moby-Dick,* although the sailors seem no less sailorly as a result) and physical tyranny to gain his will; he dominates through sheer will. He is kingly in the best sense of the metaphor. Symbol of the great Nantucket whalemen, Ahab is a captain cast in heroic mold. It is true that some of Ahab's verbal virtuosity may have been suggested by the tongue-lashings of the captain so offensive to J. Ross Browne

in receipt of a letter from my brother Herman dated August 1841 at Santa Martha, coast of Peru — He was then in perfect health, & not dissatisfied with his lot. The fact of his being one of a crew so much superior in morale & early advantages to the ordinary run of whaling crews affords him constant gratification."

[31] Writing of a voyage in 1849–50, Samuel Millett said: "I begin to learn something of their characters . . . like most sailors they are very profane for there is not one of them, even the officers, but use profane language to such an extent that they never utter a sentence without curses."

in *Etchings of a Whaling Cruise*; if so, the influence was general, and Melville purified and ennobled his source.[32] Ahab is a Nantucketer; he is a shrewd and daring captain, but he is cut from different cloth from that of the whaling captains of Melville's memory or of his "numerous fish documents." Ahab is a tragic hero.

9

"This dreamer of the avenging dream"

AHAB fulfills the Aristotelian formula for a tragic hero. Not that Melville had ever read the *Poetics*, but then, Aeschylus and Sophocles and Shakespeare had not studied Aristotle either. Wherever and whenever there is a great tragic character in drama, fiction, or life, he conforms to the Aristotelian formula. The nightingale unable to read a textbook resembles nevertheless the ornithologist's description of his species.

It would be easy to prepare a detailed case showing Melville's realization in Ahab of Aristotle's formula for a tragic hero; one or two instances may suffice. In setting down the dictum that "Tragedy is an imitation of personages better than the ordinary man," Aristotle stipulated that the tragic hero should be a king or a noble — at least of high estate. This law was natural enough in the *Poetics;* the Greek drama which furnished Aristotle his materials for analysis contained nothing but such heroes. Melville, an American democrat writing a book about the American institution of whaling, had no titular king to set up as his hero. Melville was forced into metaphor.[33] Ahab no less than Agamemnon

---

32 Although the speech at the mainmast, the delayed appearance of the captain, and the violence of Captain A —— in *Etchings* may have given hints to Melville for Ahab, these hints were completely altered. Browne's captain had a "sneaking, hang-dog look" — a far cry from Ahab — and "he did not altogether realize my expectations."

33 Nathaniel Hawthorne, in *Tanglewood Tales,* contemporary with *Moby-Dick,* ironically described the gluttonous followers of Ulysses in Circe's palace

or Oedipus is a superior person, and, as Captain Peleg hissed in Ishmael's ear before the voyage, "Ahab of old, thou knowest, was a crowned king." Ishmael, realistically looking on ragged Ahab, acknowledged his metaphorical royalty:

> But Ahab, my Captain, still moves before me in all his Nantucket grimness and shagginess; and in this episode touching Emperors and Kings, I must not conceal that I have only to do with a poor old whale-hunter like him; and, therefore, all outward majestical trappings and housings are denied me. Oh, Ahab! what shall be grand in thee, it must needs be plucked at from the skies, and dived for in the deep, and featured in the unbodied air!

And after all, what were the Aeschylean kings but half-barbarians, or what was Colonus but a dirty little village — and yet the artist has made them bridge the vast of time. What is needed is not Hollywood's conception of kingliness, which is meretricious, but the great artist's passionately felt knowledge — by which he imposes exaltation upon the shagginess of a grime-streaked whale hunter, and sees him *sub specie aeternitatis.* Ahab is Melville's unconscious answer to Tocqueville's criticism "that poets of democratic ages can never, therefore, take any man in particular as the subject of a piece; for an object of slender importance, which is distinctly seen on all sides, will never lend itself to an ideal conception."

Ahab, tragic center of *Moby-Dick,* is noble in person as well as kingly in command. Scarred "not in the fury of any mortal fray, but in an elemental strife at sea," he was a heroic figure of man:

> His whole high, broad form, seemed made of solid bronze, and shaped in an unalterable mould, like Cellini's cast Perseus. Threading its way out from among his grey hairs, and con-

seated on their twenty thrones, while one of them whispers, "Our good hostess has made kings of us all. . . . Ha! do you smell the feast? I'll engage it will be fit to set before two-and-twenty kings." And twenty-five years later another American novelist employed irony in dealing with kings, allowing two worthless tramps to style themselves King and Duke, while their human superiors, Huck Finn and Jim (waif and slave), treated them with innocent (Jim) or ironic (Huck) admiration. Basically, Mark Twain was of course asserting the nobility of the human spirit; implying, not stating, the innate worth of Huck and Jim.

tinuing right down one side of his tawny scorched face and neck, till it disappeared in his clothing, you saw a slender rod-like mark, lividly whitish. It resembled that perpendicular seam sometimes made in the straight, lofty trunk of a great tree, when the upper lightning tearingly darts down it, and without wrenching a single twig, peels and grooves out the bark from top to bottom ere running off into the soil, leaving the tree still greenly alive, but branded. Whether that mark was born with him, or whether it was the scar left by some desperate wound, no one could certainly say. By some tacit consent, throughout the voyage little or no allusion was made to it, especially by the mates. But once Tashtego's senior, an old Gay-Head Indian among the crew, superstitiously asserted that not till he was full forty years old did Ahab become that way branded, and then it came upon him, not in the fury of any mortal fray, but in an elemental strife at sea. Yet, this wild hint seemed inferentially negatived, by what a grey Manxman insinuated, an old sepulchral man, who, having never before sailed out of Nantucket, had never ere this laid eye upon wild Ahab. Nevertheless, the old sea-traditions, the immemorial credulities, popularly invested this old Manxman with preternatural powers of discernment. So that no white sailor seriously contradicted him when he said that if ever Captain Ahab should be tranquilly laid out — which might hardly come to pass, so he muttered — then, whoever should do that last office for the dead, would find a birth-mark on him from crown to sole.

So powerfully did the whole grim aspect of Ahab affect me, and the livid brand which streaked it, that for the first few moments I hardly noted that not a little of this overbearing grimness was owing to the barbaric white leg upon which he partly stood. It had previously come to me that this ivory leg had at sea been fashioned from the polished bone of the sperm whale's jaw. "Aye, he was dismasted off Japan," said the old Gay-Head Indian once; "but like his dismasted craft, he shipped another mast without coming home for it. He has a quiver of 'em."

Ahab's two physical infirmities had strange origins: one in the personal experience of Melville, the other in his reading. The famous Pittsfield elm furnished the scar, at least so says J. E. A. Smith, Melville's Pittsfield friend: "Thus in

'Moby Dick' he incorporates in three or four lines of his portrait of 'Captain Ahab,' a graphic picture of the old elm of Pittsfield Park." [34] And in another place, Smith described the tree as follows: "But, in 1841, the lightning scored a ghastly wound down its tall, straight trunk, and began to dry up its life-blood. Limbs fell away from time to time; and the thunderbolt again scathed it." [35]

The use of the scarred tree to create a symbol of blasted man is the result of Melville's enlarging imagination. It is of a pattern with Hawthorne's symbolism, save that with Hawthorne the symbolism became dominant, whereas with Melville the graphically present object is primary, the symbolism secondary. One curious parallelism is to be seen between Ishmael and Ahab. Ishmael by his very name is the symbol of the wanderer in life's desert; even more tragically, Ahab by his scar is Cain, cursed by life to wander eternally, unsatisfied.

Ahab's second infirmity, his amputated leg, is in keeping with traditional one-legged sea captains popular in fiction. Or was Ahab the one to establish the tradition? The amputated leg does not appear in the whaling documents used by Melville,[36] but in his copy of Beale's *Natural History of the Sperm Whale* he marked a passage describing the amputation by Beale of the right arm of one of the mates. Melville even underlined the words "his best friend, his right arm." The passage occurs towards the end of Beale's book, at a point far from the cetological section, which takes up the first one hundred and ninety-seven pages. Melville was obviously impressed by the words — no other markings appear for many pages before or after. It may be possible, therefore, that the story of amputation in Beale suggested

---

[34] *Biographical Sketch of Herman Melville* (Pittsfield, 1891), p. 14. Incidentally, the tree blew down in 1861, the tenth anniversary of its having become Ahab.

[35] *The History of Pittsfield* (Pittsfield, 1869), vol. I, p. 36.

[36] In Robert Jarman's *Journal of a Voyage to the South Seas, in the "Japan," Employed in the Sperm Whale Fishery, under the command of Captain John May* (Beccles, 1848), pp. 104–107, is an account of a whaleman so badly injured by the flukes of a whale that one leg had to be amputated at the knee. Melville, I feel sure, did not know this book.

to Melville the "dismasting" of his hero to accentuate Ahab's heroism and fortitude and to serve as a symbol of the mutilation imposed by tragic circumstance on all men.

The Pittsfield elm supplied Ahab's scar; Beale's zoological treatise may have suggested the amputation of Ahab. Melville made his gigantic conception out of strange stuff; the tragic hero Ahab is created from ordinary materials as the poet's creation of Helen of Troy from a brow of Egypt.

Carefully, Melville delayed the appearance of his hero. Anticipation is stirred in Ishmael even as in the readers. Even before boarding the *Pequod* for the voyage, Ishmael had heard rumors which had shaped an heroic picture of Ahab. Nor was he let down when first he saw Ahab: "Reality outran apprehension." Ishmael's reaction was representative of the entire crew's:

> There was an infinity of firmest fortitude, a determinate, unsurrenderable wilfulness, in the fixed and fearless, forward dedication of that glance. Not a word he spoke; nor did his officers say aught to him; though by all their minutest gestures and expressions, they plainly showed the uneasy, if not painful, consciousness of being under a troubled master-eye. And not only that, but moody stricken Ahab stood before them with a crucifixion in his face; in all the nameless regal overbearing dignity of some mighty woe.

Mutilated, scarred, Ahab is the leader without benefit of oath and fist. The only suggestion of physical violence is one which never really occurred but was dreamt by Stubb. In some ways as incongruous and amusing as Bottom's celebrated dream — and in some ways not — Stubb's dream underlines Ahab's compelling power. The metaphor of Ahab as a king to Knights and Squires is restated in comic terms — even as the pastoralism of Touchstone parodies that of the exiled Duke. Having dreamed that Ahab kicked him, Stubb describes his dream to Flask in a kind of Launcelot Gobbo dialogue:

> "Captain Ahab kicked ye, didn't he?" "Yes he did," says I — "right *here* it was." "Very good," says he — "he used his ivory leg, didn't he?" "Yes, he did," says I. "Well then," says

he, "wise Stubb, what have you to complain of? Didn't he
kick with right good will? It wasn't a common pitch pine leg
he kicked with, was it? No, you were kicked by a great
man, and with a beautiful ivory leg, Stubb. It's an honor; I
consider it an honor. Listen, wise Stubb. In old England the
greatest lords think it great glory to be slapped by a queen,
and made garter-knights of; but, be *your* boast, Stubb, that
ye were kicked by old Ahab, and made a wise man of. Remember what I say; *be* kicked by him; account his kicks
honors; and on no account kick back; for you can't help
yourself, wise Stubb."

Besides impressiveness of person and nobility of mind,
the tragic hero, Aristotle says, must have high rank. His
removal from common men must not be too far; the tragic
hero must be one with whom the spectator may identify.
Ahab is exalted in rank — the captain of the ship, an absolute autocrat — but he is close enough to normal human
life that we may identify with his tragedy. "Ahab," Captain
Peleg told Ishmael, "has his humanities," and speaking for
us all, Ishmael acknowledged a feeling of "sympathy and sorrow" for his captain. We identify with Ahab most deeply,
because he has the supreme quality of life, the courage which
leads him to reach out for life itself, even driving it into
a corner in order to get fast to it. In Ahab we see life clari-
fied, directed towards a sharply defined goal, life made pur-
posive. But Ahab's desire is at once heroic, tragic, and un-
avoidable. Ortega y Gasset put it: "There is no escape; man
cannot help striving for certainty. This distinguishes him
from animals and gods." An exile from home for most of
forty years, a familiar of the loneliness of the sea, maimed
cruelly in face and limb and spirit by life, Ahab still retains
with intensity the deepest desire to fulfill his avenging
dream. His focused will is admirable, and yet, like any
great virtue, it has its defect. It is Ahab's tragic flaw.

Ahab, then, is a tragic hero, noble in spirit and person,
animated by a heroic dream, but Ahab has also the tragic
weakness, the blindness, which drives him and all who follow him to their ultimate damnation. Even as Oedipus
blindly pursues the truth, completely heedless of the por-

tents warning him that it is not well to find the truth, so Captain Ahab hunts the White Whale in revengeful rage, heedless of the prudent words of his mates, blind to the omens of the squid, the flying fish, the undelivered letter, the ships, and of Fedallah's ambiguous prophecies. Ahab's tragic flaw, his *hybris,* is his drive to self-assertion, or as John Freeman put it: "Ahab's cardinal sin is that of selfhood and single vision."

Ahab is positive that *he* can capture the White Whale, although his own former experience and that of the whaling captains he meets tell him otherwise. He would have done well to ponder Blake's words on man's dreams of selfhood through self-reliance:

I will go down to self-annihilation and eternal death
Lest the Last Judgement come and find me unannihilate,
And I be seized and given into the hands of my own Self-
    hood.

Ahab attempts to find, against all advice and direction, the One, and becomes an example of the soul lost in the search for truth — truth regardless. He is described in *Pierre*:

But the example of many minds forever lost, like undiscoverable Arctic explorers, amid those treacherous regions, warns us entirely away from them; and we learn that it is not for man to follow the trail of truth too far, since by so doing he entirely loses the directing compass of his mind; for arrived at the Pole, to whose barrenness only it points, there, the needle indifferently respects all points of the horizon alike.

Ahab's folly, then, is in trying to come to close quarters with life. "True philosophy," Edmund Scherer says, "has never consisted in probing all problems, but often on the contrary eluding them. We are skirting the abyss: beware of vertigo." Ahab deceives himself; the extreme dogmatist and absolutist, positive of his own wisdom, lacking in humility, always does. Ahab will not accept illusion as an integral part of reality, but must tear away all the veils from the goddess. Ahab has not learned what Jonathan Swift found, that happiness is the state of being perpetually well deceived. He is spiritually tortured because he will not discriminate between the accessible and the inaccessible in nature. Goethe told Eckermann, in words which Melville probably read:

> He who does not know it torments himself, perhaps his life long, about the inaccessible without ever coming near the truth. But he who knows it, and is wise, will confine himself to the accessible; and, while he traverses this region in every direction, and confirms himself therein, will be able to win somewhat even from the inaccessible, though he must at last confess that many things can only be approached to a certain degree, and that nature has ever something problematical in reserve, which man's faculties are insufficient to fathom.

In Ahab we see the ravages of immeasurable ambition. Ahab is a figure from the Renaissance; Christopher Marlowe might have created him in blank verse, for Ahab is the Nantucket counterpart of Tamburlaine and Doctor Faustus, "still climbing after knowledge infinite." Ahab is the Wandering Jew seeking ever, and unavailingly, to find peace; he is tortured man trying to capture a fragment of eternity from the flux of events. Ahab is Man after the Fall, his innocence lost, seeking ever to recapture the primal bliss, the final answer, even in the white mass of a sperm whale. In his refusal to accept the human limitation, in his disregard of the social tie, Ahab is guilty of self-love, and self-reliance. Ahab suffers from Emerson's "goitre of egotism." Ahab has not learned that only by exorcising selfhood may one achieve it. Ahab had not heard, as had Ishmael, nor would he have heeded, the sermon by Father Mapple in which the law of self-annihilation was proclaimed. To save one's life, one must lose it; this is the paradox of the world's greatest religions; it is the lesson of *Billy Budd*, Melville's "testimony of acceptance." Implied rather than stated, it is the overarching lesson of *Moby-Dick*.

Ahab's tragedy arises from his isolation, from his aloneness. Aristotle believed that "To live alone one must be either an animal or a god." Ahab is the vulnerable god who will not accept the limitations of life, and of self. He is the doom-driven man no less than Macbeth, than Othello, than Orestes. He is described by Melville in *Pierre*:

There is a dark, mad mystery in some human hearts, which, sometimes, during the tyranny of a usurper mood, leads them to be all eagerness to cast off the most intense beloved bond, as a hindrance to the attainment of whatever transcendental object that usurper mood so tyrannically suggests. Then the beloved bond seems to hold us to no essential good; lifted to exalted mounts, we can dispense with all the vale; endearments we spurn; kisses are blisters to us; and forsaking the palpitating forms of mortal love, we emptily embrace the boundless and the unbodied air. We think we are not human; we become as immortal bachelors and gods; but again, like the Greek gods themselves, prone we descend to earth; glad to be uxorious once more; glad to hide these god-like heads within the bosoms made of too-seducing clay.

Weary with the invariable earth, the restless sailor breaks from every enfolding arm, and puts to sea in height of tempest that blows off shore. But in long night-watches at the antipodes, how heavily that ocean gloom lies in vast bales upon the deck; thinking that that very moment in his deserted hamlet-home the household sun is high, and many a sun-eyed maiden meridian as the sun. He curses Fate; himself he curses; his senseless madness, which is himself. For whoso once has known this sweet knowledge, and then fled it; in absence, to him the avenging dream will come.

Pierre was now this vulnerable god; this self-upbraiding sailor, this dreamer of the avenging dream.

"Doom," says Auden, "is dark and deeper than any sea-dingle." The "dark, mad mystery" of Ahab and his "usurper mood" makes him cast off the "beloved bond," but makes him into the "self-upbraiding sailor." Ahab is the vulnerable god seeking invulnerability. With the exaggeratedness of Manfred or Childe Harold, he is nevertheless close to modern readers still attracted by the romantic egoist seeking self-fulfillment in the solitudes of the sea or the mountains. "It is not human beings I like, but what devours them," said Gide in a passage which explains the fascination Ahab holds for the readers of *Moby-Dick*.

In considering Ahab, let us also remember Santayana's wise words: "The life of tragic heroes is not good; it is misguided, unnecessary, and absurd."

IV.

The Cetological Center

1

"Out of the trunk grow the branches"

AN ABRUPT CHANGE of direction in *Moby-Dick* takes place at the thirty-second chapter. From the sharp, swift description of New Bedford and Nantucket and from the narrative speed of the adventures of the seaport, we move suddenly into bibliographical considerations of a pseudo-scholarly nature. From comedy and drama we turn to exposition. Melville deliberately and abruptly hauled in sail.

The shift from rapid narrative to detailed exposition was intentional, not haphazard, and thoroughly realized by the author, as the following sentences indicate:

> Already we are boldly launched upon the deep; but soon we shall be lost in its unshored, harborless immensities. Ere that come to pass; ere the Pequod's weedy hull rolls side by side with the barnacled hulls of the leviathan; at the outset it is but well to attend to a matter almost indispensable to a thorough appreciative understanding of the more special leviathanic revelations and allusions of all sorts which are to follow.

Unambiguous in its statement of artistic plan, the passage says in effect: "We are now well along in our story; before long we shall be moving among wonders difficult to believe but having hard reality; therefore, a few facts about the whaling industry may serve a useful narrative as well as informational function." The cetological center recognizes the truth of Thoreau's dictum: "we are enabled to apprehend at all what is sublime and noble only by the perpetual instilling and drenching of the reality that surrounds us." Melville recognizes that while reality may at times seem fabulous, in art it must always be credible. The cetological center of *Moby-Dick* is the keel to Melville's artistic craft.

Except for the one chapter, "The Advocate" (24), the plot

of *Moby-Dick* has moved through thirty-one chapters without deviation and with constantly tightening tension. In order to build to the first great climax of the book — the doubloon scene at the main-mast — Melville must momentarily change pace, descend to a *pianissimo*. Nothing is more fatiguing, either in art or in life, than unrelieved tension or than continuous and unbroken excitement. Melville later acknowledges this, obliquely, when he mentions Ahab's recognition that although his men consent to pursue the White Whale with him, nevertheless they must be allowed diversion, for instance, to hunt for other whales along the way. The reader of a book or the spectator of a serious drama is like an archer's bow; he may prudently endure the taut state for a short time only. In Shakespearean tragedy, for example, the fourth acts are breathing places for the spectators after the climactic heights of the third acts, quiet moments in which motion seems suspended while years unroll in stretches of expository dialogue. The pianissimo fourth acts prepare the spectators for the thunderous fortissimi of the culminating fifth acts. Thus *Macbeth* and *Hamlet*. And similarly, *Moby-Dick*. Having set the sails of the *Pequod,* with reduced canvas, her bow plunging towards the South Seas, home of the Sperm Whale and of the great White Whale, Melville abandons for a time the maniacal captain and his mad design, in order to concentrate upon the minutiae of the very world in which Ahab is the human and heroic center. In this way only could Melville make credible old Ahab's crazy scheme, and give verisimilitude to the climax of *Moby-Dick*. The world of fantastic strangeness is best approached through the archway of the familiar and known; thus, what seems improbable can become probable. Whaling is the tonic chord to which we turn again and again, finally concentrating on one particular whale.

Something more than the necessity of adequate motivation, however, compelled Melville's shift from narrative into detailed description: the arcana of whaling, necessary to the atmosphere of the book, was mystery to the English and American millions. Now approaching the whaling episodes the narrative would have been half meaningless without the patient and graphic descriptions of materials and processes which Melville supplied. In creating a whaling epic in which the chief actor is himself a whale, the audience — landsmen most of them — must be able to tell a whale from a handsaw, and to know the routines of the whaleman's life. In fiction the law of identification is basic, and only from exact knowledge concerning the whale's ways and the whalemen's habits could Melville stimulate within his readers a real identification with the great fish and with the whalemen adventurers from Nantucket. In other words, in any book of adventure built on such a special area of life, as philately, campanology, or baseball, there are always certain necessary details of the methods and manner peculiar to them, which require expository treatment before the narrative may effectively proceed. Note also that these cetological data were the core of the original "whaling voyage," the book which Melville had begun back in the spring of 1850.

Whaling was the productive subject, but only to the person saturated in cetological fact.[1] In 1850, Americans as a whole were not familiar with whaling, much less with whales; their ignorance was probably even greater than that of twentieth-century Americans. It is true that previously there had been attempts to describe the whaleman's life, but in the main both the whaleman and the whale were figures of mystery. Even later this was so. Writing towards the end of the century, Frank Bullen complained that public ignorance concerning whaling required him to describe processes which clogged the narrative flow of his book, *The Cruise of the Cachalot.*

---

[1] But novels by and about whalemen have not been distinguished. Aside from J. C. Hart's *Miriam Coffin,* already mentioned, one should note *The Adventures of William Avery,* by the author of *The Black Velvet Bracelet, Annette Warrington,* etc., etc. (Boston, 1833). Later novelettes of equal incompetence are Harry Halyard's *Wharton the Killer! or, The Pride of the Pacific: A Tale of the Ocean* (Boston, 1848); *Harry Harpoon: or, The Whalemen's Yarn* (New York, n.d.) (DeWitt's *Stories of the Sea*); Roger Starbuck's *The Golden Harpoon, or, Lost Among the Floes, A Story of the Whaling Grounds* (New York, 1865) (Beadle's Dime Novels, 83); and C. W. Waddell's "The Tonokomoth Tiger," *People's Favorite Magazine,* XXXVI (10 November, 1921), [113]–128. A number of other, less lurid, stories have been published; a bibliography is needed.

If the public of Bullen's day (1899) was uneducated in cetology, how much more ignorant were Melville's readers. And while it is true that public interest in whaling was on the increase when Melville wrote, nevertheless the publications of his contemporaries, Beale, Bennett, Browne, and Cheever, scarcely constituted a wide popular literature on the subject. There was a good reason why *Moby-Dick* had been first conceived as a "whaling voyage" — it met a real educational need.

Perhaps as Mauron observes, "A novel ought to be living but not impartial or exact; it is not a source of information." Nevertheless, defying this dictum, *Moby-Dick* is a whaling handbook; it is document as well as art. In *Moby-Dick* we have the best popular introduction ever written on the subject of the American sperm-whale fishery.[2] Considering the information available to Melville in the eighteen-fifties, the account is complete. Considering the limited research then completed, *Moby-Dick* is accurate. Later books are fuller in fact, but not in *essential* fact. Almost no new information discovered by whalemen in the past ninety years invalidates Melville's basic data. For Melville, speaking as a whaleman himself, was too careful a writer to report solely from his limited experiences; whenever possible he rested on the most reliable authorities available to him. When those authorities contradicted each other or showed signs of uncertainty about their facts, Melville put forward the information in a tentative, often humorous, statement — one far from dogmatic. Melville's conjectures — and whaling still furnishes vast room for speculation — have been proved sound. *Moby-Dick* may be relied on for its cetological and whaling fact. The general reader feels the authority behind Melville's account of the American sperm-whale fishery, an authority acknowledged by modern writers on the subject. W. J. Dakin, author of *Whalemen Adventurers,* termed *Moby-Dick* "the

---

[2] Almost fifty years ago in his now famous article of Melville appreciation Archibald MacMechan said: "This book is at once the epic and the encyclopaedia of whaling. It is a monument to the honour of an extinct race of daring seamen; but it is a monument overgrown with the lichen of neglect." "'The Best Sea Story Ever Written,'" *Queen's Quarterly*, VII (October, 1899), 130.

great whaling classic," while Ashley, the greatest modern authority on whaling, has extended his tributary wreath to Melville in *The Yankee Whaler*, saying: "There could be no truer picture of whaling or finer story of the sea than Herman Melville's 'Moby-Dick.' "

The cetological center of *Moby-Dick* is neither digressive nor diversive; it is not an intrusion. "Out of the trunk the branches grow," — the trunk of Melville's novel is the "whaling voyage" with which he began in February, 1850. From the whaling center, Melville works out to the symbolical and metaphysical circumference. The scientific accuracy of the exposition supports and enriches the poetic and narrative sections of the novel. The large accumulation of data serves, does not interfere with, the narrative and thematic ends of the epic. Zoological, economic, and nautical facts are fixed in an esthetic context. Every natural fact is given a new, a larger dimension. Melville does not record whaling fact like an encyclopedist. Every real detail from harpoon to cutting tackle is somehow assimilated into the exciting story of the *Pequod* and of the spiritual quest of Ishmael and Ahab. Exposition, narration, and metaphysical insight are skillfully interwoven — then colored with a somber and rich tragic vision of man's fate.

With a documentary base, *Moby-Dick* is a work of art. Nowhere is there waste in *Moby-Dick*; every concrete detail serves a double and triple purpose. The exposition is the foil against which the story, like a star i' the darkest night, sticks fiery off indeed. No detail is unleavened. For instance, as will shortly be shown in detail, even such a chapter as "The Specksynder," at first seemingly irrelevant, contributes to the designed effect of the whole novel. In a strange and remarkable way, our quickly and easily acquired information about harpoons and lances, whaleboats and lines, blubber and bones, the pursuit of the whale and the flight from the whale, informs [3] us so thoroughly and profoundly concerning whaling life that we identify ourselves with the

---

[3] Melville wrote in *The Confidence-Man*: "It is with fiction as with religion; it should present another world, and yet one to which we feel the tie."

Pequod crew as they abandon themselves to the delirious pursuit of the albino whale so soon to destroy them. Ahab's mad scheme seems reasonable enough to win our subscription. Through knowledge acquired in the cetological center we say, at last, with Ishmael: "I was he whom the Fates ordained to take the place of Ahab's bowsman."

2

"My numerous fish documents"

THE CETOLOGICAL CENTER of *Moby-Dick* begins almost like a formal essay, with bibliography, definition, and classification, except that Melville's tone is mocking and his procedure high-spirited. He was free from precedents; the bibliography of whaling was haphazard in the eighteen-fifties, and even to-day there is no complete bibliography on the subject.[4] Melville was not a professional scholar, but he wanted to find accurate and authoritative facts. He worked well against odds. His own library in Pittsfield was probably quite small, but he was fortunate to have free access to Evert Duyckinck's large library and to the collections of the New York Library Society, of which he was a member. The student of whaling may be grateful for Melville's diligence in research; the reader of *Moby-Dick* is rewarded by Melville's ingenious and imaginative use of his facts.

If the general structure of "Cetology" seems formal, the details were highly informal. The following list of authors is impressive, but one must admit that it does not meet elementary bibliographical requirements:

4 A modern bibliography is badly needed. Most students must depend on the "List of Sources" appended to the various modern studies of whales and whaling. There is, however, a superb critical bibliography covering the printed materials to 1840 by Joel Asaph Allen, "Preliminary List of Works and Papers Relating to the Mammalian Orders Cete and Sirenia," *Bulletin of the United States Geological and Geographical Survey of the Territories,* VI (1881), [399]–562. In compiling his bibliography Allen made use of D. Mulder Bosgood's *Bibliotheca Ichthyologia et Piscatoria* (Harlem, 1873).

Nevertheless, though of real knowledge there be little, yet of books there are a plenty; and so in some small degree, with cetology, or the science of whales. Many are the men, small and great, old and new, landsmen and seamen, who have at large or in little, written of the whale. Run over a few: — The Authors of the Bible; Aristotle; Pliny; Aldrovandi; Sir Thomas Browne; Gesner; Ray; Linnaeus; Rondeletius; Willoughby; Green; Artedi; Sibbald; Brisson; Marten; Lacépède; Bonneterre; Desmarest; Baron Cuvier; Frederick Cuvier; John Hunter; Owen; Scoresby; Beale; Bennett; J. Ross Browne; the Author of Miriam Coffin; Olmstead; and the Rev. T. Cheever. But to what ultimate generalizing purpose all these have written, the above cited extracts will show.

If one were to read what these men said about whales and whaling, one would be well along in understanding the subject. Few people have done so, and certainly Melville himself was acquainted with most of these men by name only, not with their works. No library then accessible to him along the entire Eastern seaboard contained all the titles on his list, and very few libraries today contain the majority of these names.[5] Nor does Melville say that he *had* read them; he merely lists them. But the hasty reader gathers the impression that Melville's list was compiled from firsthand investigation. Such was not the situation. Melville took the larger number of his references from Thomas Beale's *Natural History of the Sperm Whale*. Every author up to J. Ross Browne is mentioned or quoted in Beale's work. And rapid research shows that whereas Melville did consult, and use, all the authors from J. Ross Browne to the end of the list, he probably used none of the early ones. At no place in *Moby-Dick* does Melville display the slightest familiarity with the whaling materials gathered by Aristotle, Artedi, Green, Willoughby, Aldrovandi, and Ray, although there is much usable information to be had from them. Certainly, had Melville seen the outlandish whale pictures in Aldrovandi he would have mentioned them sarcastically in his chapters on whaling iconography.

[5] The finest collecting of whaling and piscatorial books in America, so far as I know, is the Fearing Collection in the Harvard College Library. The New Bedford Public Library, the Library of Congress, and the New York Public Library have excellent if less extensive holdings.

Melville was not at ease in foreign languages.[6] He may have had a slight reading knowledge of Latin and French, recalled from studies at high school, but he obviously did not know those languages or others well enough to work his way through the important whaling documents written in Dutch, French, Latin, and German. His satire of Scoresby's familiarity with the Dutch writers, for instance, suggests that Melville was conscious of his own ignorance. More generally than students have realized, Melville relied on secondary sources; but so blandly does he quote Cuvier, Linnaeus, and others that we credit him with primary research, when investigation shows that he had dexterously removed his allusions from citations in Beale, Bennett, Browne, or Scoresby, Jr. Therefore, when Melville says, "I have swam through libraries," we must take his remark with reservations. Fortunately, the whaling authors which he could find, or did use, were first-rate authorities. Melville's full boast is, in a way, justified: "I have swam through libraries and sailed through oceans; I have had to do with whales with these visible hands; I am in earnest; and I will try." Research among the best available books on whaling, personal experience on the whaling grounds, and a supreme literary skill — what better qualifications could one have for writing a "whaling voyage"? And add a penetrating vision of the tragedy of life and we have *Moby-Dick*.

Five books furnished Melville with the bulk of his whaling data. These books play such an important part in the discussion to follow that a few words about each is in order.

The primary source book for Melville in composing the cetological section of *Moby-Dick* was Thomas Beale's *Natural History of the Sperm Whale*. Melville secured his personal copy on 10 July, 1850, paying Putnam's $3.38.[7] The care

[6] Such a statement would explain why he made such little use, *if any*, of Frederick Cuvier's valuable whale book, *De l'histoire naturelle des cétaces, ou recueil et examen des faits dont se compose l'histoire naturelle de ces animaux* (Paris, 1836).

[7] This valuable book was bought in 1945 by Mr. Perc Brown, of Montclair, New Jersey. He has generously allowed me to examine the volume and to copy Melville's markings and notes. Unfortunately, at some time in its his-

with which he read the book is attested by the many check-marks throughout the book as well as the comments scribbled in the margins. It is a good book, still required reading for cetologists. Even by 1850 it had achieved the status of an authority. In 1843 a reviewer said that Beale "supplies by far the most copious and satisfactory information on the subject"; and Beddard, writing in our century, called the *Natural History* "the classic in its [the whale's] habits and pursuits." Melville's praise is in fundamental agreement with these two critics. Linking Beale with Bennett, Melville wrote:

> There are only two books in being which at all pretend to put the living sperm whale before you, and at the same time, in the remotest degree succeed in the attempt. Those books are Beale's and Bennett's; both in their time surgeons to the English South-Sea whale-ships, and both exact and reliable men. The original matter touching the sperm whale to be found in their volumes is necessarily small; but so far as it goes, it is of excellent quality, though mostly confined to scientific description.

Melville's specific debts to Beale will be enumerated at length; his general debt — and probably to Bennett, also, though to a much smaller degree — was in his arrangement of whaling materials in chapter groups. Beale's fifteen headings: "External form and peculiarities of the Sperm Whale," "Habits of the Sperm Whale — Feeding," "Swimming," "Breathing," "Other actions of the Sperm Whale," "Herding, and other particulars of the Sperm Whale," "Nature of the Sperm Whale's Food," "Anatomy and Physiology of the Sperm Whale" (divided into twenty-five sections, which

tory, a vandal erased many of Melville's pencil markings; but since not many words were erased — the vandal objected more to the checkmarks — and since by holding the book to the light one may see where the erasures occurred, it is still possible to follow Melville through the book. It is to be hoped that a future examination of the markings under infra-red rays may bring out some of these erasures.

Melville owned what is called the second edition of Beale. In reality it is a first edition. Printed in 1835, the so-called first edition was but a little pamphlet of sixty pages out of which grew the expanded and altered *Natural History*. This 1835 edition is quite rare; the 1839 is not.

leave no part of the whale undescribed), "Of Spermaceti, etc.," "Of Ambergris," "Rise and Progress of the Sperm Whale Fishery," "Description of the Boats, with various Instruments employed in the capture of the Sperm Whale," "Chase and capture of the Sperm Whale," "Of the 'cutting in' and 'trying out,' " "Of the favourite places of resort of the Sperm Whale," were followed, except for necessary variations in narrative structure, by Melville in *Moby-Dick*.[8] Comparing the chapter headings of *Moby-Dick* with this list from Beale, one sees how closely Melville followed, either by accident or design, Beale's grouping. At the same time one notices how freely Melville adapted the groupings to the demands of art, and how his love of metaphor compelled him to change Beale's prosaic wording into graphic figures of speech: e.g. "the battering ram" and "the Heidelburgh Tun" for Beale's "Of the Cranium" and "Of the lower jaw." If, as Melville objected, Beale was limited by his scientific approach, Melville in borrowing from him readily remedied that defect.

When Melville coupled Bennett with Beale as "exact and reliable," he might have added that his personal obligation to Frederick Debell Bennett's *A Whaling Voyage Round the Globe, from the Year 1833 to 1836* (London, 1840) was second only to his debt to Thomas Beale's *Natural History of the Sperm Whale*. Both men, as Melville stated, had written from firsthand knowledge; although they were not professional whalemen, they had at least taken a field trip to the haunts of the sperm whale to see and to dissect the great fish for themselves. Unlike the whalemen, neither Beale nor Bennett was inclined to spin a pretty yarn, nor were they, too, like many scientists, inspired to speak at second hand. Lacépède, Bonneterre, and other cetologists, had done no more whaling than Simple Simon; in contrast, Beale and Bennett went out to the whale to report objectively what they saw, to sift with care that which they heard. In the history of whale research they have an important place; in

[8] Melville of course varied Beale's sequence to suit his own convenience, discussing the subjects listed by Beale in an order as follows, roughly: 1, 15, 13, 7, 2, 14*a*, 8, 4, 3, 6, 10, 9, 14*b*, and 5, 8, 11, and 12 variously.

the history of the American novel they unwittingly played a part.

We have already recognized Melville's debt to Browne's *Etchings of a Whaling Cruise,* in that it was the book which probably led Melville to preparatory research for a whaling book. Why Melville did no more than list Browne without further comment is puzzling. Either he must have felt that Browne's book was essentially a *rifacimento* of other writers' labors, or he may have thought that he had sufficiently recognized *Etchings* in the review which he wrote for Duyckinck's *Literary World.* Or perhaps Melville was embarrassed by the similarities of passages in *Moby-Dick* to passages in *Etchings.* We shall study these similarities shortly.

Melville's fourth source book, the Reverend Henry T. Cheever's *The Whale and His Captors* (1850), contributed much less to *Moby-Dick* than did those of Beale, Bennett, and Browne. It may be that the book appeared too near the composition of *Moby-Dick* for Melville to bother with incorporating many of Cheever's suggestions. But the lively and dramatic account of the whale fishery helped Melville out in at least two places in his own whaling epic.

The sperm whale and the sperm-whale fishery were the subject of four books written in the fifteen years preceding *Moby-Dick.* Melville knew them well; he acknowledged their merits; and yet his was a well-considered remark, and true, when he wrote: "As yet, however, the sperm whale, scientific or poetic, lives not complete in any literature. Far above all other hunted whales, his is an unwritten life." He meant that Beale, Bennett, Browne, and Cheever together had the parts; no one had the whole. For Melville was creating that book at the time.

One other source book was invaluable to Melville, but it did not deal with the sperm whale. Writing a book about the sperm-whale fishery, Melville employed his skill in praising the Cachalot to the derogation of its chief rival, the Right Whale of Arctic waters. (And embarrassingly, this valuable book dealt almost exclusively with the Greenland Whale.) To counteract this potent book, Melville, taking a suggestion from Thomas Beale's words in the *Natural History of the Sperm Whale —*

The Greenland whale, or *Balaena mysticetus,* has so frequently been described in a popular manner, that the public voice has long enthroned him as monarch of the deep, and perhaps the dread of disturbing such weighty matters as a settled sovereignty and public opinion may have deterred those best acquainted with the merits of the case from supporting the more legitimate claims of his southern rival to this pre-eminence —

transformed Beale's words into a stirring announcement of his whaling intention in *Moby-Dick*:

And here be it said, that the Greenland whale is an usurper upon the throne of the seas. He is not even by any means the largest of the whales. Yet, owing to the long priority of his claims, and the profound ignorance which, till some seventy years back, invested the then fabulous or utterly unknown sperm-whale, and which ignorance to this present day still reigns in all but some few scientific retreats and whale-ports; this usurpation has been every way complete. Reference to nearly all the leviathanic allusions in the great poets of past days, will satisfy you that the Greenland whale, without one rival, was to them the monarch of the seas. But the time has at last come for a new proclamation. This is Charing Cross; hear ye! good people all, — the Greenland whale is deposed, — the great sperm whale now reigneth!

This chronicler of the despised Greenland Whale was William Scoresby, Jr., author of the two-volume classic, *An Account of the Arctic Regions with a History and Description of the Northern Whale Fishery* (1820). His learned study, a storehouse of materials, was plundered by Melville. Scoresby has justly been called the father of Arctic science. He is certainly the outstanding English authority on the Greenland whaling fishery, and his two closely packed volumes are the fullest account of whaling ever written by a genuine whaleman gifted with scientific caution and restraint. Immediately after publication, *An Account of the Arctic Regions* became the standard whaling reference. Most of the popular accounts of whaling published in the periodical press from 1820 to 1850 took their information straight from Scoresby,[9] often not acknowledging the source and not even changing the wording. Even today after the researches of one hundred years, the value of his book is almost as great as in 1820. While perhaps no whaling library is complete without Beale and Bennett, the cornerstone of that library must be Scoresby's *An Account of the Arctic Regions*.

Melville's admiration for Scoresby was genuine but grudging. He was, Melville admitted, "a real professional harpooner and whaleman. . . . On the separate subject of the Greenland or right-whale, he is the best existing authority." Why then did Melville seize several opportunities to satirize or parody the saintly old whaleman's pages — parody the entire point of which is partly hidden? Perhaps Melville was amused at the explorer's lack of humor. Another artistic defect, to Melville, was that Scoresby had packed his volumes heavily with dry and often irrelevant fact. He did not bother to marry fact to human history. Lastly, since Scoresby was the celebrant of the Right Whale, rival to the Sperm Whale in the attention of the public, Melville's campaign to glorify the Sperm Whale made it necessary, he felt, for him to laugh at anything concerned with *Balaena mysticetus*. "Scoresby," Melville wrote in reproof, "knew nothing and says nothing of the great sperm whale, compared with which the Greenland whale is almost unworthy mentioning." For this reason does Scoresby posthumously suffer the slings of outrageous satire in *Moby-Dick*.

A Melville dig at Scoresby is before us in "Cetology." In classifying whales, Melville mentioned the narwhale [10] — a fish found only in Arctic waters which Melville knew nothing about at first hand. For whatever information Melville

---

9 The accounts of the whale fishery published in *The Mariner's Library, or Voyager's Companion* (Boston, 1840), pp. 331–346, and *The Mariner's Chronicle: Containing Narratives of the Most Remarkable Disasters at Sea* (New Haven, 1834), pp. 410–412, are but two instances of unacknowledged "borrowings" from Scoresby which I have seen.

10 No. 210 of the Hull Museum Publications has a discussion of narwhale tusks which is interesting; even better is Morton P. Porsild, "Scattered Observations on Narwhales," *Journal of Mammalogy*, III (1922), 8–12. Melville also knew, but apparently did not use, the discussion of narwhale anatomy in William Scoresby's *Journal of a Voyage to the Northern Whale-Fishery* (Edinburgh, 1823), pp. 136–142.

picked up about narwhales, he seems to have relied almost completely on Scoresby's long description and his engraved plate of the narwhale. Not satisfied with using Scoresby's information, Melville insisted on his secret joke, with heavy humor calling Scoresby "Charley Coffin" and giving Scoresby's account a humorous twist of fact. For instance, in describing the narwhale's peculiar long horn, Scoresby had added a suggestion as to its use:

> it is not improbable but it may be used in piercing thin ice for the convenience of respiring, without being under the necessity of retreating into open water. It cannot, I conceive, be used as many authors have stated, in raking their food from the bottom of the sea.

Taking this passage into *Moby-Dick* Melville made characteristic additions:

> What precise purpose this ivory horn or lance answers, it would be hard to say. It does not seem to be used like the blade of the sword-fish and bill-fish; though some sailors tell me that the Narwhale employs it for a rake in turning over the bottom of the sea for food. Charley Coffin said it was used for an ice-piercer; for the Narwhale, rising to the surface of the Polar Sea, and finding it sheeted with ice, thrusts his horn up, and so breaks through.

And then came the extra touch Melville always felt called upon to add:

> But you cannot prove either of these surmises to be correct. My own opinion is, that however this one-sided horn may really be used by the Narwhale — however that may be — it would certainly be very convenient to him for a folder in reading pamphlets.

Scoresby will help out Melville several times, and on each occasion Melville will satirize him under a pseudonym. "Charley Coffin" and "sailors" are but the beginning.

The five whaling books by Thomas Beale, the Reverend Henry Cheever, J. Ross Browne, Frederick Debell Bennett, and William Scoresby, Jr., by no means close the list of Melville's "numerous fish documents." [11] They are, however, with the addition of Olmstead's *Incidents of a Whaling Voyage*, the key books for studying the cetology of *Moby-Dick*. They will be referred to frequently in this study. From them Melville borrowed facts and ideas with lavish freedom, his strange mind ticketing the oddest materials for development in his whaling novel. Melville's borrowings do not in any way make him liable to the charge of plagiarism; whatever he took he transformed; the practice and authority of Shakespeare, his great master, gave sanction to his method of transfer. Out of Beale's and Bennett's sows' ears Herman Melville made silk purses. Imagination amended bare and unpromising fact. In Goethe's words to Eckermann:

> It is, in fact, utter folly to ask whether a person has anything from himself, or whether he has it from others; whether he operates by himself, or operates by means of others. The main point is to have a great will, and skill and perseverance to carry it out.

And an organizing, enlivening imagination.

3

"The classification of the constituents of a chaos"

WHALING CLASSIFICATION in the eighteen-fifties was almost as disorganized as whaling bibliography. What little had been

---

11 Although I have examined all the numerous fish documents, especially those prepared for a general public, I have not found satisfactory evidence that Melville borrowed from them. One of the most helpful to him would have been Henry William Dewhurst's *The Natural History of the Order Cetacea, and the Oceanic Inhabitants of the Arctic Regions* (London, 1834), written by a careful scientist retelling as fully and as entertainingly as possible the facts about whales and whaling. For instance, he mentions on page 54 that the Dutch whalemen at Smeerenberg had hot rolls for breakfast, information which had Melville seen he would scarcely have neglected (cp. "The Decanter"). Dewhurst's book also has information on whale skeletons and fossils which Melville obviously had not read in preparation of his chapters on these subjects. The rarity of this book today (at least in the United States) may indicate a similar rarity in Melville's day.

written on the subject was liable to error; the learned doctors fought among themselves like the two priests fighting over the measurements of the whale skeleton in *Moby-Dick*.

To classify whales in any sort of popular system was a formidable task.[12] For two reasons, Melville met the problem head on. First, it probably pleased his sense of humor to enter the field cluttered up by the professional zoologists; he was the amateur mockingly attempting what the experts had bungled — or even sidestepped. Secondly, he undoubtedly felt that since he was committed to the cause of the sperm whale, it behooved him to make a sharp distinction between the sperm whales and their cousins so similar in appearance. He plainly stated his intention in "Cetology." To most people all whales are alike. The sheep must be separated from the goats:

> Now the various species of whales need some sort of popular comprehensive classification, if only an easy outline one for the present, hereafter to be filled in all its departments by subsequent laborers. As no better man advances to take this matter in hand, I hereupon offer my own poor endeavors. I promise nothing complete; because any human thing supposed to be complete must for that very reason infallibly be faulty. I shall not pretend to a minute anatomical description of the various species, or — in this place at least — to much of any description. My object here is simply to project the draught of a systematization of cetology. I am the architect, not the builder.
>
> But it is a ponderous task; no ordinary letter-sorter in the Post-Office is equal to it. To grope down into the bottom of the sea after them; to have one's hands among the unspeakable foundations, ribs, and very pelvis of the world; this is a fearful thing. What am I that I should essay to hook the nose of this leviathan! The awful tauntings in Job might well appal me. "Will he (the leviathan) make a covenant with thee? Behold the hope of him is vain!" But I have swam through libraries and sailed through oceans; I have had to do with whales with these visible hands; I am in earnest; and I will try. There are some preliminaries to settle.

[12] Actually, the sperm whale was not properly described and classified until Clusius did so in 1605.

Melville was an architect where even Beale backed down. But Bennett had made a classification of whales, and this Melville found helpful. The reason for the scientists' uncertainties is obvious: the extreme difficulty of finding enough specimens to justify one's classes. Whales are not captured as readily as lizards or dogs. The first formal classification of whales was that by John Ray in 1671; one hundred and fifty years later there was still confusion. Few scientists had known live whales firsthand. Too few of them had had the chance to dissect stranded whales along shore. None before Beale had studied the whale on the whaling grounds or had seen one cut up, fresh captured, aboard a whaling ship. Scientists either repeated the errors of previous reporters, or imagined new errors with which to mislead the public. They were like the painters in Daumier's cartoon: the first painting a tree, but the second copying the painting of the tree — only, the whale-classifiers continued the chain-borrowing down the years. The confusion was bemoaned by a scientist as late as 1830: this was Edward Pigeon, in a book possibly seen by Melville:

> Myriads of sailors have caught and divided whales, who perhaps have never had the opportunity of properly contemplating one in its entire state. Yet naturalists have deemed themselves able to compose the history of these animals, from the vague descriptions and the ruder figures given by such uninstructed observers. No critical accuracy, no correct deduction, could exist in such compilations for want of the proper basis of well-authenticated facts. Consequently we find the history of the cetacea, on the one hand, meagre in the extreme, and, on the other, swarming with contradictions, and confusions of nomenclature.[13]

And how is one to seize on the whales for sorting them? Beale mentions that Brisson had distinguished seven species of sperm whales, depending on their dorsal fins, spout holes,

13 *The Animal Kingdom arranged in Conformity with its Organization, by the Baron Cuvier . . . with additional Descriptions of all the Species hitherto named, and of many not before noticed,* by Edward Griffith and others. Volume XI (London, 1830): *The Fossil Remains of the Animal Kingdom,* by Edward Pigeon, Esq., p. 147. Melville owned the 1834 edition of this book, now in the Berkshire Athenaeum, Pittsfield, Massachusetts.

and form of their teeth; Linnaeus had reduced the species to four, characterized by the teeth of the lower jaw; Bonneterre then increased them to six species, depending on dorsal fins and teeth; Lacépède again increased the species to eight, subdivided into three groups; and Desmarest followed him, only adding one more species, "the characters of which," Beale added witheringly, "he obtained from some Chinese drawing, upon the fidelity of which no dependence can of course be placed." With such contradiction among the most celebrated cetologists — Melville had read Beale's account of the contradictions — one may imagine the difficulties facing Melville, no zoologist, in categorizing all the whales of the seven seas. Beale said that the job was "utter confusion":

> Great contradictions and dissensions have also at various times originated among naturalists, relative to the number of the species of this whale; yet notwithstanding the ingenious reasoning of some, and the bold and truthlike observations of others, with the close attention to the subject of such men as Green, Aldrovandus, Willoughby, Rondelet, Artedi, Ray, Sibbald, Linnaeus, Brisson, Marten, and a crown of other distinguished naturalists, from the impossibility of any of these great men making continuous observations upon this interesting animal, the subject was still doomed to remain an apparently impenetrable mystery.

In the light of Beale's sense of frustration, we see how much Melville must have enjoyed entering the arena, with no scientific reputation at stake. "It is," he wrote adventurously, "some systematized exhibition of the whale in his broad genera, that I would now fain put before you. Yet it is no easy task. The classification of the constituents of a chaos, nothing less is here essayed."

Although Beale considered the difficulties of the classification problem at great length, and furnished materials towards a system, he refused to commit himself, perhaps privately justifying himself with the excuse that he was writing only about the Sperm and not the Right Whale. Bennett was bolder and attempted a classification, a trinitarian one, in fact, which may have suggested to Melville his own triadic arrangement of whales. Melville had the advantage over Beale and Bennett in that he was no scientist; whereas they had to consider soberly every little detail, Melville could generalize, could harmonize his materials through humor and anecdote; and furthermore, he knew that a system compiled for the convenience of the readers of a whaling novel need not be scrupulously complete nor finically exact. Melville's audience was in general much different from Beale's and Bennett's.

Facing the difficulty before him, Melville resorted to quotations from four cetological experts all alluding to the mystery of whale groupings. First Melville quoted Scoresby: "No branch of Zoology is so much involved as that which is entitled Cetology"; then quoted Cuvier: "All these incomplete indications but serve to torture us naturalists"; [14] John Hunter: "Unfitness to pursue our research in unfathomable waters"; and Lesson: "A field strewn with thorns." What is amusing about these four quotations is that although they sound as though Melville had surgically removed them directly from their original contexts, they had actually been quoted together on an unnumbered page in the front part of Beale's *Natural History of the Sperm Whale*; instead of ransacking a large whaling library, Melville had merely lifted his authorities from Beale's convenient cache of quotations.

Just before he classified "the grand divisions of the entire whale host" Melville penned his famous definition of a whale; the contracted definition of expanded meditation, he called it: "To be short, then, a whale is a *spouting fish with a horizontal tail.*" This is a satisfactory definition and may have been original with Melville. On the other hand, Melville's expanded meditation may have been assisted by a suggestion from Frederick Cuvier appearing in Todd's *Cyclopedia of Anatomy and Physiology*:

> Aristotle, from his anatomical knowledge, was aware of the essential differences between the Whales and the Fishes, but it is not absolutely necessary to seek for internal characters to establish the real distinction which subsists between these dif-

[14] This was Melville's translation of the French passage quoted in Beale: "Toutes ces indications incomplètes ne servent, qu'à mettre les naturalistes à la torture."

ferent denizens of the deep; the horizontal position of the tail-fin at once distinguishes the cetacean from the fish, in which it is vertical.[15]

Whatever his source, Melville neatly described the whale so that the practical whalemen in the whale fishery were satisfied — if not the zoologists expostulating that the whale was no fish but a mammal. This Melville knew perfectly well, but he let his definition be shaped by the common characteristics and by familiar experience, not by laboratory information. In *The Animal Kingdom* (1830) Edward Pigeon admitted "In fact the Cetacea have altogether the external form of fishes, with the exception that in the latter the fin of the tail is vertical."

Melville decided that there was nothing to do "but to take hold of the whales bodily, in their entire liberal volume, and boldly sort them that way. And this is the Bibliographical system here adopted; and it is the only one that can possibly succeed, for it alone is practicable." Melville divided the whales into three classes: folio, octavo, and duodecimo. Certainly Melville's grouping is the most practical one for a literary man, especially since he was led to it by the half-hidden pun ("volume") , and by the character he had humorously assumed as the "sub-sub-librarian" of the "Extracts" prefixed to his novel.

It would have been practically impossible for Melville to work out any other — a scientific — system; the bibliographical "alone is practicable." Beale devoted three pages to a discussion of former classification methods which had tried to distinguish the whales according to humps, baleen, or fins. At the end of his long exploration of possibilities he concluded:

> So that they resemble each other in some respects, and differ so widely in other parts of their formation, and also in their habits, that they necessarily belong to distinct classes of beings and convince me, that they cannot properly be arranged in families, from the form or situation of their fins, humps, teeth, or baleen.

15 Volume I (London, 1835–1836), p. 594. Beale refers to the book.

Though the passage sounds new-coined by the reflective author, when one reads Melville's words, the debt to Beale is immediately apparent:

> ... yet it is in vain to attempt a clear classification of the Leviathan, founded upon either his baleen, or hump, or fin, or teeth; notwithstanding that those marked parts or features very obviously seem better adapted to afford the basis for a regular system of Cetology than any other detached bodily distinctions which the whale, in his kinds, presents. How then? The baleen, hump, back-fin, and teeth; these are things whose peculiarities are indiscriminately dispersed among all sorts of whales, without any regard to what may be the nature of their structure in other and more essential particulars. Thus, the sperm whale and the humpbacked whale, each has a hump; but there the similitude ceases. Then this same humpbacked whale and the Greenland whale, each of these has baleen; but there again the similitude ceases. And it is just the same with the other parts above mentioned. In various sorts of whales, they form such irregular combinations; or, in the case of any one of them detached, such an irregular isolation; as utterly to defy all general methodization formed upon such a basis. On this rock every one of the whale-naturalists has split.

Melville might well have quoted Goethe's words to Eckermann, 8 October, 1827: "The ornithologists are probably delighted when they have brought any peculiar bird under some head; but still Nature carries on her own free sport, without troubling herself with the classes marked out by limited men," for in a sense part of "Cetology" is a parody of the efforts of limited men to pigeonhole the phenomena of Nature.

Under the Folio whales Melville described the Hump Back, Razor Back, Sulphur Bottom, omitting special descriptions of the Sperm and Right Whales since they were destined for a full dissection in later pages of *Moby-Dick*. For the Octavoes, "the whales of middling magnitude," he described the Grampus, the Black Fish, the Narwhale; and for the Duodecimo, "the smaller whales," he included the Huzza Porpoise, the Algerine Porpoise, and the Mealy-Mouthed Porpoise, with an additional paragraph lumping together "a rabble of uncertain, fugitive, half-fabulous whales, which, as an American whaleman, I know by reputation, but not personally."

Melville let his fancy loose in his description — not that he falsified facts but that he embellished them with imagery and humor and irony. I have already shown how he parodied Scoresby in describing the Narwhale. Other uses of sources are dimly seen. In describing the Black Fish, Frederick Bennett had written: "the angles of the lips are curved upwards, giving the physiognomy of the animal an innocent, smiling expression." Melville changed this to read in *Moby-Dick*: "His voracity is well known, and from the circumstances that the inner angles of his lips are curved upwards, he carries an everlasting Mephistophelean grin on his face." Undoubtedly the picture which accompanied Bennett's description attracted his attention to the smile, and strengthened his reworking of Bennett's words. Other borrowings may possibly be traced but they are small ones and add nothing significant to the record, being more suitable as footnotes to an edition of *Moby-Dick*.[16]

With the elementary cetological material disposed of, Melville returned to his story to strengthen his characterization of Ahab in "The Specksynder" (33) and "The Cabin-Table" (34).

4

"An officer called the Specksynder"

With the bibliographical and classification matters settled, Melville moved back to the characters of his story so that the next few chapters deal with Ahab and his men. Special

[16] For instance, Melville's sentence on the Grampus, "By some fishermen his approach is regarded as premonitory of the advance of the great sperm whale," is almost a quotation from Bennett, p. 238: "their appearance is supposed to indicate the resorts of the Cachalot."

care was necessary, for the leading figures of *Moby-Dick* were, after all, not merely officers on a whaling voyage; they were the central figures in a great tragic drama. This necessity led Melville to a series of chapters in which he strategically stresses the "largeness" of his characters, especially the captain, through outright statement, humorous episode, and symbolic overtone. The first of these chapters, for instance, seems completely out of place if it is not seen in its larger purpose. "The Specksynder" (33) describes an officer in the Greenland Whale Fishery, but unknown to whaleships hunting the sperm whale in Pacific waters. None of the books on South Seas whaling had told Melville about the specksynder, nor had he come across one aboard the *Acushnet* or any other whaling ship. His source of information was William Scoresby, Jr.'s *An Account of the Arctic Regions*:

> At this period, each ship carried two principals; the Commander, who was a native, was properly the navigator, as his chief charge consisted in conducting the ship to and from Greenland; the other, who was called by the Dutch *Specksynder,* or cutter of the fat, as his name implies, was a Biscayan, and had the unlimited control of the people in the fishery; and indeed every operation belonging to it was confided to him. When, however, the fishery became better known, the commander likewise assumed the superintendence of the fishery. The office of specksioneer is now the principal harpooner, and has the "oering of the fat," and extracting or boiling of the whale; but he serves entirely under the direction of the commander of the vessel.

Melville's description follows Scoresby's closely:

> . . . originally in the old Dutch Fishery, two centuries and more ago, the command of a whale-ship was not wholly lodged in the person now called the captain, but was divided between him and an officer called the Specksynder. Literally this word means Fat-Cutter; usage, however, in time made it equivalent to Chief Harpooneer. In those days, the captain's authority was restricted to the navigation and general management of the vessel; while over the whale-hunting department and all its concerns, the Specksynder or Chief Harpooneer reigned supreme. In the British Greenland Fishery, under the cor-

rupted title of Specksioneer, this old Dutch official is still retained, but his former dignity is sadly abridged. At present he ranks simply as senior Harpooneer; and as such, is but one of the captain's more inferior subalterns.

The revelation of Melville's source for "The Specksynder" does not explain, however, why he devoted an entire chapter to an antiquarian detail foreign to the fishery which he was celebrating in *Moby-Dick*. But in *Moby-Dick* nothing is useless, even the most minute whaling fact is made to serve a larger purpose. It is with reference to the character of Ahab that "The Specksynder" becomes significant. In describing an officer employed on other whaleships, Melville implies that on the *Pequod* there could be no division of authority, and that captain and specksynder must be one when there was an Ahab aboard. Though whaleships in the past may have carried two commanders, now only one commander was needed, whether on the decks of the *Pequod* or in the boats following the harpooned whale. In other words, Melville implies, Ahab dominates through power of personality and skill of craft, and not through established, legalized office, or from usage and custom. Ahab, he says in effect, needed no resort to rank to gain his will; he compels by leadership. Ahab, though "least given to that sort of shallowest assumption . . . the only homage he ever exacted, was implicit, instantaneous obedience."

Melville carries the point further: "Be a man's intellectual superiority what it will, it can never assume the practical, available supremacy over other men, without the aid of some sort of external arts and entrenchments, always, in themselves, more or less paltry and base." Most kings and emperors, he adds, necessarily resort to mechanical supports for the authority, which uphold the monarch even though he be of idiot mentality. But when such supports uphold a man possessing "an imperial brain; then, the plebeian herds crouch abased before the tremendous centralization." That Melville was deliberately pointing up the personal greatness of Ahab for his rôle as tragic hero is shown in a subsequent sentence: "Nor, will the tragic dramatist who would depict mortal indomitableness in its fullest sweep and direct swing, ever forget a hint, incidentally so important in his art, as the one now alluded to." With Melville's hint — in which Ahab is seen as both captain *and* specksynder, — we need not be surprised at Ahab's magnificent domination over his crew so that at all times they "crouch abased before the tremendous centralization."

How consciously Melville worked out his portrait of the dominating, yet isolated, Ahab, appears in the chapter immediately following "The Specksynder." "The Cabin-Table" (34) is a description of the table formalities among the officers of the *Pequod,* with an episode, a humorous obbligato, of poor Flask caught short in the red tape of etiquette, and forced to go hungry at the table — a scene in the spirit of Sancho Panza's frustrated feast as Governor in *Don Quixote.* But even as we laugh at Flask's plight, we do not forget the silent, lonely figure of Ahab at the head of the table — it is his cabin and although the mates and harpooners have every right to be there during mealtime, they seem like interlopers. Ahab in society is a lonely man, not to be touched by normal social duties. The point is made in the concluding paragraph of the chapter:

> . . . in the cabin was no companionship; socially, Ahab was inaccessible. Though nominally included in the census of Christendom, he was still an alien to it. He lived in the world, as the last of the Grisly Bears lived in settled Missouri. And as when Spring and Summer had departed, that wild Logan of the woods, burying himself in the hollow of a tree, lived out the winter there, sucking his own paws; so, in his inclement, howling old age, Ahab's soul, shut up in the caved trunk of his body, there fed upon the sullen paws of its gloom!

"The Cabin-Table" may describe ship etiquette, but the mind fastens on the lonely Ahab, while the humorous and grotesque performance about him only accentuates his isolation. Thus the "isolatoes" theme appears again, as if played by the bassoons in a strange, dancing figure.

5

"It is exceedingly pleasant the mast-head"

As we have just seen, "The Cabin-Table" (34) pictured
Ahab in his isolation, and, by extension, suggested the life of
the impassioned seeker whose monistic search leads him away
from social ties and obligations. It is a picture of the lonely
man intent upon seizing the meaning of life in one potent
answer. Strange though the suggestion at first may seem,
Melville's subsequent chapter, "The Mast-Head" (35), is
another study of loneliness to be placed beside the picture of
"The Cabin-Table." It too portrays the danger of monism.
But where "The Cabin-Table" was a blending of tragic
grimness with farcical humor, "The Mast-Head" combines
an innocent picture of blissful solitude with a caustic criticism of certain American ideals. Melville's ability to manufacture much from little is effectively illustrated as we see
him spin satire and philosophy from the description of an
ordinary, everyday experience of the whaleman's life. Writing from personal recollection and from his recent reading
about the mastheads on whaling ships, Melville extended
what might have been a brief paragraph into one of his
longest and subtlest chapters, what might have been simple
exposition into a nostalgic-ironic remembrance of things past
and of things timeless, all embellished with pseudo-history
and parody. Seldom has so much owed to so little. Seldom
in literature has a single "fact" as unassuming as the mast-
head of an American whaleship produced such a delightful
set of literary variations.

Before moving into the symbolical meanings of the mast-
head, Melville first described its function, adding a facetious
decoration of pseudo-history to include Saint Simeon Stylites,
Napoleon, Washington, and Nelson as standers of mastheads
— metaphorical ones at least — although he admitted that
"their spirits penetrate through the thick haze of the future,
and descry what shoals and rocks must be shunned" — a re-
verse statement of Emerson's famous dictum that "An insti-

tution is the lengthened shadow of a man." Briefly, the mast-head was the lookout, high up the three masts, for whales. "In most American whalemen," said Melville, "the mast-heads are manned almost simultaneously with the vessel's leaving her port." [17] This information was sufficient if mere fact was his intention, but one of the longer chapters in *Moby-Dick* unfolds from it. Why? Mainly, it seems, because Melville enjoyed intensely the experience of standing in the masthead and getting away from the crowding of the deck. One may take as almost autobiographical Ishmael's words: "For one, I used to lounge up the rigging very leisurely, rest-ing in the top to have a chat with Queequeg, or any one else off duty whom I might find there." *Redburn* and *White-Jacket* both testify to Melville's pleasure in riding the rigging, engaging in leisurely, anecdotal chat with his ship-mates — or later, his journal of the trip to London in 1849 tells of his indulging in metaphysical discussion high above the decks of the *Southampton.*

But even while he had the stimulation of pleasant memory to guide him in the factual part of his chapter on the mast-head, Melville kept his eye on his numerous fish documents. One example is sufficient for illustration: Melville said,

> . . . the worthy Obed tells us, that in the early times of the whale fishery, ere ships were regularly launched in pursuit of the game, the people of that island erected lofty spars along the sea-coast, to which the look-outs ascended by means of nailed cleats, something as fowls go upstairs in a hen-house.

The concluding, homely image is a characteristic Melville addition to Obed Macy's straightforward description:

> To enable them to discover whales at a considerable dis-tance from the land, a large spar was erected, and cleats fixed to them, by which the whalemen would climb to the top, and there keep a good look out for their game.

[17] Apparently an echo of Thomas Beale's, "From the commencement of the voyage, men are placed at each mast-head, who are relieved every two hours, an officer is also placed on the fore-top-gallant-yard, consequently there are four persons constantly on the look-out during the day, from the most elevated parts of the ship."

With historical material disposed of, Melville moved on to another element of mastheads. The sensory delights of the masthead and the feeling of "sublime uneventfulness" aroused in the apprentice in the lookout are delightfully described in *Moby-Dick*:

> In the serene weather of the tropics it is exceedingly pleasant the mast-head: nay, to a dreamy meditative man it is delightful. There you stand, a hundred feet above the silent decks, striding along the deep, as if the masts were gigantic stilts, while beneath you and between your legs, as it were, swim the hugest monsters of the sea. . . . There you stand, lost in the infinite series of the sea, with nothing ruffled but the waves. The tranced ship indolently rolls; the drowsy trade winds blow; everything resolves you into languor. For the most part, in this tropic whaling life, a sublime uneventfulness invests you; you hear no news; read no gazettes; extras with startling accounts of commonplaces never delude you into unnecessary excitements; you hear of no domestic afflictions; bankrupt securities; fall of stocks; are never troubled with the thought of what you shall have for dinner — for all your meals for three years and more are snugly stowed in casks, and your bill of fare is immutable.

Reminiscent as these words obviously are of Melville's own experience of the lookout on the *Acushnet*,[18] one must, however, note that Melville has in effect rewritten a passage from J. Ross Browne's *Etchings of a Whaling Cruise*. The rhythmical felicity of Melville's words is far above Browne's simpler statement:

> The mast-head was a little world of peace and seclusion, where I could think over past time without interruption. There was much around me to inspire vague and visionary fancies: the ocean, a trackless waste of waters; the arched sky spread over it like a variegated curtain; the sea-birds wheeling

---

[18] Later in *Moby-Dick*, Chapter 61, Melville expressed again the dream effect of the lookout watch:

"It was my turn to stand at the foremast-head; and with my shoulders leaning against the slackened royal shrouds, to and fro I idly swayed in what seemed an enchanted air. No resolution could withstand it; in that dreamy mood losing all consciousness, at last my soul went out of my body; though my body still continued to sway as a pendulum will, long after the power which first moved it is withdrawn."

in the air; and the myriads of albacore cleaving their way through the clear, blue, waves, were all calculated to create novel emotions in the mind of a landsman. It was here I could cast a retrospective glance at my past life. . . .

Whenever I became so wrapped up in these visionary dreams as to forget that I was not placed at the masthead for that special purpose, the loud harsh voice of the captain would arouse me, with a friendly hint to 'keep a sharp lookout for whales, or he'd wake me up with a rope's end.' To be suddenly startled from a delicious revery, abounding in those ethereal and refined fancies which Rousseau has so beautifully described as part of the inspiration derived from an elevated atmosphere; to have one's happiest dreams of home dissipated by an allusion to 'ropes'-ends,' suggesting thoughts of the mode in which they are usually applied, is not so romantic as one might suppose.

Melville rewrote Browne's paragraph a second time in "The Mast-Head," making it far more complex and far more extended in its implications than the serene and dreamlike passage which I have just quoted. Melville turns Browne's description into a satire of the starry-eyed romantic who unaware of the "uprising fin of some discernible form" would escape reality through Rousseauistic revery:

And let me in this place movingly admonish you, ye shipowners of Nantucket! Beware of enlisting in your vigilant fisheries any lad with lean brow and hollow eye; given to unseasonable meditativeness; and who offers to ship with the Phaedon instead of Bowditch in his head. Beware of such an one, I say: your whales must be seen before they can be killed; and this sunken-eyed young Platonist will tow you ten wakes round the world, and never make you one pint of sperm the richer. Nor are these monitions at all unneeded. For nowadays, the whale-fishery furnishes an asylum for many romantic, melancholy, and absent-minded young men, disgusted with the carking care of earth, and seeking sentiment in tar and blubber. Childe Harold not unfrequently perches himself upon the mast-head of some luckless disappointed whale-ship, and in moody phrase ejaculates: —

"Roll on, thou deep and dark blue ocean, roll!
Ten thousand blubber-hunters sweep over thee in vain."

Very often do the captains of such ships take those absent-minded young philosophers to task, upbraiding them with not feeling sufficient "interest" in the voyage; half-hinting that they are so hopelessly lost to all honorable ambition, as that in their secret souls they would rather not see whales than otherwise. But all in vain; those young Platonists have a notion that their vision is imperfect; they are short-sighted; what use, then, to strain the visual nerve? They have left their opera-glasses at home.

"Why, thou monkey," said a harpooneer to one of these lads, "we've been cruising now hard upon three years, and thou hast not raised a whale yet. Whales are scarce as hen's teeth whenever thou art up here." Perhaps they were; or perhaps there might have been shoals of them in the far horizon; but lulled into such an opium-like listlessness of vacant, unconscious reverie is this absent-minded youth by the blending cadence of waves with thoughts, that at last he loses his identity; takes the mystic ocean at his feet for the visible image of that deep, blue, bottomless soul, pervading mankind and nature; and every strange, half-seen, gliding beautiful thing that eludes him, every dimly-discovered, uprising fin of some undiscernible form, seems to him the embodiment of those elusive thoughts that only people the soul by continually flitting through it. In this enchanted mood, thy spirit ebbs away to whence it came; becomes diffused through time and space; like Cranmer's sprinkled Pantheistic ashes, forming at last a part of every shore the round globe over.

There is no life in thee, now, except that rocking life imparted by a gently rolling ship; by her, borrowed from the sea; by the sea, from the inscrutable tides of God. But while this sleep, this dream is on ye, move your foot or hand an inch; slip your hold at all; and your identity comes back in horror. Over Descartian vortices you hover. And perhaps, at mid-day, in the fairest weather, with one half-throttled shriek you drop through that transparent air into the summer sea, no more to rise for ever. Heed it well, ye Pantheists!

Never content, as we have seen, with the straightforward retelling of his own experiences nor with a mere repetition of other men's words, Melville has compelled everyday whaling fact and whaling experience to carry a load of extra meaning and meditation. "Meditation and water are wedded forever," Melville tells us in the opening chapter of *Moby-Dick*, speaking perhaps for all men and certainly for himself. Seen from the heights of the lookout, the sea became to him "thought-suggesting" as it did years later to Logan Pearsall Smith:

> When I walk to the side of the thought-suggesting sea, when I sit on the sand not far from the margin of the incoming or retreating tide, I often gaze on that waste of undulating water until it assumes in my eyes a moral meaning — seems to lie there on the page of Nature's book in an immense and shining metaphor, re-presenting the instability and transience of all things in the stream of Time. And the waves, as they hasten toward the pebbled shore, remind me, as they have reminded others, of our own moments hastening to their end.
>
> But as they keep on reiterating monotonously the lesson, and my thoughts ebb and flow to their melancholy music, they seem to efface and wash away their own monitions; my sense of the transience of things proves itself but a transient reflection; and reclining there in the shade of my white cotton sun umbrella I float agreeably off into an oblivion of Time, the Sea and Mortality.

Much of what Smith describes is said in Melville's chapter on a simple whaling office.

Perhaps, as Melville has warned us, it is "vain to popularize profundities," but a word concerning his deeper meanings is necessary for a full understanding of *Moby-Dick*. The paragraphs descriptive of the dreamer in the masthead may well bear the weight of another interpretation: that they here constitute an implicit satire of the unitarian point of view, especially as manifest in the Transcendental philosophy of the Over-Soul. Melville seems to say that transcendental harmony, in which the personal identity is lost in infinity,[19] is deceptively seductive. It is unable to account

---

19 As great a prose poet as Melville, perhaps, Baudelaire expressed this same "vast delight of gazing fixedly, drowning one's glance in the immensity of sky and sea" in his prose-poem "*Confiteor* of the Artist," in which, like Melville above, he pointed out that "in the grandeur of reverie the *ego* is lost." Baudelaire's short prose-poem might well serve as an epigraph for Melville's Mast-Head chapter.

for the evil and repellent facts of life; in other words, the shark swimming in the sea (the "uprising fin") may not be explained away glibly, Melville says, as "the embodiment of those elusive thoughts that only people the soul." Emerson's famous sentence, "When I behold a rich landscape, it is to know why all thought of multitude is lost in a tranquil sense of unity," presents a point of view which, whether or not he was aware of Emerson's precise statement, Melville satirizes in his portrait of the young Platonist whose spirits have ebbed away, diffused through time and space, the thought of multitude (the waves) lost in the "enchanted mood." [20]

Melville's personal antipathy (allied with sympathy) towards pantheistic revery is revealed in his letter to Hawthorne, June, 1851, written during the last stages of the composition of *Moby-Dick*. Discussing Goethe's phrase, "Live in the all," Melville says sarcastically:

> That is to say, your separate identity is but a wretched one, — good; but get out of yourself, spread and expand yourself, and bring to yourself the tinglings of life that are felt in the flowers and the woods, that are felt in the planets Saturn and Venus, and the Fixed Stars. What nonsense! Here is a fellow with a raging toothache. "My dear boy," Goethe says to him, "you are sorely afflicted with that tooth; but you must *live in the all,* and then you will be happy!" As with all great genius there is an immense deal of flummery in Goethe, and in proportion to my own contact with him, a monstrous deal of it in me.

[20] William James described these pseudo-Platonians dreaming in the lookout: "In many persons, happiness is congenital and irreclaimable. 'Cosmic emotion' inevitably takes in them the form of enthusiasm and freedom. I speak not only of those who are animally happy. I mean those who, when unhappiness is offered or proposed to them, positively refuse to feel it, as if it were something mean and wrong. We find such persons in every age, passionately flinging themselves upon their sense of the goodness of life, in spite of the hardships of their own condition, and in spite of the sinister theologies into which they may be born. From the outset their religion is one of union with the divine. The heretics who went before the Reformation are lavishly accused by the church writers of antinomian practices, just as the first Christians were accused of indulgences in orgies by the Romans. It is probable that there never has been a century in which the deliberate refusal to think ill of life has not been idealized by a sufficient number of persons to form sects, open or secret."

As an indication that his interest was not entirely against the unitarian concept of the "all," Melville added in a postscript a delightful qualification of his initial sarcasm:

> N.B. This "all" feeling, though, there is some truth in. You must often have felt it, lying on the grass on a warm summer's day. Your legs seem to send out shoots into the earth. Your hair feels like leaves upon your head. This is the *all* feeling. But what plays the mischief with the truth is that men will insist upon the universal application of a temporary feeling or opinion.[21]

These words to Hawthorne were not, however, Melville's first indictment of the "all-sayers"; two years before, in *Mardi*, Melville had referred sarcastically to "those orthodox systems which ascribe to Oro [God] almighty and universal attributes every way, those systems, I say, destroy all intellectual individualists but Oro, and resolve the universe into him. But this is heresy."

Melville's collocation of masthead sitting and the All is made much clearer in the nineteenth chapter of *White-Jacket*, "The Jacket Aloft." Mentioning that White Jacket was "of a meditative humor, and at sea used often to mount aloft at night and . . . give loose to reflection," Melville praises the pleasures of such reflection and adds:

> And it is a very fine feeling, and one that fuses us into the universe of things, and makes us a part of the All, to think that, wherever we ocean-wanderers rove, we have still the same glorious old stars to keep us company; that they still shine onward. . . . Aye, aye! we sailors sail not in vain. We expatriate ourselves to nationalize with the universe; and in all our voyages round the world, we are still accompanied by those old circumnavigators, the stars, who are shipmates and fellow-sailors of ours — sailing in heaven's blue, as we on the

21 I have not yet traced the exact passage of Goethe's which Melville had in mind, although in one of the few Goethe texts accessible to him in English, Margaret Fuller's translation of *Conversations with Goethe in the last years of His Life,* translated from the German of Eckermann (Boston, 1839), Melville might have read, " 'Did not God inspire the bird with this all-powerful love for his young, and did not similar impulses pervade all animate nature, the world could not subsist. But even so is the divine energy every where diffused, and divine love every where active' " (p. 405).

azure main. Let genteel generations scoff at our hardened hands, and finger-nails tipped with tar — did they ever clasp truer palms than ours? . . . Oh, give me again the rover's life — the joy, the thrill, the whirl! Let me feel thee again, old sea! Let me leap into thy saddle once more. I am sick of these terra firma toils and cares; sick of the dust and reek of towns. . . . But when White-Jacket speaks of the rover's life, he means not life in a man-of-war, which, with its martial formalities and thousand vices, stabs to the heart the soul of all free-and-easy honorable rovers.

Melville then tells of a scene in which the sailors, seeing the white jacket aloft, had taken it to be the ghost of an old shipmate and had lowered the halyards in fear. In symbolic terms, White Jacket had almost fallen from his blissful reveries in the masthead down to the ocean or the deck — to what is called in *Moby-Dick* the Descartian vortices. The passage in *White-Jacket* illuminates the later, greater passage in *Moby-Dick*.

The masthead sitter, the dreamer, is tempted into belief in the One and into forgetfulness of the Many. To Melville the All-sayers were the New England Transcendentalists, and since *Moby-Dick* implicatively attacks their type of idealism, a word about them is in order.

Moby-Dick is a Geiger-counter, delicately sensitive to the intellectual radiations of mid-nineteenth-century America. Its strongest oscillation was to the Panglossian optimism then prevailing, especially in the Transcendentalism of New England.

Transcendentalism in New England is difficult to describe; to define it with Polonian precision is to waste both night and day. "What is popularly called Transcendentalism among us, is Idealism," Emerson wrote in the *Dial*, "Idealism as it appears in 1842." Emerson's vagueness of description is understandable. Transcendentalism had many faces, but whether the term was used to describe a philosophy of individualism, a religious attitude towards life, a collection of individual lunacies, or man's intuitive understanding of Truth, it was fundamentally, to quote Emerson again, "a protest against usage, and a search for principles." No more definite than that, Transcendentalism may be briefly labeled as "an enthusiasm, a wave of sentiment, a breath of mind," as its chief historian, Frothingham, described it; while Santayana summed it up best of all: "Transcendentalism is an attitude or a point of view rather than a system."

If the definition of New England Transcendentalism is uncertain, equally indeterminate is its precise origin. It would be safest to classify New England Transcendentalism as a mixture made up of many simples; or as cloth which, though made from several foreign threads, was woven on New England looms and was a thoroughly native product.

Although the Transcendental band was small, its effect was widespread; whether it received enthusiastic support or met with disapproval, American intellectuals did not look at it with lack-luster eye. To men outside the Transcendental circle, the spiritual leader and the chief symbol of the movement in America was Ralph Waldo Emerson — and so he was to Herman Melville.

The word "transcendental" does not appear often in *Moby-Dick*, but seldom in the reflective passages are we far from some of Transcendentalism's favorite ideas. How did these ideas reach Melville? Probably by the usual routes: newspapers and periodicals, conversations, and lectures. Transcendentalism was in the air; everyone praised or satirized it. Undoubtedly the Concord Transcendental group was frequently discussed at the table of Melville's father-in-law, Chief Justice Shaw of Massachusetts. Even as early as *Mardi* (1849), Melville had formed an unfavorable opinion of Transcendental thought because "those systems, I say, destroy all intellectual individualities but Oro [God], and resolve the universe into him."

Probably the main source of Melville's knowledge of the Transcendental movement was Nathaniel Hawthorne. Hawthorne was well acquainted with the Transcendental leader, Emerson, having been his friend and neighbor in Concord. Hawthorne had also been for a short time a member of the Transcendental colony at Brook Farm, and he had married one of the most enthusiastic of the Transcendental bluestockings, Sophia Peabody. Despite his close association with the group, Hawthorne was ambivalent in his attitude, admiring and disapproving at the same time. Writing in *Mosses from an Old Manse*, the book which had enthralled Melville in July, 1850, Hawthorne reflected on Transcendental reformers and their ilk in the sketch "The Hall of Fantasy," finding it "good for the man of unquickened heart to listen to their folly. . . . My faith revived even while I rejected all their schemes." During the long and wonderful talks between Hawthorne and Melville [22] in the years 1850–51, the two must have discussed Emerson, Thoreau, and Transcendentalism. Hawthorne's tolerant sympathy for a movement with which he could not fully agree is similar to Pierre's friendship for the eccentric Charles Millthorpe, or to the following mockery in *Pierre*:

> Their mental tendencies, however heterodox at times, are still very fine and spiritual upon the whole; since the vacuity of their exchequers leads them to reject the coarse materialism of Hobbes, and to incline to the airy exaltations of the Berkeleyan philosophy. . . . These are the glorious paupers from whom I learn the profoundest mysteries of things; since their very existence in the midst of such terrible precariousness of the commonest means of support, affords a problem on which many speculative nut-crackers have been vainly employed. Yet let me here offer up three locks of my hair, to the memory of all such glorious paupers who have lived and died in this world. Surely, and truly I honour them — noble men often at bottom — and for that very reason I make bold to be gamesome about them; for where fundamental nobleness is, and fundamental honour is due, merriment is never accounted irreverent.

Like Hawthorne, Melville respected the sincerity and good intentions of the Transcendentalists even while he mocked them as misguided men blind to the brute facts of existence.

---

[22] Both of these men were Transcendentalists in that they believed in a spirit transcending man's knowledge, in a world of reality beyond the world of phenomena, but to use the term thus broadly would lead to a discussion of Melville's religious thought. Transcendentalism is here restricted to its special development by the New England group. As to Melville's beliefs see William Braswell, *Melville's Religious Thought* (Durham, North Carolina, 1943).

Even though they sought oneness with the Over-Soul without an understanding of tragic experience, their essential shallowness was redeemed by the enthusiasm with which they supported their faith. In their tolerant attitude towards the Transcendentalists, Hawthorne and Melville implicitly foreshadow the later remark of William Graham Sumner, "A society needs to have a ferment in it; sometimes an enthusiastic delusion or an adventurous folly answers the purpose."

Transcendental dreaming, living in the benevolent All, is the antithesis of materialism. Melville indicates this by the closing words of warning in "The Mast-Head" to the Pantheistic dreamer to be awake for whales lest he fall into "the Descartian vortices." It is not easy to be certain of precisely what Melville meant by the "Descartian vortices." Some help may be found, perhaps, in *Pierre*. Describing the Apostles, the group of "poor, penniless devils" who live "in the region of blissful ideals," Melville stresses their Platonic idealism ironically at odds with their material poverty:

> Often groping in vain for their pockets, they cannot but give in to the Descartian vortices; while the abundance of leisure in their attics (physical and figurative), unite with the leisure in their stomachs, to fit them in an eminent degree for that undivided attention indispensable to the proper digesting of the sublimated Categories of Kant; especially as Kant (can't) is the one great palpable fact in their pervading impalpable lives.

Here, certainly, the Descartian vortices are the brute, material (and often evil) facts of life. The Apostles are unmistakably the Transcendentalists, as all students of *Pierre* agree, and the association of the Descartian vortices (material necessities) with impractical idealism in *Pierre* assures us that a similar association in *Moby-Dick* implies the same satirical object.

The Pantheistic revery of the masthead is, as suggested before, in symbolical antithesis to the Descartian vortices. The Pantheistic revery is the concentration on Unity, on the One; the Descartian vortices represent multiplicity. The greenhorn whaleman in the lookout becomes lost in infinity and fails to sight whales. Pantheism neglects the "uprising fin" [23] as the multitudinous waves merge into one dreamy, blissful sensation of the All. Unity is the delusion of youth careless of distinctions. Said Henry Adams: "The older the mind, the older its complexities, and the further it looks, the more it sees, until even the stars resolve themselves into multiples; yet the child will always see but one." The opposite extreme of multiplicity is the revulsion from the early worship of unity; it may be just as bad, even worse, than Pantheistic revery, which is at least a shallow but not ignoble enthusiasm. Multiplicity does not order the concrete facts of day-to-day experience; too close scrutiny of every fact reveals evil in so many forms that the mind is destroyed. As Amiel wrote in his journal: "On whatever side one looks one feels besieged by the infinity of infinities. A serious look at the universe is terrifying. Everything seems so relative that one does not know what has real value." The mature human mind must be able to discern unity in multiplicity, must be neither Pantheistic dreamer nor the youth falling into the Descartian vortices; the mature mind must maintain a sharp lookout for whales even as it relishes the ride high in the cross-trees of the ship.

Once again, obliquely, through the description of mastheads, the problem of the One and the Many has turned up as a major theme in *Moby-Dick*.

As if he had not made "The Mast-Head" complex enough already with his implicit criticism of the New England Transcendentalists in particular and of Platonian idealism in general, Melville further complicated the chapter — and enlivened it, too — by throwing in a parody to boot. Discussing the origins of the masthead, Melville saw in one of

[23] Read William James's indictment of too strong a stress on ideal harmony in a letter to George H. Palmer, 2 April, 1900: "Moreover, when you come down to the facts, what do your harmonious and integral ideal systems prove to be? in the concrete? Always things burst by the growing content of experience. Dramatic unities; laws of versification; ecclesiastical systems; scholastic doctrines. Bah! Give me Walt Whitman and Browning ten times over, much as the perverse ugliness of the latter at times irritates me, and intensely as I have enjoyed Santayana's attack. The barbarians are in line of mental growth, and those who do insist that the ideal and the real are dynamically continuous are those by whom the world is to be saved."

his "numerous fish documents" an excellent opportunity to fill out his chapter, none too strong in historic facts, with additional historical material carrying humorous overtones. The butt of his satire was William Scoresby, Jr., who in *An Account of the Arctic Regions* had described with filial pride the crow's nest, an invention of his father's [24] for making the Greenland Fishery lookouts more comfortable and efficient. Melville pounced upon Scoresby's long, prideful account,[25] parodying its pedantry as well as its piety, its over-particularity. Even without knowledge of the parody, one enjoys the mockery of Melville's paragraphs, but an awareness of the parodic intent, hidden to all but the source hunter or the student of whaling, enhances one's relish of the humor. Also, smiling over Melville's sarcastic commentary on academic verbosity, one enjoys another refutation of the charge (itself humorless) that *Moby-Dick* is a book without humor, and that Melville's was a humorless mind. Such a judgment is a howler of the enormity of Doctor Johnson's words on "Lycidas." One might better keep in mind Doctor

[24] Captain William Scoresby, Sr., father of the whale chronicler, was "probably the most successful whaler and ice navigator that ever lived. In all his total of thirty voyages as commander into the dangerous Arctic waters he never lost a ship. He invented the top-gallant 'crow's nest'; (the first one built in 1807 and in use ever after), the ice drill, and numerous things connected with the operations of whaling. He was the first on record after Hudson to trace the east coasts of what was then called 'West' Greenland, as distinguished from Spitsbergen, at that time called Greenland and 'East' Greenland." *Seven Log-Books Concerning the Arctic Voyages of Captain William Scoresby, Senior, of Whitby, England.* Issued on facsimile by The Explorers Club of New York, with reproductions in color of portraits in oil of Captain William Scoresby, Senior, and Captain William Scoresby, Junior, D. E. Introductory Brochure. Edited by Frederick S. Dellenbaugh (New York: The Explorers Club, 1917), p. 1. — William Scoresby, Jr., told the crow's-nest story again, even as *Moby-Dick* was being written, in *Memorials of the Sea. My Father: Being records of the adventurous life of the late William Scoresby, Esq. of Whitby* (London, 1851), pp. 135–139. The crow's nest was also described in *Voyages and Adventures of Jack Halliard, in the Arctic Ocean* (Boston, 1839), pp. 9–10, by a man who says that he had sailed with the elder Scoresby. It is also described in Henry William Dewshurst, *The Natural History of the Order Cetacea*, etc. (London, 1834), p. 53, along with an amusing picture of the crow's-nest.

[25] The source of "The Mast-Head" parody was discovered ten years ago by F. B. Adams, Jr., in "The Crow's Nest," *Colophon*, N. S. II (Autumn, 1936), 148–154.

Johnson's words on Shakespeare's fatal love for quibbles and insist that *Moby-Dick* is too divertingly humorous and that Melville was only too ready to follow the trail of a jest.

The story picks up again after the quiet tone and the metaphorical ruminations of "The Mast-Head." Having cast away his pipe, symbol of peace of mind and of spiritual quiet ("This thing that is meant for sereneness"), Ahab summons his men before the quarter-deck to enlist the sworn support of the crew to make the White Whale, Moby Dick, spout black blood. "The Quarter-Deck" (36) is one of the most powerful narrative sections of the entire novel, rising to a pitch of intensity and wildness not to be reached again until "The Candles" (119). But the wildness of "The Quarter-Deck" is not the wildness of uncontrol; the scene has been discussed at length by various commentators, by none more brilliantly than F. O. Matthiessen in *American Renaissance*. These observations, familiar to many students of Melville, need not be here repeated; we will pause only to consider briefly one implication of Ahab's words, now made famous by frequent quotation. Ahab addresses the crew, his sentences pointed at Starbuck:

> "Hark ye yet again — the little lower layer. All visible objects, man, are but as pasteboard masks. But in each event — in the living act, the undoubted deed — there, some unknown but still reasoning thing puts forth the mouldings of its features from behind the unreasoning mask. If man will strike, strike through the mask! How can the prisoner reach outside except by thrusting through the wall? To me, the white whale is that wall, shoved near to me. Sometimes I think there's naught beyond. But 'tis enough. He tasks me; he heaps me. I see in him outrageous strength, with an inscrutable malice sinewing it. That inscrutable thing is chiefly what I hate; and be the white whale agent, or be the white whale principal, I will wreak that hate upon him."

The ambiguity of these passionate words may not be untangled in a paragraph, if at all, but some interpretation will be useful in relating the passage to the themes and motifs evolving before our minds in the novel. If, as the opening chapter said, the concern of Ishmael was to drive the

November drizzle from his soul and to go forth to see the White Whale, shadowily imagined by him, a similar concern for the White Whale, precisely and concretely imagined, is displayed by Ahab. Both men are symbolically in search of the answer to the final mysteries. Both have perceived the necessity of looking beyond phenomena for that answer. Ahab now openly refers to the forces felt behind all phenomena. Having been lacerated by life through the White Whale, he thinks of those forces as malevolent, seeing in them, or in their cetological embodiment, Moby Dick, "outrageous strength, with an inscrutable malice sinewing it." He does not know whether the force perceived was the final source — "be the white whale agent, or be the white whale principal" — but Ahab was aware of the demonic and evil power in the universe whether it be Moby Dick or beyond him. It has been argued that Ahab is Melville's portrait of the self-reliant man seeking to fulfill the "law of his being" according to Emerson's directive. We see this egotistic compulsion at work in the present chapter, for despite the ominous warning of "the subterranean laugh," a "foreboding invocation," Ahab will not heed the "admonitions and warnings" because he must assert his selfhood against the will of the crew. As Ishmael says, with Ahab in mind, "the innermost necessities in our being, these still drive us on." This is the fatality of rampant self-reliance.

Fiendish dedication of the crew to the will of Ahab completes "The Quarter-Deck." The contrasting quiet of the succeeding, and short, chapter "Sunset" (37), from the crowded deck to the solitary cabin of Ahab, is worth noting. The former scene of physical violence is now matched with a scene of psychological unrest as Ahab soliloquizes on the success of his exhortation to the crew. In Ahab's soliloquy Melville reinforces the individualism theme recurrent in the novel: "I thought to find one stubborn, at the least; but my one cogged circle fits into all their various wheels, and they revolve. Or, if you will, like so many ant-hills of powder, they all stand before me; and I their match. . . . What I've dared, I've willed; and what I've willed, I'll do!" The one potentially stubborn spirit, Starbuck, admits in his parallel soliloquy, "Dusk" (38), that "My soul is more than matched; she's over-manned; and by a madman! . . . aye, he would be a democrat to all above; look, how he lords it over all below!" and even as he shudders at the "latent horror" in life he desperately prays for the support of "ye blessed influences." Ahab's and Starbuck's soliloquies are of course revelations of the two sides of the coin, the opposition of forces: Ahab and Individualism against Starbuck and Society; Free Will *versus* Necessity. In "First Night Watch" (39) we have the soliloquy of Stubb, who reveals himself as the unthinking man unaware of implications and ready to accept whatever comes, to surrender his will to the whim of Ahab. Stubb is the mass, happy to be led.

According to the central philosophical canons of Herman Melville and Nathaniel Hawthorne, Ahab has now committed the Unpardonable Sin. Through the unchecked assertion of his own private will, his overbearing self-reliance, Captain Ahab has violated or destroyed the will of his men. His is the gravest of all the sins of man. It is no wonder then that the scene aboard the *Pequod* grows incredibly wild, as though a witches' sabbath were being held. Individual members of the crew come frontstage and utter their lines and then sink back into the obscurity of their anonymity; each is the representative of a segment of the world, a not accidentally gathered league of nations. Each one has frankly committed himself to an act which is against his own personal impulse; in other words, each has forsworn his own self-reliance in order that the extreme of Ahab's egoism may be fulfilled. It is no wonder then that little Pip, the little colored cabin boy, ironically has the last word on these unholy celebrations as he shivers in terror at what his dim brain discerns:

Here have I heard all their chat just now, and the white whale — shirr! shirr! — but spoken of once! and only this evening — it makes me jingle all over like my tambourine — that anaconda [26] of an old man swore 'em in to hunt him! Oh, thou

[26] This is a curious figure of speech which possibly becomes clearer when we know that in his copy of Hawthorne's *Mosses,* Melville generously marked

big white God aloft somewhere in yon darkness, have mercy on this small black boy down here; preserve him from all men that have no bowels to feel fear!

Pip called it "bowels to feel fear"; at the other extreme, Father Mapple would have called it humility. Whatever the name, Ahab does not have it.

The doubloon is nailed to the mast as a reward to him who first sights the White Whale. Ahab enlists his heathen crew to hunt for Moby Dick. Having thus set the stage, Melville turns to the great whale so that his readers may know just what Ahab is really after.

6

"The history of that murderous monster"

THOUGH *Moby-Dick* is a monument to the greatest whale that ever swam the seven seas, it is not, however, the biography of that fish, since it reconstructs but one episode from Mocha Dick's career. But even though the climax of *Moby-Dick* is fiction, it sprang from a vortex of tradition traceable through an odd assortment of records. Mocha Dick was a real whale, destroying Pacific shipping during the very years that Melville was a harpooner on the *Acushnet*.

No less an authority than Coleridge has assured us that poetic faith requires a "willing suspension of disbelief." Greatest of the apparent improbabilities of *Moby-Dick* is the bare suggestion that whales, seemingly all alike in appearance, could be distinguished as individuals, and then, that any individual whale could be found in the uncharted vastness of the ocean. Melville met this grave improbability in "The Chart" (40) and in "Moby-Dick" (41). To prepare his readers for facts which he himself, as an ex-whaleman, was willing to accept, Melville wrote an essay in five informative chapters (41–45), attempting to clew his bold fiction to the

the story of Roderick Ellison; "Egoism, or The Bosom Serpent." Thus in Pip's words Ahab is metaphorically described as suffering from the evil of egoism.

firm facts of record. "It is well known in the Sperm Whale Fishery," he told his readers, "however ignorant the world ashore may be of it, that there have been several memorable historical instances where a particular whale in the ocean has been at distant times popularly recognisable." Melville's chapter on Moby Dick stacks up reasons why whalemen both knew and feared the White Whale, and why whalemen never for a moment doubted both his actuality and the stories carried far and wide concerning his destructive power. "Not all of them," Melville says, "knew of his existence" and "only a few of them, comparatively, had knowingly seen him; while the number who as yet had actually and knowingly given battle to him, was small indeed." The reason for this immediate unfamiliarity, Melville added, was the very nature of the whaling voyage, with its penetration to wide and unknown spaces far removed in time, so that the irregularity of home returns had "long obstructed the spread through the whole world-wide whaling fleet of the special individualized tidings concerning Moby Dick." But Melville makes his point: though the events he describes seem like fantastic fiction, nevertheless they rest on a cetological foundation.

Unfortunately, the documentary evidence from which Melville pieced the concept of the destructive sperm whale, and of one special whale in particular, was as little known to the general public as was the sight of Mocha Dick to whalemen in general. That the sperm whale was destructive Melville already knew; he needed authority to give conviction to his picture of the terror whale. He resorted to the few bits of evidence to be gleaned from the fish documents. Proclaiming the "tested reality of his [the sperm whale's] might" as seen in widespread rumor, Melville turned to the writers:

> . . . we find some book naturalists — Olassen and Povelson — declaring the Sperm Whale not only to be a consternation to every other creature in the sea, but also to be so incredibly ferocious as continually to be athirst for human blood. Nor even down to so late a time as Cuvier's, were these or almost similar impressions effaced. For in his Natural History, the

Baron himself affirms that at sight of the Sperm Whale, all fish (sharks included) are "struck with the most lively terrors," and "often in the precipitancy of their flight dash themselves against the rocks with such violence as to cause instantaneous death."

Once more in tracking Melville's sources, we discover his habit of blandly quoting or citing an authority in such manner as to suggest that he was using the primary source. But here Melville is not quoting Cuvier, or Olassen and Povelsen, at first hand. Melville has leaned on Beale's *Natural History of the Sperm Whale,* putting together two passages separated from each other in Beale by only one paragraph. For "Olassen and Povelsen," Melville read in Beale:

> While the sperm whale has been quietly searching the ocean depths for his food, and avoiding with the greatest care and timidity the slightest danger or rencontre of any kind, he has been represented by Olassen and Povelsen as the most savage and ferocious of all marine animals; for not only, according to their accounts, does the cachalot constantly thirst for the blood of every fish in the sea, but actually possesses a relish for human flesh, which we are led to suppose they wished to satiate, when these historians assert that they seized, and upset with their jaws, a boat which contained some seamen, whom they speedily devoured.

It is more than coincidence that Beale's one citation from Olassen and Povelsen should be the one also made by Melville in *Moby-Dick*! And for the citation from Baron Cuvier, Melville merely had to read on to Beale's next page, where he found the following passage waiting removal to *Moby-Dick*:

> Yet the Baron Cuvier, in the compilation of its natural history, which he has obtained from many incorrect sources, states: — "the terrible arms, the powerful and numerous teeth with which nature has provided the cachalot, render it a terrific adversary to all the inhabitants of the deep, even to those which are most dangerous to others; such as the phocae, the balaenopterae, the dolphin, and the shark. So terrified are all these animals at the sight of the cachalot, that they hurry to conceal themselves from him in the sands or mud, and often

in the precipitancy of their flight, dash themselves against the rocks with such violence as to cause instantaneous death. It is not therefore surprising," says Cuvier, "if the myriads of fishes on which this tyrant preys, are struck with the most lively terror at his presence."

What is most amusing about Melville's "gathering" of evidence (to support his account of the terror of the sperm whale) is that he builds up a case from scientific writers quoted by Beale, although Beale had been anxious to show how wrong those authorities had been. Melville accepts the quotations as satisfactory because they support the picture of the destructive sperm whale so necessary to his narrative. Beale, on the contrary, argued that "not only does the sperm whale in reality happen to be a most timid and inoffensive animal as I have before stated, readily endeavoring to escape from the slightest thing which bears an unusual appearance, but he is also quite incapable of being guilty of the acts of which he is so strongly accused." But can any one familiar with the whole tone of *Moby-Dick* question the strategy of Melville in quoting Beale's arguments for his own different conception and his own artistic purpose?

It is a pity that Melville never put together in a short story or sketch the anecdotes which he must have picked up on the whaling grounds concerning the exploits of Mocha Dick, the White Whale. With a history amazing in its actuality, Mocha Dick should have had a biography written for him by the same man who established his immortality through a single feat, and that fictional.

Mocha Dick — why Melville changed the name to Moby Dick has never been satisfactorily explained [27] — was a bona fide whale, the "terror whale of the Pacific," of awesome size and with a reputation for terror and malice justifying his selection as the villain of a novel. Mocha Dick had proclaimed unremitting warfare on the sons of men, and some twenty years before the Civil War the far reaches of the Pacific rang with rumors of his deeds.

[27] One writer said that "Apparently the famous whale was sometimes referred to as 'Mocha' and sometimes as 'Moby.'" I find no earlier use of the name "Moby" than Melville's novel.

No one may say when Mocha Dick was born. Apparently his history goes back by a happy coincidence to just about 1819–20, the time of Herman Melville's birth. For one whaling writer stated that it was Mocha Dick who sank the whaleship *Essex* in 1820. Perhaps this famous feat should not be credited to Mocha Dick; Owen Chase, principal recorder of the event, makes no mention in his *Narrative* of the whiteness of the attacking whale — a detail which undoubtedly would have been recorded if seen. But since the *Essex's* sinking is one of the classics of the sea; and since the whale which did sink her was as mighty and malicious as ever Mocha Dick was; and since the *Essex* story furnished Melville with the dramatic climax of *Moby-Dick,* the cautious biographer of the White Whale must describe the event even while he reservedly files it in the Mocha Dick dossier under "Doubtful."

The whaleship *Essex* sailed from Nantucket, Captain George Pollard in command, on 12 August, 1819, to cruise the Pacific Ocean for sperm whales. She was "a good, substantial vessel," her first mate, Owen Chase, wrote, "she had a crew of twenty-one men, and was victualled and provided for two years and a half." The prospect for a voyage of two and one half years was over-optimistic. On 20 November, 1820, in latitude 40° S. and longitude 119°, the *Essex* lowered three boats when the lookout's cry "Thar she blows" dropped down to the ears of the lolling whalemen. In short order the mate's boat became fast to a large spermaceti whale, but was stove in when the whale's flukes struck her amidships near the waterline. Owen Chase was forced to cut the line connecting his boat with the whale, and to make his way back to the hovering ship for repairs. Nailing a piece of canvas over the hole, the crew returned to the hunt, while Chase remained with the ship. Almost immediately an enormous sperm whale, "about eighty-five feet in length," surfaced twenty rods off the ship's weather bow, spouted two or three times and disappeared, only to emerge in three seconds, heading directly for the *Essex* at a deliberate pace of about three knots an hour. Trouble threatening, Chase ordered the helm hard up, hoping to sheer off and avoid a head-on collision. Before the order could be executed, the mighty battering ram, the head of the sperm whale, struck the ship just beyond the fore-chains "such an appalling and tremendous jar, as nearly threw us all on our faces. The ship brought up as suddenly and violently as if she had struck a rock and trembled for a few seconds like a leaf." The whale passed on beneath the *Essex*, grazing her keel, and came up to the leeward side. After resting a moment, he then turned from the ship. Recovering from his amazement, Chase estimated that the pumps would have to be manned. Alarmed at the settling of the ship, he ordered the whaleboats to return. During this time, and some distance away, the great whale thrashed the water violently as if in pain and fury.

Before the boats could get back the crew shouted, "Here he is — making for us again." Surely enough, one hundred rods away the whale bore down with doubled speed, his course marked by a wake of white foam a rod wide. Rearing his vast head high above the water he struck the *Essex* a second blow which completely stove in her bow. The *Essex* was doomed. The situation of the crew was desperate with the mainland more than a thousand miles away, the nearest island inhabited by ferocious cannibals, and only two thirty-foot whaleboats to carry them across the stormy Pacific. The story of their epic voyage to the South American coast, of the intense suffering, of the cannibalism they practiced, of the death of most of the men — all of it is an epic of the sea, outside the biography of Mocha Dick. He — if it was he — had done his work and had gone his way to find other worlds to conquer. The men of the *Essex* were left to face the horrible consequences.

The *Essex* was sunk in 1820. It is barely possible that the whale which sent her to the bottom was the same whale which breached a few years later with terrifying results. Whales do live to be fifty or sixty years old, and the records relevant to Mocha Dick's history fall between 1820 and 1859, a span of thirty-nine years.

At any rate, by 1834 the great White Whale of the Pacific was established in sea tradition; in that year Ralph Waldo Emerson struck up a stagecoach conversation with a sailor who told him a yarn about a white whale, Old Tom by name, which, after wreaking terrible destruction, had finally been killed off Payta Head by a fleet of whaleships specially organized to capture him.[28]

Possibly referring to the same episode told to Emerson is J. N. Reynolds's narrative, first printed in the *Knickerbocker Magazine* for May, 1839.[29] It tells of the pursuit and capture of a

> renowned monster, who had come off victorious in a hundred fights with his pursuers, was an old bull whale, of prodigious size and strength. From the effect of age, or more probably from a freak of nature, as exhibited in the case of the Ethiopian Albino, a singular consequence had resulted — *he was white as wool!* Instead of projecting his spout obliquely forward, and puffing with a short, convulsive effort, accompanied by a snorting noise, as usual with his species, he flung the water from his nose in a lofty, perpendicular, expanded volume, at regular and somewhat distant intervals; its expulsion producing a continuous roar, like that of a vapor struggling from the safety-valve of a powerful steam engine. Viewed from a distance, the practised eye of the sailor only could decide, that the moving mass, which constituted this enormous animal, was not a white cloud sailing along the horizon. On the spermaceti whale, barnacles are rarely discovered; but upon the head of this *lusus naturae*, they had clustered, until it became absolutely rugged with the shells. In short, regard him as you would, he was a most extraordinary fish; or, in the vernacular of Nantucket, 'a genuine old sog,' of the first water.

[28] Robert Forsythe first noted this in "Emerson and 'Moby-Dick,'" *Notes and Queries*, CLXXVII (23 December, 1939), 457–458.

[29] Reprinted by Scribner's in 1932 with illustrations by Lowell Leroy Balcom. I believe that it appeared in book form later, published in Maine. An abridgment of it was reprinted in *The Sea. Narratives of Adventure, Shipwreck, Tales and Sketches, Illustrative of Life on the Ocean* (Edinburgh, 1840), pp. 131–135.

Interesting in himself as well as in his influence on Melville, Reynolds is the subject of two scholarly articles: Robert F. Almy, "J. N. Reynolds: A Brief Biography With Particular Reference to Poe and Symmes," *The Colophon*, N. S. II (Winter, 1937), 227–245; and, Aubrey Starke, "Poe's Friend Reynolds," *American Literature*, XI (May, 1939), 152–159. As the instigator of the South Seas expedition finally commanded by Wilkes, Reynolds described his great plan in *Pacific and Indian Oceans: The South Sea Surveying and Exploring Expedition, etc.* (New York, 1841).

Reynolds's account pushes the biography back to 1810 when Mocha Dick had been encountered near the island of Mocha [30] — whence, of course, his name. The story which Reynolds tells is of the pursuit of Mocha Dick by a resolute and audacious blubber hunter determined to catch the famous fish. The resolution of the whaleman is contrasted with the windy boasting of a crew member constantly belittling whalemen because he had once been a sealer. The story ends with the glorious victory of the whaling captain over the white whale. Mocha Dick was cut up and rendered into one hundred barrels of oil (a "normal" whale usually brought about 40 barrels); he "measured more than seventy feet from his noddle to the tips of his flukes" and twenty harpoons were lodged in his blubber. So wrote J. N. Reynolds.

It is of course impossible that Mocha Dick was killed, for he is deathless. Every reader of *Moby-Dick* knows this. The Mocha Dick of record was at his work of destruction only a year after the publication of the slander by Reynolds. On 5 July, 1840, he breached the surface of the sea to become real news, not far from his home territory, the island of Mocha, off Chile in latitude 38° 28′ S.[31] The *Desmond,* an English whaling ship, was sailing 215 miles west of Valparaiso when her lookouts sighted a lone whale two miles away. Immediately, according to habit, boats were lowered and the pursuit began. Instead of sounding, or swimming away, the whale came directly *towards* the boats to meet them. The whale was Mocha Dick. He struck the first boat head on and destroyed it. After sounding for fifteen minutes he suddenly emerged beneath the second boat and lifted it thirty feet in the air. Chewing the planks of the boat with lordly leisure, Mocha Dick at last swam off in a northerly

[30] Six miles off the coast of Chile latitude 38° 38′ South and longitude 75°. A description of this island is in *Chile and Peru in 1824* (Boston, 1824), pp. 70–71; in Capt. James Colnett, *A Voyage to the Atlantic and Round Cape Horn into the Pacific Ocean* (London, 1798), pp. 29–30, and in J. N. Reynolds's story (see previous note).

[31] The story which follows was printed in the Detroit *Free Press*, Sunday, 6 March, 1892. It was reprinted, minus the headline, as an appendix in John Freeman, *Herman Melville* (London, 1926), pp. 189–195.

direction, leaving behind him two dead whalemen. The men aboard ship reported him to be the largest whale they had ever seen, easily identifiable by an eight-foot scar across his head.

Two months later Mocha Dick struck again. On 30 August, 1840, the Russian ship *Sarepta* encountered him 500 miles south of his battle with the *Desmond*. Two boats, immediately after they had successfully killed another lone whale, not our hero, saw a large whale breach between them and their ship. Righting himself after a spectacular leap Mocha Dick struck out towards the two boats. One of them quickly retreated behind the dead whale for safety; Mocha Dick caught the other with a wide sweep of his jaw and knocked it to matchwood. Content with this he came to a rest beside the dead whale, allowing the second boat to slip back to the ship unharmed. The *Sarepta* hung around for three hours in the hope that Mocha Dick would leave the dead whale so that they might claim their prize, but, after a fruitless wait, sailed away. Two days later a Nantucket ship found the dead whale unguarded and secured it. Mocha Dick had swum away to other adventures.

Next, Mocha Dick bedeviled a British ship. In May, 1841, the *John Day* was trying out blubber east of the Falkland Islands when early in the afternoon an enormous whale breached within three hundred feet of the ship. The waves created by his fall to the ocean made the ship roll as if "in a gale." Identifying the whale as Mocha Dick the men, with more courage than sense, decided to capture him. They lowered three boats, and the first mate soon harpooned him. Then the trouble began. Feeling iron, perhaps for the first time, Mocha Dick sounded and ran for three miles, finally slewing around to attack the boat, which was still fast to him. The unexpected move caught the boat unprepared and Mocha Dick swam directly over it. With deliberate malice he stopped and beat the submerged boat with his great flukes (which measured, it was said, twenty-eight feet across). Nothing was left of the boat but splinters, two men were killed. Observing the other two boats pursuing him the wily whale settled down to await his prey. One of the boats picked up the floating line. The act was brave and foolhardy. Mocha Dick came up directly under the boat, knocked the bottom out of it, and sent two more men to their deaths. Enough was enough: the third boat returned to the ship, and the captain, despite a previous vow to capture the White Whale, retreated with a wisdom that Ahab might later have emulated.

Such dramatic encounters with such an easily identified whale became part of the whaling tradition of the Sperm Whale Fishery.[32] Dauntless captains vowed, Ahab-like, to capture the leviathan; more prudent ones, Starbuck-like, decided to avoid him. For seventeen months nothing was seen of Mocha Dick. Some whalemen assumed that he was dead.

As if to substantiate Melville's description of him as "not only ubiquitous but immortal (for immortality is but ubiquity in time) . . . hundreds of leagues away, his unsullied jet would once more be seen," Mocha Dick surprised one and all by appearing off the coast of Japan. Here he fought the most destructive and dramatic battle of his recorded career.

A lumber ship blown from her course by a heavy gale was making her way back to the coast when shortly after daylight a large whale breached two miles away. Since it was none of their concern the crew paid little heed to a sight common in whaling grounds. Imagine their surprise, then, fifteen minutes later, as they saw a whale bearing down on them full speed. They made no effort to avoid the impact. Mocha Dick struck the ship in the stern, wrecking her instantly and carrying away pieces of the wreckage in his jaw. Hastily the men threw together a raft from the lumber of their ship, but they did not need it, for the lumber kept her afloat even though she was submerged to her decks.

---

32 J. N. Reynolds's story said "his celebrity continued to increase, until his name seemed naturally to mingle with the salutations which whalemen were in the habit of exchanging, in their encounters upon the broad Pacific; the customary interrogatories almost always closing with 'Any news from Mocha Dick?' Indeed, nearly every whaling captain who rounded Cape Horn, if he possessed any professional ambition, or valued himself on his skill in subduing the monarch of the seas, would lay his vessel along the coast, in the hope of having an opportunity to try the muscle of this doughty champion, who was known never to shun his assailants."

At this point three whaling vessels hove into sight, an international galaxy containing the Scottish *Crieff,* the English *Dudley,* and the Amercian *Yankee.* The three ships had known about Mocha Dick but had thought him dead. By the time they reached the wrecked lumber ship Mocha Dick had disappeared. The *Crieff,* the *Dudley,* and the *Yankee* agreed to cooperate in a hunt to rid the oceans of the monstrous terror. Even as they planned, Mocha Dick, as if in contempt of confederations, breached a mile to windward. Wallowing around on the surface of the sea for a moment, he then turned to face the ships, quietly waiting to see whether they would accept the challenge to battle. Each ship sent out a boat, and followed this up with another: six boats in all. At the drawing of lots the *Yankee* had won the chance of darting the first iron. The wily old whale sank suddenly just as the boats approached him. His history made the men cautious; they feared, and rightly, that Mocha Dick would try to breach beneath one of their boats just as he had done in his fights with the *Sarepta* and the *Desmond.* Only this alertness on their part saved the crews when Mocha Dick emerged twenty minutes later. As Mocha lay wallowing, the mate of the *Yankee* put a harpoon into him. For five minutes the whale played dead; then, with dramatic speed he acted. He rushed for and ran right over the Scottish boat. Then he turned for the English boat, and caught it with a scythe-like swing of his great jaw. He lifted his head out of water, boat between his jaws, and at one bite crunched it into chips and chewed the life out of two men. In the meantime the crews of the stove boats were swimming in the water, frantically trying to avoid the wide sweeps of Mocha Dick's lethal flukes. Two of them were killed as the great tail struck savagely; the rest of the men were rescued by the brave arrival of the reserve boats.

As a sort of diversion in this battle, Mocha Dick turned his attention once more to the lumber ship. Swimming at a speed estimated to have been thirty miles an hour, he headed for the ship, towing behind him the boat, still intact, which had made fast to him. A battering ram, he struck the lumber ship with such force that she turned bottom up. The men dragged behind in the boat were forced to cut the line in order to avoid a collision. Mocha Dick then sounded and the men in the boat headed back for their ship. Mocha Dick breached again, this time under the bow of the Scottish ship, *Crieff*. Fortunately for her, Mocha Dick missed his aim by a matter of inches, coming so close to her that he carried away the jib boom and bowsprit. Falling back to the ocean, Mocha Dick turned upon the boat rowing for the *Yankee*. To save their lives the boat-crew dived overboard just before the White Whale "picked the light craft up and chewed it as a horse does his oats."

By now a storm was blowing up so that the men were all recalled to the ships. The three crafts beat a retreat as inglorious as that of Cleopatra's fleet at Actium before the Roman galleys. Three ships and ninety men had bowed to the might of Mocha Dick.

Skipping over the *Essex* sinking — a doubtful attribution to Mocha Dick — we may add up the real record. It is impressive: fourteen stove boats, nineteen planted harpoons absorbed in his blubber, and the death of thirty men. Mocha Dick sank a lumber ship, a French merchantman, and an Australian trader, and stove in three whaleships so badly that they were almost lost. Melville may not have known these statistics, but he did not exaggerate when he wrote: " . . . there was enough in the earthly make and incontestable character of the monster to strike the imagination with unwonted power."

If Mocha Dick was ubiquitous in space — for he was encountered in most of the main whaling grounds — he was not equally ubiquitous in time, for in August, 1859, off the coast of Brazil, Mocha Dick, old and worn out by years and by battle, was taken in by a Swedish whaler. He was said to have been one hundred feet long (the average sperm whale is about sixty feet); his jaw measured twenty-six feet. His massive head was badly scarred and his right eye was blinded. He succumbed with almost no struggle.

*   *   *   *

The exploits of a demon whale in the Pacific appear in

two interesting and unreliable documents which should be briefly considered. Three years before the publication of *Moby-Dick* there was printed in Boston a lurid novelette by Doctor Louis A. Baker, *Harry Martingale: or, Adventures of a Whaleman in the Pacific Ocean.* The early part of the little volume tells of the capture of a famous Pacific whale who

> had earned for himself a much-dreaded reputation, by his pugnacious disposition, which, in the frequent conflicts which he had been engaged in, had ever brought himself off the conqueror, and many ships now absolutely refused to lower their boats to attack him. He was a remarkable whale and easily known by a very peculiar white spot on the back, exactly between his fins, and he never could be caught napping, but seemingly always on the look-out for danger; he never would allow a boat to approach him, he hastened to meet them, and numberless were the stories which every ship had to relate, of boats smashed to pieces by the spotted whale.

According to the story, this spotted whale was captured after a terrific struggle in which several boats were smashed. The blubber yielded eighty barrels of oil. Baker's book is, of course, a piece of fiction of the dime-novel class, but it is interesting as an outgrowth of a widespread whaling legend shortly to be recorded in *Moby-Dick*.[33]

The sober record above recounted seems to require that as historians we accept 1859 as the year of Mocha Dick's death. Another and later romancer would not let Mocha Dick die. Captain Barnacle — obviously a pseudonym — wrote a small pamphlet, *Pehe Nu-e, The Tiger Whale of the Pacific*,[34] in which he alleged that the Tiger Whale had appeared in many places and over many years, under various names: Timor Tom, New Zealand Jack, Mocha Dick, and "as ren-

[33] There is also *Harry Halyard, The Doom of the Dolphin: or, The Sorceress of the Sea. A Tale of Love, Intrigue, and Mystery* (Boston, 1848), which tells about a boat being stove in by the flukes of a monstrous whale, a "regular old white-head eighty barrel fellow" (p. 83).

[34] This pamphlet was first noted by J. H. Birss, " 'Moby-Dick' under Another Name," *Notes and Queries*, CLXIV (25 March, 1933), 206. The picture of this tiger-whale which I have reproduced in this book is the earliest picture of "Moby Dick."

dered by some authors, Moby Dick." The phrase just quoted gives *Pehe Nu-e* away as a cheap imitation of *Moby-Dick*. In *Pehe Nu-e* not only do we have the demonic whale, but we also have the crippled, vengeful sea captain, Uncle Joe Bailey, who for thirty years had hunted the fish. Bailey, however, was successful as Ahab had not been, for Moby Dick fell to his harpoon. *Pehe Nu-e* was published in 1877, twenty-six years after its great original.

One imagines the ironic amusement with which Melville might have read the lurid rehash of his own masterpiece.[35]

But Melville would insist, rightly, that neither Harry Martingale nor Uncle Joe Bailey was any more successful in capturing Moby Dick than was Ahab.[36] And the capture of Mocha Dick in 1859 by a Swedish whaleship is merely a matter of physical record.[37] As Mr. F. V. Morley has said: "There are two kinds of whales — the whales that are classified as cetaceans, and those that are enlarged into ideas." Mocha Dick was one; Moby Dick is both. Through Melville, Moby

[35] Another sea story, by J. S. Sleeper writing under his pseudonym of "Hawser Martingale," involving whaling was *Mark Rowland. A Tale of the Sea* (Boston, 1867). A sperm whale hits the bargue *Loon* on the starboard bow "with all the force of a gigantic battering-ram," so that the crew takes to the boats. I feel Sleeper had in mind either the *Essex* disaster or *Moby-Dick* in writing his trashy novel. Mocha Dick has appeared in fiction in recent years, in Irwin Shapiro's *How Stormalong Captured Mocha Dick* (New York, 1942), a book for children.

[36] Another appearance of Moby Dick was at a Navy air firepower show held in the summer of 1946 at the Patuxent River Naval Air Base, when his name was given to a rocket propulsion unit looking like a gas canister 105 inches long and 17 inches in diameter, and with a power thrust of 66,000 pounds for two seconds.

Mr. Jay Leyda informs me that the following statement appeared in the *Berkshire County Eagle*, 21 July, 1854: "Capture of Moby Dick. Moby Dick is 'tuk.' The terror of the whalemen, the imperial tyrant of the seas, in the decrepitude of age and sickness has fallen into the hands of his puny enemies and is no more. Like many another conqueror he allowed his 'vaulting ambition to overleap itself,' and perished of his own victories. But although dead, he still liveth *a burning and shining light*."

[37] In the Mocha Dick tradition is E. J. Pratt's narrative poem "The Cachalot" which tells of the destruction of a ship by a spermaceti whale. Pratt's poem is powerful. "In the crushing of the ship by the whale," Professor E. K. Brown writes, "what Pratt sees is Nature imposing her strength to rend the complex contrivances of artificial society, the primitive overpowering the intellectual."

Dick has been absolved of mortality. Readers of *Moby-Dick* know that he swims the world unconquered, that he is ubiquitous in time and place. Yesterday he sank the *Pequod*; within the past two years he has breached five times; from a New Mexico desert, over Hiroshima and Nagasaki, and most recently, at Bikini atoll.

7

"A large wrinkled roll of yellowish charts"

EVEN THOUGH Melville's forty-first chapter, "Moby-Dick," speaks but little of the specific exploits of the White Whale, it does effectively drive home to us the feeling that Moby Dick was an actuality, a monster of lethal potency — even to the extent of being a ship-destroyer. Chapter 41 is one part of Melville's attempt to convince readers that the fantastic events of his fiction might be felt as reasonable probabilities. The whale instead of being an object of mild curiosity becomes also an object of terror. To enhance the sense of terror, Melville created the celebrated chapter on "The Whiteness of the Whale" (42). A subtle study in evocative symbolism from an imagination searching far for illustrations and analogies, "The Whiteness of the Whale" moves with muted beauty of phrase and paragraph,[38] piling up "linked analogies" which range the worlds of space and mind, overpowering our sensibilities with the incomprehensible terrors of the whale, so that we return a convinced "No" to the question with which the chapter closes: "Wonder ye then at the fiery hunt?"

May, however, the symbolism of the White Whale be stated in a phrase? pinned by a word as a butterfly is pinned

---

38 Of "The Whiteness of the Whale" Peter Quennell said: "That chapter alone would entitle Herman Melville to be called a great poet." W. H. Hudson was so stirred by Melville's discussion of whiteness that he devoted an entire chapter, "Snow, and the Quality of Whiteness," to the subject in *Idle Days in Patagonia*.

to a board? Critics have tried to compress its meaning; subtle and interesting interpretations of Moby Dick's significance pad the Melville bibliography. This is not the place, certainly, to recapitulate their many theories, although it might be pointed out that most of them have gone astray by not keeping the text of *Moby-Dick* before them as a control. "Moby-Dick" and "The Whiteness of the Whale" should serve as a check, not as a goad, to the critical imagination. And the primary mistake is that people interpret the statements made in these two chapters about the symbolism of the White Whale as being the symbolic meaning held by Melville himself. Identifying Melville with Ahab, they interpret Ahab's crazed viewpoint as the author's. Read what the whale meant to Ahab, noting the words which I have italicized:

> Small reason was there to doubt, then, that ever since that almost fatal encounter, Ahab had cherished a *wild* vindictiveness against the whale, all the more fell for that in his *frantic morbidness he* at last came to identify with him, not only all *his* bodily woes, but all *his* intellectual and spiritual exasperations. The White Whale swam before him as the *monomaniac* incarnation of all those malicious agencies which *some* deep men feel eating in them, till they are left living on with half a heart and half a lung. That intangible malignity which has been from the beginning; to whose dominion even the modern Christians ascribe one-half of the worlds; which the ancient Ophites of the east reverenced in their statue devil; — Ahab did not fall down and worship it like them; but *deliriously transferring* its idea to the abhorred white whale, he pitted himself, *all mutilated,* against it. All that most maddens and torments; all that stirs up the lees of things; all truth with malice in it; all that cracks the sinews and cakes the brain; all the subtle demonisms of life and thought; all evil, to *crazy Ahab,* were visibly personified, and made practically assailable in Moby Dick. *He* piled upon the whale's white hump the sum of all the general rage and hate felt by his whole race from Adam down; and then, as if his chest had been a mortar, he burst his hot heart's shell upon it.

This much-quoted passage is not obscure; it states that to the crazy Ahab — not necessarily to anyone else: Stubb, Queequeg, or Ishmael, etc. — Moby Dick is the personification of

Evil. Ahab's reaction, Melville says, is not the normal sort of response; it is that of one scarred and maimed by life. It is the monomania of the paranoid. To Mankind in general, the White Whale in *Moby-Dick* must symbolize something else. And the representative Man in *Moby-Dick* is Ishmael — so, what did the Whale signify to him?

Ishmael says towards the end of "Moby-Dick" that the crew of the *Pequod* "aboundingly responded to the old man's ire," and seemed "specially picked and packed by some infernal fatality to help him to his monomaniac revenge," but even as he says this he wonders at the "evil magic" which was able to seize their souls so securely — to Ahab and crew the great fish "seemed the gliding great demon of the seas of life." Ishmael says that he cannot explain the spell, to do so would be "to dive deeper than Ishmael can go," and he frankly adds, "I gave myself up to the abandonment of the time and the place; but while yet all a-rush to encounter the whale, could see naught in that brute but the deadliest ill."

It would be wrong to accept the White Whale as Ishmael's symbol of Evil, however. In the opening lines of "The Whiteness of the Whale" he says: "What the white whale was to Ahab, has been hinted; what, at times, he was to me, as yet remains unsaid." In other words, Ahab's view was Ishmael's only when he was immediately under the magnetic spell of the crazed Captain — and it is Ishmael, significantly, who escapes this spell, who survives the sinking of the *Pequod.*

What was the meaning of the White Whale to Ishmael? The answer, ambiguous though it is, is to be found stated most explicitly in "The Whiteness of the Whale," set in deliberate contrast against the previous chapter in which Ahab's viewpoint had been stated. The secret of the whale is in his whiteness, his lack of color. Explaining the varied symbols which the world has adopted for white, Melville shows it to be a shifting symbol, used at one time for joy and innocence, as at bridals, and for terror and emptiness, as in lepers or at Polar wastes. White is many things, never one alone. Like any good symbol it is fluxional; to state its meaning flatly is to make it disappear, like an iridescent bubble seized by the child's grasping fingers. White as symbol is like Life itself; one may hope, finally, to find its meaning, but one never will. But there are, whether for good or ill no one may say, some who strive to find the single answer, always eluding them, like the silvery jet which spouted so tantalizingly before the *Pequod* crew. White, like Life, includes Evil, but to see it that way only is to be an Ahab. White, like Life, includes Joy, but to see it that way only is to be a Transcendental optimist. The White Whale is Life itself with its Good and its Evil; it is the final Mystery which no man may know, and which no man should pursue unrelentingly. To lift the veil of the Goddess is destruction to the disciple of Truth and Life; it is no accident that Melville elsewhere in his novel alludes to this myth of the Statue at Sais. Ishmael momentarily accepts Ahab's interpretation; later, one notes, he sees from a soberer, a more profound point of view and is willing to accept Life as it may come.[39] Ishmael perceives that the White Whale must be left alone; that illusion alone will sustain life. Recently Eugene O'Neill has held audiences in a theater for four hours to make this point; Melville did it almost a century earlier (other artists had done it long before, especially the Greeks) but through a symbolized whale, an emblematic hunt, and through implication.

Chapters 41 through 46 are in substance an essay on the actual and lethal might of Moby Dick, in which Melville amasses evidence to make credible the strange narrative into which he has plunged his readers. But as he gathers his data, Melville pauses for a thirty-five-line chapter, "Hark" (43), to pick up for a second the narrative thread. He tells of the

39 In an excellent, short pamphlet, *Herman Melville: The Tragic Vision and the Heroic Ideal* (Cambridge, Mass., 1939), p. 22, Stanley Geist says: "For Ahab alone the White Whale is a terrible incarnation: for the rest of the *Pequod's* crew, Moby Dick is another whale to be harpooned, slaughtered, and cooked down to oil — with a gold doubloon reward for the man who first sights him." But it should be pointed out that, though the men may not have Ahab's tragic vision, and to them the whale may be just another whale — however, they *do* willingly pursue Moby Dick for three strenuous days; some of Ahab's desire is theirs, perhaps by contamination to be sure, and for a brief time they too are heroic, they too have the tragic vision.

surprise of one of the men who thinks he hears a human sound under the hatches. Later it is learned that it was a real though unintelligible outcry from one of the pagan crew specially hired for Ahab's whaleboat. The brief chapter is a skillful dissonance — a short phrase played by the basses whereby curiosity is aroused, expectation heightened as we return to the essay on the might of Moby Dick.

The surprise of the *Pequod's* crew upon hearing Ahab's announcement that they have all shipped to hunt the White Whale, parallels the surprise with which readers receive the news that they, too, are participants of this incredible hunt for an individual fish. It would seem at first thought that Sir Thomas Browne had as much chance of learning the sirens' song as did Ahab of capturing a lone whale in the uncharted vastness of the Pacific. Again, then, Melville had some explaining to do; "The Chart" (44) establishes Ahab's rationale. Ahab's single-minded purpose is justified by reference to general whaling lore.

Melville reports his understanding of the technical problem: "Now, to any one not fully acquainted with the ways of the leviathans, it might seem an absurdly hopeless task thus to seek out one solitary creature in the unhooped oceans of this planet. But not so did it seem to Ahab," and, Melville must have hoped, not so to his readers. We follow Ahab into his cabin as he studies his "large wrinkled roll of yellowish sea charts." In writing "The Chart" (44) Melville seems to have meditated: "I know from *my* whaling experiences that Ahab's dream is not unattainable, but my readers do not. If I acquaint this land-bound public with information known to veteran whaling men, they will believe even as the *Pequod* crew believed." There are more things in Heaven and in the Pacific than are dreamt of in a layman's philosophy.

"The Chart" did not spring full-blown from Melville's brain; it was a growth from ideas suggested in the fish documents — from two books in particular: Wilkes's *Narrative* and Maury's *Sailing Directions*.

Commodore Charles Wilkes's exploring expedition to the South Seas was one of the important historical events of the mid-nineteenth century. The first large, genuinely scientific expedition sponsored by the government of the United States, it sailed through Antarctica and the Pacific, charting tides and currents, charting new islands and territories, and gathering a vast fund of new information about unknown places of the globe. It was first conceived by J. N. Reynolds (historian, incidentally, of Mocha Dick), but was soon taken from his hands and given to Wilkes and the original scheme was enlarged so that the United States might make a good showing in the imperialistic race going on in the South Seas. Wilkes's expedition fired the imagination of Americans who up to now, save through Captain Porter, perhaps had been unable to identify on a national scale with the Polynesian myth first stirred to life by Captain Cook's voyages. With Wilkes's expedition, Oceania became a fashion in conversation; it prepared the way for *Typee* the next year, for *Typee* cast the spell of fiction over the real world newly made known by Wilkes.

Melville's personal copy [40] of Commodore Wilkes's *Narrative of the U.S. Exploring Expedition . . . 1838–1842* (Philadelphia, 1845) has not turned up, but that he had read many parts of this important book is unquestionable. Its light fell across *Typee*. But in writing *Moby-Dick*, Melville made special and significant use of the last chapter of the final volume, the essay on "Currents and Whaling." Discussing the relationship between ocean currents and the migration of whales, Wilkes said:

> It may at first sight appear singular that subjects apparently so dissimilar as currents and whaling should be united to form the subject of one chapter. Before this conclusion, however, we trust to establish satisfactorily that the course of the great currents of the ocean, sweeping with them the proper food of the great cetaceous animals, determines not only the places to which they are in the habit of resorting, but the seasons at which they are to be found frequenting them.

Melville dramatized this statement by connecting it with Ahab's solitary studies:

[40] In John Wiley's statement of accounts with Melville is listed for 17 April, 1847, "1 Wilkes U.S. Exploring Expedition 6 vols sheep 21.00."

But not so did it seem [improbable] to Ahab, who knew the sets of all tides and currents; and thereby calculating the driftings of the sperm whale's food; and, also, calling to mind the regular, ascertained seasons for hunting him in particular latitudes; could arrive at reasonable surmises, almost approaching to certainties, concerning the timeliest day to be upon this or that ground in search of his prey.

Wilkes supplied a second usable idea to Melville. Proposing that reports should be collected from many captains so that useful information might be compiled from the findings, Wilkes said:

In particular, simultaneous observations in different parts of the ocean, and their continuance for months or even for the whole year, were requisite to render the results, that I believe I have attained, more satisfactory and conclusive. Enough however has I hope been done to excite the curiosity and rouse the attention of future navigators, by whose labours a sufficient number of facts may be collected upon which to found a theory that will admit of no question.

This Melville kept without appreciable changes:

So assured, indeed, is the fact concerning the periodicalness of the sperm whale's resorting to given waters, that many hunters believe that, could he be closely observed and studied throughout the world; were the logs for one voyage of the entire whale fleet carefully collated, then the migrations of the sperm whale would be found to correspond in invariability to those of the herring-shoals or the flights of swallows. On this hint, attempts have been made to construct elaborate migratory charts of the sperm whale.

And in applying Wilkes's generalities about currents and whaling charts to his own novel, Melville made particular in Ahab such an abstract paragraph as this from the *Narrative*:

. . . it is obvious that we do not know enough of the natural history of his favourite food, nor of the rate and course of all the submarine polar currents, to enable us to predict with certainty the seasons at which he will be found in particular parts of the ocean. This can be learned by observation alone, and long experience has taught those who are skilful in the whale-fishery the position of the favourite haunts of their prey, and the times at which they are most likely to be met there.

Thus, Wilkes supplied Melville authority for portraying Ahab, learned as he was in whaling lore, with the prescience to anticipate the migrations of Moby Dick, to follow the great fish to the feeding grounds at "the time at which they are most likely to be met there." Instead of this pursuit being an improbability, it proves to be but another sample of Ahab's surpassing skill in the whaling industry, a true specimen of the Nantucket whaling captain able to follow where others would falter and fail.

Wilkes's suggestion of a whaling chart compiled out of the reports from all possible whaling captains was not long in coming into being. Whether or not it was Wilkes who had suggested it to him, or whether it was merely the great success of his own previous researches in trade winds, Matthew Fontaine Maury, Director of the Naval Observatory in Washington, made a whaling chart to show the main whaling migrations and the best whaling grounds. Although the chart as such was not published until after the publication of *Moby-Dick*, Melville discovered that such a chart was being made, and he passed the word along in a last-minute footnote in his whaling novel, saying: "Since the above was written, the statement is happily borne out by an official circular, issued by Lieutenant Maury, of the National Observatory, Washington, April 16th, 1851. By that circular, it appears that precisely such a chart is in course of completion; and portions of it are presented in the circular." This "circular" to which Melville alluded was the second edition of Matthew Maury's *Explanations and Sailing Directions to Accompany Lieut. Maury's Investigation of the Wind and Current Charts* (Washington, 1851), an immensely important book in the history of the sea, for its suggested trade routes enabled the new clipper ships to save days from their traveling time. It is a pity that Maury's handsome whaling chart was not issued before the publication of *Moby-Dick,* for

Melville would have enjoyed it and would maybe have discussed it briefly there.[41]

Exemplar of the whaling captains later useful to Matthew Maury, old Ahab wisely concentrated his pursuit during what was called the "Season-on-the-Line," for there, report had it, "Moby Dick had been periodically descried, lingering in those waters for awhile, as the sun, in its annual round, loiters for a predicted interval in any one sign of the Zodiac." (Thus, symbolically, Moby Dick becomes a great natural force.) Bennett's *Whaling Voyage Round the Globe* had told Melville that "large parties of these whales have been remarked to affect particular spots at distinct times," information corroborative of Wilkes's predictions and of his whaling and current chart; and both Beale and Bennett included lists of the best whaling grounds, with an account of the best seasons for hunting whales throughout the Atlantic and Pacific oceans.

Ahab working over his charts [42] is a picturesque dramatization conceived by Melville to give probability to his wild narrative, a dramatization occurring to him as he read Wilkes's *Narrative* and Maury's "circular." [43] Ahab and his

41 Unfortunately it was never really very useful, because the good whaling grounds of one year were the exhausted ones of the next, and it was impossible in those pre-radio days to gather information fast enough to keep the chart up to date, and thereby useful. A fine copy of Maury's chart inscribed by him to Edward Everett may be seen in the Boston Public Library. Making his survey, Maury used the *Acushnet* log, an abstract of which is now in the Agricultural Department Library, Washington, and is now being edited by Wilson L. Heflin.

42 The Boston Public Library has two maps of the Pacific, on which have been drawn the route of whaleships, along with some indication of success or failure in the whale hunt by three New Bedford ships.

43 Several men had tried to determine the chief feeding grounds of whales, and also their migration habits. By their own admission, the students have had doubtful results. Charles Hanson Towne made several charts of nineteenth-century whaling grounds, four of which I have seen at the Peabody Museum, Harvard. There is an excellent article by Remington Kellogg, "What is Known of the Migrations of Some of the Whalebone Whales," *Smithsonian Institution Annual Report* (1927–1928), pp. 467–494, with several distribution charts and an excellent bibliography. See also D. F. Echricht and J. Reinhardt, "On the Greenland Right Whale *(Balaena mysticetus* Linn.) with especial Reference to Its Geographical Distribution and Migrations in Times Past and Present, and to Its External and Internal Characteristics, *Ray Society* (1866), pp. 1–150; J. E. Gray, "On the Geographical Dis-

hare-brained scheme are not made realistic in terms of the everyday explorer; rather, familiar exploration is adduced to give a rational basis to Ahab's scheme so that we may accept it as possible.

From "Moby-Dick" (41) to "The Affidavit" (45) Melville variously but undeviatingly attempts to prove that his basic plot — the hunt for a single whale in the oceans of the world — is not completely fantastic, but that it has enough sense in it to justify it. Ahab, in other words, is an intelligent whaleman and his madness is but north-nor'west. "The Affidavit" is the last of his series, and unlike the earlier chapters, it is straightforward exposition — blended, of course, with Melville mockery and humor. "The Affidavit" is a sort of footnote to the preceding chapter, "The Chart," in which we saw Ahab poring over his yellowish maps in order to trace the whereabouts of Moby Dick, for this last takes up the subject of individual whales and the historical evidence for their destructiveness.

The evidence of the whale's lethal might is not neatly docketed in an archive nor was such evidence in Melville's day gathered in a single book. Melville had to study his fish documents and piece together his affidavit from hints and suggestions, and a few bare facts. It is no wonder that he elected the casual technique in doing so: "I care not to perform this part of my task methodically; but shall be content to produce the desired impression by separate citations of items, practically or reliably known to me as a whaleman; and from these citations, I take it — the conclusion aimed at will naturally follow of itself."

As a beginning, he testifies that single whales have been harpooned only to escape, but later to be captured by the

tribution, Migration, and Occasional Habitats of Whales and Dolphins (Cete)," *Annals of Natural History*, 4th Series, II, 98–104; J. E. Gray, "On the Geographical Distribution of the Balaenidae or Right Whales," *Annals of Natural History*, 4th Series, I, 242–247; V. A. Arsenyev, *Distribution and Migration of the White Whale in the Far East* (Vladivostok, 1939). Mention should be made of attempts by a British scientific expedition to tag whales with metal disks shot into the blubber much as birds are tagged for migration studies. See D. W. T., "The Voyages of the *Discovery*," *Nature*, 140 (25 September, 1937), 529–532.

same captain, who thereupon recovered his old harpoon. "I have," says Melville-Ishmael, "personally known three instances . . . in two of them I saw the whales struck; and, upon the second attack, saw the two irons with the respective marks cut in them, afterwards taken from the dead fish." Authentic as this sounds, it is undoubtedly a fabrication on Melville's part, although the basic fact that such things occurred was true enough.[44] Melville had never had such an experience, even though he says:

> In the three-year instance, it so fell out that I was in the boat both times, first and last, and the last time distinctly recognized a peculiar sort of huge mole under the whale's eye, which I had observed there three years previous. I say three years, but I am pretty sure it was more than that. Here are three instances, then, which I personally know the truth of; but I have heard of many other instances from persons whose veracity in the matter there is no good ground to impeach.

Melville could not have "personally" known three such instances, because he was not in the whale fishery for three years' time. Furthermore, the humorous reference to the mole under the whale's eye proves that he was telling a tall tale. And finally, the episode he relates at length about "the three-year instance" he had read in Scoresby's *An Account of the Arctic Regions,* so that the "persons whose veracity in the matter there is no good ground to impeach" are none other than William Scoresby, Jr. — always the butt of a Melville jest — and Cheever.[45]

Secondly, Melville proves "that there have been several memorable historical instances where a particular whale in the ocean has been at distant times and places particularly cognisable . . . not only did each of these famous whales enjoy great individual celebrity — nay, you may call it oceanwide renown; not only was he famous in life and now is immortal

---

[44] A Captain Paddock struck a whale in 1802. It escaped, and in 1815 Paddock captured the same whale, recovering his iron.

[45] Cheever tells about Captain Bunker's experience in recovering from a captured whale a blubber-kept harpoon, "the identical one he had lost five years before, having on it the ship's name and his own private mark."

in forecastle stories after death, but he was admitted into all the rights, privileges, and distinctions of a name." While aboard the *Acushnet* Melville no doubt heard many stories, reliable and unreliable, from the glib lips of his shipmates, about particular whales of great renown. Unprovable though it is, it is probable that Melville first heard of Mocha Dick himself while on the whaling grounds. But it is also true that Melville found references to mighty whales of the past in one of his most reliable source books. Discussing further these individual whales, Melville said:

> Was it not so, O Timor Tom! thou famed leviathan, scarred like an iceberg, who so long did'st lurk in the Oriental straits of that name, whose spout was oft seen from the palmy beach of Ombay? Was it not so, O New Zealand Jack! thou terror of all cruisers that crossed their wakes in the vicinity of the Tattoo Land? Was it not so, O Morquan! King of Japan, whose lofty jet they say at times assumed the semblance of a snow-white cross against the sky? Was it not so, O Don Miguel! thou Chilian whale, marked like an old tortoise with mystic hieroglyphics upon the back! In plain prose, here are four whales as well known to the students of Cetacean History as Marius or Sylla to the classic scholar.
>
> But this is not all. New Zealand Tom and Don Miguel, after at various times creating great havoc among the boats of different vessels, were finally gone in quest of, systematically hunted out, chased and killed by valiant whaling captains.

But Melville was wrong: these individual whales were not familiar to all "students of Cetacean History." If they were, the students failed to leave any records of such celebrated whales, for the "numerous fish documents" are quite unrewarding to the searcher — save for Thomas Beale, in a chapter which Melville marked up freely because of his interest in its contents. And among the pages marked (the name of Timor Jack was underlined) was page 183 on which Melville had read:

> Numberless stories are told of fighting whales, many of which, however, are probably much exaggerated accounts of the real occurrences. A large whale, called "Timor Jack," is the

hero of many strange stories, such as of his destroying every boat which was sent out against him, until a contrivance was made by lashing a barrel to the end of the harpoon with which he was struck, and whilst his attention was directed and divided amongst several boats, means were found of giving him his death wound.

In the year 1804, the ship "Adonis," being in company with several others, struck a large whale off the coast of New Zealand, which "stove" or destroyed nine boats before breakfast, and the chase consequently was necessarily given up. After destroying boats belonging to many ships, this whale was at last captured, and many harpoons of the various ships that had from time to time been sent out against him were found sticking in his body. This whale was called "New Zealand Tom," and the tradition is carefully preserved by whalers.[46]

The differences between Melville's passage and Beale's are interesting. Melville changed Beale's "Timor Jack" to "Timor Tom," for although he had underlined the name in his copy of Beale, he probably wanted an alliterative name — though it is of course possible that Beale was in error and that Melville was merely correcting him. And Melville also changed "New Zealand Tom" to "New Zealand Jack," probably because his first change made it advisable for him not to have two Toms. Also, Melville added Morquan and Don Miguel, names so far not found among the whaling books, so that I tentatively assume that they came from Melville's memory rather than from Beale. But Beale's passage supplied Melville with much of his chapter. For instance, Mel-

---

[46] Bennett has accounts of two individual whales, as Melville knew: "A few Cachalots have been noted individually as animals dangerous to attack. One was thus distinguished on the cruising ground off the coast of New Zealand, and was long known to whalers by the name of 'New Zealand Tom.' He is said to have been of great size; conspicuously distinguished by a white hump; and famous for the havoc he made amongst the boats and gear of ships attempting his destruction. A second example, of similar celebrity, was known to whalers in the Straits of Timor. He had so often succeeded in repelling the attacks of his foes as to be considered invincible, but was at length dispatched by a whaler, who, forewarned of his combative temper, adopted the expedient of floating a cask on the sea, to withdraw his attention from the boats; but notwithstanding this *ruse*, the animal was not destroyed without much hard fighting, nor until the bow of one of the boats had been nipped off by his jaws."

ville, like Beale, goes on to discuss specific acts performed by great whales, and mentions the *Essex* tragedy. Of course Melville knew the *Essex* story from his copy of Owen Chase's *Narrative* — the book given him by his father-in-law, Lemuel Shaw, in April, 1851 — and he did not need Beale's information. In fact, in a long footnote Melville quoted directly from Chase's pamphlet the passages dealing with the malevolence and vengefulness of the whale which sank the *Essex*.

But Melville brings forward examples of the whale's strength not to be found in Beale. He alludes to the loss of the *Union,* adding no information because "the authentic particulars of this catastrophe I have never chanced to encounter, though from the whale hunters I have now and then heard casual allusions to it." This is a strange statement, indicating that Melville had not read his "worthy Obed" Macy's *History of Nantucket* with any care, for there he would have found a detailed account of the sinking of the *Union.* Melville's third example, of Commodore J——'s sloop-of-war, is as yet untraced, but it should turn up in time to research, for it sounds like an anecdote taken from Melville's reading. Melville's next instance is related with pride, from Langsdorff's *Voyages,* because as he says, his own uncle, Captain John DeWolf, was commanding the ship at the time a large whale struck her and jarred her considerably. Melville also quotes Lionel Wafer's experience, from Captain William Dampier's *Voyages Round the World,* when a whale badly jarred their ship; and then he concludes his instances with the episode of the *Pusie Hall*:

> In more than one instance, he has been known, not only to chase the assailing boats back to their ships, but to pursue the ship itself, and long withstand all the lances hurled at him from its decks. The English ship Pusie Hall can tell a story on that head; and, as for his strength, let me say that there have been examples where the lines attached to a running sperm whale have, in a calm, been transferred to the ship, and secured there; the whale towing her great hull through the water, as a horse walks off with a cart.

The story of the *Pusie Hall* is taken directly from Bennett's account:

In the year 1835, the ship Pusie Hall encountered a fighting whale, which after injuring and driving off her four boats, pursued them to the ship, and withstood for some time the lances hurled at it, by the crew, from the bow of the vessel, before it could be induced to retire: in this affair a youth in one of the boats was destroyed by a blow from the whale, and one of the officers was severely lacerated by coming in contact with the animal's jaw.

Melville probably took the story of a whale pulling a ship from Scoresby's excellent account of such an advenure by the *Royal Bounty of Leith,* on 28 May, 1817, in an astounding exhibition of brute strength when the whale pulled the ship behind him for several hours, even though at one time the sails were set against him.

In reading about the perils of the whale fishery, Melville did not make use of several vivid anecdotes of death or brutal maiming, especially in his favorite "fish documents": Browne, Beale, Bennett, Cheever, and Scoresby. Significantly, only one of the *Pequod's* crew is killed before the final tragedy. Melville did not want to distract the reader's attention from the central and overwhelming tragedy; he deliberately, it would seem, passed over this interesting material.

Connected with unusual tragedy, *Moby-Dick* not only treated of a whale sinking a ship, but it was published almost at the moment that word came through to America that another ship had suffered a similar fatality. Almost as if to accompany the *Pequod,* the New Bedford whaleship *Ann Alexander* while sailing in lat. 5° 50′ south, long. 102° west, was struck by the battering ram of a spermaceti whale. The ship sank rapidly while the men took to the boats. Fortunately, and unlike the men of the *Essex,* they were rescued on the second day following. This occurred on 20 August, 1851, but word did not reach the United States until 4 November. The sensational event could not have been timed better had Harper Brothers been able to plan it. It is no wonder that upon hearing the news of the sinking, Herman Melville wrote to Duyckinck expressing his surprise:

Your letter received last night had a sort of stunning effect on me . . . the Whale had almost completely slipped me for the time (and I was the merrier for it) when Crash! comes Moby-Dick himself (as you justly say) and reminds me of what I have been about for part of the last year or two. It is really and truly a surprising coincidence, to say the least. I make no doubt it *is* Moby-Dick himself, for there is no account of his capture after the sad fate of the Pequod about fourteen years ago ——

Ye Gods! What a Commentator is this Ann Alexander whale. What he has to say is short and pithy but very much to the point. I wonder if my evil art has raised this monster.

"Ye Gods!" indeed.[47]

The "Affidavit" closes with an account, from Propontius, of a sperm whale once known to have attacked Mediterranean shipping. But as will be shown later, Melville took this material from Kitto's *Cyclopedia of Biblical Literature,* not from the Latin author. The "Affidavit" closes the five chapters of warning, of foreshadowing. We are fully prepared for trouble when the boats are lowered and the men make fast to a whale. Now, having carefully prepared us for perilous action, Melville quickly narrates a dramatic scene involving Ishmael and his *Pequod* friends.

8

"A sight full of quick wonder and awe"

THE AHAB described to us for the past few chapters is clearly not the whaling captain first shaped for the "whaling voyage" begun in 1850. Then he was probably just from Nantucket; now he is instead from humanity, American style. The Ahab we have seen intently scanning the charts or, merely by his

[47] For a more recent ship sinking by a whale see Thomas H. Jenkins, *Bark Kathleen Sunk by a Whale, as Related by the Captain* (New Bedford, Mass., 1902) . In Elisha Dexter's *Narrative of the Loss of the Whaling Brig William and Joseph, of Martha's Vineyard* (Boston, 1848) , is a statement that the *Two Generals* of Charleston, South Carolina, and the *Essex* of Nantucket were also stove in by whales. Melville apparently did not know this rare and obscure pamphlet.

presence, silencing the mates at the cabin table is a great advance over the whaling captains of the "fish documents." In his passion and power Ahab is the heroic character for tragic drama on a cosmic scale. Chapters 42 to 46, it would seem, were added to the original "whaling voyage" *after* the summer of 1850, when the long year of "revision" was begun.

The long section which follows the Ahab portrait is set in the whaling grounds and carries us out into the whaleboats to pursue the sperm whale. This is certainly a section of the novel which Melville was ready to send to Bentley in July, 1850. This old section had to be connected with the new material, the "whaling voyage" with the tragic point of view, but Melville must have found it a difficult problem to join his new conceptions of character and idea onto the plot and exposition of the original whaling voyage. However difficult the joining, there is no sign of his struggle, for it is practically impossible to trace any parts or pieces in *Moby-Dick* serving as connectives between the old form and the new vision.

One may suggest, however, that "Surmises" (46) is such a connective; that it is one of those "shanties" of chapters which Melville told Hawthorne that he was constructing early in the summer of 1851, shortly before sending his manuscript to the printers. A shanty, he explained, was but a connecting building. In other words he was at work smoothing off his novel, connecting main parts more firmly, making articulation more effective. "Surmises" falls between the Ahab section and the first lowering for whales. On close examination it appears to have been placed there to connect the two radically different structures, architecturally unifying old and new to make them congruous parts of the larger whole. For the two sections *are* strikingly (and effectively) unlike. The Ahab scenes take place in a lurid or dark light; they have an intensity and passion which is terrifying; they have a nimbus of demonism. The whale-hunt scenes are, primarily, placed in the sunlight, among the rising and falling waves of the wide ocean; and only as Ahab or Fedallah appear in them do they have other than an atmosphere of health and normality — violence, yes, but a violence which is the result of healthy animal activity and not of human madness. These sunlit scenes punctuate tragic quality.

"Surmises" is a shanty. It is the modulation whereby we shift from the mystery of the minor to the openness of the major key. It effects with shocking speed one of those transitions which are part of the dramatic quality of *Moby-Dick*; even as Shakespeare, in *I Henry IV* for instance, passes from scene to contrasting scene to give variety and brilliance to his history. Attractive as this technique is to us today, it appealed also to one reader in 1851, the reviewer of *Harper's New Monthly Magazine,* who was responsible for the most intelligent contemporary criticism of Melville's book. He wrote:

> These sudden and decided transitions form a striking feature of the volume. Difficult of management, in the highest degree, they are wrought with consummate skill. To a less gifted author, they would inevitably have proved fatal. He has not only avoided their dangers, but made them an element of great power. They constantly pique the attention of the reader, keeping curiosity alive, and presenting the combined charm of surprise and alternation.

In "Surmises" the transition is skillfully and with psychological insight effected through the contriving brain of shrewd old Ahab. Ahab, "by nature and long habituation far too wedded to a fiery whaleman's ways, altogether to abandon the collateral prosecution of the voyage," realizes that his men might not be held to his monomaniac purpose alone, but should be allowed to hunt other whales, it being "requisite that temporary interests and employments should intervene and hold them healthily suspended for the final dash." With his awareness that their knight-errantism might lapse, he decides to let them "have food for their more common, daily appetites" and so the order is given to keep a sharp lookout for any whale. Men are like tools and will rust unless used; even the highest resolves must share the company of the mundane. Ahab thus plays to the ordinary interests and desires — for gold as well as for adventure — and returns the crew to the commonplace level of life, to disarm them so that he may later use them when Moby Dick spouts before the lookout's startled eyes.

The *scherzo* follows the *andante*. "Surmises" symbolically explains Melville's own technical procedure. In order to hold the attention of his audience he must take them from the strange, lightning-flecked storm created in his plot and give reassurance by the common everyday activities so sanative in effect. Like Ahab, Melville will not, of course, allow us to forget entirely the main narrative goal for which we are headed, but we shall approach that goal through activities which do not greatly disturb, and which equip us in time to enjoy with greater zest the final pursuit of the White Whale. Melville the artist was just as vigilant in strategy as was Ahab the hunter of Moby Dick.

The whale hunt itself begins with dramatic speed, but first there is a quiet prelude. In the opening of "The Mat-Maker" (47) the sailors are lazily lounging about the decks on a sultry afternoon. "Each silent sailor seemed resolved into his own invisible self" [48] save for Ishmael and Queequeg, who were "mildly employed weaving what is called a sword-mat, for an additional lashing to our boat." The crew is suddenly startled from this indolent quiet and inactivity as the cry of "There she blows" drops "like a wing" from the masthead. The *Pequod* churns into activity as the men race for the boats and lower rapidly to hunt the sperm whale.[49]

The metaphysical magic of Melville's mat-maker scene has been commented on satisfactorily and sensitively by F. O. Matthiessen in *American Renaissance,* so that further analysis on my part would be supererogatory, save to point out that the reflections on Free Will, Necessity, and Chance are consonant with the themes as already developing in *Moby-Dick.* The determination of what constitutes selfhood involves [49] a

48 The "isolato" motif stated by Melville with deliberate casualness.

49 Further discussion of the metaphysical meaning of "The Mat-Maker" may be found in Carvel Collins, "Melville's 'Moby-Dick,'" *Explicator,* IV (February, 1946) , no. 27, and G. Giovannini, "Melville's 'Moby-Dick,'" *Explicator,* V (October, 1946) , no. 7. It will be seen that much of what I say and imply about Ishmael agrees with Mr. Giovannini's statement: "Between the usual interpretation in terms of the will determined and W. H. Auden's in terms of pure possibility . . . stands that of Ishmael, who qualifies Ahab's remarks on fatalism by a reference to the hero's determination and wilfulness."

serious consideration of the part played in human affairs by
Chance, Free Will, and Necessity. But what at this time is
interesting about the passage with which "The Mat-Maker"
opens is not only the way in which Melville has disarmingly
woven his metaphysical thread into the whaling mat, but also
that the mat itself, along with the weaver idea, was undoubtedly suggested to him by a passage in Francis Olmsted's
Incidents of a Whaling Voyage, published just ten years before *Moby-Dick.* Olmsted wrote:

> There is always plenty of work to be done aboard a ship, to
> employ the men in the watch upon the deck. When there is
> nothing else to do, they pick to pieces old ropes, and splice
> together the separate yarns, which are then twisted together
> and form *spun yarn.* . . . Three yarns are also spun together
> by means of three spindles to which motion is communicated
> by large tooth wheels acting upon three smaller ones.
>
> All the shrouds and stays of a ship are carefully protected
> from the friction of the running rigging, by being "served"
> or wound around with spun yarn. Some of them are covered
> with *mats* of spun yarn woven very neatly together. These
> are usually homemade, and the process of manufacture is as
> follows.
>
> A number of spun yarns corresponding to the required
> breadth of the mat, are stretched parallel to one another across
> the deck, passing through a frame work of parallel bars, which
> retains every other one and allows the remainder to move
> freely between them. The person who works the frame, car-
> ries it down, and consequently, the spun yarns retained by the
> bars, are thrown down below the level of the other; the weaver
> stands ready with two balls of twine, which he passed across
> the yarns between the separate ranks, and the work is ren-
> dered compact by means of the *sword,* a long thin piece of
> hard wood, playing between the ranks of spun yarn. The
> frame is now raised, and the same steps are repeated, until the
> mat is finished.

Never was borrowing repaid at greater interest than by Melville in his revision:

> I was the attendant or page of Queequeg, while busy at the
> mat. As I kept passing and repassing the filling or woof of
> marline between the long yarns of the warp, using my own

hand for the shuttle, and as Queequeg, standing sideways, ever and anon slid his heavy oaken sword between the threads, and idly looking off upon the water, carelessly and unthinkingly drove home every yarn: I say so strange a dreaminess did there then reign all over the ship and all over the sea, only broken by the intermittent dull sound of the sword, that it seemed as if this were the Loom of Time, and I myself were a shuttle mechanically weaving and weaving away at the Fates. There lay the fixed threads of the warp subject to but one single, ever returning, unchanging vibration, and that vibration merely enough to admit of the crosswise interblending of other threads with its own. This warp seemed necessity; and here, thought I, with my own hand I ply my own shuttle and weave my own destiny into these unalterable threads. Meantime, Queequeg's impulsive, indifferent sword, sometimes hitting the woof slantingly, or crookedly, or strongly, or weakly, as the case might be; and by this difference in the concluding blow producing a corresponding contrast in the final aspect of the completed fabric; this savage's sword, thought I, which thus finally shapes and fashions both warp and woof; this easy, indifferent sword must be chance — aye, chance, free will, and necessity — no wise incompatible — all interweavingly working together. The straight warp of necessity, not to be swerved from its ultimate course — its every alternating vibration, indeed, only tending to that; free will still free to ply her shuttle between given threads; and chance, though restrained in its play within the right lines of necessity, and sideways in its motions directed by free will, though thus prescribed to by both, chance by turns rules either, and has the last featuring blow at events.

∗   ∗   ∗   ∗

Thus we were weaving and weaving away when I started at a sound so strange, long drawn, and musically wild and unearthly, the ball of free will dropped from my hand, and I stood gazing up at the clouds whence that voice dropped like a wing. High aloft in the cross-trees was that mad Gay-Header, Tashtego. His body was reaching eagerly forward, his hand stretched out like a wand, and at brief sudden intervals he continued his cries.

But Melville's magic wand was waved over more than Olmsted as he wrote this passage. In his copy of Beale's

Natural History of the Sperm Whale, Melville placed a checkmark beside the following paragraph:

> Let the reader suppose himself on the deck of a South-seaman, cruising in the North Pacific Ocean at its Japanese confine — he may be musing over some past event, the ship may be sailing gently along over the smooth ocean, every thing around solemnly still, with the sun pouring its intense rays with dazzling brightness; suddenly, the monotonous quietude is broken by an animated voice from the mast-head, exclaiming "there she spouts." The captain starts on deck in an instant, and inquires "where away?" but perhaps the next moment every one aloft and on deck can perceive an enormous whale lying about a quarter of a mile from the ship. . . . But while they have been looking, a few seconds have expired — they rush into the boats, which are directly lowered to receive them — and in two minutes from the time of first observing the whale, three or four boats are down, and are darting through the water with their utmost speed towards their intended victim, perhaps accompanied with a song from the headsman, who urges the quick and powerful plying of the oar.

Beale's paragraph may be seen as having furnished the general setting and the suggestion of dramatic change incorporated by Melville in the Ishmael-Queequeg scene. Both *Moby-Dick* and the *Natural History of the Sperm Whale* open with the scene of monotonous quiet; in both is the contrast between the revery and the sudden activity following the masthead cry. Beale's "musing over some past event" becomes in *Moby-Dick* "each silent sailor seemed resolved into his own invisible self," a change which much better fitted the idea into Melville's study of the isolation of all men. The separated sailors curiously re-echo the scene of the silent worshipers in Father Mapple's church, each an isolated self, and none more turned in on himself than Father Mapple.

Beale's "musings" may have encouraged or stimulated Melville into incorporating some of his own musings — his "ontological heroics" he termed them to Hawthorne — such as those he enjoyed while in passage to London when, according to his journal, 7 December, 1849, the second night at

sea, he and his shipboard friend, G. Adler, indulged themselves to a late hour in discussion "of 'fixed Fate, Free-Will,
foreknowledge absolute' &c." Queequeg is a strange substi-
tution for men like Adler or Hawthorne, and such subjects
are strange ones for a whaling book. Nevertheless, Melville
knew that "meditation and water are wedded forever" and
he has performed the ceremony in "The Mat-Maker." [50]

"The First Lowering" (48) follows "The Mat-Maker"
with only the break of chapter separation. The scene is vigorous, fast-moving, dramatic. It is one of the set paintings of
the novel; it is like a whaling print. Or perhaps it might be
better to imagine Melville's whale hunt in terms of the
motion picture, so eventful, so pulsing with excitement is the
story from Tashtego's cry to the return to the ship.

For the general structure of "The First Lowering" Melville drew on J. Ross Browne's *Etchings of a Whaling Cruise,*
with changes suggested by passages from Beale's *Natural History.* Browne's description of the whale chase has a sequence
of events similar to that found in *Moby-Dick*: the cry from
the lookout, the pell-mell rush for the boats, the lowering,
the approach on to the whale, the excited urging of the
boatsteerers, the harpooning of the whale, the desperate
struggle to land the great fish, the unexpected squall, the
danger of separation from the ship. This abbreviated list of
parallels might have occurred, one may suppose, even if Melville had never read *Etchings,* since the procedure in pursuing the whale was routine (familiar to Melville) throughout
the southern fishery. But knowing Melville's familiarity with
Browne, and that he had borrowed from Browne before, one
may scarcely question that Melville kept his eye on Browne's
narrative in order to shape his own. This seems undebatable
when comparing Melville's surging paragraph beginning "It
was a sight full of quick wonder and awe" with the similar
passage which he wrote years before in preparing his review
of Browne's book for the *Literary World.*[51]

[50] Lest one think that Melville's interest in Beale was not so close as I have
suggested, he should keep in mind that Melville marked this section of the
Natural History (chapter XIII) with more checks and with more marginalia (now erased) than any other section of the book.

[51] See p. 17.

But Thomas Beale's thirteenth chapter still remained open on Melville's desk even as he utilized ideas from Browne. In both Beale and Browne appears the sudden squall which strikes the boat, and in both is the suggestion of imminent danger through the threatened approach of night separating the boat crew from the mother ship. In *Etchings* the squall strikes just as dusk approaches and

> When the squall abated, we came to under the lee of the whale, and looked to leeward for the barque. Not a speck could be seen upon the horizon! Night was rapidly approaching, and we were alone upon the broad, angry ocean!

Fortunately for the men, the ship draws alongside just as darkness encircles them, and they are saved — even so it occurs, with differences, in *Moby-Dick*. But Melville enhanced his scene by adding details from Beale's much fuller account of the danger; in the *Natural History of the Sperm Whale* Melville marked the following passage — a tap which was an accolade:

> . . . and therefore when half-past nine P.M. came, we made up our minds that they were all lost; and as the wind howled hoarsely through the rigging, and the waves beat savagely against our ship. . . . There were not many on board who did not think of home on that dreadful night — there were not many among us who did not curse the sea, and all sea-going avocations; while with the same breath, they blessed the safe and cheerful fireside of their parents and friends who resided at home, and which at that moment they would have given all they possessed but to see. But at the moment despair was firmly settling upon us, a man from aloft called out that he could see a light right ahead of the ship, just as we were "going about," by which we should have gone from it. We all looked in that direction, and in a few minutes we could plainly perceive it; in a short time we were close up with it, when, to our great joy, we found the captain and all the men in the boats, lying to leeward of the dead whale, which had in some measure saved them from the violence of the sea. They had only just been able to procure a light, having unfortunately upset all their tinder through the violent motion of the boats, by which it became wet — but which they succeeded

in igniting after immense application of the flint and steel —
or their lantern would have been suspended from an oar
directly after sunset, which is the usual practice when boats
are placed under such circumstances.

The details which passed from Beale [52] to Melville may be
seen in the far more vivid sketch in *Moby-Dick*:

> Though completely swamped, the boat was nearly un-
> harmed. Swimming round it we picked up the floating oars,
> and lashing them across the gunwale, tumbled back to our
> places. There we sat up to our knees in the sea, the water
> covering every rib and plank, so that to our downward gazing
> eyes the suspended craft seemed a coral boat grown up to us
> from the bottom of the ocean.
>
> The wind increased to a howl; the waves dashed their buck-
> lers together; the whole squall roared, forked, and crackled
> around us like a white fire upon the prairie, in which, uncon-
> sumed, we were burning; immortal in these jaws of death! In
> vain we hailed the other boats; as well roar to the live coals
> down the chimney of a flaming furnace as hail those boats in
> that storm. Meanwhile the driving scud, rack, and mist, grew
> darker with the shadows of night; no sign of the ship could be
> seen. The rising sea forbade all attempts to bale out the boat.
> The oars were useless as propellers, performing now the office
> of life-preservers. So, cutting the lashing of the waterproof
> match keg, after many failures Starbuck contrived to ignite the
> lamp in the lantern; then stretching it on a waif pole, handed
> it to Queequeg as the standard-bearer of this forlorn hope.
> There, then, he sat, holding up that imbecile candle in the
> heart of that almighty forlornness. There, then, he sat, the
> sign and symbol of a man without faith, hopelessly holding up
> hope in the midst of despair.
>
> Wet, drenched through, and shivering cold, despairing of
> ship or boat, we lifted up our eyes as the dawn came on. The
> mist still spread over the sea, the empty lantern lay crushed
> in the bottom of the boat. Suddenly Queequeg started to his
> feet, hollowing his hand to his ear. We all heard a faint
> creaking, as of ropes and yards hitherto muffled by the storm.
> The sound came nearer and nearer; the thick mists were
> dimly parted by a huge, vague form. Affrighted, we all sprang

[52] Cheever, pp. 172–174 and pp. 220–224, has accounts of the separation of
a boat from the ship but Melville does not seem to have made use of them.

into the sea as the ship at last loomed into view, bearing right down upon us within a distance of not much more than its length.

Floating on the waves we saw the abandoned boat, as for one instant it tossed and gaped beneath the ship's bows like a chip at the base of a cataract; and then the vast hull rolled over it, and it was seen no more till it came up weltering astern. Again we swam for it, were dashed against it by the seas, and were at last taken up and safely landed on board. Ere the squall came close to, the other boats had cut loose from their fish and returned to the ship in good time. The ship had given us up, but was still cruising, if haply it might light upon some token of our perishing, — an oar or a lance pole.

The writing is splendid in its graphic realism, but it achieves true magnificence in Melville's perception of the scene as a symbol of man's terrifying loneliness amidst the hostile forces of the universe, of man's pathetic care for the flickering light of hope even as universal darkness engulfs him, of man's attempt to make a heaven in hell's despite.

This brief account of Melville's particular adaptations from Beale and Browne in the construction of "The First Lowering" does not pretend to be exhaustive in revealing Melville's fundamental transformation of source materials.[53] Only a close reading of Browne's, Beale's, and Melville's chapters side by side, can show how remarkably brilliant Melville's scene [54] is — because of the dramatization through Stubb, Daggoo and Flask, Ishmael and Queequeg, and because of the piling up of images, the enlivening style — in comparison with the workaday accounts of the author's fish documents. Melville's first lowering reaches far beyond his sources because of what an 1893 critic described as "the healthy, wholesome, [and] rude but terrible realities" of *Moby-Dick*.

As was his habit, Melville followed the brilliant, exciting

[53] Olmsted's *Incidents of a Whaling Voyage* has points of similarity between the whale-pursuit scenes, but none so striking or demonstrable as those in Beale and Bennett.

[54] I cannot help wondering whether or not Walt Whitman was familiar with Melville's "The First Lowering" and that he had *Moby-Dick* in mind when he wrote his lines on the whaleman in "A Song of Joys."

episode of "The First Lowering" with a chapter treating of the same subject — the dangers of the whale fishery — but in an entirely different key and of a greatly different length. "The Hyena" (49) is Ishmael's brief, ironic comment concerning the rigors of hunting whales. "The Hyena" is short, humorous, explicit. It describes an Ishmael who, having considered idly of Necessity and Chance in the weaving scene, now, after strenuous experiences, follows up his reflections with a philosophical conclusion: that he will accept the consequences of his whaling life no matter what Fate or Chance should bring. For when the storm-soaked boat crew has clambered in great relief aboard the rescuing *Pequod,* Ishmael, finding out that such grim experiences were "an unalterable law in this fishery," draws up his will, vowing to accept "tranquilly and contentedly" what Fate has in store for him "and the devil fetch the hindmost." [55]

Melville's favorite habit of sliding his philosophical themes into the narrative or humorous sections of *Moby-Dick* is illustrated for a second time in "The Hyena." Having made his will, Ishmael "felt all the easier; a stone was rolled away from my heart. Besides, all the days I should now live would be as good as the days that Lazarus lived after his resurrection." In other words, Ishmael's acceptance of the sea and its consequences — of life, for which with Melville the sea is ever the symbol — has resulted for him in a symbolic resurrection. Death and rebirth was a favorite theme with Melville from 1849, the time of *Mardi,* until 1891, the year of *Billy Budd* and of its author's death. The theme is important in *White-Jacket, Clarel,* and the poems. Death and rebirth is the enveloping theme of *Moby-Dick,* touched on in several scenes, and culminating in rich restatement in the Epilogue, when Ishmael floats on his strangest of life preservers, Queequeg's old coffin. In "The Spirit-Spout," so that the reader may not miss the connection of

---

[55] Ishmael's acceptance of the rude shattering of his romantic illusions about whaling fit into some words of Freud: "Illusions commend themselves to us because they save us pain and allow us to enjoy pleasure instead. We must therefore accept it without complaint when they sometimes collide with a bit of reality against which they are dashed to pieces."

the Lazarus allusion with Ishmael's experience, Melville closes the chapter with a statement almost explicit: "I survived myself; my death and burial were locked up in my chest." And characteristically, the pun on "chest" brings together the physical will and the "will," the stoical acceptance of all that life may offer, which is locked up within Ishmael's own bosom (chest). The philosophical themes of *Moby-Dick* are thus woven by Melville's imagination into the actual dangers of the fishery.

"The First Lowering" and "The Hyena" have introduced materials for further elaboration, mysteries requiring explanation. "Fedallah" (50) describes the leader of the strange boat crew, "pagan leopards" which had first burst upon the sight of the *Pequod* crew at the time of the first lowering. The men back on shipboard, Ishmael has time in which to reflect. Willing, at least momentarily, to accept Ishmael's statement that Fedallah remains "a muffled mystery to the last," we will not discuss him until a later chapter. But having described Fedallah in a special chapter, Melville then proceeded to show him in action — for it is Fedallah who sights the spirit-spout. Direct from the comfortable, if rigorous, world of the whale hunt we move back (still in pursuit of a whale) to the world of strangeness and mystery, to the inexplicable, back to Ahab. Ahab will misread the meaning of the silvery spout; we must try to interpret it more accurately. The audience can always see the gathering doom when the tragic hero is unable to read the signs.

Furthermore, in "The Hyena" we have one of the few occasions in which Ishmael speaks as himself rather than as the dramatic surrogate of Melville. And whenever Ishmael thus comes front stage to speak in his own person and about his own person, he has been brought forward by Melville in order to restate, either implicitly or explicitly, important thematic material. Just as "The Hyena" fulfills in structural counterpoint the length, the tone, and the meaning of "The First Lowering," so Ishmael is thematically related to Ahab. Ahab, symbol of the egoistic, tortured spirit, fights against fate all through the novel and destroys both himself and his crew. He will not accept stoically but must fight fiercely; he too has pondered Free Will, Fate, and Chance. He must know all — and find Moby Dick. Ishmael, on the other hand, has thus early in the journey learned to accept what the sea and Fate bring forth. Ishmael who had started out with a November drizzle in his soul and a grimness about the mouth, can now laugh — hyenalike indeed, but a laugh and not a snarl — at Fate. Having learnt stoic endurance, Ishmael alone among the *Pequod* crew will survive, saved by his coffin barque. Says Ishmael in "The Hyena": "There is nothing like the perils of whaling to breed this free and easy sort of genial, desperado philosophy; and with it I now regarded this whole voyage of the Pequod, and the great White Whale its object" — a far different point of view from Ahab's relentless, unhumorous determination to bathe in the hot blood of Moby Dick. "There is no alternative," says Berdyaev, "but to shoulder the burden of history and culture, the burden of the terrifying, distressing and degraded world." No alternative but Ahab's mad one. Ishmael has attained the inner harmony unrealized by Ahab, because he has come to terms with his environment as his great captain never could do.[56] Ishmael has subdued his sense of outrage in the face of events; Ahab's expands to the point of self-destruction.

9

"A silvery jet was seen"

MELVILLE left no explanation of the meaning of *Moby-Dick*. He was too much the artist ever to leave a "key" to his works, recognizing that they must, finally, speak their own

[56] Ishmael found out, as Ahab could not, the truth later expressed by William James: "To give up pretensions is as blessed a relief as to get them gratified; and where disappointment is incessant and the struggle unending, this is what men will always do. The history of evangelical theology, with its conviction of sin, its self-despair, and its abandonment of salvation by works, is the deepest of possible examples, but we meet others in every walk of life. There is the strangest lightness about the heart when one's nothingness in a particular line is once accepted in good faith."

messages, or the lesser artist he. Even for the confused and complex *Mardi* he refused annotation, saying that "Time, which is the solver of all riddles, will solve the riddle of 'Mardi.'" He was right. But in connection with "The Spirit-Spout" (51) we come close to a Melville explanation — close, but not too close — of what his symbolism meant in *Moby-Dick*. Soon after the novel was published, Mrs. Hawthorne wrote an appreciative letter in which she suggested to Melville the possible allegorical significance of his work. We do not have her letter, but his reply is of great interest:

> It really amazed me that you should find any satisfaction in that book. It is true that some *men* have said that they were pleased with it, but you are the only *woman*. . . . But, then, since you, with your spiritualizing nature, see more things than other people, and by the same process, refine all you see, so that they are not the same things that other people see, but things, which while you think you but humbly discover them, you do in fact create them yourself — therefore, upon the whole, I do not much marvel at your expressions concerning Moby Dick. At any rate, your allusion to the "Spirit Spout" first showed to me that there was a subtle significance in that thing — but I did not, in that case, mean it. I had some vague idea while writing it, that the whole book was susceptible of an allegorical construction, & also that parts of it were — but the specialty of many of the particular subordinate allegories were first revealed to me after reading Mr. Hawthorne's letter, which, without citing any particular examples, yet intimated the part-&-parcel allegoricalness of the whole.

Melville does not deny allegorical possibilities, general or particular, in *Moby-Dick*, although he suggests that the meanings which Mrs. Hawthorne found had not been intended by him. Thus he avoids the problem of conscious and unconscious intention.

In dealing with Melville's acknowledgment of an "allegorical construction" in *Moby-Dick*, it might be well to consider the nature of effective symbolism. Symbolism is an aftereffect. The symbolical significance of the *thing* presented is always secondary to the original, immediate description, and grows out of it, hovering over it like an impalpable presence. Symbolism suggests; it does not flatly state. It is fluid, oblique, shadowy; it is not, like allegory, mechanical equation, for when precise equivalents are established the "life" and "spirit" evaporate from the work of art — as in the *Faerie Queene*. And when the symbolical meaning becomes unfortunately the primary concern of the artist, the resultant work of art will be vague and amorphous, lacking, as Melville would say, in bread and ale. Effective symbolism is implicit, not exposed. Symbolism is like quicksilver in the hand, not to be had by the hard, clutching grasp. "Symbols," said Emerson, "are fluxional."

Since the letter which Sophia Hawthorne wrote to Melville has probably been destroyed, we shall never know just how she explained to its amused author the symbolical meaning of "The Spirit-Spout." One may only invite Melville's irony by supplying one's own interpretation in lieu of any other.

"The Spirit-Spout" may be understood by placing it in relationship to the episode, and the chapters, immediately preceding it — chapters to which an interpretation has already been suggested. We saw Ishmael learning through danger and imminent death from the flukes of the whale, to accept stoically the destruction of life, to submit to Fate. Thus Ishmael contrastingly accentuates Ahab's egoism. Ahab will not submit to life, but boastingly calls himself Fate's lieutenant, to be the instrument of revenge on Moby Dick. Ahab forgets to whom vengeance belongs. "The Spirit-Spout" is another statement of the fate awaiting the overly self-assertive man. In his egoistic desire for the black blood of the great Whale Ahab becomes the victim of delusion, mistaking the spirit-spout for Moby Dick's fountain. Night after night he and his men (for delusion is contagious) see the strange sights which ever disappear as they approach it: "this solitary jet seemed for ever alluring us on." The spirit-spout is the symbol of delusion; it is the hope which allures; it is the power-dream of Tamburlaine, the knowledge-dream of Faustus. And just as it was Mephistopheles who led Faustus on to his damnation, so Fedallah is the one who first calls Ahab's attention to the silvery spout. The spirit-spout is the Demon of the Absolute, "treacherously beckoning us on and on, in order that the monster might turn round upon us, and rend us at last in the remotest and most savage of seas." It is the phenomenon described by Yeats: "O self-born mockers of man's enterprise. . . . / Whatever flames upon the night / Man's own resinous heart has fed."

"The Spirit-Spout" and the *Pequod* move into demon-haunted waters. We are in Milton's "dark illimitable ocean,/ Without bound, without dimension, where length, breadth and height, / And Time and place are lost." At first the spout is sighted while the ship advances through serene but lifeless seas — the lifelessness of the Arctic ice-closed seas of silvery sheen which entranced Coleridge's ill-fated crew — but in due time "this desolate vacuity of life" gives "place to sights more dismal than before" as they near the Cape of Good Hope. Read Melville:

> Nor with the immemorial superstition of their race, and in accordance with the preternaturalness, as it seemed, which in many things invested the Pequod, were there wanting some of the seamen who swore that whenever and wherever descried; at however remote times, or in however far apart latitudes and longitudes, that unnearable spout was cast by one self-same whale; and that whale, Moby Dick. For a time, there reigned, too, a sense of peculiar dread at this flitting apparition, as if it were treacherously beckoning us on and on, in order that the monster might turn round upon us, and rend us at last in the remotest and most savage seas.
>
> These temporary apprehensions, so vague but so awful, derived a wondrous potency from the contrasting serenity of the weather, in which, beneath all its blue blandness, some thought there lurked a devilish charm, as for days and days we voyaged along, through seas so wearily, lonesomely mild, that all space, in repugnance to our vengeful errand, seemed vacating itself of life before our urn-like prow.
>
> But, at last, when turning to the eastward, the Cape winds began howling around us, and we rose and fell upon the long, troubled seas that are there; when the ivory-tusked Pequod sharply bowed to the blast, and gored the dark waves in her madness, till, like showers of silver chips, the foam-flakes flew

over her bulwarks; then all this desolate vacuity of life went away, but gave place to sights more dismal than before.

Close to our bows, strange forms in the water darted hither and thither before us; while thick in our rear flew the inscrutable sea-ravens. And every morning, perched on our stays, rows of these birds were seen; and spite of our hootings, for a long time obstinately clung to the hemp, as though they deemed our ship some drifting, uninhabited craft; a thing appointed to desolation, and therefore fit roosting-place for their homeless selves. And heaved and heaved, still unrestingly heaved the black sea, as if its vast tides were a conscience; and the great mundane soul were in anguish and remorse for the long sin and suffering it had bred.

Cape of Good Hope, do they call ye? Rather Cape Tormentoto, as called of yore; for long allured by the perfidious silences that before had attended us, we found ourselves launched into this tormented sea, where guilty beings transformed into those fowls and these fish, seemed condemned to swim on everlastingly without any haven in store, or beat that black air without any horizon. But calm, snow-white, and unvarying; still directing its fountain of feathers to the sky; still beckoning us on from before, the solitary jet would at times be descried.

During all this blackness of the elements, Ahab, though assuming for the time the almost continual command of the drenched and dangerous deck, manifested the gloomiest reserve; and more seldom than ever addressed his mates. In tempestuous times like these, after everything above and aloft has been secured, nothing more can be done but passively to await the issue of the gale. Then Captain and crew become practical fatalists. So, with his ivory leg inserted into its accustomed hole, and with one hand firmly grasping a shroud, Ahab for hours and hours would stand gazing dead to windward, while an occasional squall of sleet or snow would all but congeal his very eyelashes together. Meantime, the crew driven from the forward part of the ship by the perilous seas that burstingly broke over its bows, stood in a line along the bulwarks in the waist; and the better to guard against the leaping waves, each man had slipped himself into a sort of bowline secured to the rail, in which he swung as in a loosened belt. Few or no words were spoken; and the silent ship, as if manned by painted sailors in wax, day after day tore on through all the swift madness and gladness of the demoniac

waves. By night the same muteness of humanity before the
shrieks of the ocean prevailed; still in silence the men swung
in the bowlines; still wordless Ahab stood up to the blast.

As one reads this passage, another influence becomes clear:
Samuel Taylor Coleridge's *Rime of the Ancient Mariner*.
The transition from the serenity of the tropic seas to the
storm-tossed seas inhabited only by strange, uncomforting
sea fowls and fish, recalls the Mariner's passage from the
cold, lifeless Antarctic to the Pacific seas, the ship spirit-
driven into waters where swim the coiling, monstrous serpents which haunt the ship. That Melville had Coleridge's
poem in mind is suggested by the passage: "and the silent
ship, as if manned by painted sailors in wax, day after day
tore on through all the swift madness and gladness of the
demoniac waves," with its verbal similarity to "As idle as a
painted ship upon a painted ocean" from the poem. Furthermore, it is more than coincidence that Melville's very next
chapter is entitled "The Albatross," a name which inevitably
brings to mind Coleridge's ominous bird. To be sure Melville's albatross is no bird but a ship, the *Goney* (the sailors'
name for the albatross), "a whaler at sea, and long absent
from home." [57] The *Pequod* hails the ship, the men anxious
for a good sociable gam, Ahab concerned only for news of
the White Whale. The *Goney* is a spectral craft, "bleached
like the skeleton of a stranded walrus," and suggests, perhaps, to the reader the spectral ship of the *Ancient Mariner*.
Rough seas and a threatening wind prevent the gam. The
two ships pass each other, unable to communicate, and the
strange, mysterious *Goney* slips away. Then a slight event
occurs — slight but ominous. Ishmael explains: "shoals of
small harmless fish, that for some days before had been
placidly swimming by our side, darted away with what
seemed shuddering fins, and ranged themselves fore and aft
with the stranger's flanks." [58] Although these strange fish

[57] I see no indication that Melville made any use of the description and
plate of the albatross in Olmsted's *Incidents of a Whaling Voyage*, but undoubtedly picture and text refreshed his memory.

[58] It is barely possible that this desertion of the *Pequod* by the fish was
suggested to Melville by the following passage from Olmsted's *Incidents of*

suggest the snakes which swam about the Mariner's ship, their symbolism is quite different. The snakes of the *Ancient Mariner* were Evil. The flying fish of *Moby-Dick* symbolize good fortune, and when they desert the *Pequod*, the men dimly suspect evil ahead. Though Ahab regards the swimming fish sadly, so intent is he on his maniacal purpose that he refuses to face the omen, and orders the men to continue the course: "Up helm! Keep her off round the world!"

This does not mean that Melville "borrowed" from Coleridge's *Rime of the Ancient Mariner*. He knew the poem, for he tells us so in a footnote in *Moby-Dick*, describing his personal reactions to the albatross as he first saw it in southern waters. What is stated is that Melville's knowledge of the *Rime of the Ancient Mariner* was so complete — for the themes of the poem are, in a very real sense, themes in the novel — that, unconsciously or consciously, he enriched his chapter by subtle allusion to and utilization of the poem. The similarities between novel and poem are general, not specific, except in the instances shown. The differences are great. One especially is important: The Mariner bitterly repents his shooting of the bird and eagerly seeks to regain the companionship of men. Ahab on the other hand is unrepentant to the end; he rejects the wedding feasts, emblem of sociality. The Mariner learns to love all life, so that he even blesses the watersnakes. From Ahab's heart all love, except for his own unswerving purpose, has been torn by the malevolence of the creature of the sea.

The *Goney* and the *Pequod* are separated by the turbulent seas and by the impetuous haste of Ahab. The full significance of this failure in communication is made clear to us in the subsequent chapter, "The Gam" (53). A gam is a friendly interchange of visits by the crews of ships encountering each other at sea. Far from home, the men eagerly exchange information and gossip and enjoy a chance to be social. It was a practice commonly indulged in by the old-

a Whaling Voyage, p. 146: "When a ship is seen to be surrounded by large schools of fish, it is a trick sometimes practised by a brother whaler to run down close to her, under pretence of speaking to her, when a part, if not the whole of the school abandon their old friend and move off with the stranger."

time whalemen on the whaling grounds, and Melville makes much of the point that such social good nature was indeed peculiar to the whaleman, and not to be found among other sailors. Therefore, in pushing on to find the White Whale, to the neglect of the ritual of the gam, Ahab was again turning his back on the group, opposing the will of his men, and setting up his own law.

In "The Gam" Melville carefully defines the term, alleging that it has not had previous definition in the dictionaries. His statement is true, but Melville might have added that other men, whaling writers, had explained the term for the benefit of landsmen. In 1841, Francis Olmstead discussed the gam in his *Incidents of a Whaling Voyage*, and three years later a Stephen Curtis also explained the term.[59] Melville certainly knew Olmstead's work; he probably did not know Curtis's. He had also read J. Ross Browne's description in *Etchings of a Whaling Cruise*: "When two whalers meet on any of the whaling-grounds, it is usual to have a 'gam,' or mutual visit, for the purpose of interchanging the latest news, comparing reckoning, discussing the prospect of whales, and enjoying a general chit-chat." And before *Moby-Dick* was finished another description of the gam was published, from which Melville took the idea for his chapter: the adoption of the rôle of lexicographer. The Reverend Henry Cheever wrote in *The Whale and His Captors* (1850):

> Had Noah Webster ever gone a whaling, he would have been able to add some five or six notable and genuine English words to his Dictionary, which may never be known off salt water unless we record them here. . . .
> *Gam* is the word by which they designate the meeting, exchanging visits, and keeping company of two or more whale ships, or a sociable family of whales. Thus we *gammed* two

[59] *Brief Extracts from the Journal of a Voyage performed by the Whale Ship M —— Y, of New Bedford, Massachusetts, commencing May 25, 1841, and terminating August 1, 1844* (Boston, 1844), p. 20. Curtis's voyage, it will be seen, was almost exactly the same time as Melville's. Curtis describes brutality aboard his whaleship, and he also has some interesting details about Nukahiva, all of which would have interested Melville, but I cannot see that he was acquainted with the book at all.

days on the New Zealand whaling ground with the Niantic
of Sag Harbor. One day the captain of the Niantic spent
with us, the next our captain spent on board the Niantic, the
boats' crews *gamming* together at the same time in the forecastle, and the ships meeting and having a *gam* in the ship
that was left of her captain.

These *gams* are very pleasant interludes in a whaleman's
life, when abroad upon the desert ocean, without change of
society or scene, a thousand miles from land. It is peculiarly
grateful for a rusty and barnacled old ship, that has been
absent thirty or more months, to have a *gam* of a day with
a fresh competitor just arrived out with all the news from
home. Such a *gam* gives matter of talk and old newspaper
reading for a month, and nobody can tell how pleasant it is
but one that has experienced it. A shipmaster has a chance
to exchange counsel, and tell stories, and let himself be familiar with somebody that's new, and he is always the milder,
and better pleased with himself and all about him, for some
days after such a *gam*.

With Olmsted, Browne, and Cheever — the last especially
— in mind, Melville wrote:

But what is a *Gam*? You might wear out your index-finger
running up and down the columns of dictionaries, and never
find the word. Dr. Johnson never attained to that erudition;
Noah Webster's ark does not hold it. Nevertheless, this same
expressive word has now for many years been in constant use
among some fifteen thousand true born Yankees. Certainly,
it needs a definition, and should be incorporated into the
Lexicon. With that view, let me learnedly define it.

GAM. Noun — *A social meeting of two (or more) Whaleships, generally on a cruising-ground; when, after exchanging
hails, they exchange visits by boats' crews: the two captains
remaining, for the time, on board of one ship, and the two
chief mates on the other.*

Although Melville borrowed from others, and from his own
experience, to define the word, he has placed his stamp on it
so that it is to his and not the prior definitions that we turn.
Melville's method of adapting Browne's and Cheever's materials is characteristic of the graphic imagination: the finger

running up and down the pages of the dictionary, the metaphor of the ark for Noah Webster's great work, and the
mocking paragraphs in which Melville glorifies the sociable
whaleman as against the unsocial merchant sailor.

Melville called the crew members "isolatoes," their captain being an isolato of isolatoes. But where they wanted
the companionship of the gam, Ahab cared for it only so
long as it afforded him information of the whereabouts of
Moby Dick: "He cared not to consort, even for five minutes,
with any stranger captain, except he could contribute some
of that information he so absorbingly sought." Melville's
informative account of a genial whaling custom is more than
a retelling of other men's descriptions or of his own memories; it is an implied criticism of the completely unsocial
self-reliance of Ahab in neglecting the ordinary social decen-
cies which constitute a civilized world.

10

"Unpainted to the last"

MELVILLE had a scattered and miscellaneous fund of information about whaling iconography, gathered through wide
but unsystematic reading, but somehow his factual scraps
come together into a graceful and readable three-chapter
essay. The information is injected at this point in the novel
because shortly we shall see the whale through the professional whaleman's eyes as it lies chained beside the ship,
and therefore we might well first see the whale as *popularly*
conceived and misconceived. Beside the errors of the fish
documents, the accuracy of *Moby-Dick* will stand in striking
contrast.

Melville made a clear and amusing essay by his skill in
arrangement. Reading a passage in Scoresby's *An Account
of the Arctic Regions:*

Besides, the drawings hitherto given of many of the whale tribe are so unlike, and so preposterous, that they tend rather to mislead than to assist the practical zoologist. . . . Hence, also, as another step towards an improved system of Cetology, I have confined my engravings, as well as my descriptions, to those animals which have come immediately under my own examination, or have been sketched by persons on whose accuracy and faithfulness I could fully depend; while drawings and descriptions that I have met with, where the least doubtful, have been altogether rejected . . .

— Melville took the idea of dividing his pictures into two groups: those unscientifically done, no matter by whom, and those done accurately. The first group of course predominated, and where Scoresby conscientiously rejected them, Melville described them in judicious but amusing phrases. Melville also added a chronological method of arrangement, so that we begin with "the oldest Hindoo, Egyptian, and Grecian sculptures" and come straight down the ages, mocking the Elephanta Cave carving ("more like the tapering tail of an anaconda, than the broad palms of the true whale's majestic flukes"), Guido Reni's whale ("a strange creature"), the whale decorating an abridged edition of Goldsmith's *Animated Nature* ("an amputated sow"), and, Frederick Cuvier's whale ("not a Sperm Whale, but a squash"). "Of the Monstrous Pictures of Whales" (55) is an amusing account of pictorial incompetence.

The second part of the essay, "Of the Less Erroneous Pictures of Whales and the True Pictures of Whaling Scenes" (56), narrows Melville's field of discussion, for accurate whale pictures were few in his day. He says, "I know of only four published outlines of the great Sperm Whale; Colnett's, Huggins's, Frederick Cuvier's, and Beale's. In the previous chapter Colnett and Cuvier have been referred to. Huggins's is far better than theirs; but, by great odds, Beale's is the best. . . . Of the Right Whale, the best outline pictures are in Scoresby; but they are drawn on too small a scale to convey a desirable impression." Melville sounds more authoritative in this statement than he had reason to be. Colnett's outline he certainly knew. He may have known

Huggins's, but it is to be found only on Huggins's whaling print, to which Melville does not refer, and which it is doubtful that Melville had seen. It is much more probable, and consistent with Melville's frequent practice, that he studied Beale's outline which carries the words beneath: "Huggins and Beale." Cuvier's he probably saw not in Cuvier's book but in Beale, on the same page where Huggins's had appeared. The accompanying picture shows what Melville studied, and why he was justified in calling Cuvier's whale a "squash."

Melville studied the whaling pictures in Beale with interest. On page twelve of his copy, he made an index of Beale's pictures, obviously so that he might rapidly and frequently turn to them. For the small picture of three whales prefacing the second chapter, Melville wrote: "There is some sort of mistake in the drawing of Fig: 2. The tail part is wretchedly cropped & dwarfed, & looks altogether unnatural. The head is good." And on the title-page, referring to the plate facing, he wrote: "Turner's pictures of whales were suggested by this book." But in *Moby-Dick*, as the result of his study indicated in his marginalia, Melville said: "All Beale's drawings of this whale are good, excepting the middle figure in the picture of three whales in various attitudes [i.e. "Fig: 2"], capping his second chapter. His frontispiece, boats attacking Sperm Whales, though no doubt calculated to excite the civil skepticism of some parlor men, is admirably correct and life-like in its general effect."

Melville selects for admiring approval the two Garnery engravings and one by Durand. His descriptions correctly tell their excellence; the prints are today among the most prized by whaling-print collectors.[60] Any illustrated edition of *Moby-Dick* would gain by their reproduction.

The third chapter in Melville's iconographic essay is sufficiently summed up in its title: "Of Whales in Paint; in Teeth; in Wood; in Sheet-Iron; in Stone; in Mountains; in Stars" (57). The most interesting paragraph deals with

---

[60] For a general article on whaling prints see Charles D. Childs, " 'Thar She Blows.' Some Notes on American Whaling Pictures," *Antiques,* July, 1941, pp. 20–23.

scrimshaw (Melville calls it "skrimshandering"), the native art of whalemen in which they carved or painted whalebone and whale teeth, or shaped walking sticks and other objects during the long periods of calm on their cruises. The Jonathan Bourne Whaling Museum in New Bedford has an entire room devoted to scrimshaw articles, fascinating to the student of folk art.

But what, we may ask, keeps Melville's essay on whaling pictures from being digressive? He shows his purpose as he extenuates the errors of the inaccurate whale artists — the whale can never be captured, even by pencil or brush. (The art of Daguerre was not well enough developed to warrant consideration. But when, incidentally, was the first whaling photograph?)

But these manifold mistakes in depicting the whale are not so very surprising after all. Consider! Most of the scientific drawings have been taken from the stranded fish; and these are about as correct as a drawing of a wrecked ship, with broken back, would correctly represent the noble animal itself in all its undashed pride of hull and spars. Though elephants have stood for their full-lengths, the living Leviathan has never yet fairly floated himself for his portrait. The living whale, in his full majesty and significance, is only to be seen at sea in unfathomable waters; and afloat the vast bulk of him is out of sight, like a launched line-of-battle ship; and out of that element it is a thing eternally impossible for mortal man to hoist him bodily into the air, so as to preserve all his mighty swells and undulations. And, not to speak of the highly presumable difference of contour between a young sucking whale and a full-grown Platonian Leviathan; yet, even in the case of one of those young sucking whales hoisted to a ship's deck, such is then the outlandish, eel-like, limbered, varying shape of him, that his precise expression the devil himself could not catch.[61]

---

[61] By coincidence, the year Melville wrote this, another whaling writer thousands of miles away, wrote: "Even whalers in general know little more of them than their oil. While a lion or a tiger has become quite a vulgar animal in our menageries, there are few persons who have seen a live cetacean in captivity. . . . At least, in the present railroad times, when a live hippopotamus is sporting in the midst of London, the most of the external aspect of a cetacean that any Cockney has yet seen, has been presented to his

"In fact," Melville adds later, "as the great Hunter says, the mere skeleton of the whale bears the same relation to the fully invested and padded animal as the insect does to the chrysalis that so roundingly envelopes it." Melville's reference to the "great Hunter" is to Doctor John Hunter, the distinguished eighteenth-century medical man, whose careful dissections of whales, written up in a famous essay in the *Philosophical Transactions*, laid the groundwork for scientific whale anatomy. Melville read his whale reports not in Hunter's collected *Works*, but in the long quotations from Hunter which Beale included in the *Natural History of the Sperm Whale*. Discussing the whale's skeleton, Beale quoted exclusively from Hunter, including the following passage:

> The bones alone (says Hunter) in many animals, when properly articulated into what is called the skeleton, give the general shape and character of the animal. Thus a quadruped is distinguished from a bird, and even one quadruped from another, it only requiring a skin to be thrown over the skeleton to make the species known; but this is not so decidedly the case with this order of animals, for the skeleton in them does not give us the true shape. An immense head, a small neck, few ribs, and in many a short sternum, and no pelvis, with a long spine terminating in a point, require more than a skin laid over them to give the regular and characteristic form of the animal. The bones of the anterior extremity give no idea of the shape of a fin, the form of which wholly depends upon its covering. The different parts of the skeleton are so enclosed, and the spaces between the projecting parts are so filled up as to be altogether concealed, giving the animal externally a uniform and elegant form, resembling an insect enveloped in its chrysalis coat.

wondering gaze by some distorted skin. And this is one of the reasons why the figures of the sperm whale by Beale and Frederick Cuvier are so widely different from each other, as to make it almost incredible that they should have been intended for the same species. By such missshapen masses of stuffing so little accurate information is afforded to the zoologist, that he is of necessity obliged to have recourse to the skeleton." William Wall, *History and Description of the Skeleton of a New Spermaceti Whale, Lately set up in the Australian Museum* (Sidney, 1851), p. 1.

One does not need to see Melville's copy of Beale, in which this passage is checked and a marginal note (now erased) added, to be aware of his debt to Hunter's words both for information and for simile. But Melville's additional use of the scientific statement is characteristic humor in *Moby-Dick:*

> This peculiarity is strikingly evinced in the head, as in some part of this book will be incidentally shown. It is also very curiously displayed in the side fin, the bones of which almost exactly answer to bones of the human hand, minus only the thumb. This fin has four regular bone-fingers, the index, middle, ring, and little finger. But all these are permanently lodged in their fleshy covering, as the human fingers in an artificial covering. "However recklessly the whale may sometimes serve us," said humorous Stubb one day, "he can never be truly said to handle us without mittens."

As he so often does throughout the novel, Melville completes a progression from deft exposition to humorous commentary, to serious statement whereby the expository information is brought into significant relationship with the theme:

> For all these reasons, then, any way you may look at it, you must needs conclude that the great Leviathan is that one creature in the world which must remain unpainted to the last. True, one portrait may hit the mark much nearer than another, but none can hit it with any very considerable degree of exactness. So there is no earthly way of finding out precisely what the whale really looks like. And the only mode in which you can derive even a tolerable idea of his living contour, is by going a whaling yourself; but by so doing, you run no small risk of being eternally stove and sunk by him. Wherefore, it seems to me you had best not be too fastidious in your curiosity touching this Leviathan.

Passages like this may not have symbolical overtones, may not carry metaphysical and ethical implications, but it would certainly be a cautious or a lumbering mind which insisted on mere literal interpretation as being sufficient. In the light of what Melville says later about the whale's head, one may have pleasure in considering for oneself the kind of curiosity, and the object of it, Melville is here hinting. Time does not permit me to explicate here.[62]

11

"Brit, the minute, yellow substance"

AS THE AUTHOR of a book intended to present the whale "complete" to the reader, Melville felt required to include a description of the whale's food. Then and now, information on the subject was scanty, based on hearsay, guesswork, and limited observation. In two short paragraphs Melville might have told us everything scientifically known or hypothesized about the Right Whale's and the Sperm Whale's food. Instead he wrote two full chapters, expanding the small whaling topic, not by adding new factual data — such he did not have — but by weaving his few facts, supplied to him by Beale and Bennett, chiefly, into the main cloth of his narrative. Exposition and narrative reinforce one another. Furthermore, Melville saw that he might state once more his favorite antithesis of the sea, symbol of the half-known life, against the land, symbol of the known, the secure. By extending physical fact to narrative need, and thence to metaphysical perception, Melville made two bare paragraphs — sufficient had exposition been his sole intent — flower into two complex chapters. Instead of writing a prosaic account of whale food, Melville poetically and dramatically embel-

---

62 Accepting Melville's own restraint ("I am strongly tempted here to enter upon those still more monstrous stories" of whales) I must omit consideration of the "monstrous stories" which Melville had read, knowing, however, that there were many more which Melville did not know but would have enjoyed (see, for instance, some of those collected in Fletcher S. Bassett, *Legends and Superstitions of the Sea and of Sailors* [London, 1885], pp. 202 ff.) Probably the reason, other than space, which made him "pass that matter by" was that his own whaling story was taxing to our credulity, and that his attempt to bring it into the reader's sense of probability would be harmed by the inclusion of whalemen's yarns. Still, he had to omit a lot of interesting material.

lished the naked fact, adding the large, ominous implications foreshadowing the fate of the *Pequod* — implications which extend beyond the covers of *Moby-Dick* into life itself.

"Brit" (58), subject of the first of the two whale-food chapters, Melville explains as a "minute, yellow substance, upon which the Right Whale largely feeds." It is widely known to naturalists as plankton. Melville describes how the Right Whale, swimming through large areas of ocean discolored by infinite quantities of these minute shrimplike creatures, takes them into his cavernous mouth along with the sea water. Shutting his mouth, or rather, letting down the long pieces of hair-fringed whalebone (not possessed by the Sperm Whale), the Right Whale pushes the water out while the whalebone serves as a hairy sieve to retain the microscopic molluscs. At his lordly leisure, the whale then swallows the brit down a gullet so narrow, Melville adds, that a tuppenny roll would choke him.

Dispensed with admirable brevity in Melville's short, introductory paragraph, this information is but a beginning. What interested Melville far more than the fact was an idea growing out of the physical phenomenon. For Melville it was a miracle of Nature thus to provide the mightiest of monsters with the minutest of foods. Besides being an ironic antithesis it was yet another example, and a striking one, of the profound mystery of the sea itself, engendering in Melville a sense of wonder at man's ignorance and at the plenitude of life. As a sailor gazing speculatively over the billowing Pacific from the masthead of the *Acushnet,* Melville had reflected much concerning the multiplicity of phenomena and the inscrutability of Nature. "Brit" presents us some of that reflection. Melville's own, old, personal experience was probably recalled to his mind by Bennett's *A Whaling Voyage,* where he read: "We cannot fail to be impressed with a truly magnificent idea of the profusion of animal life which must necessarily exist in the ocean's depths, though invisible to man." If Bennett's single, significant sentence awakened old (and strengthened) reflection within Melville, or if it acted catalytically upon his sense of wonder, suggesting the theme of the sea as "an everlasting incognita," Bennett's passage was really no more than an undeveloped hint, a nudge in the ribs — though it stirred the powerful imagination of Melville, sharply aware of the tragic destiny of man adrift among the terrors of life's unknown, to magnify and to enrich the bare words of Bennett into the famous directive in *Moby-Dick*:

> Consider the subtleness of the sea; how its most dreaded creatures glide under water, unapparent for the most part, and treacherously hidden beneath the loveliest tints of azure. Consider also the devilish brilliance and beauty of many of its most remorseless tribes, as the dainty embellished shape of many species of sharks. Consider once more, the universal cannibalism of the sea; all whose creatures prey upon each other, carrying on eternal war since the world began.
>
> Consider all this; and then turn to this green, gentle, and most docile earth; consider them both, the sea and the land; and do you not find a strange analogy to something in yourself? For as this appalling ocean surrounds the verdant land, so in the soul of man there lies one insular Tahiti, full of peace and joy, but encompassed by all the horrors of the half known life. God keep thee! Push not off from that isle, thou canst never return.

Consider the perfection of this passage; how its every sentence gleams with color and life, shifting iridescently from the enameled richness of the first sentence to the gentler tones of the second paragraph. Consider also the sharpness of technique, how each repetition of the imperative verb forces the attention back to the dread implications of the images. Consider once more those very implications with their unsparing sense of the sharkishness of life. Consider all this, and then turn back to the innocent, prosaic sentence of Bennett's, honest and direct, but uncomprehending of the significance of the thing described. Melville's cadenced lines — equally honest, but subtly contrived — penetrate to the core of life; they are fully aware of what Yeats has called "That dolphin-torn, that gong-tormented sea." A single, particular fact — the food of the Right Whale — has led us to a universal truth. Immensity has clustered about the microscopic brit.

The chapter "Brit" is but half of Melville's description

of the whale's food. After all, the Sperm Whale, too, must be fed. In the second of his two chapters, then, Melville carries on with the subject and antiphonally continues the *mare incognitum* theme so powerfully invoked in the pages on "Brit." To present the food of the Sperm Whale Melville adopted a different technique — dramatic, by way of an episode, in contrast with the expository statements of his preceding chapter — just as the Sperm Whale was dramatic, to Melville, and the Right Whale expository.

The facts about the Sperm Whale's food were conjectural, an even greater mystery than the Right Whale's. Cetologists of Melville's day — and now — felt certain of only one fact — that Moby Dick and his fellows fed almost exclusively on the giant squid hidden in the unexplored depths of the ocean, a creature reputed to be as monstrous as the Sperm Whale himself.[63] The squid was the Kraken of mythology, the subject about which Melville facetiously suggested a new novel. In *Moby-Dick* our introduction to the squid is not didactic but vividly dramatic, in an episode which leads us back to the primary thread of Melville's story: the pursuit of Moby Dick himself. When the *Pequod* crew mistakes the squid for the White Whale, we are assured that our author has not forgotten the course of his main story. Rather we admire the way in which he has strengthened it.

Slowly gliding through the Java seas "one transparent blue morning," the *Pequod* is electrified by Daggoo's cry from the masthead: "There! there again! there she breaches! right ahead! The White Whale, the White Whale!" Four boats put out in pell-mell haste, each crew racing for the honor of darting the first harpoon into the flank of Moby Dick. As the men draw close to the white mass undulating on the sea's surface, they are struck with terror; instead of a whale, they stare at a giant squid, seldom seen by men — and then fatally:

[63] There is an excellent illustrated article on squid by Roy Waldo Miner, "Marauders of the Sea," *The National Geographic Magazine*, LXVIII (August, 1935), 185–207, which also includes eight color life studies by Else Bostelman. See also W. Gregory Walker, "Sperm Whale and Squid," *Discovery*, 18 (1937), 308–312, which includes a photograph of a sperm whale's head with the squid marks showing plainly.

. . . we now gazed at the most wondrous phenomenon which the secret seas have hitherto revealed to mankind. A vast pulpy mass, furlongs in length and breadth, of a glancing cream-color, lay floating on the water, innumerable long arms radiating from its centre, and curling and twisting like a nest of anacondas, as if blindly to clutch at any hapless object within reach. No perceptible face or front did it have; no conceivable token of either sensation or instinct; but undulated there on the billows, and unearthly, formless, chance-like apparition of life.

As the squid sinks "with a low sucking sound," [64] Starbuck explains the significance of what they have seen to the questioning Flask (and to us): "The great live squid, which, they say, few whale-ships ever beheld, and returned to their ports to tell of it." Certainly to the *Pequod*. The scene is shocking and terrifying to the *Pequod* crew, as our remembrance, upon seeing, let us say, Pierre Roy's painting, *Danger on the Stairs,* of the presence of evil in the familiar —on the commonplace stairway where a long, blood-chilling snake curves round the turn of the stairs.

Again, what might have been an unimportant fact about the whale's food has suddenly become an important part of the narrative structure, an integral part of the emotional structure, and an unforgettable bit of foreshadowing. The very fate of the *Pequod* is hinted to the crew; even dauntless Ahab is struck silent. Both readers and crew sense the fate of the ship. The squid is as much a promise of things to come as an appearance of the Weird Sisters in *Macbeth*. And like Macbeth, Ahab, blinded by *hybris,* refuses to accept the inevitable restriction of life. Ahab's is the delusion of appearances. Or the delusion of him who, seeing, will not understand.

The dramatic irony of *Moby-Dick* has been strongly reinforced. Echoes reverberate. The blankness and whiteness

---

[64] Did the sentence in Francis Olmsted's *Incidents of a Whaling Voyage,* "The entire animal consists of a flabby mass of a white color, not unlike very stiff *blanc mange,"* help Melville in describing the "vast pulpy mass"? Olmsted's was one of the few descriptions of the squid which I have been able to find in Melville's "numerous fish documents."

of the squid call to mind the great chapter on the whiteness of the whale, now taking on terrible, new meaning.

Ahab withholds his harpoon from the squid. He does not learn from this portent to stay his dart from Moby Dick's white side. Melville, we have seen, always adapted his whaling materials to the larger thematic and narrative necessities of the novel. The squid information is almost a complete transmutation; nowhere else are his sources more fully concealed. Here the hunt of parallel passages and borrowings is more like sparse gleaning. One may safely assume, however, that Melville relied in good part on the squid information in Beale and Bennett. In Melville's copy, Beale's chapter on the "Nature of the Sperm Whale's Food" is marked at several places. He needed the chapter, for information in accessible books was scarce; it was the longest and most informative essay on the squid which he could find outside the learned sources.

One particular trace of borrowing from Beale may be suspected. Admitting that the facts about the Sperm Whale's diet being the squid were inferential, Melville cited as fact that the whale in moments of excitement disgorged "what are supposed to be the detached arms of the squid; some of them being thus exhibited exceeding twenty and thirty feet in length." This is Melville's variation of Beale's statement that authorities had reported squid specimens ranging from eighteen to twenty-seven feet in length.

Beale assisted Melville in another traceable matter: the allusion to Bishop Pontoppidan's description of the kraken,[65] commonly supposed to be the giant squid. In *Moby-Dick* we read:

> There seems some ground to imagine that the great Kraken of Bishop Pontoppodan may ultimately resolve itself into Squid. The manner in which the Bishop describes it, as alternately rising and sinking [Melville's "undulating"], with

[65] In his poem "The Aeolian Harp" Melville again referred to the "kraken": "Overwashed by every wave / Like the slumbering kraken"; and in his letter to Hawthorne of November, 1851: "So, now, let us add Moby Dick to our blessing, and step from that. Leviathan is not the biggest fish; — I have heard of Krakens."

some other particulars he narrates, in all this the two correspond. But much abatement is necessary with respect to the incredible bulk he assigns to it.

But Beale's squid chapter was long, detailed, and really digressive, considering that his subject was the "Nature of the Sperm Whale's Food." At least it was digressive to Melville,[66] who rejected the very materials that his interested mind made him check. Melville was writing a whaling novel and not an essay for naturalists.

Bennett, too, served Melville well. When, for instance, we read in *Moby-Dick* that "By some naturalists who have vaguely heard rumors of the mysterious creature, here spoken of, it is included among the class of cuttle-fish, to which, indeed, in certain external respects it would seem to belong, but only as the Anak of the tribe."

We may know that the reference to "some naturalists" is probably to Bennett, who had written in *A Whaling Voyage*:

> Their ordinary food is the cuttle-fish, or "squid," . . . Amongst the examples thus rejected we find solid masses of enormous size and weight, though evidently but mere fragments of the body of some vast cuttle-fish, and probably of that kind termed the "gigantic squid" — an animal with which naturalists are but little acquainted; but which has been known to attain such huge dimensions, that, when spread out beneath the surface of the sea, it has alarmed navigators by its resemblance to a reef, or shoal.

Melville artfully changed the "shoal" or "reef" into Daggoo's mistaken identification of the squid with Moby Dick.

But neither Beale nor Bennett cared for the implications, the overtones, of their subject — the squid as a terror symbol, as an omen. This is Melville's artistic enlargement of zoological fact. The dietary information had its place, but to Melville it became really important when seen as another illus-

---

[66] One episode which Melville marked — along the margins of two pages — in Beale's book told of Beale's encounter with an octopus and his terror at the experience: "A sensation of horror pervaded my whole frame when I found this monstrous animal had affixed itself so firmly upon my arm. Its cold slimy grasp was extremely sickening." But Melville rejected the scene except for the terror connotations woven into his "Squid" chapter.

tration that the ocean's "most dreaded creatures glide under water for the most part, and treacherously hidden beneath the loveliest tints of azure." Melville's manipulation of Beale's and Bennett's pages bears out the truth of Emerson's dictum, "The poorest experience is rich enough for all the purposes of expressing thought," for out of prosing pages of scientific discourse, Melville's creative imagination brought forth the "Squid" chapter, instinct with the terrors of the deep, with what William James called "the vast slow-breathing unconscious Kosmos with its dread abysses and its unknown tides."

12

"The magical, sometimes horrible whale-line"

MELVILLE'S ACCOUNT of "The Line" (60) turns out, as we now might expect, to be both a clear description of the whale line and a metaphor. The whale line is a physical fact and a "linked analogy." The chapter is short, describing (*a*) the English whale line, (*b*) the American, (*c*) the whale line's use, and (*d*) the metaphorical extension of the physical object. Also, here is the first of another doublet, for as the author says in the opening paragraph, he mentions the whale line because of "the whaling scene shortly to be described, as well as for the better understanding of all similar scenes elsewhere presented." When we read the next chapter, we notice the emphasis given to the whale line, just as promised. We also recall "The Line" as we read the closing episode of Ahab's life, just as we will remember the line's "hempen intricacies" when we see the corpse of Fedallah entwined by the rope around Moby Dick's back. There is almost no expository fact in *Moby-Dick* which does not have some narrative or thematic function besides.

Beale and Bennett furnished Melville with information for his chapter. Although the description of the American manila rope, which had superseded the English hemp, was perhaps from Melville's memory — there is no description of one in the whaling books he used — nevertheless, for his description of the hemp rope Melville adapted the following passage from Bennett:

> The whale-line, provided for British South-Seamen, combines so completely the best qualities of cordage, that it may be regarded as the height of perfection in our rope manufacture. It is constructed of the best hemp, slightly but uniformly imbued by the vapour of tar; is two inches in circumference; and composed of three strands; each strand containing seventeen yarns, each of which is calculated to sustain the weight of one hundred and twelve pounds. Of this line, 220 fathoms is the ordinary complement of each boat. It is coiled, continuously, in two tubs, and in neat and compact horizontal layers, or "sheaves," each extremity of the line being kept exposed, the one for attachment to the harpoons, the other (which is provided with a loop, or "splice,") for connecting it to the line of a second boat, should any probability arise that its entire length would be taken out by the whale.
>
> When ready for running, the commencement of the line is passed over the logger-head at the stern, and thence forward, over the oars, to be fastened to the harpoons in the bow; about fifteen fathoms, termed "box-line," being kept coiled in the head, or box, of the boat, to accompany the harpoon when it is first darted. At the spot where the box-line commences, a mark, commonly a piece of red cloth, is attached, to enable the whaler to judge at what distance the boat may be from the harpoon, and consequently from the whale, when the sea is turbid with blood.

Melville's enrichment and vivification of Bennett's description is an illustration of expository writing at its best. Memory as well as imagination have been added to the "source" passage:

> The line originally used in the fishery was of the best hemp, slightly vapored with tar, not impregnated with it, as in the case of ordinary ropes; for while tar, as ordinarily used, makes the hemp more pliable to the rope-maker, and also renders the rope itself more convenient to the sailor for common ship use; yet, not only would the ordinary quantity too much stiffen the whale-line for the close coiling to which it must be subjected;

but as most seamen are beginning to learn, tar in general by no means adds to the rope's durability or strength, however much it may give it compactness and gloss.

Of late years the Manilla rope has in the American fishery almost entirely superseded hemp as a material for whale-lines; for, though not so durable as hemp, it is stronger, and far more soft and elastic; and I will add (since there is an aesthetics in all things), is much more handsome and becoming to the boat, than hemp. Hemp is a dusky, dark fellow, a sort of Indian; but Manilla is as a golden-haired Circassian to behold.

The whale-line is only two thirds of an inch in thickness. At first sight, you would not think it so strong as it really is. By experiment its one and fifty yarns will each suspend a weight of one hundred and twenty pounds; so that the whole rope will bear a strain nearly equal to three tons. In length, the common sperm whale-line measures something over two hundred fathoms. Towards the stern of the boat it is spirally coiled away in the tub, not like the worm-pipe of a still though, but so as to form one round, cheese-shaped mass of densely bedded "sheaves," or layers of concentric spiralizations, without any hollow but the "heart," or minute vertical tube formed at the axis of the cheese. As the least tangle or kink in the coiling would, in running out, infallibly take somebody's arm, leg, or entire body off, the utmost precaution is used in stowing the line in its tub. Some harpooneers will consume almost an entire morning in this business, carrying the line high aloft and then reeving it downwards through a block towards the tub, so as in the act of coiling to free it from all possible wrinkles and twists.

In the English boats two tubs are used instead of one; the same line being continuously coiled in both tubs. There is some advantage in this; because these twin-tubs being so small they fit more readily into the boat, and do not strain it so much; whereas, the American tub, nearly three feet in diameter and of proportionate depth, makes a rather bulky freight for a craft whose planks are but one-half inch in thickness; for the bottom of the whale-boat is like critical ice, which will bear up a considerable distributed weight, but not very much of a concentrated one. When the painted canvas cover is clapped on the American tub-line, the boat looks as if it were pulling off with a prodigious great wedding-cake to present to the whales.

Both ends of the line are exposed; the lower end terminating in an eye-splice or loop coming up from the bottom against the side of the tub, and hanging over its edge completely disengaged from everything. This arrangement of the lower end is necessary on two accounts. First: In order to facilitate the fastening to it of an additional line from a neighboring boat, in case the stricken whale should sound so deep as to threaten to carry off the entire line originally attached to the harpoon. In these instances, the whale of course is shifted like a mug of ale, as it were, from the one boat to the other; though the first boat always hovers at hand to assist its consort. Second: This arrangement is indispensable for common safety's sake; for were the lower end of the line in any way attached to the boat, and were the whale then to run the line out to the end almost in a single, smoking minute as he sometimes does, he would not stop there, for the doomed boat would infallibly be dragged down after him into the profundity of the sea; and in that case no town-crier would ever find her again.

Before lowering the boat for the chase, the upper end of the line is taken aft from the tub, and passing round the logger-head there, is again carried forward the entire length of the boat, resting crosswise upon the loom or handle of every man's oar, so that it jogs against his wrist in rowing; and also passing between the men, as they alternately sit at the opposite gunwales, to the leaded chocks or grooves in the extreme pointed prow of the boat, where a wooden pin or skewer the size of a common quill, prevents it from slipping out. From the chocks it hangs in a slight festoon over the bows, and is then passed inside the boat again; and some ten or twenty fathoms (called box-line) being coiled upon the box in the bows, it continues its way to the gunwale still a little further aft, and is then attached to the short-warp — the rope which is immediately connected with the harpoon; but previous to that connexion, the short-warp goes through sundry mystifications too tedious to detail.

But what gives the chapter importance is Melville's metaphor of the whale line as one of the dangers threatening all men, death being ready to seize suddenly any one of us even as the loop of the whale line seizes the whaleman — even, as we are to find, Ahab. Melville comes out into the open with his point, with an ironic and unexpected twist in the last sentence:

All men live enveloped in whale-lines. All are born with halters round their necks; but it is only when caught in the swift, sudden turn of death, that mortals realize the silent, subtle, ever-present perils of life. And if you be a philosopher, though seated in the whale-boat, you would not at heart feel one whit more of terror, than though seated before your evening fire with a poker, and not a harpoon, by your side.

As if especially to illustrate the place of the whale line in the industry, Melville's succeeding chapter, "Stubb Kills a Whale" (61) dramatizes again the hunt for the Sperm Whale. We see, of course, the whale line whizzing through the chocks, terrifyingly hinting of sudden death to each member of the boat crew. But the scene is much larger than mere illustration for the previous exposition; it is an exciting piece of narrative. As he tells his story, Melville holds in mind the expository necessities. Since he wishes to keep the dramatic struggle moving without pause, however, he put the expository addition in two footnotes. The first footnote discusses the "head out" progress of the whale, and is little but Beale's original description, simplified, embellished by a simile or so. Melville had made a long marginal mark beside Beale's account of the Sperm Whale's head, and a few paragraphs later he read:

One of the peculiarities of the sperm whale, which strikes at first every beholder, is the apparently disproportionate and unwieldy bulk of the head; but this peculiarity, instead of being, as might be supposed, an impediment to the freedom of the animal's motion in his native element, is, in fact, on the contrary in some respects very conducive to his lightness and agility, if such a term can with propriety be applied to such an enormous creature; for a great part of the bulk of the head is made up of a large thin membranous case, containing, during life, a thin oil of much less specific gravity than water; below which again is the junk, which, although heavier than the spermaceti, is still lighter than the element in which the whale moves; consequently the head taken as a whole, is lighter specifically than any other part of the body, and will always have a tendency to rise at least so far above the surface as to elevate the nostril or "blowhole" sufficiently for all purposes of respiration, and more than this, a very slight effort on the part of the fish would only be necessary to raise the whole of the anterior flat surface of the nose out of the water; in case the animal should wish to increase his speed to the utmost, the narrow inferior surface, which has been before stated to bear some resemblance to the cutwater of a ship, and which would in fact answer the same purpose to the whale, would be the only part exposed to the pressure of the water in front, enabling him thus to pass with the greatest celerity and ease through the boundless track of his wide domain.

Melville compressed this to one succinct footnote:

It will be seen in some other place of what a very light substance the entire interior of the sperm whale's enormous head consists. Though apparently the most massive, it is by far the most buoyant part about him. So that with ease he elevates it in the air, and invariably does so when going at his utmost speed. Besides, such is the breadth of the upper part of the front of the head, and such the tapering cut-water formation of the lower part, that by obliquely elevating his head, he thereby may be said to transform himself from a bluff-bowed sluggish galliot into a sharp-pointed New York pilot-boat.

The other footnote, explaining why water was poured over the loggerhead, said: "in the old Dutch fishery, a mop was used to dash the running line with water," a bit of information which Melville had found in Scoresby's *Arctic Regions*.

But the main part of the chapter would seem to have been written straight from imagination unhampered by sources. To the contrary. It would be tedious to attempt to show in detail just how Melville made use of his fish documents in building up his narrative of Stubb's pursuit of a sperm whale; having already shown the process at length in the discussion of "The First Lowering," it can merely be stated that Melville's narrative is a blend of an episode from Browne's *Etchings of a Whaling Cruise,* Beale's *Natural History of the Sperm Whale* (of a passage which Melville checked and on which he wrote two marginal comments, now erased and unreadable), and his own aroused imagination and skillful pen.

13

"A meat-pie nearly one hundred feet long"

AFTER STUBB'S WHALE has been hauled wearily to the side of the *Pequod* and chained there, Stubb impulsively longs to eat some whale meat. He orders the colored cook [67] to prepare a whale steak for his supper on deck. When the steak is cooked, Stubb chews appreciatively on the meat, and while he smacks his lips loudly, the sharks snap even more loudly at the whale chained alongside. Stubb's banquet and the sharks' feast are ironic commentaries on each other, a grotesque antiphonal. At first Stubb pays no attention to the monsters below, but finally he is disturbed by their noise, and he orders the cook to tell the sharks that "they are welcome to help themselves civilly, and in moderation, but they must keep quiet." Lantern in hand, the old darkey leans far over the rail to admonish the sharks. He tells them to stop "dat noise . . . dat dam smackin' ob de lip!" Pretending to be shocked at such language Stubb orders the cook to "talk to 'em gentlemanly." In more controlled phrases the sermon — for such it proves to be — continues. "You is sharks, sartin; but if you gobern de shark in you, why den you be angel; for all angel is not'ing more dan de shark well goberned." Such sound advice follows that Stubb cries out, "Well done, old Fleece, that's Christianity," but the sermon changes to Stubb's catechism of the cook upon the fate of his soul, and with a final benediction — profane and remarkable — the episode closes.

Stubb's supper, a wild scene, is pertinent and meaningful. Melville's wild passages are never uncontrolled, nor are they included as mere ornament or filigree. Melville was not a literary Rossini or Von Suppé. His violence is incremental. Even in moments of extravagance, his novel moves forward. The cook's comment on Stubb, "I'm bressed if he ain't more

---

[67] Perhaps a development from the cook on the *Acushnet*, with maybe a suggestion from Bennett's cook: "a greater grumbler, or a more disagreeable animal, I never had the misfortune to meet."

of shark dan Massa Shark hisself," — a "sage ejaculation" says Melville — shrewdly tickets the episode. The gluttony of the sharks (obvious symbols of heedless cruelty) parallels Stubb's gluttony for whalemeat. Dog eat dog. While the cook preaches on the Golden Rule to the sharks, Stubb pays no attention to its meaning to himself. The sermon comes from lips parroting a message uncomprehended, and is addressed to creatures, human and marine, equally uncomprehending. If you have never seen sharks devouring a dead sperm whale by night, "then suspend your decision about the propriety of devil-worship, and the expediency of conciliating the devil." But, says Melville, the vulturism of the world is not confined to unhuman beings alone. Stubb with all his gluttonous brutality is a revelation of the evil at the heart of man.

Strangely, Melville places the cook's sermon so that it recalls Father Mapple's sermon to the whalemen of the Seaman's Bethel. The cook's sermon is the anti-masque (always satiric and parodic) to the masque (lyric and serious). And though placed in a whaling setting graphic and concrete, on the boards of the *Pequod*, the ship is the world even as the Seamen's Bethel is a part of the world.

By a perfectly natural turn, the author then discusses the whale as an article of food. Again Melville follows his practice of the two-chapter presentation of a subject, each chapter with a different approach to the topic. "The Whale as a Dish" (65) is the expository accompaniment to the dramatic "Stubb's Supper" (64).

It may not have been Scoresby's statement, including as it does the suggestive word "banquet," "but a dead whale is an easy prey, and affords a fine banquet to this insatiable [shark] creature," which had led Melville to compose "Stubb's Supper"; but it was certainly Scoresby's information which helped Melville considerably in compiling "The Whale as a Dish."

Scoresby's statement that "the flesh, and particularly the tongue, was publicly sold in the markets of Bayonne, Cibourne, and Beariz, and that it was esteemed a great delicacy" led Melville to write: "It is upon record, that three centuries ago the tongue of the Right Whale was esteemed a great delicacy in France, and commanded large prices there." [68] But Melville's third paragraph shows his imagination not only taking over material but secretly satirizing the material in the transfer. Pointing out that "a meat-pie nearly one hundred feet long" must take away the appetite of most people, Melville wrote:

> Only the most unprejudiced of men like Stubb, nowadays partake of cooked whales; but the Esquimaux are not so fastidious. We all know how they live upon whales, and have rare old vintages of prime old train oil. Zogranda, one of their most famous doctors, recommends strips of blubber for infants, as being exceedingly juicy and nourishing.

In the person of old Zogranda, the doctor, Melville satirized William Scoresby, Jr., authority on Esquimau life, who had described — not "recommended" — the eating habits of the Esquimaux:

> The Esquimaux eat the flesh and the fat of the whale, and drink the oil with greediness. Indeed, some tribes who are not familiarized with spirituous liquors, carry along with them in their canoes in their fishing excursions, bladders filled with oil, which they use in the same way, and with a similar relish, that a British sailor does a dram. They also eat the skin of the whale raw, both adults and children; for it is not uncommon, when the females visit the whale-ships, for them to help themselves to pieces of skin, preferring those with which a little blubber is connected, and to give it as food to their infants, who suck it with apparent delight.

Scoresby has been translated to Captain Sleet and to Zogranda; he will suffer further transformation. To Scoresby Melville might have murmured the lines about Doctor Fell.

The next whale dish mentioned was sperm whale's brains.

---

[68] Since the above was written, Willard Thorp's edition of *Moby-Dick* (New York: Oxford University Press, 1947) has appeared. In a footnote on p. 282 he suggests that "The porpoise sauce and the grant to the monks of Dunfermline, Melville probably found in Sir Robert Sibbald's *History . . . of Fife and Kinross,* Cuparfife, 1803, p. 116, n. 1." He also suggests, and rightly, that Zogranda is a misspelling of the name of Dr. Sangrade from Le Sage's *Gil Blas.*

Browne, and not Scoresby, was Melville's informant. Describing the trying-out process, Browne, in *Etchings of a Whaling Cruise,* told of the crew feasting on the whale being tried:

> About the middle of the watch they get up the bread kid, and, after dipping a few biscuits in salt water, heave them into a strainer, and boil them in the oil. It is difficult to form any idea of the luxury of this delicious mode of cooking on a long watch-night. Sometimes, when on friendly terms with the steward, they make fritters of the brains of the whale mixed with flour, and cook them in the oil. These are considered a most sumptuous delicacy. Certain portions of the whale's flesh are also eaten with relish, though, to my thinking, not a very great luxury, being coarse and strong.

Melville changed Browne's paragraph to serve as information and satire:

> In the case of a small Sperm Whale the brains are accounted a fine dish. The casket of the skull is broken into with an axe, and the two plump, whitish lobes being withdrawn (precisely resembling two large puddings), they are then mixed with flour, and cooked into a most delectable mess, in flavor somewhat resembling calves' head, which is quite a dish among some epicures; and every one knows that some young bucks among the epicures, by continually dining upon calves' brains, by and by get to have a little brains of their own, so as to be able to tell a calf's head from their own heads; which, indeed, requires uncommon discrimination. And that is the reason why a young buck with an intelligent looking calf's head before him, is somehow one of the saddest sights you can see. The head looks a [*sic*] sort of reproachfully at him, with an "Et tu Brute!" expression.

Whether or not Melville's satire is, as Anderson suggests, "a sly thrust at the epicure of 1841," it is a slyly humorous dig at the fish-eat-fish behavior of mankind which Melville had just satirized in the cook's sermon to the sharks. "Cannibals? who is not a cannibal?" Melville asks facetiously in this chapter, a question which he had considered at length and with understanding in *Typee* and *Mardi.* But Stubb was even worse than a normal cannibal, for "Stubb, he eats the whale by its own light, does he? and that is adding insult to injury, is it?" And with this mocking tone the two food chapters come to their amusing conclusion.[69]

14

"And thus the work proceeds"

IN THE MAIN, chapters 66 to 72 constitute a single group dealing with the problems of cutting up the whale and storing the blubber. The various steps are described in faithful detail, but in general these chapters are the best answer to those people objecting to the cetological center as being "nothing but whaling." Melville describes harsh and grim whaling work, to be sure, but if one will read the descriptions of the same process in Browne, Beale, and Bennett, one will see how significant are Melville's. Melville's superiority is not merely of information, but also of sheer descriptive power, to begin with. For example, "Cutting In" (67), almost unique in *Moby-Dick* as a chapter of pure exposition unaccompanied by humorous or metaphysical ornamentation, tells about the simple process of flensing the whale. Here again it is undoubtedly true that Melville was not unmindful of his fish documents. His copy of Beale shows this; the fourteenth chapter, "Of the 'Cutting In' and 'Trying Out,' " is well marked although, unfortunately, the markings and the marginal comments have been erased. He checked such a passage in Beale:

69 Melville far from exhausted the subject of "The Whale as a Dish." Even today in parts of this starving world whale meat is in demand, as it was during World War I. Whale meat is a substitute for low-grade beef; it is quite nutritious, containing over thirty per cent protein, six per cent fat, and less than two per cent ash. For the United States Bureau of Fisheries, Lewis Radcliffe edited a ten-page circular, *Whales and Porpoises as Food* (With thirty-two recipes furnished by American Pacific Whaling Co.; Mrs. Evelene Spencer; Delmonico; chef, Palace Hotel, San Francisco; Mrs. Henry B. Ward; chef, Nueces Hotel, Corpus Christi; Victory Kitchen, San Antonio; Gedney's restaurant, San Marcos; and Mrs. Charles S. Smith). Washington, 1918. See also George L. Sparks, ["Porpoise as Food"] *Bulletin of the United States Bureau of Fisheries,* V (1885), 215.

After the hook is inserted it is drawn upon by the pullies to which it is attached, and a tension being exerted upon the fat, or blubber as it is termed, it is then cut by the spade in a strip about two or three feet broad, in a spiral direction around the body of the whale, which being drawn up by means of the windlass acting upon pullies which are fixed to the "main-top," it is removed much in the same way that a spiral roller or bandage might be; of course, as the "blanket pieces" ascend, the body of the whale performs a rotary motion, until the whole is stripped off to the tail or flukes.

And he also had read, and remembered, the following from Bennett:

The windlass being put in motion, the blubber is raised and put on the stretch when its separation from the carcase being assisted by the spades, and the whale at the same time revolving slowly in the water, it is peeled off in a spiral direction, or as the rind from an apple, and in one continuous sheet about four feet in breadth; but as the elevation of the cutting-falls does not permit a "blanket-piece" higher than the main-mast to be received on board at one time, the sheet, when it has attained that height, is divided, and lowered down the main-hatchway into a room set apart for its reception, whilst a second set of pulleys raises a piece of similar size.

And possibly Melville recalled Browne's description, especially the words, "the blanket-pieces are stripped off in a spiral direction, running down towards the flukes; the whale turning at every heave of the windlass," but all of these descriptions do not add up to Melville's powerful description. His graphic imagination has seized wanted details, incorporating with them memories from *Acushnet* days, so that we see the cutting tackles as "this vast bunch of grapes," the hawserlike rope twisting and winding about, the enormous blubber hook; and we feel every step in the process, our muscles adjust to the tipping ship, our eyes see the toiling sailors and our ears hear their wild chantey, as image illuminates fact, as fact is made metaphor. For instance, in grasping the sensory vividness of such words as: —

More and more she leans over to the whale, while every gasping heave of the windlass is answered by a helping heave from the billows; till at last, a swift, startling snap is heard; with a great swash the ship rolls upwards and backwards from the whale, and the triumphant tackle rises into sight dragging after it the disengaged semicircular end of the first strip of blubber. Now as the blubber envelopes the whale precisely as the rind does an orange, so it is stripped off from the body precisely as an orange is sometimes stripped by spiralizing it. For the strain constantly kept up by the windlass continually keeps the whale rolling over and over in the water, and as the blubber in one strip uniformly peels off along the line called the "scarf," simultaneously cut by the spades of Starbuck and Stubb, the mates; and just as fast as it is thus peeled off, and indeed by that very act itself, it is all the time being hoisted higher and higher aloft till its upper end grazes the main-top; the men at the windlass then cease heaving, and for a moment or two the prodigious blood-dripping mass sways to and fro as if let down from the sky, and every one present must take good heed to dodge it when it swings, else it may box his ears and pitch him headlong overboard.[70]

— we realize the difference between the concrete imagination of genius and the workmanlike competence of the naturalists. Nowhere in literature has a process been described more memorably than in "Cutting In."

In "The Blanket" (68) Melville's imagination continued to describe harsh details both read about and remembered. "I have given no small attention to that not unvexed subject, the skin of the whale," he says, but he found the answers to the problem in Beale and Bennett especially. The skin of the whale is his blubber, he concluded, as though there were another point of view. Perhaps there was, for he had read in Scoresby: "The skin of the body is slightly furrowed, like the water-lines in coarse laid paper. . . . The cuticle, or that part of the skin which can be pulled off in sheets after it has

---

[70] See the excellent photographs of the process in *Cutting in a Whale*. A series of twenty-five photographs taken on board the bark *California* (New Bedford, 1903), or the photographs reproduced in Albert Cook Church, *Whale Ships and Whaling* (New York, 1938). This second book, and George Francis Dow, *Whale Ships and Whaling, A Pictorial History of Whaling During Three Centuries* (Salem, 1925); and Clifford W. Ashley, *The Yankee Whaler* (Garden City, New York, 1942), are the indispensable pictorial books on all phases of whaling life.

been a little dried in the air, or particularly in frost, is not thicker than parchment." This skin, Melville says in a long paragraph (he does not use Scoresby's words), is really only "as the skin of the skin, so to speak; for it were simply ridiculous to say, that the proper skin of the tremendous whale is thinner and more tender than the skin of a new-born child." Even though this statement contradicts Scoresby and Bennett,[71] nevertheless Melville had the authority of Beale, who quoted a Professor Jacob of Dublin in a passage which Melville marked: " . . . that structure in which the oil is deposited, denominated blubber, is the true skin of the animal, modified certainly for the purpose of holding this fluid oil, but still being the true skin."

Melville accepted the authority of this statement and for him the blubber was the skin of the whale. But the paragraphs which he extends from this definition are from a pictorial imagination. On the skin are numberless straight marks and scratches which remind Melville variously of Italian line engravings (Melville was always interested in art), of "the famous hieroglyphic palisades on the banks of the Upper Mississippi" (near Galena, where Melville visited in 1840), or of the glacial scrapings on certain New England rocks noted by Agassiz. This blubber-skin is like an Indian poncho slipped over the head, it is a counterpane, a blanket — Melville thought ever in metaphors. And finally, in characteristic manner, he moralized:

> It does seem to me, that herein we see the rare virtue of a strong individual vitality, and the rare virtue of thick walls, and the rare virtue of interior spaciousness. Oh, man! admire and model thyself after the whale! Do thou, too, remain warm

71 Bennett wrote: "The essential parts which compose the integuments are the same as in quadrupeds. The *epidermis,* or scarf-skin, is exceedingly delicate; being no thicker than the membrane known as 'gold-beaters'-skin. It is transparent, of a pale-brown colour, and, after the death of the whale, is easily detached from the body.

"Beneath this covering is a thick layer of colouring matter, or *rete mucosum,* (the 'black-skin' of whalers,). . . . When exposed to the air, its surface hardens, becomes polished, and may be repeatedly peeled off in sheets, which are sometimes preserved by sailors and exhibited as the 'skin of the whale.' "

among ice. Do thou, too, live in this world without being of it. Be cool at the equator; keep thy blood fluid at the Pole. Like the great dome of St. Peter's, and like the great whale, retain, O man! in all seasons a temperature of thine own.

Such a passage defensive of individualism should be remembered when we observe Melville's attack upon false individualism, as revealed in Ahab, or when we see Melville's stress upon the social norm. As Melville added to his moralizing: "But how easy and how hopeless to teach these fine things."

"The Funeral" (69) continues, or should conclude, the process of flensing the blubber from the whale. The carcass is unchained from the ship, to float away, "the water round it torn and splashed by the insatiate sharks, and the air above vexed with rapacious flights of screaming fowls, whose beaks are like so many insulting poniards in the whale." The whale "floats on and on, till lost in infinite perspectives." Fact has become tremulous with implication through the infinite perspectives with which Melville's mind saw a mere fish carcass. J. Ross Browne was satisfied to write — and it was sufficient for straight exposition — "The carcass of the whale, when stripped of its blubber, is cast loose, and soon sinks from the want of its buoyant covering. I have seen it float astern, however, some distance without sinking," but this was but Melville's springboard. What Browne's limited eyes saw differed from Melville's vision:

There's a most doleful and most mocking funeral! The sea-vultures all in pious mourning, the air-sharks all punctiliously in black or speckled. In life but few of them would have helped the whale, I ween, if peradventure he had needed it; but upon the banquet of his funeral they most piously do pounce. Oh, horrible vultureism of earth! from which not the mightiest whale is free.

Melville's lines are concentrated in evocative power. His reiteration of "most," the paradox of sea vultures and air sharks, and the deliberate use of archaic words like "ween" and "peradventure," all reinforce the Hamletian insight. "Nor is this the end," Melville says:

Desecrated as the body is, a vengeful ghost survives and hovers over it to scare. Espied by some timid man-of-war or blundering discovery-vessel from afar, when the distance obscuring the swarming fowls, nevertheless still shows the white mass floating in the sun, and the white spray heaving high against it; straightway the whale's unharming corpse, with trembling fingers is set down in the log — *shoals, rocks, and breakers hereabouts: beware!* And for years afterwards, perhaps, ships shun the place; leaping over it as silly sheep leap over a vacuum, because their leader originally leaped there when a stick was held. There's your law of precedents; there's your utility of traditions; there's the story of your obstinate survival of old beliefs never bottomed on the earth, and now not even hovering in the air! There's orthodoxy!

There indeed, but it takes a relating and penetrating mind to elaborate a simple physical fact into a profound metaphor. Sedgwick says that this "passage contains the spectrum of the book, of which it is so small a particle." He is right (except that other particles in *Moby-Dick* do likewise; as Lewis Mumford showed, "The Doubloon" is equally a spectrum). But it is this continual awareness of spiritual and intellectual relationships which gives *Moby-Dick* its vastness. The whale is an enormous animal not only because he is sensed as the symbol of infinite distances and immeasurable depths. It is no accident that in the next chapter occurs the famous sentence, "O Nature, and O soul of man! how far beyond all utterance are your linked analogies; not the smallest atom stirs or lives in matter, but has its cunning duplicate in mind." Not Browne's mind, nor Beale's, nor Bennett's, nor Cheever's, nor Scoresby's — but in the poet's mind: Aeschylus, Dante, Shakespeare, and Melville.

"The *Jeroboam's* Story" (71) [72] is a strange and disturbing episode which brings us back to the main stem of the story: the hunt for Moby Dick. The *Pequod* encounters the *Jeroboam* of Nantucket. Under the control of wild Gabriel

[72] I skip over "The Sphynx" (70), except to wonder what was Melville's inspiration for writing what is one of the most beautiful and poetic sentences in all of his work: "An intense copper calm, like a universal yellow lotus, was more and more unfolding its noiseless measureless leaves upon the sea."

("He had been originally nurtured among the crazy society of Neskyeuna Shakers, where he had been a great prophet"), the crew believed him a prophet, and took his cracked ravings seriously. He warns Ahab against the pursuit of the White Whale, "pronouncing the White Whale to be no less a being than the Shaker God incarnated." The *Jeroboam* incident is an omen to which Ahab pays no attention.

The Prophet Gabriel is of course from Melville's familiarity with Shakers, both in the Watervliet colony near Albany, and in the colony near Pittsfield. The whaling documents, however, furnished one part of the chapter. When the *Jeroboam's* men were in the boats pursuing Moby Dick, one of the men was destroyed by the flukes of the great whale. Melville tells the story:

> Now, while Macey, the mate, was standing up in his boat's bow, and with all the reckless energy of his tribe was venting his wild exclamations upon the whale, and essaying to get a fair chance for his poised lance, lo! a broad white shadow rose from the sea; by its quick, fanning motion, temporarily taking the breath out of the bodies of the oarsmen. Next instant, the luckless mate, so full of furious life, was smitten bodily into the air, and making a long arc in his descent, fell into the sea at the distance of about fifty yards. Not a chip of the boat was harmed, nor a hair of any oarsman's head; but the mate for ever sank.

The entire episode was taken from Bennett's *A Whaling Voyage Round the Globe*:

> The boats were close together, and Captain Stavers had but just remarked to his mate, that as the whale was nearly dead he would leave him to complete its destruction whilst he harpooned the loose Cachalot, when the tail of the latter passed, with the rapidity of lightning, over, and in front of his boat, and simultaneously, Mr. Young, though a large and strong man, was seen flying through the air at a considerable height, and to the distance of nearly forty yards from the boat, ere he fell into the water, where he remained floating motionless on the surface for a few moments, then sank, and was seen no more. There can be no doubt that his death was instantaneous. A native of the Society Islands plunged into the water imme-

diately the accident occurred, and endeavored to save the body of his unfortunate officer, but it had sunk before he could swim to the spot where it fell. No injury was sustained by any other person in the boat; nor was the boat itself injured, beyond a portion of the bow being broken off, and the thigh-board, which was torn from its place and accompanied the body of the unfortunate mate, so powerful was the impulse it had received.

It will be seen, however, that Melville changed Bennett's story but slightly — to have the boat completely unharmed — but he added further information which showed how completely he wanted to use Bennett's information on the perils of the whaling industry. Melville wrote:

It is well to parenthesize here, that of the fatal accidents in the Sperm-Whale Fishery, this kind is perhaps almost as frequent as any.[73] Sometimes, nothing is injured but the man who is thus annihilated; oftener the boat's bow is knocked off, or the thigh-board, in which the headsman stands, is torn from its place and accompanies the body. But strangest of all is the circumstance, that in more instances than one, when the body has been recovered, not a single mark of violence is discernible; the man being stark dead.

The last bit of information Melville took from Bennett's account of a man flipped from a boat by the whale's flukes: "his body floated on the water, and was immediately rescued and conveyed to the ship; but, although no external marks of injury were any where visible, all attempts to restore animation were of no avail, for life was totally extinct."

The final chapter in the essay on cutting up the whale, is "The Monkey-Rope (72). Melville must backtrack. A description of the comings and goings of the crew necessitates this sort of technique; as he says: "There is no staying in any one place; for at one and the same time everything has

---

[73] Cp. Bennett: " . . . but human life is chiefly endangered when the tail of the animal is swept rapidly through the air, and either descends upon the boat, cutting it down to the water's edge, or encounters in its *trajet* some of the crew standing up, as the headsman, or harpooner, who are destroyed and carried away by the blow; and this last is the most common, as well as the most sudden and awful calamity in the fishery."

to be done everywhere. It is much the same with him who endeavors the description of the scene. We must now retrace our way a little." He tells how Queequeg dexterously descends to the slippery, rolling whale and inserts the blubber hook in the hole previously cut by the spade. Having made the insertion, Queequeg on occasion had to stay down there:

> But in very many cases, circumstances require that the harpooneer shall remain on the whale till the whole flensing or stripping operation is concluded. The whale, be it observed, lies almost entirely submerged, excepting the immediate parts operated upon. So down there, some ten feet below the level of the deck, the poor harpooneer flounders about, half on the whale and half in the water, as the vast mass revolves like a tread-mill beneath him. . . . You have seen Italian organ-boys holding a dancing-ape by a long cord. Just so, from the ship's steep side, did I hold Queequeg down there in the sea, by what is technically called in the fishery a monkey-rope, attached to a strong strip of canvas belted round his waist.
>
> It was a humorously perilous business for both of us. For, before we proceed further, it must be said that the monkey-rope was fast at both ends; fast to Queequeg's broad canvas belt, and fast to my narrow leather one. So that for better or for worse, we two, for the time, were wedded; and should poor Queequeg sink to rise no more, then both usage and honor demanded, that instead of cutting the cord, it should drag me down in his wake. So, then, an elongated Siamese ligature united us.[74] Queequeg was my own inseparable brother; nor could I any way get rid of the dangerous liabilities which the hempen bond entailed.

Keeping this in mind (along with a later paragraph in which Queequeg's peril from the cutting spades and from the sharks is vividly depicted), one might well imagine that Melville developed his scene from Olmsted's description of the monkey rope.[75] Melville's old memories were stirred. Olmsted wrote:

[74] A favorite allusion of Melville's.

[75] Although the monkey rope was standard protection in the whale fishery so that Melville's mind was probably jogged rather than informed in reading Olmsted.

To point the hook into the orifice made for it, one of the boatsteerers, having upon his feet a pair of woollen stockings to prevent his slipping, jumps overboard, guarded by a rope passing under his arms, and tended by one of the men upon deck. It is no very easy matter to introduce the hook into the proper place, while the sea is dashing the whale against the ship and the waves are breaking over him; so that a man runs the risk of being strangled, or of being bruised by the concussion of the animal with the vessel. The danger of being horribly mutilated by the sharks that assemble in great numbers during the "cutting in," attracted by the scent of blood, is by no means inconsiderable. They are so voracious that notwithstanding the deep gashes they receive from the cutting spades, they rush upon the whale, and tear off large masses of blubber with their formidable jaws. Several times I trembled for the safety of the man who was endeavoring to fix the blubber hook into the proper place, as a large shark came up within a few inches of his leg, and once I thrilled with horror as one of the ravenous monsters turned over in the attitude of one seizing one of his limbs in his terrible teeth; but at this moment a pull upon the rope extricated the man from his perilous situation.

Whether Melville consciously "used" Olmsted's description of the life-saving rope is not of very great importance. What is more to the point is that Melville did not describe the experience in the same way Olmsted did. The experience in Melville gains secondary and tertiary significance. It reverberates. It recalls the close friendship between Queequeg and Ishmael in the Spouter Inn. The monkey rope (the metaphor is no doubt Melville's — it is nowhere in the fish documents) becomes a superb symbol of human brotherhood:

So strongly and metaphysically did I conceive of my situation then, that while earnestly watching his motions, I seemed distinctly to perceive that my own individuality was now merged in a joint stock company of two: that my free will had received a mortal wound; and that another's mistake or misfortune might plunge innocent me into unmerited disaster and death. Therefore, I saw that here was a sort of interregnum in Providence; for its even-handed equity never could have sanctioned so gross an injustice. And yet still further pondering — while I jerked him now and then from between the whale and the ship, which would threaten to jam him — still further pondering, I say, I saw that this situation of mine was the precise situation of every mortal that breathes; only, in most cases, he, one way or other, has this Siamese connexion with a plurality of mortals. If your banker breaks, you snap; if your apothecary by mistake sends you poison in your pills, you die.

Ishmael has previously pondered the question of free will — as he and Queequeg wove the mat — and now, further into the problem, he perceives that free will is a relative term in a social world. And Ishmael looks on Queequeg as a symbol, too, saying: "Are you not the precious image of each and all of us men in this whaling world? That unsounded ocean you gasp in, is Life; those sharks, your foes; those spades, your friends; and what between sharks and spades you are in a sad pickle and peril, poor lad."

Melville's most profoundly *human* comprehensions of life may be found at those few and precious episodes when Ishmael and Queequeg are together. One of the tragedies of Melville's own life was that he never found a Queequeg for companionship, or that when he did, Hawthorne was forced by circumstances to move elsewhere.

15

"Laying their heads together"

Beginning with the seventy-third chapter, "Stubb and Flask kill a Right Whale; and Then Have a Talk Over Him," Melville composed an eight-chapter section which an anthologist might gather under the supplied title, "Craniological and Spinal Considerations Touching Whales." These eight chapters deal precisely with what their specific titles and the suggested unifying title indicate: the cranial features of Right

Whales and Sperm Whales. It would not be *Moby-Dick,* however, had not the author used physical facts, drawn largely from the fish documents, for the purposes of humor, satire, and metaphysics. Melville composed a jigsaw group out of anatomy, zoology, general whaling lore, nineteenth-century phrenology, and the Platonic concept of the One. Only cabbages and kings are omitted. Disconnected as these subjects might seem to be, they are unified by the meta-physical theme of *Moby-Dick,* and particularly by the ceto-logical fact now before us: two whale heads in equipoise sus-pended on the *Pequod.* Nor is any of this material inorganic; it all relates to Ahab's search for the White Whale.

The Sperm Whale having been cut up, the main part of the carcass had been released to float away, food for the sharks and a delusion to foolish navigators who, seeing it from a distance, log the sight as shoals and reefs to be placed on a chart. Thus, Melville implies, Man records error if he is unable to comprehend the show of things.

But the *Pequod* tilts perilously with the Sperm Whale's head chained on one side:

> It must be borne in mind that all this time we have a Sperm Whale's prodigious head hanging to the Pequod's side. But we must let it continue hanging there a while till we can get a chance to attend to it. For the present other matters press, and the best we can do now for the head, is to pray heaven the tackles may hold.

Is Melville indirectly saying in the last sentence, "I have a number of side matters requiring consideration so that I must interrupt my story, but I trust that this temporary abandonment of my main narrative won't strain too greatly the attention of the reader"?

As any writer knows, nothing is more effective in descrip-tion than a well-sustained comparison between two objects similar in kind but different in appearance. It is the "Look on this picture, then on that" device employed in *Hamlet*; it is the "Before and After" technique of the advertising man. Any whaling writer describing the head of the Sperm Whale could do so most graphically by contrasting it with that of the Right Whale. In formally placing the two heads against each other —

> Of the grand order of folio leviathans, the Sperm Whale and the Right Whale are by far the most noteworthy. They are the only whales regularly hunted by man. To the Nantucketer, they present the two extremes of all the known varieties of the whale. As the external difference between them is mainly observable in their heads; and as a head of each is at this moment hanging from the Pequod's side; and as we may freely go from one to the other, by merely stepping across the deck: — where, I should like to know, will you obtain a better chance to study practical cetology than here?

— Melville had undoubtedly been influenced by Beale's similar method and statement: "It is in this shape of the head that the sperm whale differs in the most remarkable degree from the Greenland whale, the shape of whose head more resembles the porpoise."

Beale developed his comparison for two pages, crammed with information which Melville somehow incorporated in various places in *Moby-Dick*. We may be certain that Beale's cautious paragraphs served as the main factual guide and the cetological control for Melville's capering and fanciful chapters on craniology.

The counterbalancing head of the Right Whale was captured by Stubb and Flask at Ahab's express command. The capture was soon effected, but only after a struggle Homeric in character, culminating as follows:

> Meantime, they hauled more and more upon their lines, till close flanking him on both sides, Stubb answered Flask with lance for lance; and thus round and round the Pequod the battle went, while the multitudes of sharks that had before swum round the Sperm Whale's body, rushed to the fresh blood that was spilled, thirstily drinking at every new gash, as the eager Israelites did at the new bursting fountains that poured from the rock.
> At last his spout grew thick, and with a frightful roll and vomit, he turned upon his back a corpse.

Interestingly, the exciting scene does more than introduce

the Right Whale's head into the story; it subtly foreshadows the climactic scene of *Moby-Dick,* for as the Right Whale rushes through the water, dragging the two boats after him, he heads directly for the *Pequod*: "So close did the monster come to the hull, that at first it seemed as if he meant it malice; but suddenly going down in a maelstrom, within three rods of the planks, he wholly disappeared from view, as if diving under the keel." For the time the *Pequod* is safe — a Right Whale would not be allowed to sink her! — but the danger from the whale is emphasized, as if in preparation for the final scene of the book. The coming event already casts its shadow.

But it soon appears that the capture of the Right Whale's head was far more than a rhetorical device for Melville. As the "foul lump of lard" is towed to the ship, Flask observes, "Did you never hear that the ship which but once has a Sperm Whale's head hoisted on her starboard side, and at the same time a Right Whale's on the larboard; did you ever hear, Stubb, that that ship can never afterwards capsize?" Flask's authority for this information is doubtful: "I heard that gamboge ghost of a Fedallah saying so, and he seems to know all about ships' charms. But I sometimes think he'll charm the ship to no good at last." Stubb concludes that Fedallah must be the Devil in disguise. The clowns can see what the King will not; one is reminded of the insight of the Fool as against the blindness of Lear. Fedallah, like the Weird Sisters, was a master of ambiguity.

Suddenly, but not unexpectedly, Melville gives the two whale heads a philosophical meaning: The *Pequod* regains her balance when the Right Whale's is hung on the larboard:

> As before, the Pequod steeply leaned over towards the sperm whale's head, now, by the counterpoise of both heads, she regained her even keel; though sorely strained, you may well believe. So, when on one side you hoist in Locke's head, you go over that way; but now, on the other side, hoist in Kant's and you come back again; but in very poor plight. Thus, some minds for ever keep trimming boat. Oh, ye foolish! throw all these thunder-heads overboard, and then you will float light and right.

The opposition of Locke and Kant is significant: the utilitarian and the idealist. Melville has considered the opposition of viewpoints once before in *Moby-Dick,* in the section of "The Mast-Head," dealing with the starry-eyed Platonist lost in the One, but in danger of tumbling into the Descartian vortices, the Many. Now the antithesis is again made by means of the grotesque symbols of whale heads hanging to an old whaleship. The point will be made at least twice more in this craniological section. It is an ironic commentary that Melville, who had been searching the philosophers for help, rejects the very philosophers whom he had consulted. To find Truth, he seems to say, one should not consult the sages — they only lead one to extremes, cause one to tip precariously; they are the cause of bias. Do not strain (as the *Pequod* strains) to support the wisdom of the books; be yourself, discard the philosophers, and like Queequeg, you will "float light and right."

Or it is possible to suggest another tentative interpretation of Melville's startling paragraph, to give it a nationalistic bent. America had been founded on the social contract of John Locke, a horological point of view which was counterbalanced in American life by the chronometrical view, found in Kantian individualism. The Right Whale thus stands for the concept of the Social, the Sperm Whale for the Individual — a polarity central to American history.

But philosophical — Life — truth is ever ambiguous, as Melville says again and again, either indirectly in *Moby-Dick,* or directly in *Pierre* the following year. Both Ahab and Fedallah come up on deck to look at the newly captured Right Whale's head. We observe Fedallah

> ever and anon glancing from the deep wrinkles there to the lines in his own hand. And Ahab chanced so to stand, that the Parsee occupied his shadow; while, if the Parsee's shadow was there at all it seemed only to blend with, and lengthen Ahab's. As the crew toiled on, Laplandish speculations were bandied among them, concerning all these passing things.

The Laplandish speculations concerning Melville's meanings must include one more. Melville has restated as in a coda his symbolism of Fedallah as the Devil and of Ahab's domination by the powers of Evil. The united shadows of Ahab and Fedallah represent the union of Ahab with the Devil. Ahab is a Faustian character, not from an evil will but, ironically, from good will. In his search for Truth (the White Whale), he is betrayed, as are all men who pursue the Demon of the Absolute. Melville will repeat this point again in the seven chapters to follow. We are by no means through with the cetological craniums.

From interpretation let us return to the more mundane source-hunting. Melville's craniological details closely follow Beale's *Natural History*.[76] Even the order of the details is similar. Like Beale, Melville discussed first the head as a whole, then the eyes, the ears, the spine, and the jaw. Unlike Beale, Melville embellished the facts with anecdote, analogy, and wit, so that the tedious exposition sparkles with the picturesque and dramatic additions. Compare, for instance, what Beale (quoting Doctor John Hunter)[77] says about the whale's ear:

> This organ consists of the same parts as in the quadruped, an external opening, with membrani tympani, an Eustachian tube, a tympanum with its processes, and the small bones. There is no external projection forming a funnel; we can easily assign a reason why there should be no projecting ear, as it would interfere with progressive motion, but the reason why it is not formed as in birds is not so evident. The external opening begins by a small hole scarcely perceptible, situated on the side of the head a little behind the eye; it is much longer than in other animals, in consequence of the size of the head being so much increased beyond the cavity which contains the brain. The Eustachian tube opens on the outside of the upper part of the fauces. . . . Dr. Alderson has remarked of the sperm whale, that "there was no external ear, but

[76] Melville put two checkmarks, now erased, beside Beale's opening sentence on the whale's cranium: "The gigantic skull of this animal forms than a third of the whole length of the skeleton; it is wedge-shaped, and begins with a very thin edge anteriorly, and rises gradually in height, forming an angle. . . . " He made other checkmarks at odd places throughout the discussion which followed.

[77] In Beale, Melville underlined, now erased, "the great John Hunter," and made a checkmark, now erased, in the margin.

simply a small circular opening, about nine inches, posteriorly to the posterior canthus of the eye, which just admitted the finger."

Nor is this all, but it is sufficiently long to reveal the dullness and authenticity of Melville's source. Anxious to put the whale "livingly," as he put it, before us, Melville rewrote Beale completely in the following paragraph in *Moby-Dick*:

> But the ear of the whale is full as curious as the eye. If you are an entire stranger to their race, you might hunt over these two heads for hours, and never discover that organ. The ear has no external leaf whatever; and into the hole itself you can scarcely insert a quill, so wondrously minute it is.[78] It is lodged a little behind the eye. With respect to their ears, this important difference is to be observed between the Sperm Whale and the Right. While the ear of the former has an external opening, that of the latter is entirely and evenly covered over with a membrane, so as to be quite imperceptible from without.

Detail after detail from Beale and Bennett become transformed as Melville wrote. Describing the whale's eye, he said: "Far back on the side of the head, and low down, near the angle of either whale's jaw, if you narrowly search, you will at last see a lashless eye, which you would fancy to be a young colt's eye; so out of all proportion is it to the magnitude of the head." This sentence seems to have been suggested by Bennett's remark that

> The eye of the cachalot is small and placed far back on the head, above and between the pectoral fin and angle of the lower jaw. Its situation is chiefly marked by a raised portion of integument around it.

— and from Beale's repeated comparison of the eye to that of a "quadruped," particularized by Melville as a colt.

Beale's (Hunter's) sentences stick close to scientific fact. Such a passage as

[78] Francis Olmsted, *Incidents of a Whaling Voyage*, p. 59, wrote: "The *ear* is a funnel shaped cavity situated between the eye and the lower jaw, of so minute a size, as hardly to admit one's little finger."

The lower jaw is 16 feet 10 inches long, and forms, in its whole length, a slight arch, with the convexity downwards; it is armed with forty-eight formidable teeth, twenty-four on each side. The lower jaw is formed of two lateral pieces, which form a cylindrical symphysis anteriorly, etc.

— is vastly less interesting than Melville's vivacious account of the same:

Let us now with whatever levers and steam-engines we have at hand, cant over the Sperm Whale's head, so that it may lie bottom up; then, ascending by a ladder to the summit, have a peep down the mouth; and were it not that the body is now completely separated from it, with a lantern we might descend into the great Kentucky Mammoth Cave of his stomach. But let us hold on here by this tooth, and look about us where we are. What a really beautiful and chaste-looking mouth! from floor to ceiling, lined, or rather papered with a glistening white membrane, glossy as bridal satins.

But come out now, and look at this portentous lower jaw, which seems like the long narrow lid of an immense snuff-box, with the hinge at one end, instead of one side. If you pry it up, so as to get it overhead, and expose its rows of teeth, it seems a terrific portcullis; and such, alas! it proves to many a poor wight in the fishery, upon whom these spikes fall with impaling force. But far more terrible is it to behold, when fathoms down in the sea, you see some sulky whale, floating there suspended, with his prodigious jaw, some fifteen feet long, hanging straight down at right-angles with his body; for all the world like a ship's jib-boom.

The picture of the Sperm Whale deep in the ocean, his long jaw suspended at right angles from his body to serve as a gleaming magnet to attract the squid, was drawn from Beale's account of the whale's feeding habits. The simile of the Mammoth Cave, evoking as it does the image of dark winding caverns, was Melville's concentration into one phrase of Beale's six-page description of the many stomachs and intestinal passage in the Sperm Whale. Dull fact became a lively metaphor.

Beale and Bennett were thoroughly familiar with the head of the Sperm Whale; they knew very little about the Right

Whale. Scoresby had to serve Melville the information needed at this point in his comparison, and many of Melville's cranial details are traceable to *An Account of the Arctic Regions*, the factual base on which Melville constructed "The Right Whale's Head" (75). The comparison of the Right Whale's head to a shoemaker's last or the spiracles on the head to "*f*-shaped spout holes" passed from Scoresby to Melville. For instance, the *f*-shaped spout holes became an elaborate simile: "If you stand on its summit and look at these two *f*-shaped spout-holes, you would take the whole head for an enormous bass viol, and these spiracles, the apertures in its sounding-board." Scoresby's description of the whale's lip, "The lips are composed almost entirely of blubber, and yield from one to two tons of pure oil each," became the following in *Moby-Dick*:

> But if this whale be a king, he is a very sulky looking fellow to grace a diadem. Look at that hanging lower lip! what a huge sulk and pout is there! a sulk and pout, by carpenter's measurement, about twenty feet long and five feet deep; a sulk and pout that will yield you some 500 gallons of oil and more.

Melville translated Scoresby's two tons into the 500 gallons of *Moby-Dick* when he noted on the same page in Scoresby that "The ton or tun of oil, is 252 gallons wine measure." And it might be suggested that Melville's later modulation into the comparison of the Sperm Whale's head with the Heidelburgh Tun might have begun with Scoresby's "wine measure."

When Melville moved into the great mouth of the Right Whale, he struck off a strange metaphor: "Upon my word were I at Mackinaw, I should take this to be the inside of an Indian wigwam." But the metaphor came from no literary source; it was out of the travels of its author, Herman Melville, who visited Illinois in 1840, making the trip to Galena by way of the Mackinaw straits.[79] Another metaphor,

79 Having been attracted to the problem of whether or not Melville did visit Illinois before going to the South Seas, by the subtitle of his poem "Prairie Maize (Illinois in 1840)," I found out that Henry Murray had already established the fact in the preparation of his exhaustive study

but this time from a fish document, was utilized to convey a clear picture of the interior of the whale's mouth. Describing the great lengths of whalebone through which the Right Whale strained off the water from its food, Melville called them "Venetian blinds," and repeated the image a second time. Melville had taken the simile from Henry Cheever's *The Whale and His Captors*. And a third figure of speech was from his own observation, for in repeating Scoresby's information that in the whalebone certain markings revealed the whale's age, Melville added, "as the age of an oak by its circular rings."

Scoresby, Beale, and Bennett were Melville's primary sources of information concerning the whale's head. More profound reading and thought assisted him in the elaboration of his materials. Towards the end of his long cranial comparison (far longer and more complete than here indicated), Melville with a bold wit concluded, "This Right Whale I take to have been a Stoic; the Sperm Whale, a Platonian, who might have taken up Spinoza in his latter years." Here is a cryptic passage, meaningless unless we know what Melville meant by "Platonian" and "Spinoza." [80]

Rightly or wrongly, Melville associated Platonism with neo-Platonism. Furthermore, he seemed to equate Transcendentalism with Platonism, or saw the New England Transcendentalists as descendants of Platonic thought, for he called Emerson a "Plato who talks thro' his nose." The basic logic of the Transcendentalist's belief in the Over-Soul (the Platonic Idea) was that since the Over-Soul is all good, then all earthly phenomena, itself part of the all-enveloping Over-Soul, must be good, and therefore evil is an illusion. To Melville, the Transcendentalist and his ancestor Plato

of Melville, yet to be published. Mentor Williams, who has made a study of travelers' routes to Illinois, tells me that the most probable route that Melville would have taken would have been by way of Mackinaw.

[80] Merton Sealts, Jr., in an unpublished doctoral dissertation, "Melville's Reading in Ancient Philosophy," Yale, 1942, discusses Melville's Platonism at length, showing that Melville always distinguished between Plato and Socrates, and that in later years Melville looked more favorably on Plato's work. It is to be hoped that Dr. Sealts will complete his investigations, as at present planned, and publish his valuable study.

were pure absolutists, men sidestepping the intrusive fact of evil.

To Melville, Spinoza was equally the victim of illusion. Melville could not have known Spinoza at first hand; there was no English translation of the *Ethics* before the composition of *Moby-Dick,* and Melville could not hurdle the language barrier. Merton Sealts has suggested that Melville may have used a dictionary of philosophy in studying Spinozan doctrine. Positive proof is lacking. There can be little question, however, of Melville's familiarity with and fondness for Pierre Bayle's *Dictionary.* There Melville had undoubtedly read the article (with its many footnotes) on Spinoza, who serves as an object of bitter attack on the part of Bayle. To the great French skeptic, Spinoza was indeed God-drunk in his overemphasis on Unity, on the One. Take the following passage, for example:

> He supposes that there is but one substance in nature, and that this only substance is endowed with infinite attributes, and among others, with extension and thought. Afterwards, he affirms, that all bodies in the universe are modifications of that substance, as it is extended; and that for instance, the souls of men are modifications of that substance, as it thinks: so that GOD, the necessary and most perfect Being, is the cause of all things that exist, but does not differ from them. There is but one Being, and one Nature, and that Being produces in itself, and by an immanent action, whatever goes by the name of cause and subject; He produces nothing but what is his own modification. This is the most extravagant hypothesis that can be thought of. The most infamous things sung by the heathen Poets against Jupiter, and against Venus, do not come near the horrid notion Spinoza gives us of GOD. For the Poets did not ascribe to the gods all the crimes that are committed, all the infirmities of mankind; but, according to Spinoza, there is no other agent, nor other patient but GOD, with respect to physical and moral evil. Let us observe some of the absurdities of the system.

And "observe" is what Bayle does, at length and with scorn; his list of these absurdities is comprehensive and forceful. God, Bayle says, cannot be reduced to so many parts and still be indivisible; if God is all and all is God, then when ten thousand Turks (God) fight ten thousand Germans (God), God is committing an evil act and is, furthermore, fighting against himself. Bayle adds pungently:

> Lastly, that a GOD, infinitely good, infinitely holy, infinitely free, who could make creatures always holy, and always happy, should rather chuse to make them criminal, and eternally miserable, is a thing that shocks reason; and so much the more, because it cannot reconcile man's free-will with the quality of a Being created out of nothing.

If Melville's knowledge, or even part of it, about Spinoza [81] came mainly from Bayle's *Dictionary*, it is understandable why Melville referred to the Sperm Whale as a Platonian who has become, in later years, a follower of Spinoza. All the way through *Moby-Dick* it is suggested, or hinted, that the Sperm Whale may on occasion be seen as a symbol of the Absolute, or the All. He might, in this passage, be held as an emblem of God, or of Unity, or of the Over-Soul — of the Eternal Being which Plato, and the Transcendentalists, and Spinoza, termed Absolute Beauty and Good. The Sperm Whale, Melville says ironically, is a Platonian turned Spinozan; and *the* great Sperm Whale, object of Ahab's search, is the Absolute of Absolutes, a delusion which is embodied elsewhere in the spirit-spout, the squid, and now the head hanging to the side of the *Pequod*.

This association of Plato and Spinoza appears a year later in Melville's *Pierre*, in a passage re-echoing the criticism from Bayle's pen: "Away, ye chattering apes of a Sophomorean Spinoza and Plato, who once didst all but delude me that night was day, and pain only a tickle." Here the point not clearly made in *Moby-Dick* is explicitly stated:

---

[81] As early as *Mardi* (his first "philosophical" novel) Melville refers to Spinoza as "the Jew that rejected the Talmud, and his all-permeating principle, to which Goethe and others have subscribed." In his copy of Matthew Arnold's *New Poems*, p. 174, Melville wrote "Spinoza" against Arnold's lines: "What are we all, but a mood / . . . of the life / of the Being in whom we exist, / Who alone is all things in one." William Braswell in his article "Melville as a Critic of Emerson," *American Literature*, IX (November, 1937), 317–334, shows that Melville's criticism of Emerson followed the same line, explaining Melville's association of Platonism with Transcendentalism.

Plato (as Melville interpreted him) and Spinoza had not met the problem of Evil.[82] Such was Bayle's criticism of Spinoza's philosophy. Spinozism, Platonism and the like, were intellectual systems which dissolved all difficulties in the goodness of God; hence, they were heartless. As Pierre further expostulates, addressing the "inconceivable coxcomb of a Goethe," "Corporations have no souls, and thy Pantheism, what was that? Thou wert but the pretentious, heartless part of a man." The passages from *Pierre* illuminate the cryptic sentence in *Moby-Dick*.[83] Furthermore, Melville has not introduced an altogether new theme in his novel; he has restated, rather, in a cetological setting, some of the criticism suggested in such a chapter as "The Mast-Head" — criticism pervasive throughout the entire novel.

Pursuing his craniological considerations further, Melville pushed on into the next chapter, "The Battering-Ram" (76), the nature of which is indicated in the metaphorical title. By stressing the "compacted collectedness" of the Sperm Whale's head, Melville wishes us to realize that which we might doubt, but which is terribly true:

> I would have you investigate it now with the sole view of forming to yourself some unexaggerated, intelligent estimate of whatever battering-ram power may be lodged there. Here is a vital point; for you must either satisfactorily settle this matter with yourself, or for ever remain an infidel as to one of the most appalling, but not the less true events, perhaps anywhere to be found in all recorded history.

His allusion in the last line is to the *Essex*, sunk by the "battering-ram" of a Sperm Whale in the Pacific. And Art

---

[82] Years later Melville referred to these people in *Clarel* (II, 244 ff.):

> All recognition they forgo
> Of Evil; supercilious skim
> With spurious wing of seraphim
> The last abyss.

[83] In *Pierre*, Melville satirizes in Charlie Milthorpe, who has proudly contributed to the "Spinozaist" [*The Dial*?]: "And you know how very few can understand the Spinozaist; nothing is admitted there but the Ultimate Transcendentals." And as late as *Clarel*, Spinoza is still the "visionary" of "starry brow."

will imitate Life, Melville adapting the "true event" to make it even truer.

"The Battering-Ram" is primarily physiological in nature. The metaphor "battering-ram" as applied to the Sperm Whale came from Henry Cheever's book. The various physical details undoubtedly came from Beale and Bennett, but the verbal similarities are slight and perhaps unimportant. What gives significance to the chapter, or what gives it breadth, is the shift from fact to symbol from the physical reality of the Sperm Whale's head to the metaphor of destruction, of irresistibility. Be prepared to accept any battering feat from this great fish:

> ... when I shall hereafter detail to you all the specialities and concentrations of potency everywhere lurking in this expansive monster; when I shall show you some of his more inconsiderable braining feats; I trust you will have renounced all ignorant incredulity, and be ready to abide by this; that though the Sperm Whale stove a passage through the Isthmus of Darien, and mixed the Atlantic with the Pacific, you would not elevate one hair of your eye-brow. For unless you own the whale, you are but a provincial and sentimentalist in Truth. But clear Truth is a thing for salamander giants only to encounter; how small the chances for the provincials then? What befel the weakling youth lifting the dread goddess's veil at Lais?

The reader's attention is stirred by the allusion to the veiled statue at Sais (the spelling in *Moby-Dick* is a typographical error). Coming as it does at the close of a passage in which Melville points the way to a symbolical interpretation of his great whale, we may well wonder whether the allusion does not throw light on the symbolism. You must "own the whale," says Melville, meaning that you must accept its infinite power without question. The whale would seem to be a symbol of "Truth," an ambiguous abstraction sought for by Ahab, and a year later just as eagerly sought for by Pierre though not in the form of a whale. It is the "sentimentalist in Truth" who refuses to "own" the whale; that is, it is the "sentimentalist" (the ardent, over-eager) who will not "own" but must instead try to capture the "Truth."

The experience of the youth at Sais is a warning to such sentimentalists, Melville says. As one who owned Bulwer Lytton's translation of Schiller's *Poems and Ballads* (1844), Melville had read, and marked, "The Veiled Statue at Sais." It is the story of a young man, a sentimentalist in the truth, who visits Sais, in Egypt, to study the secret lore of the priesthood. Impatiently the learner seeks further and further, anxious to find the truth that was "changeless and indivisible." Coming upon a veiled statue of gigantic size, the impetuous student asks the old priest what form is concealed beneath the veil. He is told, "Truth." The disciple argues that since "Truth" is the object of his quest he may now end the search, but instantly he is warned by his mentor never to lift the veil. Alone, at night, the disciple visits the veiled statue. Debating whether or not to see "truth" against the advice of his elder, he finally gives in to temptation:

> He speaks, and with the word, lifts up the veil.
> Would you inquire what form there met his eye?
> I know not, — but, when day appear'd, the priests
> Found him extended senseless, pale as death,
> Before the pedestal of Isis' statue.
> What had been seen and heard by him when there,
> He never would disclose, but from that hour
> His happiness in life had fled for ever,
> And his deep sorrow soon conducted him
> To an untimely grave.

The moral need not be made explicit, but it may perhaps be applied to Ahab in *Moby-Dick*, for the youth at Sais who rashly dares to lift the sacred veil is the equivalent of Ahab who rashly seeks to "see," to capture, the White Whale. Like the youth, Ahab has the mania for certainty; therefore he is a "sentimentalist in Truth." Mankind, Melville implies, should not know all; he needs the protection of an illusion. Wrote Amiel, "Isis lifts the corner of her veil, and the vertiginousness of the spectacle confounds him who beholds the great mystery." And Joubert said, "Il ne faut rien voir tout nu."

From the whole head of the Sperm Whale we now come

to a part of it, the case, described well in the opening of "The Great Heidelburgh Tun" (77):

> Regarding the Sperm Whale's head as a solid oblong, you may, on an inclined plane, sideways divide it into two quoins, whereof the lower is the bony structure, forming the cranium and jaws, and the upper an unctuous mass wholly free from bones; its broad forward end forming the expanded vertical apparent forehead of the whale. At the middle of the forehead horizontally subdivide this upper quoin, and then you have two almost equal parts, which before were naturally divided by an internal wall of a thick tendinous substance.

The metaphor of the quoin ("a solid which differs from a wedge in having its sharp end formed by the steep inclination of one side, instead of the mutual tapering of both sides") was possibly suggested to Melville by Beale's passage in "Of the Cranium," beside which Melville placed two checkmarks, a sign of his interest in the words:

> The gigantic skull of this animal forms more than a third of the whole length of the skeleton; it is wedge-shaped, and begins with a very thin edge anteriorly, and rises gradually in height, forming an angle on its upper surface, until it arrives at the posterior fourth; it then rises suddenly and forms a thin outward wall, which encloses a large crater-looking cavity, fitted for the reception of an immense mass of the junk, which, with the case, forms the whole upper portion of the head in the living animal.

The title of Melville's chapter is itself a metaphor, "The Great Heidelburgh Tun," suggested to Melville by a passage which he had read and a picture he had seen in one of his travel books. Terming the case of the whale a great tun or vat, Melville says:

> The upper part, known as the Case, may be regarded as the great Heidelburgh Tun of the Sperm Whale. And as that famous great tierce is mystically carved in front, so the whale's vast plaited forehead forms innumerable strange devices for emblematical adornment of his wondrous tun. Moreover, as that of Heidelburgh was always replenished with the most excellent of the wines of the Rhenish valleys, so the tun of the

whale contains by far the most precious of all his oily vintages; namely, the highly-prized spermaceti, in its absolutely pure, limpid, and odoriferous state.

Melville has in mind a section from the second volume of John Harriss's *Navigantium atque Itinerantium Bibliotheca. Or, a Complete Collection of Voyages and Travels,* published in two huge folio volumes in London (revised edition, 1748). In "The Travels of Mr. Maximilian Mission, through Part of Holland, etc.," Melville's eye apparently read the following words:

> This so much celebrated Tun is thirty one Foot long and twenty one high, unto which you ascend by a Pair of Stairs of fifty Steps, to a kind of Platform or Balcony of twenty Foot long, inclosed with Rails: The Elector's Arms are placed on the Front of the Tun, and *Bacchus* on the Top, attended by Satyrs, Drunkards, and such-like. Vines, Grapes, Glasses and Leather-Jacks make a great Part of the Ornaments of this Tun, in *basso relievo*. Abundance of Jests and Apothegms, relating to the same Subject, are to be seen, in *High Dutch* on divers Parts of this enormous Tun.

It is a picturesque pen which sees similarity in a vast wine vat in Germany and the case of a sperm whale in the Pacific. Melville's tone was obviously affectionate when he referred in *Moby-Dick* to "old Harriss," and this picture of the Heidelburgh Tun reveals why.

The irresistible — and artistically sound — instinct which continually made Melville dramatize his expository materials whenever possible was active again in connection with the case of the whale. Having described the large case, and how whalemen extracted the spermaceti from it by means of a bucket attached to a long pole, Melville vivifies his whaling fact by a startling episode — Tashtego's fall into the well of the case.

To Tashtego was assigned the job of dipping the spermaceti from the case hung alongside the *Pequod*. Standing on his slippery perch, he dipped out the precious oil. "On a sudden, as the eightieth or ninetieth bucket came suckingly up — my God! poor Tashtego — like the twin reciprocating bucket in a veritable well, dropped head-foremost down into this great Tun of Heidelburgh, and with a horrible oily gurgling, went clean out of sight!" Quickly Daggoo rammed a bucket into the case hoping that Tashtego would seize it to be pulled out, but instead, it was the same, Stubb said, as "ramming home a cartridge." And then, suddenly, "the enormous mass dropped into the sea, like Niagara's Table-Rock into the whirlpool," slowly sinking with Tashtego entombed within. The hapless savage is saved by Queequeg, who, diving after the descending case, reaching in and seizing Tashtego, deftly somersaulted him inside the oil case, presenting him in a head, not a breech, delivery. It was "agile obstetrics on the run, as you may say. Yes, it was a running delivery, so it was."

The reader knows what next to expect from Melville. Having told his story, exciting just as a sea yarn, he could not let it go without extracting more from it. Consequently he closed his narrative chapter, "Cisterns and Buckets" (78), with the cryptic paragraph:

> Now, had Tashtego perished in that head, it had been a very precious perishing; smothered in the very whitest and daintiest of fragrant spermaceti; coffined, hearsed, and tombed in the secret inner chamber and sanctum sanctorum of the whale. Only one sweeter end can readily be recalled — the delicious death of an Ohio honey-hunter, who seeking honey in the crotch of a hollow tree, found such exceeding store of it, that leaning too far over, it sucked him in, so that he died embalmed. How many, think ye, have likewise fallen into Plato's honey head, and sweetly perished there?

What does Melville mean by this? Exactly what he has meant all the way through his craniological essay and what he said particularly in the words on the Platonian-Spinozan whale head. Accepting the Sperm Whale as the symbol of Truth and/or the Absolute, and if Plato is to Melville the chief ancient believer in the transcendental One, then the Sperm Whale's head is the center of the Absolute where are hidden the riches of the supernatural mystery. To fall into the mystic Unity is sweet, even as Ishmael found the revery of the One at the mast-head, and as Emerson found it in the Over-Soul.

But it is, says Melville, a sweetness which may hurl one into the Descartian vortices, or to his death.

Two specific points require consideration. First, the entire story of Tashtego's fall may possibly have been suggested to Melville as he read Scoresby's account of the flensing of a whale in the sea's swell:

> Hence accidents in this kind of flensing, in particular, are not uncommon. The harpooners not unfrequently fall into the fish's mouth, when it is exposed by the removal of a surface of blubber; where they might easily be drowned, but for the prompt assistance which is always at hand.

It might well be that Melville took this suggestion for expansion into the near-death of Tashtego, who had to be "delivered" by the prompt assistance of Queequeg; and thus Melville implicatively repeats a theme repeated throughout *Moby-Dick*: death and rebirth — the dialectic of human growth, the passage from youthful idealism into the matured and complex acceptance of reality.

Second, the simile of the case's falling into the sea "like Niagara's Table-Rock" is Melville's employment of an event occurring during the composition of *Moby-Dick,* when the table-rock of Niagara Falls fell with a tremendous crash into the whirlpool below.

Finally Melville admits defeat in trying to describe the head of the Sperm Whale. Before he gives up, however, he satirizes the phrenological craze in America, regretting that he cannot approach the whale as a phrenologist, that maybe such examination might yield results where others (the scientists) had failed. In "The Prairie" (79) he wrote:

> To scan the lines of his face, or feel the bumps on the head of this Leviathan; this is a thing which no Physiognomist or Phrenologist has as yet undertaken. Such an enterprise would seem almost as hopeful as for Lavater to have scrutinized the wrinkles on the Rock of Gibraltar, or for Gall to have mounted a ladder and manipulated the Dome of the Pantheon. Still, in that famous work of his, Lavater [84] not only

---

[84] Melville bought a copy of Lavater's *Physiognomy* (edition unknown) in London on 21 November, 1849.

treats of the various faces of men, but also attentively studies the faces of horses, birds, serpents, and fish; and dwells in detail upon the modifications of expression discernible therein. Nor have Gall and his disciple Spurzheim failed to throw out some hints touching the phrenological characteristics of other beings than man. Therefore, though I am but ill qualified for a pioneer, in the application of these two semisciences to the whale, I will do my endeavor. I try all things; I achieve what I can.

"The Nut" (80) as well as "The Prairie" both play with the phrenological idea. Although one might accept general observation of the phrenological enthusiasm about him made Melville write his satire, it is probable that this particular passage from Cheever was the immediate stimulus:

> From what may be called the top of the forehead to the roof of the mouth of this square-faced *sui generis* monster, it measured nine feet in a straight line, and there was a corresponding breadth and depth of forehead, so that, with its prodigious volume of brain (head matter), and so large a facial angle, the bust of this creature is most favorably commended to the fingers of phrenologists. Is it not a little surprising, that in the researches of comparative phrenology the cranium of the great sperm whale should be overlooked? For the matter of room, a phrenologist might keep shop in it, and light it up, if he chose, with its own brains, and there point out to visitors by the lamp-light the places in the walls and ceiling where the different organs lay. It would be like a painter at Rome who should open his studio in the Parthenon [*sic*]; the celestial gods would be eying him from the ceiling; deified men and the infernals would be looking on him from all round.

Melville's allusion to the Pantheon is probably his correction of Cheever's careless reference to it as the Parthenon. The particularization of the general idea given him by Cheever is of course characteristic of the graphic imagination of Melville, who pictures Gall climbing a ladder to the roof of the Pantheon, or who recalls specifically the (now) amusing pictures in Lavater's *Essays on Physiognomy,* wherein are discussed at length various animal crania — but not the whale's! One might suggest, hesitantly, that Lavater's remarks on foreheads stimulated Melville into writing "The Prairie," in which the final glory is given to the brow of the Sperm Whale, "pleated with riddles; dumbly lowering with the doom of boats, and ships and men," and defying the greatest readers of wrinkles: Champollion, who deciphered the mysteries of Egypt; Sir William Jones, who had mastered "thirty languages, [but] could not read the simplest peasant's face." Therefore, Melville ambiguously concluded, "how may unlettered Ishmael hope to read the awful Chaldee of the Sperm Whale's brow?" His final phrenological observation is that if one will indulge in spinal phrenology, the whale will be distinguished because of his mighty vertebrae, and the hump on his back. "I should call this high hump the organ of firmness or indomitableness in the Sperm Whale. And that the great monster is indomitable, you will yet have reason to know."

Melville's craniological essay finishes with the phrenology. To give variety he shifts back to narrative. The *Pequod* meets the *Jungfrau,* a whaleship from Bremen. The boats of the two ships set out in competitive pursuit of a huge humped bull which "seemed afflicted with the jaundice, or some other infirmity," so anguished is its spout and so twisted its course. The international competition appears elsewhere in whaling literature, scenes similar to Melville's appearing in Cheever, for instance, whose *The Whale and His Captors* was now open before him. It is possible to trace in *Moby-Dick* sections where one author has been called upon several times and then forgotten. Cheever has just given Melville his phrenological subject; he now suggests the competitive whale chase (in Cheever it is between English and Yankee crews); and we even note Melville extracting from Cheever the metaphor of the Venetian blinds for the whalebone, at the end of "The *Pequod* Meets The Virgin" (81). The *Pequod* of course wins, after an exciting chase. But excitement is not all; Melville deepens his chapter. The whale itself becomes a touching symbol.

As the boats now more closely surrounded him, the whole upper part of his form, with much of it that is ordinarily submerged, was plainly revealed. His eyes, or rather the places where his eyes had been, were beheld. As strange misgrown masses gather in the knot-holes of the noblest oaks when prostrate, so from the points which the whale's eyes had once occupied, now protruded blind bulbs, horribly pitiable to see. But pity there was none. For all his old age, and his one arm, and his blind eyes, he must die the death and be murdered, in order to light the gay bridals and other merry-makings of men, and also to illuminate the solemn churches that preach unconditional inoffensiveness by all to all.

This pitiable monster was drawn, and amplified, from Beale's simple picture:

A whale, perfectly blind, was taken by Captain William Swain, of the Sarah and Elizabeth whaler of London, both eyes of which were completely disorganized, the orbits being occupied by fungous masses, protruding considerably, rendering it certain that the whale must have been deprived of vision for a long space of time.

But if Melville took the whale from Beale's *Natural History,* the lancing of that whale by cruel Flask was probably suggested by a vivid passage in Browne's *Etchings* telling of the final flurries of a great whale maddened by pain: "He rose again, rushing furiously upon his enemies; but a slight prick of a lance drove him back with mingled fury and terror. Whichever way he turned, the barbed irons goaded him to desperation." This may have suggested the death of the blind whale to Melville:

Still rolling in his blood, at last he partially disclosed a strangely discolored bunch or protuberance, the size of a bushel, low down on the flank.

"A nice spot," cried Flask; "just let me prick him there once."

"Avast!" cried Starbuck, "there's no need of that!"

But humane Starbuck was too late. At the instant of the dart an ulcerous jet shot from this cruel wound, and goaded by it into more than sufferable anguish, the whale now spouting thick blood, with swift fury blindly darted at the craft, bespattering them and their glorying crews all over with showers of gore, capsizing Flask's boat and marring the bows. It was his death stroke. For, by this time, so spent was he by loss of blood, that he helplessly rolled away from the wreck he had made; lay panting on his side, impotently flapped with his stumped fin, then over and over slowly revolved like a waning world; turned up the white secrets of his belly; lay like a log, and died. It was most piteous, that last expiring spout. As when by unseen hands, the water is gradually drawn off from some mighty fountain, and with half-stifled melancholy gurglings the spray-column lowers and lowers to the ground — so the last long dying spout of the whale.

It is one of the memorable scenes of our national literature. The dramatic rush of events sweeps the reader along breathlessly, and the felicity of the various images — the prostrate oak, the waning world, and the concluding Homeric simile of the dying fountain — reveal Melville's craftsmanship in its most expert moment. But what gives the scene its true greatness is not technique, although that must be there, but its emphatic understanding of the dying animal. Melville's implicit attitude is made explicit by a passage from Yeats: "Nor dread nor hope attend / A dying animal." And discussing Melville's scene, Arthur Tresidder Sheppard mentioned that it had "a sense of the linking of all creation and the tears of its common fate are seen in the surge of pity when the old blind whale wakes to its danger." *Sunt lacrimae rerum.*

16

"Demi-gods and Heroes, prophets of all sorts"

"THERE ARE SOME ENTERPRISES," Melville wrote, "in which a careful disorderliness is the true method." Robert Herrick's "sweet disorder," more pleasing than precise art, and Laurence Sterne's deliberate and planned defiance of the classical proprieties in *Tristram Shandy* both find echo in

Melville's observation. The whole novel of *Moby-Dick* is an illustrious example of the "true method" of disorderly order, while the two chapters, "The Honor and Glory of Whaling" (82), and "Jonah Historically Regarded" (83), introduced by Melville's explanatory sentence, are an excellent, particular instance of the planned complexity of Melville's whaling book. Meville's two light-hearted chapters have been regarded as digressive, but, properly seen, they are an organic part of the larger structure of *Moby-Dick*. They add considerably to the cetological mosaic which Melville has for some time been patiently piecing together. They also relax the narrative tension effectively. Granting right to a spacious leisureliness, *Moby-Dick* is never really disorderly.

Melville's laughter strikes, sometimes hard, more often gently and playfully. When most facetious, as in his essay on the great heroes of the whaling past, he may be suspected of satirical intent, or of indulgence in a private joke obscured to all except those aware of his sources, the fish documents. Melville employed flippancy as a screen, much as a magician through his patter masks the fundamental machinery of his illusions. Melville's was a complex, often a devious, mind, composing a work of art on several levels of meaning at once.

"The Honor and Glory of Whaling," first of the two chapters on mock whaling history, defends the dignity and nobility of the whaleman, and his way of life, by citing illustrious whaling practitioners. Placed late in *Moby-Dick*, the chapter balances the earlier one on much the same theme, "The Advocate" (46), in which the lowly status of the whaleman had been ingeniously defended as a calumny on honorable men. Melville returns to his advocacy seemingly more impressed than ever with the "honor and glory" of whaling:

> The more I dive into this matter of whaling, and push my researches up to the very spring-head of it, so much the more am I impressed with its great honorableness and antiquity; and especially when I find so many great demi-gods and heroes, prophets of all sorts, who one way or other have

shed distinction upon it, I am transported with the reflection that I myself belong, though but subordinately, to so emblazoned a fraternity.

(With the publication of *Moby-Dick,* the modesty of Melville's last clause was unjustified; today he and his book are the boast of whalemen.)

The emblazoned fraternity which Melville was able to find is an amazing gathering including only the best names: "Perseus, St. George, Hercules, Jonah, and Vishnoo! — there's a member-roll for you! What club but the whaleman's can head off like that?"

Where previously, in "The Advocate," Melville had cited figures like King Alfred and Job, he now renews his historical survey by including mythological figures, a collection surprising even for a wide-ranging mind like his.

The emblazoned fraternity came from a strange variety of sources. Melville's literary rigadoons are generally built from experiential or literary facts, or both, so that we are entitled to ask whether or not the fish documents were used here. Certainly such knowledge as he throws out about Perseus, Saint George, and Jonah did not come to him through pure inspiration of a wintry Berkshire morning. But for once Melville had to leave his faithful assistants — Beale, Bennett, Browne, and Scoresby, Jr. — and to summon other help: John Kitto's *A Cyclopedia of Biblical Literature* (1845), and Pierre Bayle's immortal *Dictionary Historical and Critical.* Uncovering Melville's adaptations from these two books is to study rather amusingly Melville's technique of literary transmutation and construction.

To date no evidence has turned up to show whether Melville ever owned the two volumes of Kitto's *Cyclopedia,* though the work was standard decoration for English and American parlor tables. We need have no question that he knew the work fairly well, or at least certain portions of it relevant to his special interests or needs. First of all, turning to the "W's," he found the article "Whale," written by "Lieut.-Colonel C. Hamilton Smith, K. H. and K. W., F. R. and L. S., President of the Devon and Cornwall

Natural History Society, &c. &c." Here was usable material. In Smith's essay Melville found the statement that Perseus had slain a whale, not a dragon:

> It may be observed, besides, of cetaceous animals, that though less frequent in the Mediterranean than in the ocean, they are far from being unknown there. Joppa, now Jaffa, the very place whence Jonah set sail, displayed for ages in one of its pagan temples huge bones of a species of whale, which the legends of the place pretended were those of the dragon monster slain by Perseus, as represented in the Arkite mythus of that hero and Andromeda; and which remained in that spot till the conquering Romans carried them in triumph to the great city.

In "The Honor and Glory of Whaling" Melville starts out his whaleman's club with Perseus, retelling the story of Andromeda's rescue, and ending:

> And let no man doubt this Arkite story; for in the ancient Joppa, now Jaffa, on the Syrian coast, in one of the Pagan temples, there stood for many ages the vast skeleton of a whale, which the city's legends and all the inhabitants asserted to be the identical bones of the monster that Perseus slew.

These words, with others not quoted, might be described as an imperfect copy of Smith's statement in the *Cyclopedia*. It is barely possible, of course, that Melville might really have read Pliny's *Natural History*, in Latin or in translation, and seen for himself the statement:

> *Beluae cui dicebatur exposita fuisse Andromeda ossa Romae apportata ex oppido Iudaeae Ioppe ostendit inter reliqua miracula in aedilitate sua M. Scaurus longitudine pedum xl, altitudine costarum Indicos elephantos excedente, spinae crassitudine sesquipedali.*

Melville, however, needed neither Pliny's original nor a translation; Smith's statement was sufficient. Besides, the analogy between the Jonah story and the Perseus myth is made in Bayle's *Dictionary*.

Melville had earlier showed his indebtedness to Smith's

Cyclopedia article in "The Affidavit" (45). Alluding to Procopius' account of a whale in the Mediterranean, Melville had in mind the following facts from Smith:

> Procopius mentions a huge sea-monster in the Propontis, taken during his praefecture of Constantinople, in the 36th year of Justinian (A.D. 562), after having destroyed vessels at certain intervals of more than fifty years. Rondoletius enumerates several whales stranded or taken on the coasts of the Mediterranean: these were most likely all *orcas, physeters,* or *campedolios,* i.e. toothed whales, as large and more fierce than the *mysticetes,* which have balein in the mouth, and at present very rarely make their way farther south than the Bay of Biscay; though in early times it is probable they visited the Mediterranean, since the present writer has seen them within the tropics. . . . On the island of Zerbi, close to the African coast, the late Commander Davies, R. N., found the bones of a cachalot on the beach. Shaw mentions an orca more than sixty feet in length, stranded at Algiers; and the late Admiral Ross Donelly saw one in the Mediterranean near the island of Albaran.

Smith's words became, through Melville's art, the closing section of "The Affidavit":

> In the sixth Christian century lived Procopius, a Christian magistrate of Constantinople, in the days when Justinian was Emperor and Belisarius general. As many know, he wrote the history of his own times, a work every way of uncommon value. By the best authorities, he has always been considered a most trustworthy and unexaggerating historian, except in some one or two particulars, not at all affecting the matter presently to be mentioned.
>
> Now, in this history of his, Procopius mentions that, during the term of his prefecture at Constantinople, a great sea-monster was captured in the neighboring Propontis, or Sea of Marmora, after having destroyed vessels at intervals in those waters for a period of more than fifty years. A fact thus set down in substantial history cannot easily be gainsaid. Nor is there any reason it should be. Of what precise species this sea-monster was, is not mentioned. But as he destroyed ships, as well as for other reasons, he must have been a whale; and I am strongly inclined to think a Sperm Whale.

And I will tell you why. For a long time I fancied that the Sperm Whale had been always unknown in the Mediterranean and the deep waters connecting with it. Even now I am certain that those seas are not, and perhaps never can be, in the present constitution of things, a place for his habitual gregarious resort. But further investigations have recently proved to me, that in modern times there have been isolated instances of the presence of the Sperm Whale in the Mediterranean. I am told, on good authority, that on the Barbary coast, a Commodore Davis of the British navy found the skeleton of a Sperm Whale. Now, as a vessel of war readily passes through the Dardanelles, hence a Sperm Whale could, by the same route, pass out of the Mediterranean into the Propontis.

In the Propontis, as far as I can learn, none of that peculiar substance called *brit* is to be found, the aliment of the Right Whale. But I have every reason to believe that the food of the Sperm Whale — squid or cuttle-fish — lurks at the bottom of that sea, because large creatures, by no means the largest of that sort, have been found at its surface. If, then, you properly put these statements together, and reason upon them a bit, you will clearly perceive that, according to all human reasoning, Procopius's sea-monster, that for half a century stove the ships of a Roman Emperor, must in all probability have been a Sperm Whale.

For a whalemen's fraternity, then, Perseus was a logical selection. Not so convincing is the second candidate in Melville's club: Saint George. His name we associate with a dragon, not a whale. But such an identification did not bother Melville, whose humorous disposition dictated a strange argument: Saint George slew a dragon; the dragon must have been a whale, for merely to have slain a serpent would belittle Saint George's exploit. "Any man," he said, "may kill a snake, but only a Perseus, a Saint George, a Coffin, have the heart in them to march boldly up to a whale." Having federated the names of Saint George and Perseus with Coffin, Melville followed up this championship of the American whaleman:

Thus, then, one of our own noble stamp, even a whaleman, is the tutelary guardian of England; and by good rights, we

harpooneers of Nantucket should be enrolled in the most noble
order of St. George. And therefore, let not the knights of
that honorable company (none of whom, I venture to say,
have ever had to do with a whale like their great patron),
let them never eye a Nantucketer with disdain, since even in
our woollen frocks and tarred trowsers we are much better
entitled to St. George's decoration than they.

Such chauvinism is "admirable fooling." Furthermore, it
is, apparently, directly from Melville's fanciful mind. As
he intimates, none of the source books had ever described
the Saint George dragon as a whale. In need of names with
which to swell his list of distinguished whalemen, Melville
readily translated Saint George's victim into a cachalot —
a transformation no more far-fetched than that by the ancients who made Andromeda's attacking dragon into a
whale.[85]

Hercules, the third member of the select whaling fraternity, is an imaginative inclusion, suggested to Melville by a
passage from Pierre Bayle's *Dictionary Historical and
Critical.* Melville's interest in the *Dictionary* was characteristic of his intellectual bent, and opposed to that of his
fellow countrymen. The optimistic temper of America was
alien to the skeptical realism of Bayle. There is very little
evidence that Bayle directly influenced nineteenth-century
American thought. Most Americans (Emerson apparently
came to him in the eighteen-sixties) did not know him at
first hand, or knowing him, did not care for his essays. Any
influence he exerted was screened through the writings of
Locke, Hume, Voltaire, and the Encyclopedists.

To Melville, however, Bayle was a kindred spirit. Both
men possessed to a striking degree the skeptical mind. Their
mutual admiration for another great skeptic, Montaigne,
links them together; for like Montaigne, Melville and
Bayle persistently asked *que sais je,* receiving, of course,
answers as unsatisfactory as had Montaigne. Bayle's ad-

[85] Melville would have been fascinated, one feels sure, to realize some of
the mythological, folklore, and interpretative possibilities of the dragon-hero
legends, on reading an article published recently: Geza Roheim, "The Dragon
and the Hero," *American Imago,* I (March, 1940), 40–69, and (June, 1940),
61–94.

mirable detachment, his intellectual neutrality, his unre-
lenting honesty, and the courage with which he faced the
unreconcilable contradictions of life were all traits which
we find to a greater or lesser degree in Melville. Furthermore, Bayle was primarily concerned with the problem of
Evil: its origin, its hardihood, its universal appearance. Although we do not have Melville's personal copy of the
Dictionary, we may be sure that he marked with approval
such passages as: "God has removed only a portion of the
veil which conceals from us this great mystery of the origin
of evil."

From Bayle Melville undoubtedly derived inspiration and
ideas in ways impossible ever to trace. That he used Bayle
for his knowledge of Spinoza has already been suggested
earlier. And that he made Hercules into a member of the
whaling fraternity was probably owing to a statement of
Bayle's: "the heathen poets have told a story of their Hercules somewhat resembling this [Jonah]"; and a footnote
statement: "[Hercules] also was swallowed by a whale, and
remained safe in her belly excepting only that he lost his
hair, when he came out from the strong inward heat of the
creature." Equating heroic Hercules with Kit Carson and
Davy Crockett, Melville has a moment of ironic doubt
whether or not he is being quite accurate in selecting Hercules for the whale club since

> it nowhere appears that he ever actually harpooned his
> fish, unless, indeed, from the inside. Nevertheless, he may
> be deemed a sort of involuntary whaleman; at any rate the
> whale caught him, if he did not the whale. I claim him for
> one of our clan.

Melville's mocking care with these details, his disarming
seriousness — discussing ridiculous and unimportant points
— is indirectly satirical of the pedant who splits hairs of
evidence to prove or disprove a scholarly point. Furthermore, Melville's entire chapter is a satire on Comparative
Mythology — a satire startling because it pokes fun at a
field of study then in its infancy, especially in American
intellectual circles.

The fourth member of the whalemen's club is even more noteworthy than the previous three, as Melville carefully pointed out:

> Our grand master is still to be named; for like royal kings of old times, we find the head-waters of our fraternity in nothing short of the great gods themselves. That wondrous oriental story is now to be rehearsed from the Shaster, which gives us the dread Vishnoo, one of the three persons in the godhead of the Hindoos; gives us this divine Vishnoo himself for our Lord; — Vishnoo, who, by the first of his ten earthly incarnations, has for ever set apart and sanctified the whale. When Bramha [*sic*], or the God of Gods, saith the Shaster, resolved to recreate the world after one of its periodical dissolutions, he gave birth to Vishnoo, to preside over the work; but the Vedas, or mystical books, whose perusal would seem to have been indispensable to Vishnoo before beginning the creation, and which therefore must have contained something in the shape of practical hints to young architects, these Vedas were lying at the bottom of the waters; so Vishnoo became incarnate in a whale, and sounding down in him to the uttermost depths, rescued the sacred volumes. Was not this Vishnoo a whaleman, then? even as a man who rides a horse is called a horseman?

In this striking paragraph an important problem is raised to which a complete answer seems impossible: Where did Melville learn about the Matse Avatar, as he called it in Chapter 55, or about Vishnu in general? Accounts of Oriental mythology were not the normal reading diet of nineteenth-century Americans, although one may find numerous, fragmentary discussions of the subject supplementing the work of the several scholars. And the question is also raised: How did Americans in general become acquainted with the Hindu pantheon? The influence of Oriental thought upon Emerson, Whittier, Thoreau, Whitman, and the Transcendentalists has been treated in learned articles; no one has yet published a study of Melville's interest in Oriental lore. A few words on his Vishnu paragraph may initiate a fuller treatment of the subject.

We approach Melville's Orientalism through *White-*

Jacket. In that novel Jack Chase, the superior sailor, frequently and passionately quoted from the *Lusiad,* Camoëns' great epic poem treating of Vasco da Gama's famous expedition around the Cape of Good Hope to India. These quotations were drawn from Mickle's translation published in the twenty-first volume of Alexander Chalmers' *The Works of the English Poets from Chaucer to Cowper* (London, 1810). The generous critical apparatus accompanying the poem included an "Inquiry into the Religious Tenets and Philosophy of the Brahmins," an essay which unquestionably caught Melville's attention, aroused his interest in the esoteric subject, and led him to further reading. That this long article influenced Melville's spelling of some of the Hindu names (Shaster, for example) is a possibility not to be ruled out. But there are matters in Melville's Vishnu paragraph which the Mickle essay does not clarify, the Matse Avatar especially. Obviously this article merely goaded Melville into further reading. Since the main authorities cited throughout the essay were Dow and Holwell, one presumes that Melville went to them, but such a presumption is not borne out by research. Melville apparently found his Vishnuism in Thomas Maurice's *Indian Antiquities: or, Dissertations, Relative to the Ancient Geographical Divisions . . . of Hindostan,* etc. (London, 1794). Subjects alluded to by Melville, such as Zoroaster, Mithra, Isis and Osiris, Pythagoras and the doctrine of metempsychosis, the Cave of Elephanta, appear in Maurice's volumes. Their appearance does not, of course, constitute proof of Melville's use of the work. That rests on two other reasons.

First, the spelling of the first avatar, the Matse, is the same in both Maurice [86] and Melville — in no other works which Melville might have consulted, or seems to have consulted, do we find this consonance — not even between *Moby-Dick* and Maurice's other Indic study: *The History of Hindostan,*

---

[86] Thomas Maurice said that he was indebted to Pierre Sonnerat, *Voyage aux Indes Orientales et à la Chine,* 2 vols. (Paris, 1782), for his account of the ten Vishnu avatars. I do not see that Melville ever opened Sonnerat's book, although he would have enjoyed the handsome colored pictures of the avatars in Sonnerat's sumptuous work.

its Arts, and Its Sciences, etc.[87] (London, 1820). Significantly, both the *History of Hindostan* and *Indian Antiquities* have interesting plates of the Vishnu avatar, but in the first it is spelled "Matsya," and in the second "Matse."

Second, Melville's erroneous statement —

> Now, by all odds, the most ancient extant portrait anyways purporting to be the whale's, is to be found in the famous cavern-pagoda of Elephanta, in India. The Brahmins maintain that in the almost endless sculptures of that immemorial pagoda, all the trades and pursuits, every conceivable avocation of man, were prefigured ages before any of them actually came into being. No wonder then, that in some sort our noble profession of whaling should have been there shadowed forth. The Hindoo whale referred to, occurs in a separate department of the wall, depicting the incarnation of Vishnu in the form of Leviathan, learnedly known as the Matse Avatar. But though this sculpture is half man and half whale, so as only to give the tail of the latter, yet that small section of him is all wrong. It looks more like the tapering tail of an anaconda, than the broad palms of the true whale's majestic flukes.

— in Chapter 55, is stated so positively that one is half persuaded that Melville was actually looking at a drawing or picture of the Elephanta icon. Long research among the various accounts of the Cave of Elephanta written prior to *Moby-Dick* fails to produce such an account or such a picture. So far as I have been able to determine,[88] there is no

87 There are other bits in the *History of Hindostan* to make the student of Melville wonder whether its influence might not have been considerable.

The most important discussions of Indian religion before *Moby-Dick*, especially touching on Vishnu, were Horace Hayman Wilson, *The Vishnu Purana* (Bombay, 1840); Henry Thomas Colebrooke, *Miscellaneous Essays* (London, 1837), most of them, I believe, previously published in various volumes of *Asiatic Researches*; William Ward, *A View of the History, Literature, and Mythology* (London, 1847); Lieutenant Colonel Vans Kennedy, *Researches into the Nature and Affinity of Ancient and Hindu Mythology* (London, 1831); Horace H. Wilson, *Essays and Lectures Chiefly on the Religion of the Hindus* (London, 18—); John Wilson, *A Second Exposure of the Hindu Religion*, etc. (Bombay, 1834), which has information on the Matsya Avatar.

88 A bibliography of the main accounts of the Cave of Elephanta may be seen in James Burgess, *The Rock-Temples of Elephanta or Gharapuri* (Bombay, 1871).

such carving, although icons of Vishnu exist in abundance there. Melville's error, if such it be, probably occurred from hasty reading in Maurice's *Indian Antiquities* where Maurice passes rapidly, without adequate transition, from a description of the Cave of Elephanta to an account of the Matse Avatar. Only close study of Maurice's text would show that no connection between the Matse Avatar and the Cave of Elephanta was intended; the rapid reader might easily assume that Maurice was still discussing the Cave, or one aspect of it.

It would be tempting to digress into a discussion of Melville's decided interest in Oriental mythology, an interest anticipating much recent activity in England and America; but it is perhaps wisest to move along, with the reminder that the transformation of the fish-god into a whale-god was to be expected from the humorous mind which had already defined a whale as "a fish with a horizontal tail."

To the final member of his whaling fraternity Melville devotes an entire chapter, "Jonah Historically Regarded" (83). In the same satirical tone as "The Honor and Glory of Whaling," it is a mocking foray into yet another field of intellectual interest: the Higher Criticism of the Bible. Although the Higher Criticism had its rise earlier in the century, especially with the publication in 1834 of Strauss's famous life of Jesus, Higher Criticism did not achieve full growth until ten or fifteen years after the writing of *Moby-Dick*. Whaling joined with Biblical controversy! Melville's sensitivity to intellectual radiations of his time was acute.

Whether the story of Jonah in the whale's belly is myth or history is a question which has been debated for centuries, and one on which general agreement has yet to be reached. Father Mapple, it will be remembered, retold the story without one word of question. One could scarcely expect men like Stubb and Starbuck, however, to deny the evidence of their own eyes as they saw the difficulties against accepting Jonah's experience as a literal truth. Faith against skepticism. Melville takes neither side, ironically discussing the variations of belief, but perhaps in his very mockery of the skeptics siding with them. He seems to urge whalemen not to let their native skepticism disturb their faith in the miracle; doubt of the old stories of Arion on the Dolphin, and of Hercules in the whale, "did not make these traditions one whit the less facts, for all that." But the veteran whaleman — "old Sag-Harbor" Melville calls him — is a hard man to convince:

One old Sag-Harbor whaleman's chief reason for questioning the Hebrew story was this: — He had one of those quaint old-fashioned Bibles, embellished with curious, unscientific plates; one of which represented Jonah's whale with two spouts in his head — a peculiarity only true with respect to a species of the Leviathan (the Right Whale, and the varieties of that order), concerning which the fishermen have this saying, "A penny roll would choke him;" his swallow is so very small. But, to this, Bishop Jebb's anticipative answer is ready. It is not necessary, hints the Bishop, that we consider Jonah as tombed in the whale's belly, but as temporarily lodged in some part of the mouth. And this seems reasonable enough in the good Bishop. For truly, the Right Whale's mouth would accommodate a couple of whist-tables, and comfortably seat all the players. Possibly, too, Jonah might have ensconced himself in a hollow tooth; but, on second thoughts, the Right Whale is toothless.

Melville's light words are a parody of Eadie's pedantic consideration in Kitto's *Cyclopedia*:

Much profane wit has been expended on the miraculous means of Jonah's deliverance, very unnecessarily and very absurdly; it is simply said, "The Lord had prepared a great fish to swallow up Jonah." Now the species of marine animal is not defined, and the Greek Κητω is often used to specify, not the genus whale, but any large fish or sea-monster. All objections to its being a whale which lodged Jonah in its stomach from its straitness of throat, or rareness of haunt in the Mediterranean, are thus removed. . . . The Scripture thus speaks only of an enormous fish, which under God's direction swallowed the prophet, and does not point out the species to which the voracious prowler belonged. There is little ground for the supposition of Bishop Jebb, that the asylum of Jonah was not in the stomach of a whale, but in a cavity of its throat, which, according to naturalists, is a very capacious receptacle, sufficiently large, as Captain Scoresby asserts, to contain a merchant ship's jolly-boat full of men.

Old Sag-Harbor found further reasons for "his want of faith in this matter of the prophet." The third paragraph of Melville's chapter discusses gravely the effect of the whale's gastric juices on Jonah, a topic suggested to him by Smith's sober words:

> But criticism is still more inappropriate when, not contented with pointing to some assumed species, it attempts to rationalise miraculous events by such arguments; as in the case of Jonah, where the fact of whales having a small gullet, and not being found in the Mediterranean, is adduced to prove that the huge fish *dag* was not a cetacean, but a shark! Now, if the text be literally taken, the transaction is plainly miraculous, and no longer within the sphere of zoological discussion; and if it be allegorical, as some, we think, erroneously assume, then, whether the prophet was saved by means of a kind of boat called *dagh*, or it be a mystical account of initiation where the neophite was detained three days in an ark or boat, figuratively denominated a fish, or Celtic *avanc*, the transaction is equally indeterminate; and it assuredly would be derogating from the high dignity of the prophet's mission, to convert the event into a mere escape, by boat, or into a pagan legend such as Hercules, Bacchus, Jamsheed, and other deified heroes of the remotest antiquity, are fabled to have undergone, and which all the ancient mysteries, including the Druidical, symbolized. It may be observed, besides, of cetaceous animals, that though less frequent in the Mediterranean than in the ocean, they are far from being unknown there.

— as well as by Eadie's passage in the same *Cyclopedia*:

> Less, in his tract, *Von Historischen Styl der Unwelt*, supposed that all difficulty might be removed by imagining that Jonah, when thrown into the sea, was taken up by a ship having a large fish for a figure-head — a theory somewhat more pleasing than the rancid hypothesis of Anton, who fancied that the prophet took refuge in the interior of a dead whale, floating near the spot where he was cast overboard (Rosen, *Prolegom. in Jonah*, p. 328). Not unlike the opinion of Less is that of Charles Taylor, in his Fragments affixed

to Calmet's Dictionary, No. cxlv., that signifies a life-preserver, a notion which, as his manner is, he endeavours to support by mythological metamorphoses founded on the form and names of the famous fish-god of Philistia.

Melville fused the materials of Smith's and Eadie's paragraphs into a single paragraph to confute the skepticism of "old Sag-Harbor":

Another reason which Sag-Harbor (he went by that name) urged for his want of faith in this matter of the prophet, was something obscurely in reference to his incarcerated body and the whale's gastric juices. But this objection likewise falls to the ground, because a German exegetist supposes that Jonah might have taken refuge in the floating body of a *dead* whale — even as the French soldiers in the Russian campaign turned their dead horses into tents, and crawled into them. Besides, it has been divined by other continental commentators, that when Jonah was thrown overboard from the Joppa ship, he straightway effected his escape to another vessel near by, some vessel with a whale for a figure-head; and, I would add, possibly called "The Whale," as some craft are nowadays christened the "Shark," the "Gull," the "Eagle." Nor have there been wanting learned exegetists who have opined that the whale mentioned in the book of Jonah merely meant a life-preserver — an inflated bag of wind — which the endangered prophet swam to, and so was saved from a watery doom. Poor Sag-Harbor, therefore, seems worsted all round.

It might be suggested that Melville's "Old Sag-Harbor" is a personification not only of the Bible skeptics in general but also of one skeptic in particular: Pierre Bayle. Readers of Bayle's *Dictionary* are first struck by the way in which Bayle assembles and sifts contradictory opinions on a subject, rejecting sarcastically, by his severe standards, all evidence which does not meet the test of his reason. The caustic commentary which accompanies the assemblage of evidence saves Bayle from the charge of pedantry; one feels a mind, not a machine, at work. The equating of Pierre Bayle with a tough-minded whaleman is the sort of satire we find elsewhere in *Moby-Dick*. In considering the three days' journey of Jonah, Melville continues the Sag-Harbor investigation of truth:

> But he had still another reason for his want of faith. It was this, if I remember right: Jonah was swallowed by a whale in the Mediterranean Sea, and after three days he was vomited up somewhere within three days' journey of Nineveh, a city on the Tigris, very much more than three days' journey from the nearest point of the Mediterranean coast. How is that?

Melville's "if I remember right" should have been "if I read right," for as he wrote he had his eye on a passage in Bayle's *Dictionary* — from one of the long footnotes in which Bayle demolishes the work of a previous critic, and adds:

> Note, that Nineveh was built upon the river Tigris, which has no immediate communication with the Mediterranean sea. Besides, there is not water enough for such a fish in this river at the port of Nineveh. This reason, together with the surprizing miracle, we must suppose, if we say that the whale went into the ocean, and doubled the cape of Good Hope, and entred into the mouth of the Tigris, and made that pro-digious compass in three days, takes away all sorts of subter-fuge from such as would excuse Sulpicius Severus. That notion never came into his mind; he honestly believed that Nineveh was situated upon the Mediterranean sea, and erred for want of skill in Geography.

This passage from Bayle appears, considerably changed, in *Moby-Dick*:

> But was there no other way for the whale to land the prophet within that short distance of Nineveh? Yes. He might have carried him round by the way of the Cape of Good Hope. But not to speak of the passage through the whole length of the Mediterranean, and another passage up the Per-sian Gulf and Red Sea, such a supposition would involve the complete circumnavigation of all Africa in three days, not to speak of the Tigris waters, near the site of Nineveh, being too shallow for any whale to swim in. Besides, this idea of Jonah's weathering the Cape of Good Hope at so early a day would wrest the honor of the discovery of that great headland from Bartholomew Diaz, its reputed discoverer, and so make mod-ern history a liar.

And Melville added:

> But all these foolish arguments of old Sag-Harbor only evinced his foolish pride of reason — a thing still more reprehensible in him, seeing that he had but little learning except what he had picked up from the sun and the sea. I say it only shows his foolish, impious pride, and abominable, devilish rebellion against the reverend clergy. For by a Portuguese Catholic priest, this very idea of Jonah's going to Nineveh via the Cape of Good Hope was advanced as a signal magnification of the general miracle. And so it was.

Bayle had sarcastically attacked the practice of believers in attacking the beliefs of others much different, and Melville has picked up the attack on religious intolerance.

The three sentences with which "Jonah Historically Regarded" ends contains a curious error on Melville's part:

> Besides, to this day, the highly enlightened Turks devoutly believe in the historical story of Jonah. And some three centuries ago, an English traveller in old Harris's Voyages, speaks of a Turkish Mosque built in honor of Jonah, in which mosque was a miraculous lamp that burnt without any oil.

Speaking from memory, apparently, Melville thought that he had read his facts in "old Harriss's" voyage collection — used before, it will be recalled, in "The Heidelburgh Tun." Instead, the information came from Bayle's *Dictionary*, a confusion probably arising from the similarity in size (huge folio) between Harriss's and Bayle's books. In the *Dictionary* Melville had read:

> Mr Simon affirms, that the Turks have *built a very fine mosque to the honour of* Jonas, *in which there is a miraculous lamp, that burns continually without any oil or other liquor, if he will give credit to their reveries.* He says that this mosque is *in a little village, built to the honour and under the name of this Prophet.*

Melville was no scholar trying to compile a thesis on a chapter from Jonah. If he were, he omitted much curious information, facts which would have attracted him had he come across them in his readings. Bypassing such bits of knowl-

edge, that Jonah's footprints might still be seen near Naz-
areth, or that Jonah's whale is to go to Paradise because it
cast out his rider upon dry land, or that the Jonah story has,
depending upon the commentator, tremendous political and
social allegorical constructions — bypassing much interesting
information and conjecture, Melville concentrated the little
that he had learned from the Bible, from Kitto's *Cyclopedia
of Biblical Literature*, and Pierre Bayle's *Dictionary* into a
humorous discussion of the greatest whaleman of all, into
a possible satire of his own immediate sources, and into a
friendly mockery of the Higher Critics of the Bible — and
possibly into a satire of his own search for verifiable truth
in a world full of contradictory reports.

17

"The Fountain" and "The Tail"

To THE WORLD at large both in Melville's day, and our own,
the most notable characteristic of the whale was its spout,
or, as Melville calls it in his chapter on the subject, "The
Fountain" (85). Therefore, the importance of the subject
for a whaleman addressing a lay audience is rather obvious;
hence, Melville's inclusion of five factual pages on spouting.
At the time when *Moby-Dick* was written, many scientists,
even specialists on cetology, were badly confused as to the
exact nature of the fountain. Beale says, "From Pliny's
down to the present time, the notion has existed that he constantly ejects water with his breath, which has caused F. Cuvier
to indulge also in this belief, because, as he states, 'so many
persons have been witnesses of it, that he cannot for a
moment doubt the recital.'" So far as Melville was concerned, Beale settled the question once and for all with the
statement:

> I can only say, when I find myself again in opposition to
> those old and received notions, that, out of the thousands of
> sperm whales which I have seen during my wanderings in the

south and north Pacific Oceans, I have never observed one of them to eject a column of water from his nostril. I have seen them at a distance, and I have been within a few yards of several hundreds of them, and I never saw water pass from the spouthole. But the column of thick and dense vapour which is certainly ejected, is exceedingly likely to mislead the judgment of the casual observer in these matters; and this column does indeed appear very much like a jet of water, when seen at the distance of one or two miles on a clear day, because of the condensation of the vapour, which takes place the moment it escapes from the nostril, and its consequent opacity, which makes it appear of a white colour.

And Frederick Bennett, in a passage quoted by Beale, had also argued the true theory for Melville's benefit:

It is yet an unsettled point, whether the spiracles of spouting-whales have an office solely respiratory, or if they are also of use to eject the water received into the mouth together with food. In favour of the opinion that the spout is nothing more than the vapour of the breath, we may advance, — the uniform appearance of the jets, and regularity of their repetition, corresponding with the ordinary rhythm of respiration; — their being always present, and successively continued, as long as the whale remains on the surface of the water; although the animal may be at this time unoccupied with food, or even swimming with velocity, its head raised above the surface of a calm sea, and its mouth shut; — the character of the spout, which resembles a cloud, or mist, and can in no way be compared to a volume of water; — the fact, that seals, and other aquatic mammalia, as well as the herbivorous cetaceans, seize and devour their food in the water, and rise to the surface to breathe; yet do not spout, and have no peculiar provision for freeing their mouth from water, if any water be received. In the case, also, of many spouting whales, a necessity for casting water from their spiracles should rather exist in the profound depths, where they feed, than on the surface, where their business is chiefly to respire.[89]

89 The best treatment of spoutings is by Emile G. Racovitz, "A Summary of General Observations on the Spouting and Movement of Whales," in Smithsonian *Annual Reports,* Washington, 1903, I, 527–641. On p. 631 he points out that the vapor theory had been held by Fabricius (1790), Scoresby (1820), Baer (1826 and 1836), Beale (1839), and Bennett (1839), etc.

From these quotations it seems clear that Melville's basic position — indeed, his entire argument — was worked up from the pages of Beale and Bennett. His introductory statement concerning the difficulty of the problem —

> That for six thousand years — and no one knows how many millions of ages before — the great whales should have been spouting all over the sea, and sprinkling and mistifying the gardens of the deep, as with so many sprinkling or mistifying pots; and that for some centuries back, thousands of hunters should have been close by the fountain of the whale, watching these sprinklings and spoutings — that all this should be, and yet, that down to this blessed minute (fifteen and a quarter minutes past one o'clock P.M. of this sixteenth day of December, A.D. 1851), it should still remain a problem, whether these spoutings are, after all, really water, or nothing but vapor — this is surely a noteworthy thing.

— is reshaped from the fish documents, although we may be puzzled by the parenthetical addition placing Melville's writing in December, 1851. At that time *Moby-Dick* had been in print for three months and was still being reviewed. The only rational explanation is that "1851" is a typographical error. By changing one digit so that we read "1850," the passage makes sense. It would show Melville writing his eighty-fifth chapter at the time when he was most deeply in his work, December, 1850, the time of the letter to Duyckinck in which we first hear about Melville's work on the enlarged draft of *Moby-Dick* — instead of writing it after the book was published!

It was well for Melville that he had as support two such reliable authorities as Beale and Bennett, for although *Moby-Dick* would lose none of its true greatness should Melville have argued the water-spout theory, nevertheless it strengthens the book to have it correct in basic facts. Writing a book which he knew would be criticized by whalemen and other sailors, like Richard Henry Dana, Jr., Melville was wise not to make loose conjectures, except when it suited his ironic intention, in assembling his whaling lore. Consequently in such a chapter as "The Fountain" Melville stayed close to Beale's fourth chapter, "Breathing." [90] His fidelity to Beale's text is made apparent by parallel quotation:

BEALE	MELVILLE
at each breathing time the whale makes from sixty to seventy expirations, and remains, therefore, at the surface ten or eleven minutes. At the termination of this breathing time, or as whalers say, when he has had his 'spoutings out,' the head sinks slowly. . . .	. . . when I consider the otherwise inexplicable obstinacy of that Leviathan in *having his spoutings out,* as the fishermen phrase it. This is what I mean. If unmolested, upon rising to the surface, the Sperm Whale will continue there for a period of time exactly uniform with all his other unmolested risings. Say he stays eleven minutes, and jets seventy times, that is, respires seventy breaths; then whenever he rises again, he will be sure to have his seventy breaths over again, to a minute. Now, if after he fetches a few breaths you alarm him, so that he sounds, he will be always dodging up again to make good his regular allowance of air. And not till those seventy breaths are told, will he finally go down to stay out his full term below. Remark, however, that in different individuals these rates are different; but in any one whale they are alike. Now, why
When disturbed or alarmed, this regularity in breathing appears to be no longer observed; for instance, when a "bull," which when disturbed remains at the surface until he has made sixty expirations, is alarmed by the approach of the boat, he immediately plunges beneath the waves, although it may have performed half the usual number, but will soon rise again not far distant,	

90 The chapter in Melville's copy is as frequently marked as any in the book. It should be pointed out, perhaps, that much of Beale's information is incorporated into the narrative scenes, as, for instance, in "The First Lowering," where we are told that the men, waiting for the whale to rise again, could time the whale's submersion by the number of spouts per minute. Melville, in Henry James's later words, could not "imagine composition existing in a series of blocks . . . of a passage of description that is not in its intention narrative, a passage of dialogue that is not in its intention descriptive, a touch of truth that does not partake of the nature of incident."

and finish his full number of respirations.

If we then take into consideration the quantity of time that the full-grown sperm whale consumes in respiration, and also the time he takes in searching for food, and performing other acts, below the surface of the ocean, we shall find, by a trifling calculation, that the former bears proportion to the latter, as one to seven, or in other words, that a seventh of the time of this huge animal is consumed in the function of respiration.

... it is formed of the expired air, which is forcibly ejected by the animal through the blowhole, acquiring its white colour from minute particles of water, previously lodged in the chink, or fissure of the nostril, and also from the condensation of the aqueous

should the whale thus insist upon having his spoutings out, unless it be to replenish his reservoir of air, ere descending for good? How obvious is it, too, that this necessity for the whale's rising exposes him to all the fatal hazards of the chase. For not by hook or by net could this vast Leviathan be caught, when sailing a thousand fathoms beneath the sunlight. Not so much thy skill, then, O hunter, as the great necessities that strike the victory to thee!

In man, breathing is incessantly going on — one breath only serving for two or three pulsations; so that whatever other business he has to attend to, waking or sleeping, breathe he must, or die he will. But the Sperm Whale only breathes about one seventh or Sunday of his time.

The central body of it is hidden in the snowy sparkling mist enveloping it; and how can you certainly tell whether any water falls from it, when, always, when you are close enough to a whale to get a close view of his spout, he is in a prodigious commotion,

vapour thrown off by the lungs. . . .
and this column does indeed appear very much like a jet of water, when seen at the distance of one or two miles on a clear day, because of the condensation of the vapour, which takes place the moment it escapes from the nostril, and its consequent opacity, which makes it appear of a white colour, and which is not observed when the whale is close to the spectator, and it then appears only like a jet of white steam; the only water in addition is the small quantity that may be lodged in the external fissure of the spout-hole when the animal raises it above the surface to breathe, and which is blown up into the air with the spout, and may probably assist in condensing the vapour of which it is formed.

the water cascading all around him. And if at such times you should think that you really perceived drops of moisture in the spout, how do you know that they are not merely condensed from its vapor; or how do you know that they are not those identical drops superficially lodged in the spout-hole fissure, which is countersunk into the summit of the whale's head? For even when tranquilly swimming through the mid-day sea in a calm, with his elevated hump sun-dried as a dromedary's in the desert; even then, the whale always carries a small basin of water on his head, as under a blazing sun you will sometimes see a cavity in a rock filled up with rain.

Nowhere in *Moby-Dick* than in these paragraphs has Melville more closely followed a source, but even here identifying mannerisms, or habits of style, which are characteristic of Melville make their appearance. Where Beale describes in precise detail that the falling vapor acquires its white color from the minute particles of water "lodged in the chink, or fissure of the nostril," Melville describes the water as a "snowy sparkling mist" and develops Beale's chink into a figure of speech, or two of them: the whale as a camel, the chink as a small basin of water, or as a cavity in a rock filled with rain. Also, Beale's words, "a seventh of the time of this huge animal is consumed in the function of respiration" becomes with Melville, "But the Sperm Whale only breathes about one seventh or Sunday of his time," a remark which is not only reworked Beale, but it is a possible satire of a large section of the Reverend Henry Cheever's book, *The Whale and His Captors,* in which the whaleman-minister had propagandized against the constant violation of the Sabbath in the American Sperm Whale Fishery. It may also allude to William Scoresby's similar point of view piously maintained in *An Account of the Arctic Regions.*[91] Finally, the minute touches added by Melville go far to vivify the unadorned prose of the scientist; such details as the comparison of the long spouting canal with its valvular system as being "like the grand Erie Canal," a reference which drew upon personal travel by Melville over the canal. Or again, referring to the whale's voicelessness, he suddenly injects the heartfelt remark, a paraphrase of sentences from his letters to Duyckinck, "But then again, what has the whale to say? Seldom have I known any profound being that had anything to say to this world, unless forced to stammer out something by way of getting a living. Oh! happy that the world is such an excellent listener!" Except the world of 1851 was not — for *Moby-Dick,* and later, for *Pierre.*

Towards the end of the chapter, however, Melville broadens out in discussing the spout:

> Nor is it at all prudent for the hunter to be over curious touching the precise nature of the whale spout. It will not do for him to be peering into it, and putting his face in it. You cannot go with your pitcher to this fountain and fill it, and bring it away. For even when coming into slight contact with the outer, vapory shreds of the jet, which will often happen, your skin will feverishly smart, from the acridness of the thing so touching it. And I know one, who coming into still closer contact with the spout, whether with some scientific object in view, or otherwise, I cannot say, the skin peeled off from his

91 The subject, however, seems to have been one in general public consideration, as for instance, in the article "Is it right to take Whales on the Sabbath?" in *The Friend of Temperance and Seamen,* II (4 April, 1844), (37) –39, 42–43, published in Honolulu.

cheek and arm. Wherefore, among whalemen, the spout is deemed poisonous; they try to evade it.

Maybe Melville is speaking here from *Acushnet* memories, but one wonders whether the man whom Melville "knew" could have been Frederick Debell Bennett, who wrote: "During a close encounter with this whale, the latter often spouts into the boats and amongst the crew, when the exhaled fluid has been observed to be foetid in odour, and to produce an acrid effect upon the skin." Melville's allusion to "some scientific object in view" suggests the naturalist Bennett.[92]

Melville [93] the analogist closes "The Fountain" with one of his most sardonic conceits. Arguing that since sperm whales are never found close to shore they are both ponderous and profound, Melville jestingly suggests that from the heads of "ponderous profound beings, such as Plato, Pyrrho, the Devil, Jupiter, Dante, and so on, there always goes up a certain semi-visible steam, while in the act of thinking deep thoughts." In fact, he says, when writing an essay on Eternity, he had glanced into the mirror to see "a curious involved worming and undulation in the atmosphere over my head" — although, he adds, it might possibly have arisen from the fact of his having six cups of hot tea in a thin-shingled attic on a hot day. From this humorous note, he suddenly shifts to a metaphysical one, identifying the "mighty, misty monster" with the perception of finite phenomena and the infinite:

> And how nobly it raises our conceit of the mighty, misty monster, to behold him sailing through a calm tropical sea;

92 Otto von Kotzebue in his *Voyage of Discovery in the South Sea,* etc. (London, 1821), published in vol. VI of Phillips's Collection of Voyages, described the effect of the whale's spout as follows: "now and then whales made their appearance, throwing up high fountains. One . . . threw his fountain so high that the spray flew in our faces, an event which was not of the most pleasant kind, the water thrown out in this way being of a very disagreeable smell." It is of course possible that since Melville was acquainted with Kotzebue's narrative that he may have used this information along with Bennett, and also used the fountain metaphor.

93 Curiously, in Beale's discussion of the blow-hole, Melville underlined the words, now erased: "the human species alone breathe by the mouth."

his vast, mild head overhung by a canopy of vapor, engendered by his incommunicable contemplations, and that vapor — as you will sometimes see it — glorified by a rainbow, as if Heaven itself had put its seal upon his thoughts. For, d'ye see, rainbows do not visit the clear air; they only irradiate vapor. And so, through all the thick mists of the dim doubts in my mind, divine intuitions now and then shoot, enkindling my fog with a heavenly ray. And for this I thank God; for all have doubts; many deny; but doubts or denials, few along with them, have intuitions. Doubts of all things earthly, and intuitions of some things heavenly; this combination makes neither believer nor infidel, but makes a man who regards them both with equal eye.

Thus Melville has moved from the periphery of Beale and Bennett to the philosophical center of *Moby-Dick*.

There is nothing precisely like Melville's chapter "The Tail" (86), in any of his fish documents, but it was from hints in those sources that Melville wrote his account of the whale's flukes. "Other poets have warbled the praises of the soft eye of the antelope, and the lovely plumage of the bird that never alights; less celestial I celebrate a tail." Original as this seems — and is — it is possible that Melville had been amused by Beale's scientific enthusiasm, "The mode in which the tail is constructed is perhaps as beautiful, as to the mechanism, as any part of the animal." For Melville the key word was "beautiful," and at the end of his second paragraph he said, "In no living thing are the lines of beauty more exquisitely defined than in the crescentic borders of these flukes." Throughout the entire chapter Melville carries out Beale's enthusiastic note.

Beale's *Natural History of the Sperm Whale* quoted Doctor John Hunter's description of the construction of the whale's tail:

It is wholly composed of three layers of tendinous fibres, covered by the common cutis and cuticle; two of these layers are external, the other internal. The direction of the fibres of the external layers is the same as in the tail, forming a stratum about one-third of an inch thick, but varying in this respect as the tail is thicker or thinner.

The middle layer is composed entirely of tendinous fibres passing directly across between the two external ones above described, their length being in proportion to the thickness of the tail; a structure which gives amazing strength to this part.

Losing nothing of Beale's (Hunter's) fact, Melville improved the description for his chapter:

The entire member seems a dense webbed bed of welded sinews; but cut into it, and you find that three distinct strata compose it: — upper, middle, and lower. The fibres in the upper and lower layers, are long and horizontal; those of the middle one, very short, and running crosswise between the outside layers. This triune structure, as much as anything else, imparts power to the tail. To the student of old Roman walls, the middle layer will furnish a curious parallel to the thin course of tiles always alternating with the stone in those wonderful relics of the antique, and which undoubtedly contribute so much to the great strength of the masonry.[94]

The effectiveness of metaphor and analogy in achieving vividness is by the contrast between Beale's (Hunter's) and Melville's paragraphs.

It seems certain, too, that Melville reinforced his account of the tail from Bennett's words on the subject, including:

Owing to the flexibility of the tail, the movements of this fin are exceedingly extensive; whilst its power may be estimated by the gigantic bundles of round tendons which pass on either side of the loins to be inserted into its base. Whether it be wielded in sportive mood or in anger, its action is marked by rapidity and ease; and when struck forcibly on the surface of the ocean, it produces a report which may be heard at a considerable distance.

[94] Melville's next paragraph also comes from the passage which I quoted out of Beale: "But as if this vast and local power in the tendinous tail were not enough, the whole bulk of the Leviathan is knit over with a warp and woof of muscular fibres and filaments, which passing on either side the loins and running down into the flukes, insensibly blend with them, and largely contribute to their might; so that in the tail the confluent measureless force of the whole whale seems concentrated to a point. Could annihilation occur to matter, this were the thing to do it." The last sentence is almost directly out of *Ribs and Trucks*. Writing as an artist rather than a scientist, Melville was of course at liberty to sum up, or to see a conclusion, as in this closing sentence — one which links the whale's flukes with the atomic bomb.

Since the climax of *Moby-Dick* rests on the power of the whale to sink a ship, Melville extracts from Beale and Bennett the concepts of "beauty," "strength," and "flexibility" and elaborates them far beyond the scope or intention of the ordinary whaling author:

> Nor does this — its amazing strength, at all tend to cripple the graceful flexion of its motions; where infantileness of ease undulates through a Titanism of power. On the contrary, those motions derive their most appalling beauty from it. Real strength never impairs beauty or harmony, but it often bestows it; and in everything imposingly beautiful, strength has much to do with the magic. Take away the tied tendons that all over seem bursting from the marble in the carved Hercules, and its charm would be gone. As devout Eckerman lifted the linen sheet from the naked corpse of Goethe, he was overwhelmed with the massive chest of the man, that seemed as a Roman triumphal arch. When Angelo paints even God the Father in human form, mark what robustness is there. And whatever they may reveal of the divine love in the Son, the soft, curled, hermaphroditical Italian pictures, in which his idea has been most successfully embodied; these pictures, so destitute as they are of all brawniness, hint nothing of any power, but the mere negative, feminine one of submission and endurance, which on all hands it is conceded, form the peculiar practical virtues of his teachings.

A wide-ranging mind wrote this passage; one which had studied Michelangelo's art, one which knew Roman architecture and forms, and one which had read the newly translated *Conversations with Goethe* by Eckermann, which closes with the touching, and now famous, account of Eckermann gazing at the corpse of his beloved friend.

With such a range of reference for such a trivial subject as a whale's tail, Melville illustrates again the poetic mind which gathers into itself disparate experiences and imposes unity upon them.

The five motions peculiar to the tail are Melville's original list, compiled from memory and from reminders in Beale and Bennett; Melville says: "Five great motions are peculiar to it. First, when used as a fin for progression; Second, when used as a mace in battle; Third, in sweeping; Fourth, in lobtailing; Fifth, in peaking flukes." For his description of the first use, Melville seemingly called upon Bennett's description; having already used the descriptive term:

> In progression, the action of this organ is precisely the reverse of that of the tail of the lobster . . . the Cachalot, and other cetaceans, swim forward, by striking with their fluke in the contrary direction; the fin being brought beneath the body by an oblique and unresisting movement, while the act of springing it back, and straightening the tail, propels the animal ahead, with an undulating or leaping gait. When employed offensively, as in striking at a boat, the tail is curved in a direction contrary to that of the object aimed at; and the blow is inflicted by the force of the recoil.

Melville's description of the progression as "that singular darting, leaping motion to the monster when furiously swimming," and his sentence about the tail as a "mace," "In striking at a boat, he swiftly curves away his flukes from it, and the blow is only inflicted by the recoil," are both adapted from Bennett. Similarly, the account of "lobtailing" and of "peaking flukes" in *Moby-Dick* seems to have come from Beale. Writing about lobtailing, Beale said:

> Occasionally, when lying at the surface, the whale appears to amuse itself by violently beating the water with its tail; this act is called "lob-tailing," and the water lashed in this way into foam, is termed "white water" by the whaler, and by it the whale is recognized from a great distance.

One also senses all the way through "The Tail" that Melville made use, somehow, of Scoresby. Melville's leaping fancy must have been attracted to Scoresby's words:

> Sometimes the whales throw themselves into a perpendicular posture, with their heads downward, and, rearing their tails on high in the air, beat the water with awful violence. In both these cases, the sea is thrown into foam, and the air filled with vapours; the noise, in calm weather, is heard to a great distance; and the concentric waves produced by the concussions on the water, are communicated abroad to a con-

siderable extent. Sometimes the whale shakes its tremendous tail in the air, which, cracking like a whip, resounds to the distance of two or three miles.

When it retires from the surface, it first lifts its head, then plunging it under water, elevates its back like the segment of a sphere, deliberately rounds it away towards the extremity, throws its tail out of water, and then disappears.

For what Melville did with Scoresby's details and also with the accounts of peaking and breaching, the reader is referred to *Moby-Dick*. Only full quotation may do Melville's vivid descriptions justice. But one may be assured that it was Melville's reading, reinforcing his memory, which furnished him with the materials for his pen. But the reading was done by an artist who could create phrases like "the measureless crush and crash of the Sperm Whale's ponderous flukes," or who had the imaginative daring to equate the whale's tail with Miltonian grandeurs: "Out of the bottomless profundities the gigantic tail seems spasmodically snatching at the highest heaven. So in dreams, have I seen majestic Satan thrusting forth his tormented colossal claw from the flame Baltic of Hell." Or again, the reading of a man who had harpooned whales, who had "swam through libraries" of fish documents, and who had read Pierre Bayle's essay on Zoroaster, so that he could compare the peaking of a herd of flukes with the religious adoration of the fire worshipers of the East. Or finally, of a writer adumbrating mysterious meanings concerning his great subject, ending with the sardonic words:

Dissect him how I may, then, I but go skin deep. I know him not, and never will. But if I know not even the tail of this whale, how understand his head? much more, how comprehend his face, when face he has none. Thou shalt see my back parts, my tail, he seems to say, but my face shall not be seen. But I cannot completely make out his back parts; and hint what he will about his face, I say again he has no face.

Call this humor, for such it is, but it is also the restatement of one of the profoundest themes in *Moby-Dick,* the inability of man to know the final truths of life — Ahab's final inability to capture the White Whale — stated in Rabelaisian terms.

18

"Another and still stranger world"

As SEEN SEVERAL TIMES by now, it was Melville's frequent practice to gather his whaling information into sections of two chapters each, generally illustrating his subject (ambergris, the whale's food, or the whale's skeleton) by a story or by a grotesque episode in one chapter, and then expounding his expository detail in the other. Sometimes he went beyond the two-chapter section, sometimes his material could be developed within the confines of one chapter, but always he tried to blend factual information with narrative development, never really allowing any dead spots in the book. Melville's trick of developing a topic as described is exemplified most neatly in his treatment of the sociology of the whale, or what Beale titled in his similar chapter, "Herding," and what Bennett named "Natural History and habits of the Cachalot." Beale and Bennett supplied the factual base on which Melville constructed his two-chapter section, "The Grand Armada" (87) and "Schools and Schoolmasters" (88). The first of these two deserves D. H. Lawrence's praise of it as a "stupendous chapter." It renders an "account of an immense body or herd of Sperm Whales, and . . . the probable cause inducing those vast aggregations," but the pedantic tone of Melville's words is counteracted by his transformation of fact into living narrative.

"The Grand Armada," which really falls into two main parts, begins with pursuit by the *Pequod* of an enormous herd of whales swimming in varying formations, and with varying antics, through the Straits of Sunda, off Java Head, even while the *Pequod* herself becomes the quarry of Malayan pirates who, said Melville, "Time out of mind . . . have sallied out upon the vessels sailing through the straits, fiercely demanding tribute at the point of their spears." The amazing chain pursuit continues "as with glass under arm, Ahab to-and-fro paced the deck; in his forward turn beholding the monsters he chased, and in the after one the blood-thirsty pirates chasing him."

The pursuit of the pursuer is an ironic structure wide-spread in its artistic manifestations, ranging from Aeschylus's *Oresteiad* to *As You Like It* and *A Midsummer-Night's Dream* to the most recent Alfred Hitchcock picture. Perhaps its greatest appearance is in Mozart's *Don Giovanni* with the hero in pursuit of innocence, himself pursued by those he has ravaged. In *Mardi* the pursuer Taji is pursued by Hautia's maidens. In *Moby-Dick* is much the same pro-gression: the hero Ahab pursuing the innocent whales, him-self pursued by the morally destroyed. The themes of quest and flight make excellent counterpoint.

Much of "The Grand Armada" was inspired by Bennett's *A Whaling Voyage*: the *Pequod's* pursuit of the whale ar-mada, the later threat to the lives of Ishmael and Queequeg; but they were not *taken* from Bennett, they grew from de-tails which Melville had noted. It is useful to compare the rough, serviceable cotton weave of Bennett with the rich, gold-shot fabric from Melville's literary loom.

For instance, two of the dramatic scenes in "The Grand Armada" sprang from a simple, unadorned sentence in Ben-nett:

> When pursued, they may be considered to exhibit two degrees of alarm; namely, that which puts them to the top of their speed, and which often enables them to escape the boats; or a more powerful and overwhelming impression, pro-duced by the near approach of their enemies, or by one of their number being injured; when they will occasionally crowd together, stationary and trembling, or make but con-fused and irresolute efforts to escape.

Melville took the first degree of alarm, "that which puts them to the top of their speed," to create the episode of the *Pequod's* pursuit of the whale pod, adding as he did so the dramatic-ironic pursuit of the *Pequod* herself by the pirat-ical Malayans — the bloodthirsty pursued by the bloodthirsty. Melville developed Bennett's second degree of alarm, "by one of their own number being injured; when they will oc-

casionally crowd together," into the picture of the wounded
whale twisted around the line, to which is attached the razor-
keen cutting spade, "violently flailing with his flexible tail"
as he swims in convulsive fury, the spade "wounding and
murdering his own comrades." Alarmed by this danger, the
whales crowd together so as to threaten the cockleshell containing Ishmael and Queequeg.[95]

Returning to the chain pursuit, we read that the *Pequod*
finally outdistanced her pursuers. The men were at liberty
to take to the boats for the capture of the wealth swimming
close by. The boat containing Ishmael, Queequeg, and Starbuck unexpectedly becomes the center of the great whale
pod. Wonderingly and fearfully they gaze at the whales
swiftly circling their boat: "And still in the distracted distance we beheld the tumults of the outer concentric circles,
and saw successive pods of whales, eight or ten in each,
swiftly going round and round, like multiplied spans of
horses in a ring." Their gambols threaten the boat, but even
in his alarm Ishmael admires and wonders. The phenomena
of new life and imminent death are revealed to him in the
depths and on the surface of the sea.

It is strange to find that Melville's beautiful and exciting
story has its roots in Bennett's introductory paragraphs on
the whale's social habits:

> The Sperm Whale is gregarious; and usually occurs in
> parties, which are termed by whalers "schools" and "pods":
> the former name expressing the greater, and the latter the
> less number of individuals congregated together. A school may
> contain from twenty to fifty or more Cachalots, and is com-
> posed of females, or "cows," attended by their young, and asso-
> ciated with at least one adult male, or "bull," of the largest
> size, who acts as the guardian of the herd, and who, with a
> devotion highly creditable to his gallantry, generally takes a
> defensive position in the rear. . . . Two or more schools occa-

---

[95] Possibly suggested by a sentence in *Ribs and Trucks* in which when
returning in the boat from a gam, they were "suddenly surrounded by a
herd of whales — puffing and blowing and kicking up their heels, till the
water was a vortex of foam. Completely hedged in, drenched with brine from
their spiracles, menaced with immediate contact, and as immediate destruction — 'Jack,' said the captain, 'can't you hit the snortin' varmint?'"

sionally coalesce, and form very large assemblies, technically distinguished as a "body of whales." On some tracts of ocean, peculiarly favoured as their haunts, the number of Sperm Whales, seen in one large body or in many distinct schools, is beyond all reasonable conception; and could it be accurately named, would appear incredible to persons who alone consider the vast size of this animal, or who may have traversed the main for many months without noticing more than a single whale spouting in the distance. At particular times and places, however, we have seen the ocean, for several miles around the ship, strewn with a constant succession of spouts, denoting a greater number of Cachalots than, could they all have been secured, would have afforded a full cargo of oil for three or four ships.[96]

Compare Melville in "The Grand Armada" —

But here be it premised, that owing to the unwearied activity with which of late they have been hunted over all four oceans, the Sperm Whales, instead of almost invariably sailing in small detached companies, as in former times, are now frequently met with in extensive herds, sometimes embracing so great a multitude, that it would almost seem as if numerous nations of them had sworn solemn league and covenant for mutual assistance and protection. To this aggregation of the Sperm Whale into such immense caravans, may be imputed the circumstance that even in the best cruising grounds, you may now sometimes sail for weeks and months together, without being greeted by a single spout; and then be suddenly saluted by what sometimes seems thousands on thousands.

The opening of Melville's succeeding chapter, "Schools and Schoolmasters" —

Now, though such great bodies are at times encountered, yet, as must have been seen, even at the present day, small detached bands are occasionally observed, embracing from twenty to fifty individuals each. Such bands are known as schools. They generally are of two sorts; those composed almost entirely of females, and those mustering none but young vigorous males, or bulls as they are familiarly designated.

— is almost a copy of Bennett's sentences.

[96] Beale's discussion of the whale's social habits is so brief that Melville preferred Bennett's fuller account.

Bennett merely gave the factual basis for Melville's episodes; the creation of those scenes in *Moby-Dick* had to be effected by a powerful imagination able to adorn the dustiest detail with life and significance. One tires — or does one? — of reiteratively praising this passage and that scene as being remarkable in *Moby-Dick*. The entire book is so freighted; but among the great scenes few are more memorable than Ishmael's sight of the new-born whale in the depths of the sea, as their boat poised "in that enchanted calm which they say lurks at the heart of every commotion":

But far beneath this wondrous world upon the surface, another and still stranger world met our eyes as we gazed over the side. For, suspended in those watery vaults, floated the forms of the nursing mothers of the whales, and those that by their enormous girth seemed shortly to become mothers. The lake, as I have hinted, was to a considerable depth exceedingly transparent; and as human infants while suckling will calmly and fixedly gaze away from the breast, as if leading two different lives at the time; and while yet drawing mortal nourishment, be still spiritually feasting upon some unearthly reminiscence; — even so did the young of these whales seem looking up towards us, but not at us, as if we were but a bit of Gulf-weed in their new-born sight. Floating on their sides, the mothers also seemed quietly eyeing us. One of these little infants, that from certain queer tokens seemed hardly a day old, might have measured some fourteen feet in length, and some six feet in girth. He was a little frisky; though as yet his body seemed scarce recovered from that irksome position it had so lately occupied in the maternal reticule; where, tail to head, and all ready for the final spring, the unborn whale lies bent like a Tartar's bow. The delicate side-fins, and the palms of his flukes, still freshly retained the plaited crumpled appearance of a baby's ears newly arrived from foreign parts.

"Line! line!" cried Queequeg, looking over the gunwale, "him fast! him fast! — Who line him! Who struck? — Two whale; one big, one little!"

"What ails ye, man?" cried Starbuck.

"Look-e here," said Queequeg, pointing down.

As when the stricken whale, that from the tub has reeled out hundreds of fathoms of rope; as, after deep sounding, he floats up again, and shows the slackened curling line buoyantly rising and spiralling towards the air; so now, Starbuck saw long coils of the umbilical cord of Madame Leviathan, by which the young cub seemed still tethered to its dam. Not seldom in the rapid vicissitudes of the chase, this natural line, with the maternal end loose, becomes entangled with the hempen one, so that the cub is thereby trapped. Some of the subtlest secrets of the sea seemed divulged to us in this enchanted pond. We saw young Leviathan amours in the deep.

Like so many scenes in *Moby-Dick*, this one is written with the sureness of hand which suggests, to most readers, that the author must have been writing from his own firsthand knowledge. Knowing Melville's history, one is tempted to accept his account of the whale nursery as the recorded remembrance of something from his whaling past. The assumption is a pitfall for autobiographical critics, and one into which they have fallen, in the past, while interpreting scenes from *White-Jacket* or from *Typee*. Melville, let it be remembered, had a powerful imagination; again, he added thereto a practiced skill in reconstructing whole scenes within his novels from simple sentences or plain paragraphs by other writers.[97] Melville could take an inch of suggestion and make a yard of dramatic narrative. He had the invariable mark of wisdom, which is, according to Emerson, "to see the miraculous in the common." The enchanting whale nursery was constructed on the following passage from *A Whaling Voyage*:

Nothing satisfactory is known about the duration of pregnancy in this whale. We observed them copulating in August, but it is probable that no particular breeding season obtains, as we observed sucking calves during the entire eight months in the year we were engaged in cruising. The female produces one at a birth, but occasionally twins, as is usual with uniparous animals. She brings forth her young in the open ocean, and indiscriminately, on whatever spot the school may chance to be at the time of her parturition. The calf accom-

[97] Melville *had* read in Olmsted, *Incidents of a Whaling Voyage*, p. 139, of a becalmed schooner off the coast of Peru suddenly and frighteningly surrounded by a herd of whales, but I cannot see that he made use of the passage.

panies the school as soon as it is born. During a chase, it was often exceedingly interesting to observe sucklings, apparently but a few days old, leaping actively and spouting high by the side of their dams, and keeping up wonderfully well with the rapid pace of the retreating party.

Intelligent whalers, who have occasionally seen the female Cachalot in the act of suckling her young, agree very closely in their description of this process. They state, that the mother reposes upon her side, with the pectoral fin raised above the surface of the sea, while the calf, which is thus enabled to retain its spiracle in the air, receives the protruded nipple within the angle of the mouth — a part where it is reasonable to suppose that the tongue would also be found of some assistance.

There will be people who stubbornly argue that Melville may have once seen calves nursing in the Pacific Ocean, and that what he tells in *Moby-Dick* came from his photographic memory. But if this is true, then Melville was an inaccurate reporter, for the detail of whale-nursing in *Moby-Dick* — from Beale and Bennett — does not agree with physiological record. Whales do not nurse in the way Melville described. The breast of the mother whale is so retracted within the mass of blubber, and the projection of the teat is so slight, that it is physically impossible for the cub to take the nipple within the awkward and enormous cavern of his mouth. Beale and Bennett had *assumed* the act of suckling from the physiological fact of breast and milk and from the reports of whalemen; modern zoologists more accurately report that the cub whale places its mouth as close to the breast as possible while the mother whale pumps the milk into its mouth, optimistically assuming, perhaps, that all the food reaches its purposed destination.[98]

The baby whale and the umbilical cord of *Moby-Dick* had their origin in Bennett's experience, not Melville's. Bennett wrote:

[98] One of the first to realize exactly how whales suckle was Sir William Wilde, father of Oscar. (T. G. Wilson, *Victorian Doctor* [New York, 1946], pp. 80–83.) His theory has been verified by the daily observations by scientists of porpoises at the Marine Studios, Marineland, Florida.

In January, 1835, I was enabled, through the kindness of Captain Stavers, to make an anatomical examination of a foetal Cachalot, which was removed from the abdomen of its mother, and taken on board the ship. Without entering into minute particulars, I may mention the following, as the principal peculiarities noticed in this young example, which was a male, and sufficiently mature to be within a few hours of its birth. It was fourteen feet long, and six in circumference; of a deep black colour, prettily mottled with a few white-spots; and in form, as perfect as the adult whale, with the single exception that the tail-fin was crumpled on its free border, and had the corner of each fluke folded inwards. Its position in the womb was that of a bent bow — the head and tail being approximated, and the back arched. The umbilical cord (which was inserted at the posterior part of the abdomen) was five feet long, nine inches in circumference, and chiefly composed of five capacious blood-vessels.[99]

Melville's sporting day-old cub and Bennett's foetal whale were one and the same animal; they had the same measurements, both had the umbilical cord, both had the bent shape reminiscent of the womb position. And finally, both had the crumpled fins. Melville, however, added one interesting detail. Remembering his own son Malcolm, born before *Moby-Dick* was in composition, he included the simile of "the baby's ears newly arrived from foreign parts." It was the one characteristic detail out of personal experience which would help Melville make the passage his own.

Like the two whaling authorities with whom he was best acquainted, and whom he was following, Melville included

[99] Having drawn Scoresby's *An Account of the Arctic Regions* from the New York Society library, 29 April, 1850, Melville undoubtedly made use of Scoresby's similar scene:

"The sexual intercourse of whales is often observed about the latter end of summer; and females, with cubs or suckers along with them, being most commonly met with in the spring of the year, the time of their bringing forth, it is presumed, is in February or March; and their period of gestation about nine or ten months. In the latter end of April 1811, a sucker was taken by a Hull whaler, to which the fumis umbilicalis was still attached. The whale has one young at a birth. Instances of two being seen with a female are very rare. The young one, at the time of parturition, is said to be at least ten, if not fourteen feet in length. It goes under the protection of its mother, for probably a year or more. . . ."

a brief section on the breeding of the whale. He did it delicately, since, after all, he was writing not a scientific tract for scholars but a novel for Victorian readers. He packed most of his information in a footnote to the statement in the text: "We saw young Leviathan amours in the deep." Again Melville's "we" meant Ishmael and his friends and not Herman Melville and his friends; that is, the whale amours were fictional, seen only in Melville's imagination. Melville had, as was so frequently his custom, rested his fictional statement on someone else's recorded fact. This time the someone else was Bennett,[100] who had written: "Like other cetaceans, they couple *more hominum*: in one instance, which came under my notice, the position of the parties was vertical; their heads being raised above the surface of the sea." [101] Melville cut away some of this information, and humorously changing the verb, wrote: "When overflowing with mutual esteem, the whales salute *more hominum*." As Doctor Johnson said of Oliver Goldsmith: *Nullum quod tetigit non ornavit.*

The same footnote treating of whale *amours* also discussed the character of the baby whale's food. Among his fish documents Melville had found at least three descriptions of whale's milk. Bennett had written: "The mammillary gland of the female bears a close resemblance to that of the cow. It secretes a large quantity of thick milk, which has a very rich taste, and is peculiarly greasy to the touch"; while Scoresby had said: "The milk of the whale resembles that of quadrupeds in its appearance. It is said to be rich and well flavoured." But it was Beale's statement which attracted Melville's attention most: "The milk is probably very rich, for in that caught near Berkley, with its young one, the milk, which was tasted by Messrs. Jenner and Ludlow, surgeons at Sudbury, was rich like cow's milk to which cream had been added." Linking three statements together — and with a twist of humor, satirical of the devoted labors of Jenner and Ludlow — Melville amusingly summed them up: "The milk is very sweet and rich; it has been tasted by man; it might do well with strawberries."

[100] Scoresby perhaps helped, but not certainly.
[101] Described by one old sailor as "the prettiest piece of navigation I ever seen."

"Schools and Schoolmasters" is of course the expository accompaniment of "The Grand Armada," and Melville explicitly makes the association, saying: "The previous chapter has accounts of an immense body or herd of Sperm Whales, and there was also then given the probable cause inducing those vast aggregations." The two main sources of information for Melville were again Beale's *Natural History* and Bennett's *A Whaling Voyage,* but Beale was the more helpful: from him came the terms "school" (also in Bennett) and "schoolmaster" (not in Bennett). Beale wrote:

> These herds are called by whalers "schools," and occasionally consist of great numbers: I have seen in one school as many as five or six hundred. With each herd or school of females are always from one to three large "bulls" — the lords of the herd, or as they are called, the "schoolmasters." The males are said to be extremely jealous of intrusion by strangers, and to fight fiercely to maintain their rights. The full-grown males, or "large whales," almost always go alone in search of food. . . .

Melville develops this, and the rest of Beale's two pages, with Turkish-harem-Ottoman imagery, probably suggested by Beale's description of the "gallantry" of the attending males, and by Scoresby's application of "seraglio" to the female herd protected by the bull. Space does not permit quoting Melville's humorous and long elaboration of his metaphor, but the originality of his account never completely conceals from the source hunter's eye the fundamental obligation of Melville to Beale. For instance, Melville's chapter end —

> The schools composing none but young and vigorous males, previously mentioned, offer a strong contrast to the harem schools. For while those female whales are characteristically timid, the young males, or forty-barrel-bulls, as they call them, are by far the most pugnacious of all Leviathans, and proverbially the most dangerous to encounter; excepting those wondrous grey-headed, grizzled whales, sometimes met, and these will fight you like grim fiends exasperated by a penal gout.
>
> The Forty-barrel-bull schools are larger than the harem schools. Like a mob of young collegians, they are full of fight,

fun, and wickedness, tumbling round the world at such a reckless, rollicking rate, that no prudent underwriter would insure them any more than he would a riotous lad at Yale or Harvard. They soon relinquish this turbulence though, and when about three fourths grown, break up, and separately go about in search of settlements, that is, harems.

Another point of difference between the male and female schools is still more characteristic of the sexes. Say you strike a Forty-barrel-bull — poor devil! all his comrades quit him. But strike a member of the harem school, and her companions swim around her with every token of concern, sometimes lingering so near her and so long, as themselves to fall a prey.

— has been worked up out of the following passage from Beale; when, having first described at length the social feeling and concern of the female whales, he says:

The young males, or "young bulls," go in large schools, but differ remarkably from the females in disposition, inasmuch as they make an immediate and rapid retreat upon one of their number being struck, who is left to take the best care he can of himself. I never but once saw them "heave-to," and in that case it was only for a short time, and which seemed rather to arise from their confusion than affection for their wounded companion. They are also very cunning and cautious, keeping at all times a good look-out for danger; it is consequently necessary for the whaler to be extremely cautious in his mode of approaching them, so as, if possible, to escape being heard or seen, for they have some mode of communication one to another, through a whole school, in an incredibly short space of time.

"Young bulls" are consequently much more troublesome to attack, and more difficult and dangerous to kill, great dexterity being necessary to give them no time to recover from the pain and fright caused by the first blow. When about three-fourths grown, or sometimes only half, they separate from each other, and go singly in search of food.

The mosaic manner in which Melville worked up his chapter is shown by the fact that his sentence about the recklessness of the forty-barrel-bull whales (like a "riotous lad at Yale or Harvard") comes from another section of Beale's book, in which the scientist wrote: "Those young bulls which yield about forty barrels of oil, and are consequently called forty-barrel bulls, are perhaps the most difficult to destroy, and sometimes make great havoc among the men and boats."

In "The Grand Armada" and "Schools and Schoolmasters" Herman Melville used the facts from Scoresby, Beale, Bennett, and Olmsted to create a great procreative scene. Doing so he illustrated William Wordsworth's famous dictum that "the true use for the imaginative faculty of modern times is to give ultimate vivication to facts, to science, and to common life, endowing them with glories and final illustriousness which belong to every real thing and to real things only." These words describe all of *Moby-Dick*.

19

"The laws and regulations of the whale fishery"

THE INVOLVED, HUMOROUS COMPARISON of a pod of whales to a harem attended by a gallant Ottoman is gaiety enough, it would seem. But the flood-tide of Melville's good humor overflowed into another chapter, this time, strange as it may seem, on the laws and regulations of the whale fishery, "of which the waif may be deemed the grand symbol and badge." Melville had been led to refer to the laws of whaling by his allusion to the waifs and waif-poles ("The waif is a pennoned pole . . . inserted upright into the floating body of a dead whale, both to mark its place on the sea, and also as token of prior possession, should the boats of any other ship draw near") in the last chapter but one, "The Grand Armada." "Fast-Fish and Loose-Fish" seems like a strange successor to a chapter on whale amours until one realizes that Melville deliberately and sardonically used the few details on whaling fishery laws, of which there were only two, in order to satirize, among other things, amours of human beings. Men are as whales. It was for reasons of satire, then, that Melville dipped into William Scoresby's

Account of the Arctic Regions and came up with the core of a chapter ostensibly on whaling legalities.

"Perhaps [102] the only formal whaling code authorized by legislative enactment, was that of Holland. It was decreed by the States-General in A.D. 1695." Thus *Moby-Dick,* cavalierly passing by with the merest allusion to the whaling laws of Holland to which Scoresby had devoted four of his heaviest pages, to stress only the tag end of Scoresby's law information, his statement of British law. Scoresby wrote:

> Among the British whale-fishers, it does not appear that any particular laws were ever expressly laid down, for the adjusting of differences; yet custom has established certain principles, as constituting the rule of right, the legality of which is sufficiently acknowledged, by their being universally respected. The fundamental articles are two.
>
> First, That a fast-fish, or a fish in any way in possession, whether alive or dead, is the sole and unquestionable property of the persons so maintaining the connection or possession; and, secondly, That a loose fish, alive or dead, is fair game.

Not bothering to credit the British with the law, Melville transferred Scoresby's words to the American whalemen:

> Perhaps the only formal whaling code authorized by legislative enactment, was that of Holland. It was decreed by the States-General in A.D. 1695. But though no other nation has ever had any written whaling law, yet the American fishermen have been their own legislators and lawyers in this matter. They have provided a system which for terse comprehensiveness surpasses Justinian's Pandects and the By-laws of the Chinese Society for the Suppression of Meddling with Other People's Business. Yes; these laws might be engraven on a Queen Anne's farthing, or the barb of a harpoon, and worn round the neck, so small are they.
>
> I. A Fast-Fish belongs to the party fast to it.
> II. A Loose-Fish is fair game for anybody who can soonest catch it.

---

102 Melville's "perhaps" was well said, with proper caution, for there was also the Tasmanian Act Regulating Whaling, 1838! One may fancy the amusement with which Melville might also have read John Selden's weighty legal volume: *Of the Dominion, Or, Ownership of the Sea.* Translated from the Latin by Marchmont Nedham (London, 1652).

Also, observing Scoresby's definition of "fast-fish": "A fish may be said to be in possession, whenever it is connected, by any rope, pole, staff, or any other similar controllable medium, to a ship or to a boat containing one or more of her crew," Melville transferred it freely to *Moby-Dick*:

> First: What is a Fast-Fish? Alive or dead a fish is technically fast, when it is connected with an occupied ship or boat, by any medium at all controllable by the occupant or occupants, — a mast, an oar, a nine-inch cable, a telegraph wire, or a strand of cobweb, it is all the same. Likewise a fish is technically fast when it bears a waif, or any other recognized symbol of possession; so long as the party waifing it plainly evince their ability at any time to take it alongside, as well as their intention so to do.

To illustrate the way in which the courts applied the rules of fast-fish and loose-fish, Scoresby had cited at considerable length one of Lord Erskine's precedents wittily brought forward at a trial in London. The case in question involved the rights of the ship *Experiment* to a whale she had taken. Previous to the *Experiment's* capture of the whale, it had been harpooned by the crew of the *Neptune,* but they had not made fast to the carcass, so that it had got away and into the hands of the *Experiment.* The *Neptune* sued for damages. Since the case was new in the annals of the law, Erskine's precedent was an analogy. Scoresby first recorded the case for whaling history:

> He [Erskine] referred to the *crim. con.* cause tried some years ago, in which he elucidated the subject in discussion, by comparing Mrs. E. to a loose fish, whom any one had a right to seize. In that case, Mr. E. the husband, had originally harpooned the lady; he had her fast; but when he found she ran out too much line, he left her to plunge into the sea of folly and dissipation by herself, dragging the weight of her marriage vow along with her. But he did not the less abandon her because she was fastened to his boat. When he wished to recover her, or damages for her loss, it was said, — No, — he had given her up, — he had left her to her fate, and as another had harpooned her, he had a right to retain her.

One doubts that Scoresby understood Erskine's basic pun on "loose," but no one can believe that Melville missed it. Anyhow, in *Moby-Dick* he mentioned Erskine's facetious analogy, following Scoresby's words with fidelity:

> In the course of the defence, the witty Erskine went on to illustrate his position, by alluding to a crim. con. case, wherein a gentleman, after in vain trying to bridle his wife's viciousness, had at last abandoned her upon the seas of life; but in the course of years, repenting of that step, he instituted an action to recover possession of her. Erskine was on the other side; and he then supported it by saying, that though the gentleman had originally harpooned the lady, and had once had her fast, and only by reason of the great stress of her plunging viciousness, had at last abandoned her; yet abandon her he did, so that she became a loose-fish; and therefore when a subsequent gentleman re-harpooned her, the lady then became that subsequent gentleman's property, along with whatever harpoon might have been found sticking in her.

The further details of the case, especially the judgment, Melville transferred from Scoresby's record to his own, telling of the victory of the defendants as to the whale, for it was a Loose-Fish, and the award of the boat (dragged by the whale) to the plaintiffs. But as is generally true throughout *Moby-Dick*, having recorded in his customary lively fashion the basic information of his source, Melville branches out into far-reaching analogies, based on the perception that "these two laws touching Fast-Fish and Loose-Fish, I say, will, on reflection, be found the fundamentals of all human jurisprudence; for notwithstanding its complicated tracery of sculpture, the Temple of the Law, like the Temple of the Philistines, has but two props to stand on." Scoresby's tedious tale acted like a spark in Melville's gunpowder imagination. Melville's analogies radiate from his Scoresby source like the circles from a stone dropped in a pool; ethical, moral, political, and economic similitudes pour from his pen, strangely inspired by the dry facts in *An Account of the Arctic Regions*. Here are what Melville, elsewhere, called the "linked analogies" of nature; it is for these we read *Moby-Dick*, not Scoresby:

Is it not a saying in every one's mouth, Possession is half of the law: that is, regardless of how the thing came into possession? But often possession is the whole of the law. What are the sinews and souls of Russian serfs and Republican slaves but Fast-Fish, whereof possession is the whole of the law? What to the rapacious landlord is the widow's last mite but a Fast-Fish? What is yonder undetected villain's marble mansion with a door-plate for a waif; what is that but a Fast-Fish? What is the ruinous discount which Mordecai, the broker, gets from poor Woebegone, the bankrupt, on a loan to keep Woebegone's family from starvation; what is that ruinous discount but a Fast-Fish? What is the Archbishop of Savesoul's income of £100,000 seized from the scant bread and cheese of hundreds of thousands of broken-backed laborers (all sure of heaven without any of Savesoul's help) what is that globular 100,000 but a Fast-Fish? What are the Duke of Dunder's hereditary towns and hamlets but Fast-Fish? What to that redoubted harpooneer, John Bull, is poor Ireland, but a Fast-Fish? What to that apostolic lancer, Brother Jonathan, is Texas but a Fast-Fish? And concerning all these, is not possession the whole of the law?

But if the doctrine of Fast-Fish be pretty generally applicable, the kindred doctrine of Loose-Fish is still more widely so. That is internationally and universally applicable.

What was America in 1492 but a Loose-Fish, in which Columbus struck the Spanish standard by way of waifing it for his royal master and mistress? What was Poland to the Czar? What Greece to the Turk? What India to England? What at last will Mexico be to the United States? All Loose-Fish.

What are the Rights of Man and the Liberties of the World but Loose-Fish? What all men's minds and opinions but Loose-Fish? What is the principle of religious belief in them but a Loose-Fish? What to the ostentatious smuggling verbalists are the thoughts of thinkers but Loose-Fish? What is the great globe itself but a Loose-Fish? And what are you, reader, but a Loose-Fish and a Fast-Fish, too?

Ishmael said that Ahab had his humanities, but they were destroyed by his self-assertive individualism. From such a passage as this one sees how much greater were Herman Melville's humanities.

Though Melville complained about the paucity of material on whaling laws, he found sufficient to run into another
chapter, "Heads or Tails" (90), in which he satirizes legal-
istic red tape and injustice. The story is summed up in a
paragraph:

> It seems that some honest mariners of Dover, or Sandwich,
> or some one of the Cinque Ports, had after a hard chase suc-
> ceeded in killing and beaching a fine whale which they had
> originally descried afar off from the shore. Now the Cinque
> Ports are partially or somehow under the jurisdiction of a sort
> of policeman or beadle, called a Lord Warden. Holding the
> office directly from the crown, I believe, all the royal emolu-
> ments incident to the Cinque Port territories become by assign-
> ment his. By some writers this office is called a sinecure. But
> not so. Because the Lord Warden is busily at times fobbing
> his perquisites; which are his chiefly by virtue of that same
> fobbing of them.

The honest mariners start dreaming of the clothes and food
they will buy with the profits from their whale find, when
"up steps a very learned and most Christian and charitable
gentleman, with a copy of Blackstone under his arm; and
laying it upon the whale's head, he says — 'Hands off! this
fish, my masters, is a Fast-Fish. I seize it as the Lord Warden's.'" The mariners point out that the Lord Warden did
not find the fish; that they had laboriously captured it, etc.,
but they of course lose the whale to the Duke's agent. The
page of humorous dialogue closes with the sequel:

> In a word, the whale was seized and sold, and his Grace the
> Duke of Wellington received the money. Thinking that
> viewed in some particular lights, the case might by a bare
> possibility in some small degree be deemed, under the circum
> stances, a rather hard one, an honest clergyman of the town
> respectfully addressed a note to his Grace, begging him to take
> the case of those unfortunate mariners into full consideration.
> To which my Lord Duke in substance replied (both letters
> were published) that he had already done so, and received
> the money, and would be obliged to the reverend gentleman
> if for the future he (the reverend gentleman) would decline
> meddling with other people's business. Is this the still militant

old man, standing at the corners of the three kingdoms, on all hands coercing alms of beggars?

This chapter is of special interest because we can date the writing of it rather closely, finding that it was written, probably, or at least planned, before the "whaling voyage" was abandoned for the greater and more complex tragic drama we now have. Melville found out about this entire Lord Warden episode from an entry in the *Literary World*, 29 June, 1850, which read:

> An amusing anecdote is told of the Duke of Wellington, Lord Warden of the Cinque Ports. As such, he is entitled to all the "royal fish," captured and brought ashore in the adjacent waters. Some poor fishermen captured a whale in Margate Bay, and as it was of value, Dr. Wallingford addressed a letter to the Duke, endeavoring to persuade him to give up the animal to the captors, because really it was not a fish; in which assertion the doctor is fully sustained by all sound zoologists. The Duke wrote back word, that he did not see what any fellow of the College of Surgery had to do with the Warden of the Cinque Ports; that the fishermen had been paid £28 for salvage, and the balance of the proceeds of the whale aforesaid, he intended to dispose of just as he pleased, without consulting Dr. Wallingford at all! [103]

In expanding this information into a humorous scene, Melville omitted mention of the £28 granted for salvage, in order that he might stress the essential injustice of the law with which Melville headed the chapter: "De balena vero sufficit, si rex habeat caput, et regina caudam." Having illustrated the law by the story of the frustrated mariners, Melville ironically comments upon the law with the following: "But is the Queen a mermaid, to be presented with a tail? An allegorical meaning may lurk here . . . the King receiving the highly dense and elastic head peculiar to that fish, which

---

[103] I am indebted to Merton Sealts of Lawrence College for this item. In September, 1946, I had discussed with him my bafflement as to the source of Melville's episode ("both letters were published"), and the very next day he came across this news item in the *Literary World* and generously sent it to me. Melville was a subscriber to the *Literary World*.

symbolically regarded, may possibly be humorously grounded upon some presumed congeniality. And thus there seems a reason in all things, even in law." The whiplash of the last three words is not less sharp than the lash of the previous comment upon the Duke of Wellington's greedy seizure of all the perquisites resulting from his work at Waterloo. The tail of the whale carries lethal power, but so does the tail of many a Melville sentence.[104] More than a disquisition on whaling law, "Heads and Tails" is a recognition, in comic form, of the truth phrased by Carl Sandburg: "The people is a plucked goose, stripped by legalized frauds."

20

"Ambergris is a very curious substance"

IN "THE PEQUOD MEETS THE ROSE-BUD" (91) and "Ambergris" (92) Melville again follows a favorite developmental device — it might be called the doublet — in which an episode is created in order that an expository point might be explained. This technique was used in *Redburn* and *White-Jacket* and had become an identifying mark of Melville's writing.

It is questionable that Melville personally ever saw ambergris, or at least that he ever witnessed its actual discovery by whalemen. Ambergris is a rare substance eagerly sought for its value as a fixative in fine perfumes. It has aptly been

104 I think that Melville would have enjoyed reading about the differences arising between the New England whalemen and the tallow chandlers, indicated in the titles of two rare pamphlets published in 1824: *Memoirs of the Citizens of New Bedford Praying an Increase of the Duty on Imported Tallow* (Washington, 1824); and, *Memorial of Edmund Winchester, et als, Tallow Chandlers and Soap Boilers in Boston, Remonstrating against the Petition of the Nantucket and New Bedford Oil Merchants, and Praying for a Repeal of the Laws Laying Duty on Imported Tallow and Allowing Drawbacks on Exported Foreign Candles* (Washington, 1824). They may be consulted in the Fearing Collection, Harvard College Library.

called "floating gold" such is its market price.[105] Each year many people "discover" ambergris along the beach, only to learn that their valuable prize is some valueless substance. Ambergris comes from "the inglorious bowels of a sick whale," as Melville said. The Sperm Whale eats the giant squid, and at times the beak of the squid perforates the whale's intestinal wall. If the beak is not soon voided a cicatrix forms so that the intestinal passage is closed up, and the whale wastes away to his death, a goose killed by the golden egg within.

The entire story of Stubb and the *Rose-Bud* is an enjoyable bit of comic narrative preparing us for the succeeding and straightforward chapter on ambergris. The factual information came from Bennett, Beale, Scoresby, and "old Harriss"; the narrative part is from Melville's ingenious mind.

The *Pequod* meets a French whaling vessel named the *Bouton-de-Rose*, being first warned of her presence on the haze-covered ocean by "a peculiar and not very pleasant smell" arising from a blasted whale chained to the French ship. Approaching, and noting the stem piece of the ship, a carved rose, Stubb pours forth a series of jests at "the romantic name of this aromatic ship." He boards the *Rose-Bud* to talk with the captain. A Guernsey-man, serving as interpreter, is so anxious to get rid of the stinking fish that he mistranslates Stubb's sarcastic remarks so that the captain is led to believe that they will all be struck with the plague unless the whale is released. He accepts Stubb's "generous" offer to haul away the fetid fish. Stubb's offer turns out to have been from pure selfishness. No sooner is he out of sight of the French ship than he quickly draws his boat alongside the gaunt fish

> to reap the fruit of his unrighteous cunning. Seizing his sharp boat-spade, he commenced an excavation in the body a little

[105] Two interesting articles on ambergris are: A. C. Stirling and W. A. Poucher, "Ambergris: Its History, Origin, and Application," *Chemist and Druggist,* 120 (17 March, 1934), 294–295; and Robert Cushman Murphy, "Floating Gold," *Journal of the American Museum of Natural History,* XXXIII (1933).

behind the side fin. You would almost have thought he was digging a cellar there in the sea; and when at length his spade struck against the gaunt ribs, it was like turning up old Roman tiles and pottery buried in fat English loam. His boat's crew were all in high excitement, eagerly helping their chief, and looking as anxious as gold-hunters.

And all the time numberless fowls were diving, and ducking, and screaming, and yelling, and fighting around them. Stubb was beginning to look disappointed, especially as the horrible nosegay increased, when suddenly from out the very heart of this plague, there stole a faint stream of perfume, which flowed through the tide of bad smells without being absorbed by it, as one river will flow into and then along with another, without at all blending with it for a time.

"I have it, I have it," cried Stubb, with delight, striking something in the subterranean regions, "a purse, a purse!"

Dropping his spade, he thrust both hands in, and drew out handfuls of something that looked like ripe Windsor soap, or rich mottled old cheese; very unctuous and savory withal. You might easily dent it with your thumb; it is of a hue between yellow and ash color. And this, good friends, is ambergris, worth a gold guinea an ounce to any druggist.

But if the entire *Rose-Bud* episode was from Melville's imagination, at least that imagination had built around an informative paragraph in Bennett's *Whaling Voyage Round the Globe*:

It is not common for the whaler to find Ambergris in the Cachalots he destroys; nor does he, indeed, make a very rigid scrutiny of the intestines in search of it, unless a suspicion of its presence be excited by some marked peculiarity in the whale, as a torpid and sickly appearance, and the animal failing to void liquid excrement, as is usual with healthy whales, when alarmed by the sudden approach of the boats or struck by the harpoon. Some years ago the whale-ship Mary, of London, discovered a dead Cachalot floating on the ocean, and as there were no injuries on its body to account for death, that event was attributed to disease; consequently, the whale was strictly searched for Ambergris, and the captors were gratified by finding a very large quantity of that valuable drug impacted in its bowels.

It will be seen that Melville dramatized Bennett's words, adding, for reasons to be seen shortly, a conflict between a French ship and an American ship, and embellishing the whole with hearty humor. Almost everything which Bennett had written about ambergris is utilized in some way in the *Rose-Bud* episode. The appearance of the ambergris, for instance, is from Bennett's two sentences:

> It was in the state as removed from the whale; of an oval form, and pointed at each extremity; of a dull-black colour; smooth on the surface; resembled soap in texture and consistence; and was similarly unctuous to the touch. Its odour was slight and peculiar; but not decidedly fragrant, unless heat was applied.

Melville changed "soap" to the more specific "Windsor soap," and even took over the word "unctuous." And instead of giving an American dollar value to Stubb's ambergris, Melville rewrote Bennett's sentence: "The retail price it bears in London is about one guinea the ounce."

One other detail in Bennett proved of use to Melville. Bennett explained in a footnote that "ambergris has almost invariably the beaks of cuttle-fish imbedded in its substance." Melville heightened this ordinary piece of information by giving it a humorous twist:

> I have forgotten to say that there were found in this ambergris, certain hard, round, bony plates, which at first Stubb thought might be sailors' trousers buttons; but it afterwards turned out that they were nothing more than pieces of small squid bones embalmed in that manner.

There is added to the story a subtle but important vein of satire in the *Rose-Bud* episode. Professor F. O. Matthiessen has shown that the appearances of the different ships throughout *Moby-Dick* are part of the rhythmical and structural pattern of the novel. It should be further noted that the ships have been selected from different whaling industries of the world. The *Pequod*, herself representative of Nantucket whaling, meets the whaleships of the nations most important historically in whaling: Dutch, English, and French. Each part of the narrative built around these ships, and the gams they hold with the *Pequod*, subtly reveals the virtues and defects which historical research shows to have been their characteristic. The *Rose-Bud* well symbolizes the French whale fishery of the nineteenth century. French whaling, once strong and virile, thanks to help from Nantucket, had become a losing business. Lacking the intrepid dash of the Nantucketers, or the doggedness of the Dutch and English whalemen, the crappoes, as Stubb called them, had failed miserably in the fierce competition among the blubber hunters of the South Seas. Not even a lavish bounty system — one year amounting to three and one half million francs — had sufficiently primed the pump so that it could make a satisfactory return. The French whalemen were, in the words of one of their own historians, *"malpropres et indisciplines."*

Melville's story of the *Rose-Bud* is economic history as well as enlivening humor. Commonplace Stubb tweaks the noses of the French whalemen; the Yankee could outsmart any foreigner, especially a crappo — any American would testify to that. The crappoes were soft and stupid; the foul odors from the blasted whale affected their intellects so that they did not realize the treasure chained to their ship. "I well know," said Stubb, "that these crappoes of Frenchmen are but poor devils in the fishery; sometimes lowering their boats for breakers, mistaking them for Sperm Whale spouts." There is a portion of national pride wrapped up in Melville's account of Stubb's cunning. And satire, for American helpfulness has never been very far from the dollar return.

"The Pequod Meets the Rose-Bud" came from Melville's energetic mind working on a short section of Bennett's *Whaling Voyage Round the Globe*. The subsequent and accompanying chapter, "Ambergris," leaned even more heavily on another book, Thomas Beale's *Natural History of the Sperm Whale*. To save space and to show most effectively the completeness of Melville's debt to his fish document, one must resort to parallel quotations:

BEALE [106]   MELVILLE

When Captain Coffin was ex-   . . . in 1791 a certain Nan-
amined at the bar of the House   tucket-born Captain Coffin was
of Commons on the subject. . . . examined at the bar of the
                                  English House of Commons on
                                  that subject.

"The use of ambergris," says   . . . it is largely used in per-
Brande, "in Europe is now   fumery, in pastiles, precious
nearly confined to perfumery,   candles,   hair-powders,   and
though it has formerly been   pomatum. The Turks use it in
used in medicine by many emi-   cooking, and also carry it to
nent physicians. In Asia and   Mecca, for the same purpose
part of Africa, ambergris is not that frankincense is carried to
only used as a medicine and   St. Peter's in Rome. Some wine
perfume, but considerable use   merchants drop a few grains
is also made of it in cooking,   into claret, to flavor it.
by adding it to several dishes as
a spice. A great quantity of it
is also constantly bought by
the pilgrims who travel to Mecca, probably to offer it there,
and make use of it in fumiga-
tions, in the same manner as
frankincense is used in Cath-
olic countries. The Turks make
use of it as an aphrodisiac.
Our perfumers add it to scent-
ed pastiles, candles, balls, bot-
tles, gloves, and hair powder;
and its essence is mixed with
pomatum for the face and
hands, either alone or united
with musk, though its smell is
to   some   persons   extremely
offensive.

(quoting Sir Thomas Browne)
"in vain it was to rake for am-   "In vain it was to rake for Am-
bergriese in the paunch of this   bergriese in the paunch of this

---

[106] Melville made a marginal line, now erased, beside Beale's words, and
also added a checkmark, also erased, besides the erased checkmarks elsewhere in the chapter.

BEALE | MELVILLE

leviathan, as Greenland discoverers, and attests of experience dictate, that they sometimes swallow great lumps thereof in the sea — insufferable fetor denying that inquiry; and yet if, as Paracelsus encourageth, ordure makes the best musk, and from the most feted substances may be drawn the most odoriferous essences, all that had not Vespasian's nose might boldly swear here was a substance for such extractions."

Leviathan, insufferable fetor denying not inquiry." Sir T. Browne, V. E.
Now that the incorruption of this most fragrant ambergris should be found in the heart of such decay; is this nothing? Bethink thee of that saying of St. Paul in Corinthians, about corruption and incorruption; how that we are sown in dishonor, but raised in glory. And likewise call to mind that saying of Paracelsus about what it is that maketh the best musk. Also forget not the strange fact that of all things of ill-savor, Cologne-water, in its rudimental manufacturing stages, is the worst.

Melville had written about ambergris in *Mardi*, and one passage from that novel leads into the ambergris section of *Moby-Dick*. It is Media who straightens out Mohi and Yoomy by telling them exactly what ambergris is: "Listen, old Mohi; ambergris is a morbid secretion of the Spermaceti whale," but Media's words are a rewrite of Bennett's, "Ambergris is a morbid concretion in the intestines of the Cachalot, deriving its origin either from the stomach or biliary ducts." Melville-Media, however, added a metaphor: "the whale is at times a sort of hypochondriac and dyspeptic." Two years later, in Cheever's *The Whale and His Captors*, the metaphor was extended into a humorous elaboration:

The substance called ambergris, and highly prized in perfumery, is obtained from the sperm whale, being formed, it is thought, in that state of the system which calls for a cathartic. A peck of Morrison's or Brandreth's pills, or the homeopathic dose of a pound of calomel or jalap would probably remove obstructions in the creature's abdominal viscera.

Melville's vivid imagination was fascinated by Cheever's words. Working them over with care, he created one of those expansively humorous passages which are peculiarly his:

> Who would think, then, that such fine ladies and gentlemen should regale themselves with an essence found in the inglorious bowels of a sick whale! [107] Yet so it is. By some, ambergris is supposed to be the cause, and by others the effect, of the dyspepsia in the whale. How to cure such a dyspepsia it were hard to say, unless by administering three or four boat loads of Brandreth's pills, and then running out of harm's way, as laborers do in blasting rocks.

The rock-blasting image completes the history of the metaphor which arose as Melville read Bennett's scientific definitions; then, apparently, Cheever read *Mardi* (the image may have occurred independently) , and finally, Melville read Cheever. A case of bread cast upon waters.

Apparently, Melville's search for ambergris lore did not go much beyond Beale, Bennett, Cheever, and Harriss. Nor did it need to, for the two chapters in *Moby-Dick* are sufficient to their purpose as entertainment *and* information. One more phase of whaling, and the whale, has been impressed upon us.

Perhaps the chapter "Ambergris" was misnamed; perhaps Melville should have titled it "The Smell of the Whale," for such a heading would have comprehended the two halves of the chapter, since from the paragraphs on ambergris Melville moves to a discussion of the odor of whales. He states emphatically that the great fish have been badly maligned, that "whales as a species are by no means creatures of ill odor." The stigma has its rise, Melville suggests, in the practices of the Greenland whalemen, who, instead of trying-out

---

[107] Melville made a checkmark, now erased, beside Beale's words: "Ambergris appears to be nothing but the hardened faeces of the spermaceti whale, which is pretty well proved from its being mixed so intimately with the refuse of its food (the squids' beaks)."

the blubber immediately as did the South Seas whalemen, merely cut the blubber into chunks disposed in the hold, to be stored until the return home for later trying-out. What could one expect from such a practice, said Melville:

> The consequence is, that upon breaking into the hold, and unloading one of these whale cemeteries, in the Greenland dock, a savor is given forth somewhat similar to that arising from excavating an old city grave-yard, for the foundations of a Lying-in Hospital.

Melville's sentence combines an event of recent Pittsfield history and a passage from Bennett. In 1851, the old grave-yard at Pittsfield was removed to make room for a hospital. It would seem that Melville was present at some of the excavations, with senses alert to all that took place.[108] But the contrast in cleanliness of the Greenland and the South Sea fisheries was suggested to Melville by Bennett:

> South-Seamen, however, advance a step beyond their prototypes of the North, inasmuch as while they collect, they may also be said to manufacture their cargo, by the practice they pursue of separating the useful from the more cumbrous and unimportant parts of the whales they capture; and thus, (in the place of the putrified mass which composes the lading of a Greenland ship,) bringing their freight to port in a state but little less pure than when it passes into the hands of the consumer.

To conclude his chapter, Melville reserves a section for satire on Scoresby. Continuing the argument begun before, Melville says:

> I partly surmise also, that this wicked charge against whalers may be likewise imputed to the existence on the coast of Greenland, in former times, of a Dutch village called Schmerenburgh or Smeerenberg, which latter name is the one used

---

[108] The transferal of the cemetery to a new site was much in the minds of Pittsfield's citizens in 1850, and on 9 September of that year the new location was dedicated with celebrations including odes by John Hoadley and Mrs. J. R. Morewood — both close friends of Melville at this time — and a dedicatory poem by Oliver Wendell Holmes. Melville was probably in attendance. See J. E. A. Smith, *History of Pittsfield* (Springfield, 1876), II, 596–608.

by the learned Fogo Von Slack in his great work on Smells, a text-book on that subject. As its name imports (smeer, fat; berg, to put up), this village was founded in order to afford a place for the blubber of the Dutch whale fleet to be tried out, without being taken home to Holland for that purpose.

Fogo Von Slack, author of a "great work on Smells," is none other than William Scoresby, Jr., in whose *An Account of the Arctic Regions* is a section entitled "Description of Whale-Oil, and Remarks on the Causes of the Offensive Smell" — six laborious pages on the subject. And elsewhere in the book Scoresby used much space to tell about the Dutch whaling at Smeerenberg. Melville took the opportunity to supply yet another pseudonym for the pious historian of the Greenland whale.

"Nor indeed," Melville added in high spirits, "can the whale possibly be otherwise than fragrant, when, as a general thing, he enjoys such high health; taking abundance of exercise; always out of doors; though, it is true, seldom in the open air." And thus concludes Melville's ambergris section, a gallimaufry of information, satire, humor, and vivacious narrative.

The expository pages of "Ambergris" do not prepare us for the terrifying scene which Melville describes in the subsequent chapter, "The Castaway" (93). To be sure that we will not pass over the chapter lightly, Melville stresses its importance:

> . . . a most significant event befell the most insignificant of the Pequod's crew; an event most lamentable; and which ended in providing the sometimes madly merry and predestinated craft with a living and ever accompanying prophecy of whatever shattered sequel might prove her own.

The story is of Pip's brief service in Stubb's boat. In the excitement of the darting of the harpoon, Pip jumps from the boat, and is caught in the slack in the line, which wraps around his chest and neck, threatening strangulation. To save his life the line is cut, much to Stubb's disgust because it means the loss of the valuable whale. Cursing

Pip for his leap, Stubb doggedly keeps on after the whale, but when Pip jumps from the boat a second time, Pip is left behind, "another lonely castaway." Pip's plight is tragic:

> Now, in calm weather, to swim in the open ocean is as easy to the practised swimmer as to ride in a spring-carriage ashore. But the awful lonesomeness is intolerable. The intense concentration of self in the middle of such a heartless immensity, my God! who can tell it?

Thinking that Stubb had abandoned him to this lonesomeness for good, Pip loses his wits, so that when the *Pequod* rescues him, "from that hour the little negro went about the deck an idiot." And then follows a passage which Dostoevsky would have marked, and might have written:

> The sea had jeeringly kept his finite body up, but drowned the infinite of his soul. Not drowned entirely, though. Rather carried down alive to wondrous depths, where strange shapes of the unwarped primal world glided to and fro before his passive eyes; and the miser-merman, Wisdom, revealed his hoarded heaps; and among the joyless, heartless, ever-juvenile eternities, Pip saw the multitudinous, God-omnipresent, coral insects that out of the firmament of waters heaved the colossal orbs. He saw God's foot upon the treadle of the loom, and spoke it; and therefore his shipmates called him mad. So man's insanity is heaven's sense; and wandering from all mortal reason, man comes at last to that celestial thought, which, to reason, is absurd and frantic; and weal or woe, feels then uncompromised, indifferent as his God.

Would Aeschylus, creator of the mad, profound Cassandra, not join the great Russian novelist, creator of *The Idiot,* in appreciation of the psychological penetration of Melville's Pip? And would not Freud recognize, perhaps, that his concept of the Id had been anticipated or foreshadowed in this amazing passage? Could any American in 1850 other than Hawthorne and Melville have written these words? Indeed, in style they are beyond even the talents of Melville's friend, and in anticipation of future discovery they are prophetic.

Melville did **not** inject this episode of Pip's insanity

merely for the novelty of it; he saw it in relationship to events to come — so much he told us in the beginning of the chapter — and in the closing words he indicates exactly what the episode must be related to: "and in the sequel of the narrative, it will then be seen what like abandonment befell myself." When we see Ishmael afloat in his lonely coffin in the midst of the Pacific waters, we will perhaps recall Pip in the terrifying solitude. Ishmael, however, will grow to greatness from his acceptance of isolation; he will face the fact of the fundamental loneliness of the Self, and facing it, will keep his sanity where Pip lost his.

Having presented us with the tragic episode of little Pip, the "lonely castaway," Melville in the next chapter presents the counter-theme of sociality; the isolato theme is followed — and balanced — by the companionship theme in "A Squeeze of the Hand" (94). Melville describes the pleasures of squeezing the spermaceti, cooled and waiting in tubs, to be squeezed from lumps into fluid. The process, Melville says mockingly, is sheer delight after the "bitter exertion at the cutting-in."

Beyond fish documents or other sources, out of the mordant imagination of Herman Melville is "The Cassock" (95). Some day a critic will properly explain the full significance of this chapter, perhaps the most amazing in an amazing book; in the meantime, one must accept D. H. Lawrence's recognition of it as one of the greatest pieces of phallicism in all literature. Since the whaling sources give no indication, physiological or otherwise, of the facts of Melville's chapter (save, of course, for the mincer as described in such works as Browne's *Etchings* — and pictured, too) one must assume that it came from memory or from an imagination profoundly Rabelaisian. It might be added that ninety per cent of Melville's readers miss entirely the meaning of "The Cassock."

21

"Looking into the red heat of the fire"

IN "THE TRY-WORKS" (96), Melville takes up the most spectacular of all the operations in the sperm whale fishery: the trying-out of the blubber in the try-pots resting in a great brick oven built on the deck. Into these two great try-pots the crew tossed the chunks of blubber, the "bible-leaves" minced into thin slices by the "archbishoprick" in his strange cassock. Frederick Debell Bennett described the entire process succinctly in *A Whaling Voyage Round the Globe*:

> Previous to being boiled, or "tryed-out," the blubber is cleared from adhering flesh, and cut with spades into slips, or "horse-pieces," which, (after they had been "minced," or scored by a broad and thin knife, upon an elevated block of wood, termed the "horse,") are consigned to the boilers of the try-works. The "head" is first boiled, and its produce kept as distinct as possible from the "Body"; since the one is considered as Spermaceti, or "head-matter," and the other as Sperm-oil.
>
> It must be regarded as a curious circumstance, and as one highly essential to the economy of these ships, that the process of boiling the oil supplies also the fuel required for that purpose; the "scraps," or refuse from which the oil has been extracted, burning, when placed in the furnace, with a fierce and clear flame and intense heat, and being sufficient in quantity to render any other fuel unnecessary; the scraps remaining from one affair of oil being reserved to commence a second.
>
> In a dark night, the process of "trying out" in the open ocean presents a spectacle partaking much of the grand and terrific. The dense volumes of smoke that roll before the wind and over the side of the vessel, as she pursues her course through the water — the roaring of the flames, bursting in lofty columns from the works, and illuminating the ship and surrounding expanse of sea — and the uncouth garb and implements of the crew, assembled around the fires — produce a peculiarly imposing effect; though one that is not altogether to be reconciled with the ordinary character of marine scenery.

Bennett's description, especially in the last paragraph, probably contributed to Melville's account of the try-works; it is almost certain that Melville had read it. More important borrowing is to be found in comparing the words of *Moby-Dick* with J. Ross Browne's description in *Etchings of a Whaling Cruise*. Writing with a fuller feeling for the picturesque qualities of the scene than had Bennett, Browne exploited the sensational possibilities of his material at greater length and with more imaginative sweep, the allusions to Salvator Rosa and Dante, for instance, adding considerably to the superiority of his version:

> A "trying-out" scene is the most stirring part of the whaling business, and certainly the most disagreeable. . . . We will now imagine the works in full operation at night. Dense clouds of lurid smoke are curling up to the tops, shrouding the rigging from the view. The oil is hissing in the try-pots. Half a dozen of the crew are sitting on the windlass, their rough, weather-beaten faces shining in the red glare of the fires, all clothed in greasy duck, and forming about as savage a looking group as ever was sketched by the pencil of Salvator Rosa. The cooper and one of the mates are raking up the fires with long bars of wood or iron. The decks, bulwarks, railing, try-works, and windlass are covered with oil, and slime of black-skin, glistening with the red glare from the try-works. Slowly and doggedly the vessel is pitching her way through the rough seas, looking as if enveloped in flames. . . .

> . . . A trying-out scene has something peculiarly wild and savage in it; a kind of indescribable uncouthness, which renders it difficult to describe with anything like accuracy. There is a murderous appearance about the blood-stained decks, and the huge masses of flesh and blubber lying here and there, and a ferocity in the looks of the men, heightened by the red, fierce glare of the fires, which inspire in the mind of the novice feelings of mingled disgust and awe. But one soon becomes accustomed to such scenes and regards them with the indifference of a veteran in the field of battle. I know of nothing to which this part of the whaling business can be more appropriately compared than to Dante's pictures of the infernal regions. It requires but little stretch of the imagination to suppose the smoke, the hissing boilers, the savage-looking crew, and the waves of flame that burst now and then from the flues of the furnace, part of the paraphernalia of a scene in the lower regions.

Browne's passage is excellent — compact and vivid, alive to surfaces and lights. To improve on it was a challenge to Melville's subtlest skill. How he met and surpassed Browne may be seen by studying this short sample from *Moby-Dick*:

> The hatch, removed from the top of the works, now afforded a wide hearth in front of them. Standing on this were the Tartarean shapes of the pagan harpooneers, always the whale-ship's stokers. With huge pronged poles they pitched hissing masses of blubber into the scalding pots, or stirred up the fires beneath, till the snaky flames darted, curling, out of the doors to catch them by the feet. The smoke rolled away in sullen heaps. To every pitch of the ship there was a pitch of the boiling oil, which seemed all eagerness to leap into their faces. Opposite the mouth of the works, on the further side of the wide wooden hearth, was the windlass. This served for a sea-sofa. Here lounged the watch, when not otherwise employed, looking into the red heat of the fire, till their eyes felt scorched in their heads. Their tawny features, now all begrimed with smoke and sweat, their matted beards, and the contrasting barbaric brilliancy of their teeth, all these were strangely revealed in the capricious emblazonings of the works. As they narrated to each other their unholy adventures, their tales of terror told in words of mirth; as their uncivilized laughter forked upwards out of them, like the flames from the furnace; as to and fro, in their front, the harpooneers wildly gesticulated with their huge pronged forks and dippers; as the wind howled on, and the sea leaped, and the ship groaned and dived, and yet steadfastly shot her red hell further and further into the blackness of the sea and the night, and scornfully champed the white bone in her mouth, and viciously spat round her on all sides; then the rushing Pequod, freighted with savages, and laden with fire, and burning a corpse, and plunging into that blackness of darkness, seemed the material counterpart of her monomaniac commander's soul.

Stirred by his personal memories and by the graphic accounts in Browne and Bennett,[109] Melville has deepened his

---

109 And also, possibly by *Ribs and Trucks* (Boston, 1842): "but one thing, I pray thee forget not to honor with a parting glance — a night-scene around the 'try-works'; — it is too like purgatory, to be neglected. Three ovens, amidships, surmounted by three huge cauldrons of oil; the oil boiling, the

description by developing the Dantesque associations suggested in *Etchings*. Melville etches every detail with the sharpness, and the feeling for chiaroscuro, of a Rembrandt, and to the photographic fidelity of his words he adds a haunting suggestiveness Ryderesque in quality. What shows Melville's skill most completely, however, is the way in which he subordinates and unites his word-painting to the characterization of Ahab and to the emotional-philosophical currents of *Moby-Dick*. Interesting though it is in itself, the description is fused with the total structure of the novel. Here, certainly, is a single fact described not only for itself but also for its implications — a fact seen in its totality.

Although such an unforgettable bit of wit as the description of the smoke from the try-works, "It smells like the left-wing of the day of judgment," may possibly have been inspired by Browne's down-Easter who, choking with the fumes, swore: "if this warn't he——l on a small scale, he didn't know what to call it"; nevertheless, Melville's entire chapter reaches heights of meaning independent of, although extended from, fish documents. From the masterly exposition of the trying-out process Melville modulates back to his original theme, Selfhood, and to his original character, Ishmael.

Ishmael's vantage point from which he had seen the trying-out had been the tiller of the ship, apart but not far from the flaming try-pots. The physical separation suggests spiritual separation as well, which Melville subtly points up by having Ishmael describe the crew as capering fiend shapes much like flickering shapes moving about a great cauldron of evil. Watching the whalemen's sabbath, "that night, in particular, a strange (and ever since inexplicable) thing occurred to me." Ishmael fell into a doze.

ovens lapping out tongues of flickering flame; the watch clustering and flitting and gibbering, in a light now lurid, now livid — some feeding the gaping furnaces with fuel, some couchant on the windlass, 'spinning yarns'; one brandishing a mighty fork, another 'spairging about the brumstane cootie,' with a long, long ladle, and occasionally anointing the fire, till it makes the rigging and the sails and the weltering waters gleam again in its blaze; and each busy, smutty, diabolical-looking figure at hand flash into second daylight; — all, together, afford a spectacle 'beautiful as rare,' and leave nothing to be guessed at, would you fancy to yourself a 'situation' in the freehold of 'auld Nickie-Ben.' "

I was half conscious of putting my fingers to the lids and mechanically stretching them still further apart. But, spite of all this, I could see no compass before me to steer by; though it seemed but a minute since I had been watching the card, by the steady binnacle lamp illuminating it. Nothing seemed before me but a jet of gloom, now and then made ghastly by flashes of redness. Uppermost was the impression, that whatever swift, rushing thing I stood on was not so much bound to any haven ahead as rushing from all havens astern. A stark, bewildered feeling, as of death, came over me. Convulsively my hands grasped the tiller, but with the crazy conceit that the tiller was, somehow, in some enchanted way, inverted. My God! what is the matter with me? thought I. Lo! in my brief sleep I had turned myself about, and was fronting the ship's stern, with my back to her prow and the compass. In an instant I faced back, just in time to prevent the vessel from flying up into the wind, and very probably capsizing her. How glad and how grateful the relief from the unnatural hallucination of the night, and the fatal contingency of being brought by the lee!

The episode is dramatic, arising naturally but suddenly out of the rich painting of the preceding paragraphs. We may never know whether Melville was transferring journalistic fact to his novel, but it is possible to suggest that the scene may have been built from one which he had already used. The narrow escape of the *Pequod* suggests a similar event in *White-Jacket*, in which the *Neversink* is saved just in the nick of time when "Mad Jack" mutinously countermands the previous orders of Captain Claret. In *White-Jacket* Melville uses the scene to point up his contrast between the efficiency of the subordinate as against the bungling stupidity of the superior. Melville adapted this scene from a little volume entitled *Scenes in "Old Ironsides."* Possibly the idea of the ship saved at the last minute by a reversal of controls, which we have here in *Moby-Dick*, was Melville's second adaptation of an episode which had already served him well.

But whatever the source of the narrative section of "The Try-Works," Melville's manipulation of the episode is of course uniquely his own. What is the secondary meaning of the event? Ishmael, remember, said that it was "inexplicable." May it not illustrate the folly of isolation from the social norm, the sinfulness of what Hawthorne has called the Unpardonable Sin, when man has "lost his hold of the magnetic chain of humanity"? Melville makes the point obliquely through symbolism:

> Look not too long in the face of the fire, O man! Never dream with thy hand on the helm! Turn not thy back to the compass; accept the first hint of the hitching tiller; believe not the artificial fire, when its redness makes all things look ghastly. To-morrow, in the natural sun, the skies will be bright; those who glared like devils in the forking flames, the morn will show in far other, at least gentler, relief; the glorious, golden, glad sun, the only true lamp — all others but liars.

Without the capacity to sense our relatedness to our fellows we cut ourselves off from the capacity for change, and starve or destroy ourselves. One needs an awareness of one's separate identity but too complete a separation cuts us from human growth.

In the chapter on "The Mast-Head" Melville had satirized the neo-Platonic idealist, his identity lost in the infinite, dreamily unable to keep a sharp eye for the physical and harsh facts (symbolized by the whales) and therefore in imminent danger of plunging from the masthead into the Descartian vortices of the sea. If Transcendentalism errs in too great an insistence on unity and too little heeds multiety, it also errs in too great an insistence on self-reliance. Too great an emphasis on self, he says implicatively, may lead to self-destruction just as surely as too great a disregard for appearances had done. Ishmael looking at the whalemen, his fellow crew members, pitchforking the blubber, saw them pictorially and then metaphorically as devils from hell — but himself at the tiller as none. (Such confidence in his own selfhood was almost suicide — and the destruction of the crew.) These devils in the forking flames will show in the next morning's sun as human beings like himself. Man — Ishmael — may look into the fire to see the demonic shapes, but he must also recognize them as his own companions also.

The flame into which Ishmael stares resembles the lime-kiln fire into which Ethan Brand, in Hawthorne's story of that title, had too long gazed and by which he is destroyed. In both "Ethan Brand" and *Moby-Dick* the fire symbolizes the demonic and irrational forces to which Freud gave the name the "Id"; the bawdy, maenadic, and orgiastic foundations of the human personality. Amiel describes his fear at facing these terrifying, subterranean forces: "I too have been reduced to nothingness, and I shudder on the brink of the great abysses that yawn within my being, in the grip of a longing for the unknown, weakened by a thirst for the infinite, humbled before the ineffable." Ethan Brand and, momentarily, Ishmael were guilty, in Hawthorne's words, of "the sin of an intellect that triumphed over the sense of brotherhood with man and reverence for God, and sacrificed everything to its own mighty claims!" Melville had already indicated his awareness of the abysses of the human soul [110] when he wrote in *Mardi*: "To scale great heights, we must come out of lowermost depths. The way to heaven is through hell. We need fiery baptisms in the fiercest flames of our own bosoms," a passage similar in insight to Milton's famous dictum:

> The mind is its own place and in itself
> Can make a heaven of hell, a hell of heaven.

Here, in "The Try-Works," Melville implies again the necessity of the fiery baptism, for, as he says, "the sun hides not the Virginia's Dismal Swamp, nor Rome's accursed Campagna, nor wide Sahara, nor all the millions of miles of deserts and griefs beneath the moon. . . . So, therefore, that mortal man who hath more of joy than sorrow in him, that mortal man cannot be true — not true, or undeveloped." The fire of the

---

[110] Compare Nietzsche's Apothegm 146 from *Beyond Good and Evil:* "He who fights with monsters should be careful lest he thereby become a monster. And if thou gaze long into an abyss, the abyss will also gaze into thee." Some student might well study Melville's markings in his volumes of Nietzsche (written of course long after *Moby-Dick*) to see how Melville was impressed by the German writer and also to see how Melville had anticipated his thought.

primitive Self [111] must be recognized, but abandonment to it means spiritual death; Melville's warning is specific:

> Give not thyself up, then, to fire lest it invert thee, deaden thee; as for the time it did me. There is a wisdom that is woe; but there is a woe that is madness. And there is a Catskill eagle in some souls that can alike dive down into the blackest gorges, and soar out of them again and become invisible in the sunny spaces. And even if he for ever flies within the gorge, that gorge is in the mountains; so that even in his lowest swoop the mountain eagle is still higher than other birds upon the plain, even though they soar.

"Art," Fauré wrote, "is therefore a game, as the philosophers have called it. It is a matter of dancing on the edge of the abyss, or hiding it with flowers." And so, implies Melville, is Life; it is a mean between unfettered Selfhood and regimented sociality. But looking into depths of the try-works Ishmael found what Gerard Manley Hopkins later discerned:

> . . . O the mind, mind has mountains; cliffs of fall
> Frightful, sheer, no-man-fathomed.

Into these blackest gorges of Life only Catskill eagles like Shakespeare and Melville dive to explore the depths of tragic horror, then soar to the heights of human — individual and social — experience, recorded for us in ambiguous symbol.

"The Try-Works" took place in the hellish glare from the flames under the try-pots; "The Lamp" (97) is likewise a scene of shadow and flame, but it is peaceful and soothing — a scene as remarkable as it is short. Melville's expository point is, after all, a trivial one: that only in whaleships was the forecastle lighted — "the whaleman, as he seeks the food of light, so he lives in light," whereas "in merchantmen, oil for the sailor is more scarce than the milk of queens. To dress in the dark, and eat in the dark, and stumble in darkness to his pallet, this is his usual lot." It is not this explicit information which makes the chapter noteworthy; it is the opening paragraph which sketches the *Pequod* forecastle:

[111] One might keep in mind that in various fire references, Melville seems to regard it as a symbol of madness.

Had you descended from the Pequod's try-works to the Pequod's forecastle, where the off duty watch were sleeping, for one single moment you would have almost thought you were standing in some illuminated shrine of canonized kings and counsellors. There they lay in their triangular oaken vaults, each mariner a chiselled muteness; a score of lamps flashing upon his hooded eyes.

Notice that Melville does not further describe the forecastle; one gets the impression that it must have been a pleasant place. The tourist visiting the *Charles W. Morgan,* sole surviving old-time whale ship, preserved at Mystic, Connecticut, may well imagine as he descends to see the rows of wooden bunks, clean and bare and lit by electricity, that a similar scene of cleanliness (and romanticized by the soft, flickering light from the oil lamps) might have been among the old-time whale ships on the fishing grounds. But when the tourist turns to photographs of whalemen with their untrimmed beards, their grimy faces, and their bedraggled clothes; and when he remembers that in those ships cockroaches ran about with no molestation from the hardened sailors,[112] that oil, gurry, and blood dripping through the decks made the forecastle a smelly, greasy hole, and that twenty-one men with all their possessions jammed into the small space to be companions for three years — then one must realize that Melville's description does *not* say much which it might have. Why not? No doubt Melville's memories were no different in physical essentials from, let us say, those of J. Ross Browne, who wrote (and Melville had read it): "It would seem like exaggeration to say, that I have seen in Kentucky pig-sties not half so filthy, and in every respect preferable to this miserable hole: such, however, is the fact." Furthermore, in Browne's *Etchings* is a picture of the crowded forecastle in an uproar. Melville knew the picture; it shows a different world from that suggested by "The Lamp." Melville's description is different because it omits all grim details. Melville does not falsify; he selects for a

112 If Melville's memory failed him, he had Francis A. Olmsted's *Incidents of a Whaling Voyage,* p. 85, to remind him of the ubiquity and savagery of the whaleship cockroach. And his own *Omoo.*

purpose. Melville could describe filth, squalor, and disorder when it suited his purpose. Some of the descriptions in *Redburn* are Hogarthian in powerful realism. No, squalor was clearly not to his intention. In *Moby-Dick* he was celebrating, not dishonoring, the American whaleman. Brutality and filth had been sufficiently pointed out by writers like Olmsted and Browne, even as they had neglected the heroic qualities in whaling. Writing a democratic epic, Melville stresses the fundamental nobility and beauty of Ishmael's shipmates. They were savage and they were gross, but they were, for better or worse, men basically like Ishmael. Even Gulliver woke up one day to the fact that he too was a Yahoo; Melville wakes us up to the fact that the Yahoos are also we. Furthermore, by the metaphor stated early in the book in three chapters, these whalemen were Ahab's knights and squires. As we behold the sleeping faces in the forecastle we behold again the mute and chiseled kings and counselors, enshrouded in light and shadow — as are all men: kings, counselors, and whalemen.

It is not without significance that "The Lamp" with its beautiful sense of human brotherhood — stated as forcefully, but far more subtly, as Whitman later did — and sociality follows immediately, in the counterpoint so common with Melville, the unforgettable study of separateness and isolation in "The Try-Works."

The problem of self-knowledge, the delusion that we can know ourselves, comes to a kind of climax in "The Doubloon" (99). Melville directs our attention to the shining gold-piece which he had nailed to the mainmast as a reward for him who first sighted the White Whale. The coin was a doubloon marked with the signs of the zodiac, with three mountains out of which issue a tower, a flame, and a crowing cock, all surrounded by the words "REPUBLICA DEL ECUADOR: QUITO."

The place of this coin in *Moby-Dick* is roughly equivalent to the place of the images issuing from the witches' cauldron in *Macbeth*, images of the terrible truth to be but interpreted whimsically by Macbeth as portents of what he wishes to happen. He is led to his doom by his heedless willfulness.

With its various possibilities of meaning, the doubloon in *Moby-Dick*, as Ahab himself acknowledged, and should have recognized, "like a magician's glass, to each and every man in turn but mirrors back his own mysterious self." To the gold coin come in sequence Ahab, Starbuck, Stubb, Flask, Queequeg, and Pip, and to each it throws back the image of his own mind. (Significantly, Ishmael does not come to the doubloon; the symbol of Everyman, his amorphousness would have taken on form had Melville allowed him to look into the mirror.) To Ahab, "the firm tower, that is Ahab; the volcano, that is Ahab; the courageous, the undaunted, and victorious fowl, that, too, is Ahab; all are Ahab." But in his obsessive search for vengeance on Moby Dick, Ahab fails to follow the warning of the zodiacal sign on the coin, which portraying the sun entering Libra, means that it is entering the time of storms — as we realize Ahab is, and as he does too, but says foolishly, "So be it then!," and will not turn back nor furl sail.

Starbuck does not see the mountains (symbol of heroic conquest), but looks at the dark valleys and the heaven-biding peaks, seeming like the Trinity. His Christian faith reflects itself in the Quito gold. Stubb, watched by Starbuck and Pip, approaches the doubloon. Assisted by the Massachusetts almanac, he reads the history of man in the zodiacal signs:

> Come, Almanack! To begin: there's Aries, or the Ram — lecherous dog, he begets us; then, Taurus, or the Bull — he bumps us the first thing; then Gemini, or the Twins — that is, Virtue and Vice; we try to reach Virtue, when lo! comes Cancer the Crab, and drags us back; and here, going from Virtue, Leo, a roaring Lion, lies in the path — he gives a few fierce bites and surly dabs with his paw; we escape, and hail Virgo, the Virgin! that's our first love; we marry and think to be happy for aye, when pop comes Libra, or the Scales — happiness weighed and found wanting; and while we are very sad about that, Lord! how we suddenly jump, as Scorpio, or the Scorpion, stings us in the rear; we are curing the wound, when whang come the arrows all round; Sagittarius, or the Archer, is amusing himself. As we pluck out the shafts, stand aside! here's the battering ram, Capricornus, or the Goat; full tilt,

he comes rushing, and headlong we are tossed; when Aquarius, or the Water-bearer, pours out his whole deluge and drowns us; and to wind up with Pisces, or the Fishes, we sleep. There's a sermon now, writ in high heaven, and the sun goes through it every year, and yet comes out of it all alive and hearty. Jollily he, aloft there, wheels through toil and trouble; and so, alow here, does jolly Stubb.

Stubb's common sense, pragmatic attitude toward life, then, is also the reflection thrown back by the coin. It is made more amusing being written as a parody, in astrological terms and uttered by a whaleman, of Jaques's immortal seven ages of man speech.

Flask, of course, sees the coin as a mere piece of money for the purchase of cigars. Queequeg, apparently, interprets the signs of the zodiac in their physiological equivalents, glancing down at his body, and "thinks the sun is in the thigh, or in the calf, or in the bowels." He is ever the symbol of unconscious, spontaneous man, and so this reflection is in the doubloon. Fedallah, mysterious surrogate of the Powers of Darkness, merely bows in reverence to the coin — "a fire worshipper, depend upon it," says Starbuck, thinking that the Parsee is bowing before the flame issuing from the mountain, flame the symbol of the Godhood to the Zoroastrian, but the reader wonders whether Fedallah does not bow in recognition of the devilish ambiguity of the coin which betrays the men to their death.

Ironically, it is mad Pip who sees the coin most discerningly. His mutterings before the gold piece show that he dimly envisages, Cassandra-like, the day soon to be when both doubloon and ship will be at the bottom of the ocean. Furthermore, it is Pip whose babbling conjugation of the verb "to look," out of *Murray's Grammar*, sarcastically and obliquely criticizes the "looking" of the other characters who have read the doubloon: "I look, you look, he looks; we look, ye look, they look. . . . And I, you, and he; and we, ye, and they, are all bats."

Each character looking at the shining symbol views it from the limitations of his own selfhood. The physical symbol shifts meaning with the man approaching it. The world means as we see it to mean; to the silly the world is so; to the wise the world has depth. Twenty years later Melville employed the same technique in the "Mar Saba" section of *Clarel,* when each of the main characters interprets the palm tree from his idiosyncratic viewpoint. In both *Moby-Dick* and *Clarel,* Melville implies the ambiguity of appearances. The doubloon itself is an ambiguous symbol which stands for the most ambiguous of all symbols, Moby Dick himself, for he who wins the doubloon has won first sight of the White Whale. Fittingly, the ambiguous coin is the ironic prize of none other than Ahab himself.

22

"And that fine gam I had"

The two-chapter unit which was such a favorite of Melville's is again employed in "Leg and Arm: The Pequod of Nantucket, Meets the Samuel Enderby, of London" (100) and "The Decanter" (101). Melville's general subject is the English whaleship, but in "Leg and Arm" he serves up a humorous episode, a gam between the *Pequod* and the *Samuel Enderby* of London. In this gam the hard-bitten and unsmiling Ahab excitedly seeks information about the White Whale from the *Samuel Enderby's* Captain Boomer, who like Ahab had been maimed by the pursuit of Moby Dick. With humorous grotesquery Melville portrays the two captains saluting with ivory limbs, Ahab's leg crossed with Captain Boomer's ivory arm. The picture symbolizes the thematic counterpoint of the chapter. Captain Boomer describes his adventure with Moby Dick gaily, as though it had been great sport, and the details of the subsequent amputation of his arm is told light-heartedly in ironical contrast to Ahab's enraged bitterness. Impatiently Ahab stands by as Captain Boomer and his surgeon, Doctor Bunger, in spirited dialogue recall the past, until finally Doctor Bunger tells Ahab in all innocence, "So that what you take for the

White Whale's malice is only his awkwardness." Captain Boomer's suggestion that perhaps Moby Dick is best let alone, draws Ahab's passionate response: "He is. But he will still be hunted for all that. What is best let alone, that accursed thing is not always what least allures. He's all a magnet." And as Ahab hurries away from the English ship, Captain Boomer asks Fedallah, "Is your Captain crazy?," but Fedallah merely places his finger enigmatically to his lips and slides over the bulwarks into the waiting boat. It is plain that Captain Boomer is all that Ahab is not, spiritually. Maimed by life, by the White Whale, Ahab persists in tracking down Moby Dick for vengeance; Captain Boomer, likewise maimed, cheerfully accepts what life has brought him, prudently deciding not to court disaster. He accepts limitations as Ahab will not. Not heroic like Ahab, he is much more human.

"The Decanter" (101) in straightforward exposition discusses the part that the Enderbys played in the Sperm Whale Fishery. When Melville says, "How long, prior to the year of our Lord 1775, this great whaling house was in existence, my numerous fish-documents do not make plain," he is thinking especially of one fish-document, Beale's *Natural History of the Sperm Whale,* where a similar uncertainty of knowledge is expressed:

> Whether this eloquent address [Edmund Burke's] had any effect or not upon the minds of our own merchants and ship-owners in stimulating them to fit out ships for the sperm and other whale-fisheries, I am not aware, but it is certain that in the following year (1775) the first attempt was made to establish the sperm whale fishery from Britain. . . .

— a statement which Melville marked in his own copy of Beale. And reading all of Melville's second paragraph in "The Decanter":

> In 1778, a fine ship, the Amelia, fitted out for the express purpose, and at the sole charge of the vigorous Enderbys, boldly rounded Cape Horn, and was the first among the nations to lower a whale-boat of any sort in the great South Sea. The voyage was a skilful and lucky one; and returning to

her berth with her hold full of the precious sperm, the Amelia's example was soon followed by other ships, English and American, and thus the vast Sperm Whale grounds of the Pacific were thrown open. But not content with this good deed, the indefatigable house again bestirred itself: Samuel and all his Sons — how many, their mother only knows — and under their immediate auspices, and partly, I think, at their expense, the British government was induced to send the sloop-of-war Rattler on a whaling voyage of discovery into the South Sea. Commanded by a naval Post-Captain, the Rattler made a rattling voyage of it, and did some service; how much does not appear. But this is not all. In 1819, the same house fitted out a discovery whale ship of their own, to go on a tasting cruise to the remote waters of Japan. That ship — well called the "Syren" — made a noble experimental cruise; and it was thus that the great Japanese Whaling Ground first became generally known. The "Syren" in this famous voyage was commanded by a Captain Coffin, a Nantucketer.

— one is not surprised to find that Melville had carefully checked, twice, the following passage from Beale:

In 1788,[113] the grand mercantile speculation of sending ships round Cape Horn into the Pacific, in order to extend the sperm whale fishery was reserved for the bold and enterprising mind of Mr. Enderby, a London merchant and ship-owner, who fitted out, at a vast expense, the ship "Amelia," Captain Shields, which sailed from England on the 1st of September 1788, and returned on the 12th of March 1790, making an absence of one year and seven months, but bringing home the enormous cargo of 139 tons of sperm oil. . . .

In 1819, another great impulse was given to the fishery, by the indefatigable and enterprising Mr. Enderby, who had not only joined the government in 1793 in the expense of fitting out a ship, commanded by Captain James Colnett,[114] to undertake a voyage to the South Seas, with a view to extend the sperm whale fishery there; but in this year, 1819, formed the

113 Notice that Melville miscopied this date as 1778. There is in the Fearing Collection of the Harvard College Library a petition by Samuel Enderby and Sons, 1783, to be permitted to send out an expedition to the South Seas for the promoting of the whale fishery. So far as I know this important and interesting document has never been printed.

114 Melville was familiar with Captain James Colnett's own report of his expedition.

scheme, and actually fitted out at his own expense a large ship of 500 tons burthen, called the "Syren," commanded by Captain Coffin, with a crew of thirty-six seamen, for the purpose of sending her on an experimental voyage to prosecute the sperm whale fishery in that remote part of the world.

With this record of achievement, it is no wonder that Melville said: "All honor to the Enderbies, therefore, whose house, I think,[115] exists to the present day."

Melville's next paragraph is apparently one of genuine reminiscence, for he says, "The ship named after him was worthy of the honor, being a very fast sailer and a noble craft every way. I boarded her once at midnight somewhere off the Patagonian coast, and drank good flip down in the forecastle. It was a fine gam we had, and they were all trumps — every soul on board." Reminiscing, Melville tells about the good food served on the English ship, beef and dumplings and ale. Such fare, he says, "is matter for historical research. Nor have I been at all sparing of historical whale research when it has seemed needed." The specimen of research to which he obliquely alludes is the account which follows of the food served aboard the old Dutch whaleships. As might be expected, Melville's research turns out to be a satire of research. He says:

> During my researches in the Leviathanic histories, I stumbled upon an ancient Dutch volume, which, by the musty whaling smell of it, I knew must be about whalers. The title was, "Dan Coopman," wherefore I concluded that this must be the invaluable memoirs of some Amsterdam cooper in the fishery, as every whale ship must carry its cooper. I was reinforced in this opinion by seeing that it was the production of one "Fitz Swackhammer." But my friend Dr. Snodhead, a very learned man, professor of Low Dutch and High German in the college of Santa Claus and St. Pott's, to whom I handed the work for translation, giving him a box of sperm candles for his troubles — this same Dr. Snodhead, so soon as he spied

---

[115] Melville was apparently unfamiliar with Charles Enderby's *Proposals for Re-establishing the British Southern Whale Fishery, through the Medium of a Chartered Company, and in Combination with the Colonization of the Auckland Islands, as the Site of the Company's Whaling Station* (London, 1847, 3d ed.)

the book, assured me that "Dan Coopman" did not mean "The Cooper," but "The Merchant." In short, this ancient and learned Low Dutch book treated of the commerce of Holland; and, among other subjects, contained a very interesting account of its whale fishery. And in this chapter it was, headed "Smeer," or "Fat," that I found a long detailed list of the outfits for the larders and cellars of 180 sail of Dutch whalemen; from which list, as translated by Dr. Snodhead, I transcribe the following:

```
400,000  lbs.  of beef
 60,000  lbs.  Friesland pork
150,000  lbs.  of stock fish
550,000  lbs.  of biscuit
 72,000  lbs.  of soft bread
  2,800  firkins of butter
 20,000  lbs.  of Texel & Leyden cheese
144,000  lbs.  cheese (probably an inferior article)
    550  ankers of Geneva
 10,800  barrels of beer
```

Most statistical tables are parchingly dry in the reading; not so in the present case, however, where the reader is flooded with whole pipes, barrels, quarts, and gills of good gin and good cheer.

Melville's Carlylean laughter rumbles throughout his study of these tables, as he observes that each man must have had an allowance of twelve barrels of beer per two weeks, and other generous allotments. "I devoted," Melville says ironically, "three days to the studious digesting of all this beer, beef, and bread, during which many profound thoughts were incidentally suggested to me, capable of a transcendental and Platonic application." As Melville readers remember, Melville was always fond of food and drink not only for themselves but as symbols of conviviality and companionship. Not for nothing was he a member of the group around the Duyckinck punchbowl, and his letters and writings sparkle with good humor when the subject of food arises.

The satiric reference to a "transcendental and Platonic application" probably is a thrust at the unworldliness of the transcendental groups, who believed in high thinking and light feeding — as at Fruitlands with Bronson Alcott's band of disciples. One thinks of the light fare of the Apostles in *Pierre*; how Melville mocks their meagre diet, their neglect of the basic material needs of men. But not so with the Dutch whalemen.

Melville's Doctor Snodhead who had so kindly translated "Fitz Swackhammer's" ancient Dutch volume, was William Scoresby, Jr., previously labeled as Captain Sleet and Charley Coffin. In Scoresby's *An Account of the Arctic Regions* was included a long section on the history of the various fisheries, and many pages were devoted to a learned discussion of the Dutch. Melville's "innocent" misunderstanding of the meaning of "Dan Coopman" is probably a thrust at pedantic explanation of the title: "Dan Koopman (The Merchant)." "Fitz Swackhammer" is probably Melville's humorous transcription of Zorgdrager,[116] mentioned by Scoresby as author of one of the best books on Dutch whaling; or it may be a transcription of Wagenaar's *Tegenwordigen Staat der Vereenigde Nederlande* [117] that Scoresby translated for the list of supplies, which Melville took over with such glee into *Moby-Dick* — although he curtailed Scoresby's list by several items, such as nine thousand sacks of barley, etc. In extracting the long passage from Scoresby, Melville was able to indulge in two favorite jests: satire of Scoresby's pedantry, and the humor of gluttony.

23

"Annihilated antichronical Leviathans"

"THE FOSSIL WHALE" (104) concludes the cetological details in *Moby-Dick*. It is of all the chapters most certainly

[116] C. G. Zorgdrager, *Bloeyende Opkomst der Aloude en Hedendraagsche Groenlandsche Visschery.* . . . *Met byvoeging van de Walvischvangst,* etc. (Amsterdam, 1720).

[117] Jan. Wagenaar, *Vaderlandische Historie, Vewattende de Geschiedenissen der Vereenigede Nederlandien, in zonderheid die van Holland, van de vroegste tydenof: Uit de geloofwaardigste Schryvers en egte Gedenkstukken samengesteld.* 21 vols. (Amsterdam, 1749–1759).

the one written entirely by imagination based solely on research, from Melville's having "swam through libraries."
Like all of his New England neighbors, Melville undoubtedly interested himself in geological dabbling,[118] but certainly he had never seen a fossil whale nor fossil whale bones,
even though there was a good collection of them in Albany,
not far from Pittsfield, as he wrote his novel. Over his head
in paleontological waters, Melville characteristically threw
together his few shreds of facts, picked up in Autolycean
manner from various sources. The mighty whale, he says,
"affords a most congenial theme whereon to enlarge, amplify,
and generally expatiate." To do so, he adds, requires space,
for the whale's bulk is so great that only in an "imperial
folio" could he properly be treated — an echo of Melville's
earlier pun when he classified the whales according to "volume": folio, octavo, and duodecimo. Beale and Bennett had
informed him of the intricate intestinal equipment of the
whale, so that Melville wrote in admiration, "Only think of
the gigantic involutions of his intestines, where they lie in
him like great cables and hawsers coiled away in the subterranean orlop-deck of a line-of-battle ship," a sentence which
combines Melville's knowledge from Beale with memories
of his own sailor service aboard the *United States*. He adds,
"Having already described him in most of his present habita-
tory and anatomical peculiarities, it now remains to magnify
him in an archaeological, fossiliferous, and antediluvian
point of view."

Before going into his fossil facts, such as they were, Melville comically expresses his alarm in trying to write on such
a large subject as the whale. One needs placard capitals, a
condor's quill, a Vesuvian crater for inkstand, and a ponderous dictionary like Johnson's, compiled by a man bulky as
the whale. Melville admits his theme is large, but he is not
afraid: "We expand to its bulk. To produce a mighty book,
you must choose a mighty theme. No great and enduring
volume can ever be written on the flea, though many there

118 Melville's interest in fossils, as shown earlier in *Mardi* especially, is
thoroughly treated by Elizabeth S. Foster, "Melville and Geology," *American
Literature,* XVII (March, 1945), [50]–65.

be who have tried it." A humorless man would counter Melville's high spirits by adducing Fabre and Maeterlinck.

On shaky grounds as only an amateur in paleontology, Melville presents ironic credentials, boasting that his authority comes from having "been a stone-mason, and also a great digger of ditches, canals and wells, wine-vaults, cellars, and cisterns of all sorts." With this professional experience he plunges ahead, telling us that pre-Adamite whales had been discovered in various places within the last thirty years: "at the base of the Alps, in Lombardy, in France, in England, in Scotland, and in the States of Louisiana, Mississippi, and Alabama . . . in the Rue Dauphiné in Paris." This is a short statement, but it came together in Melville's mind from a variety of sources, none of them certain, but several possible. Such obscure writings as A. Rivière's *Note sur un Enorme Fossile trouvé dans la Louisiane* (Paris, 1837) and Giuseppe Cortesi's *Saggi Geologii degli Stati di Parma e Piacenza* (Rome, 1819) could have furnished Melville with the information about the Louisiana or Alp fossil whalebones, but it is far more likely that his facts came to him from secondary sources more widely accessible such as Robert Hamilton's *Mammalia. Whale, &c.* (Edinburgh, 1843), published as the eighth volume in Sir William Jardine's popular reference work, *The Naturalist's Library*.[119] There he would have found most all of his fossil citations. Again, Melville might have seen many of these references in newspaper and periodical accounts published upon the discovery and display of the most famous of the bones, described in *Moby-Dick* as a "complete vast skeleton of an extinct monster, found in the year 1842, on the plantation of Judge Creagh, in Alabama." [120] These bones had aroused public interest and scien-

[119] A short and readable account of prehistoric whales is by W. H. Flower, "On Whales, Past and Present, and Their Possible Origin," *Proceedings of the Royal Institute of Great Britain*, X (1883), 360–376. A longer account, for the specialist in paleontology, is Remington Kellogg, "The History of Whales. Their Adaptation to Life in the Water," *The Quarterly Review of Biology*, III (1928), 29–76, 174–208, including a good bibliography. Most complete is Remington Kellogg, *A Review of Archaeoceti* (Washington: Carnegie Institution of Washington, 1936).

[120] For a general, popular account of these fossil finds, and the finds preceding them, see Katherine V. W. Palmer, "Tales of Ancient Whales,"

tific controversy. One scientist, Doctor Koch, even won a pension for a Barnum-like deception which he perpetrated. Newspapers had for some time been reporting remarkable fossil finds in the South. In 1832, a Louisiana judge named Bry had found several fossil vertebrae which he had shipped to the Philosophical Society of Philadelphia. The Society in turn asked Doctor Richard Harlan to identify them. He decided that they were reptilian remains and therefore christened the animal from which they had come Basilosaurus — king of the reptiles, judging the bones to be Mesozoic. Two

Nature Magazine, 35 (April, 1942), 213–214, 221. For a picture of a zeuglodon, articulated in recent years, see James W. Gridley, "A Recently Mounted Zeuglodon Skeleton in the United States National Museum," *Proceedings of the United States National Museum,* XLIV (1913), 649–654. This skeleton is still on display in Washington. For interesting material, including some illustrations, of the fossil finds which caused such a sensation in the eighteen-forties, see the following: ((1) Richard Harlan, "Notice of Fossil Bones Found in the Tertiary Formation of the State of Louisiana," *Transactions of the American Philosophical Society,* IV (1834), 397–403. (2) Richard Owen, "Observations on the Teeth of the Zeuglodon, Basilosaurus of Dr. Harlan," *Proceedings of the Geological Society of London,* III (1838–1839), 24–28. (3) C. H. C. Burmeister, "Bemerkungen über Zeuglodon cetoides Owen's Basilosaurus Harlan's, Hydrarchos Koch's," *Allgemeine Literatur Zeitung,* Halle, 139 (June, 1847), cols. 961–984, 991–992. (4) C. G. Karus, H. B. Geinitz, A. F. Günther, and H. G. L. Reichenbach, *Resultate geologischer, anatomischer und zoologischer Untersuchungen über das unter dem Namen Hydrarchos von Dr. A. C. Koch zuerst nach Europa gebrachte und in Dresden ausgestellte grosse fossile Skelett,* Dresden and Leipzig, 1847. (5) Albert Koch, *Description of the Mussourium, or Missouri Leviathan: together with its supposed habits and Indian traditions concerning the location from whence it was exhumed: also, comparisons of the whale, crocodile and mussourium, with the leviathan, as described in 41st chapter of the book of Job* (Louisville, 1841). (6) A. C. Koch, *Hydrargos, or, Great Sea Serpent, of Alabama, 114 Feet in Broadway.* Admittance 25 cents. *Description of the Hydrargos sillimanii: (Koch) a gigantic fossil reptile, or sea serpent; lately discovered by the author, in the State of Alabama, March, 1845,* New York, 1845. (7) Charles Lyell (Letter addressed to B. Silliman), *American Journal of Science and Arts,* 2d Series, I (March, 1846), 313–315. (8) G. Lister (Letter to Jeffries Wyman on Koch's *Hydrarchos*), *Proceedings Boston Society of Natural History,* II (March, 1846), 94–96. (9) Ebenezer Emmons, "On the Supposed Zeuglodon Cetoides, of Professor Owen," *American Quarterly Journal of Agriculture and Science,* Albany, II (July, 1845), 59–63. (10) Samuel Botsford Buckly, "On the Zeuglodon Remains of Alabama," *American Journal of Science,* 2d Series, II (July, 1846), 125–129. For several of these items I am indebted to Mr. A. Wetmore of the United States National Museum. I have not studied the German titles because it is obvious that Melville had not seen them.

or three years later Judge Jonathan Creagh turned up some strange bones on his plantation in Clark County, Alabama. Harlan identified these bones, too, as Basilosaurus relics. When he visited London in 1839, he took the bones with him. Sir Richard Owen, greatest of English paleontologists, examined them and disagreed with Harlan's verdict, arguing that the teeth belonged to a sea-going mammal. Harlan agreed with Owen's conclusions and the name "Zeuglodon" was thereafter given to the prehistoric animal. It is to this historic-scientific controversy that Melville alluded when he wrote in *Moby-Dick*:

> But by far the most wonderful of all cetacean relics was the almost complete vast skeleton of an extinct monster, found in the year 1842, on the plantation of Judge Creagh, in Alabama. The awe-stricken credulous slaves in the vicinity took it for the bones of one of the fallen angels. The Alabama doctors declared it a huge reptile, and bestowed upon it the name of Basilosaurus. But some specimen bones of it being taken across the sea to Owen, the English Anatomist, it turned out that this alleged reptile was a whale, though of a departed species. A significant illustration of the fact, again and again repeated in this book, that the skeleton of the whale furnishes but little clue to the shape of his fully invested body. So Owen rechristened the monster Zeuglodon; and in his paper read before the London Geological Society, pronounced it, in substance, one of the most extraordinary creatures which the mutations of the globe have blotted out of existence.

Melville may have learned this whole story from newspapers and periodicals, but certainly not from most of the titles I have listed in my near-by footnote. Some of the bones were shipped from Alabama to Albany in 1842, and certainly Melville might well have picked up the story in visiting Albany, where the event must have been widely current in Melville's circles. These Albany bones, incidentally, were later sold for three hundred dollars to Doctor John Collins Warren of Boston; they may be seen today in the American Museum of Natural History in New York. Harlan's fossils are most of them in the Philadelphia Academy of Natural Sciences.

Melville makes no mention of Albert Koch's famous hoax.

By articulating several wagonloads of the bones, Koch was able to display, at twenty-five cents admission, a reptilian creature one hundred and fourteen feet in length, weighing so he said, seventy-five hundred pounds. This monstrous skeleton was shown in Boston in 1845, and also in New York, with publicity of a sensational nature. Melville must undoubtedly have seen it or heard about it. The better scientists showed that the skeleton had been constructed from the bones of five different individuals and from three different genera of animals. Bones were even wrongly placed; but these tides of criticism did not disturb Doctor Koch unduly. Carrying his bone pile to Europe he continued to exhibit it to his great profit.

Melville's chapter on the fossil whale was written from his desire to stress the timelessness of the whale, that it is immortal in the past as well as into the future. He says:

> When I stand among these mighty Leviathan skeletons, skulls, tusks, jaws, ribs, and vertebrae, . . . I am, by a flood, borne back to that wondrous period, ere time itself can be said to have begun; for time began with man. Here Saturn's grey chaos rolls over me, and I obtain dim, shuddering glimpses into those Polar eternities. . . . Then the whole world was the whale's; and, king of creation, he left his wake along the present lines of the Andes and the Himmalehs. Who can show a pedigree like Leviathan? Ahab's harpoon had shed older blood than the Pharaoh's. Methuselah seems a schoolboy. I look round to shake hands with Shem. I am horror-struck at this antemosaic, unsourced existence of the unspeakable terrors of the whale, which, having been before all time, must needs exist after all humane ages are over.

If passages like this and the fifty-seven others as rousing, are merely rhetorical fancy intended only to carry along a whaling story devoid of symbolical overtone, then Melville has indeed used an instrument far too great for the small task assigned to it. To demand an elaborate allegorical construction for *Moby-Dick* is indeed foolish, but to deny the emotional and metaphysical implications of such writing is the height of pedestrianism.

24

"In his unconditional skeleton"

ALTHOUGH Melville has now explained to us the appearance
of the whale from his battering-ram to his flukes, he is by
no means finished with his zoological-anatomical exposition
— he has yet to expound the whale's "interior structural features." Melville of course alludes to his next step in a lively
metaphor:

> But to a large and thorough sweeping comprehension of
> him, it behoves me now to unbutton him still further, and
> untagging the points of his hose, unbuckling his garters, and
> casting loose the hooks and the eyes of the joints of his inner-
> most bones, set him before you in his ultimatum; that is to
> say, in his unconditional skeleton.

As a harpooner and a sailor Melville had seen many whales,
but mostly their outsides. The whales were stripped of their
blubber as they lay alongside the ship, and once stripped
were cast loose to float away for the sharks. Whalemen knew
little and cared less about the whale "in his ultimatum"; his
oil and his whalebone were their main interest. Melville,
then, is now covering material about which he is almost as
ignorant, so far as experience goes, as his readers. He was
forced back to his whaling books. His feeling of factual
insecurity is discernible beneath the deception of his humor:

> But how now, Ishmael? How is it, that you, a mere oarsman
> in the fishery, pretend to know aught about the subterranean
> parts of the whale? Did erudite Stubb, mounted upon your
> capstan, deliver lectures on the anatomy of the Cetacea; and
> by help of the windlass, hold up a specimen rib for exhibition?
> Explain thyself, Ishmael. Can you land a full-grown Whale on
> your deck for examination, as a cook dishes a roast-pig? Surely
> not. A veritable witness you have hitherto been, Ishmael; but
> have a care how you seize the privilege of Jonah alone; the
> privilege of discoursing upon the joists and beams; the rafters,

ridge-pole, sleepers, and under-pinnings, making up the frame-work of Leviathan; and belike of the tallow-vats, dairy-rooms, butteries, and cheeseries in his bowels.

"A veritable witness you have hitherto been" was Melville's way of saying that up to now he has been speaking more or less from personal experience, but that from this point he must rely upon the "numerous fish documents." As he went on to say, "since Jonah, few whalemen have penetrated very far beneath the skin of the adult whale." To this, Melville added an ambiguous "nevertheless":

> nevertheless, I have been blessed with an opportunity to dis-
> sect him in miniature. In a ship I belonged to, a small cub
> Sperm Whale was once bodily hoisted to the deck for his poke
> or bag, to make sheaths for the barbs of the harpoons, and
> for the heads of the lances. Think you I let the chance go,
> without using my boat-hatchet and jack-knife, and breaking
> the seal and reading all the contents of that young cub?

This experience, of a whale on deck, may possibly have oc-curred on Melville's ship. The detail about making sheaths for the harpoon barbs is not in the whaling books Melville consulted. But, also, the dissection of a small whale cub is described in Bennett's *A Whaling Voyage Round the Globe*,[121] where five paragraphs are devoted to the anatom-ical details then discovered. Is Ishmael's experience merely Bennett's reworked?

> In January, 1835, I was enabled, through the kindness of
> Captain Stavers, to make an anatomical examination of a
> foetal Cachalot, which was removed from the abdomen of its
> mother, and taken on board the ship. Without entering into
> minute particulars, I may mention the following, as the prin-

121 He may also have had in mind William Scoresby, Jr.'s *Journal of a Voyage to the Northern Whale-Fishery* (Edinburgh, 1823), pp. 148–158, with its detailed account of the anatomy of a cub whale drawn aboard Scoresby's ship; or, furthermore, Captain James Colnett's *A Voyage Round Cape Horn into the South Seas, for the Purpose of Extending the Spermaceti Whale Fish-eries* (London, 1798), p. 80, which mentions a small whale drawn aboard "and of which I made a small drawing." (This drawing was probably the one referred to sarcastically in chapter 55 of *Moby-Dick*.)

cipal peculiarities noticed in this young example, which was a male, and sufficiently mature to be within a few hours of its birth.

As we have seen previously, Melville had been attracted to this passage to the extent of adapting material from it in his chapter "The Grand Armada." Now he will use it in a much different, and a more humorous way.

When Melville was most dependent on his fish documents for material or experiences which he himself had not encountered firsthand, he made the greatest commotion with his fancy, concealing his paucity of personal knowledge beneath a mask of parody, satire, and general grotesque playfulness. It may be assumed that Melville had never seen an articulated whale's skeleton before he wrote *Moby-Dick*. In the mid-nineteenth century, few museums owned them. We may be certain that had Melville-Ishmael seen one on display in a Boston or New York museum he would have alluded to it in his whaling book. Certainly he alluded to museum skeletons mentioned by other writers.

The whale skeleton which Herman Melville saw and from which he created his chapters "A Bower in the Arsacides" and "Measurement of the Whale's Skeleton" (103), was one articulated in his own picturesque imagination by the long, scientific description in Beale's *Natural History of the Sperm Whale*. Using Beale's truly dull information, Melville first created a fantastic pagan temple made from the whale "in his ultimatum":

> And as for my exact knowledge of the bones of the Leviathan in their gigantic, full grown development, for that rare knowledge I am indebted to my late royal friend Tranquo, king of Tranque, one of the Arsacides. For being at Tranque, years ago, when attached to the trading-ship Dey of Algiers, I was invited to spend part of the Arsacidean holidays with the lord of Tranque, at his retired palm villa Pupella; a seaside glen not very far distant from what our sailors called Bamboo-Town, his capital.
>
> Among many other fine qualities, my royal friend Tranquo, being gifted with a devout love for all matters of barbaric vertù, had brought together in Pupella whatever rare things

the more ingenious of his people could invent; chiefly carved woods of wonderful devices, chiselled shells, inlaid spears, costly paddles, aromatic canoes; and all these distributed among whatever natural wonders, the wonder-freighted, tribute-rendering waves had cast upon his shores.

Chief among these latter was a great Sperm Whale, which, after an unusually long raging gale, had been found dead and stranded, with his head against a cocoa-nut tree, whose plumage-like, tufted droopings seemed his verdant jet. When the vast body had at last been stripped of its fathom-deep enfoldings, and the bones became dust dry in the sun, then the skeleton was carefully transported up the Pupella glen, where a grand temple of lordly palms now sheltered it.

The ribs were hung with trophies; the vertebrae were carved with Arsacidean annals, in strange hieroglyphics; in the skull, the priests kept up an unextinguished aromatic flame, so that the mystic head again sent forth its vapory spout; while, suspended from a bough, the terrific lower jaw vibrated over all the devotees, like the hair-hung sword that so affrighted Damocles.

It was a wondrous sight. The wood was green as mosses of the Icy Glen; the trees stood high and haughty, feeling their living sap; the industrious earth beneath was as a weaver's loom, with a gorgeous carpet on it, whereof the ground-vine tendrils formed the warp and woof, and the living flowers the figures. All the trees, with all their laden branches; all the shrubs, and ferns, and grasses; the message-carrying air; all these unceasingly were active. Through the lacings of the leaves, the great sun seemed a flying shuttle weaving the unwearied verdure. Oh, busy weaver! unseen weaver! — pause! — one word! — whither flows the fabric? what palace may it deck? wherefore all these ceaseless toilings? Speak, weaver! — stay thy hand! — but one single word with thee! Nay — the shuttle flies — the figures float from forth the loom; the freshet-rushing carpet for ever slides away. The weaver-god, he weaves; and by that weaving is he deafened, that he hears no mortal voice; and by that humming, we, too, who look on the loom are deafened; and only when we escape it shall we hear the thousand voices that speak through it. For even so it is in all material factories. The spoken words that are inaudible among the flying spindles; those same words are plainly heard without the walls, bursting from the opened casements. There-

by have villainies been detected. Ah, mortal! then, be heed-
ful; for so, in all this din of the great world's loom, thy
subtlest thinkings may be overheard afar.

Now, amid the green, life-restless loom of that Arsacidean
wood, the great, white, worshipped skeleton lay lounging — a
gigantic idler! Yet, as the ever-woven verdant warp and woof
intermixed and hummed around him, the mighty idler seemed
the cunning weaver; himself all woven over with the vines;
every month assuming greener, fresher verdure; but himself
a skeleton. Life folded Death; Death trellised Life; the grim
god wived with youthful Life, and begat him curly-headed
glories.

The critic is tempted to explain this passage, but only a
monograph could unfold the intertwined meanings, the complexity of the metaphor which re-echoes the mat-maker
weaving earlier in the novel. The passage is poetry, evoking
through the most unusual of symbols the most universal of
experiences: the inescapable presence of Death, the sense of
Time's stanchless flow, the antiphonal of Death and Life
(which other authors have pictured by the image of the roses
in the skull). The homeliest fact, Emerson once pointed out,
may serve to illustrate the most profound truth; few facts
could be homelier than the bones of a whale, few truths more
profound than those implied in Melville's paragraphs.

The geneticist must admire the daring ingenuity of weaving disparate memories and readings into a rich pattern. The
valley of Tranque is like no valley along the Mediterranean
coast but is obviously a Marquesan or Tahitian valley from
Melville's own memorable past. Furthermore, one will never
find Tranque on any map of the Mediterranean area. It is
an obscure little island off the coast of Chile, in latitude
43° S. and longitude 73° 30′ W., along the whaling route
once traveled by Melville. We may surmise that he had once
seen or visited the island, and for private reasons dragged it
out for use in his *jeu d'esprit*. Only, he has placed Tranque
among the Arsacides, a small group of islands at the southern
tip of the Solomons, discovered in the latter part of the
eighteenth century and known to La Pérouse and Bougain-
ville, travelers whose narratives were perhaps familiar to

Melville. And the Arsacides were also the ancient Persian kings.

And finally, what gave Melville the courage to place a sperm whale's skeleton upon a Mediterranean coast? What, furthermore, suggested to him a skeleton-temple? In the article on "Whale" in Kitto's *A Cyclopedia of Biblical Literature*, Melville had read that once Commodore Davis had seen a sperm whale's skeleton on the northern shore of Africa. Furthermore, Melville had in some place encountered Leo Africanus's — the "old Barbary traveller" he called him — description of a whale temple, and he reprinted Leo Africanus's description in "The Fossil Whale" (104):

> Not farre from the sea-side they have a Temple, which they greatly esteeme and honour. Out of which, Historiographers say, that the same Prophet, of whom the great Mahumet foretold, should proceed. Yea, some there are which sticke not to affirme, that the Prophet Jonas was cast forth by the Whale upon the shoare of Messa, when he was sent to preach unto the Ninivites. The rafters and beames of the said Temple are of Whales bone. And it is a usuall thing amongst them, to see Whales of an huge and monstrous bignesse cast up dead upon their shoare, which by reason of their hugeness and strange deformitie, may terrifie and astonish the beholders. The common people imagine, that, by reason of a certaine power and vertue infused from heaven by God upon the said Temple, each Whale which would swim past it, can by no means escape death.

> Which opinion had almost persuaded me, especially when at my being there, I my selfe saw a mighty Whale cast up, unlesse a certaine Jew had told me, that it was no such strange matter: for (quoth he) there lie certaine rockes two miles into the Sea on either side, and as the Sea moves, so the Whales move also; and if they chance to light upon a rock, they are easily wounded to death, and so are cast upon the next shoare. This reason more prevailed with me, then the opinion of the people. My selfe (I remember being in this Region at the same time when my Lord the Seriffo bare rule over it,) was invited by a certaine Gentleman, and was by him conducted into a Garden, where he shewed me a Whales rib of so great a size, that lying upon the ground with the convexe or bowing side upward, in manner of an arch, it resembled a gate,

the hollow or inward part whereof aloft we could not touch
with our heads, as we rode upon our Camels backs: this rib
(he said) had laine there above an hundred yeares, and was
kept as a miracle.[122]

Melville's my Lord Tranque would seem to be an adaptation
of Leo Africanus's "my Lord the Seriffo," and the skeleton
intertwined with the verdure, an amazing enlargement of
the whale's rib in the garden.

But now we approach the scientist Beale — for Melville is
but beginning with his osteological humors. Ishmael sets out
to explore the unusual temple:

Now, when with royal Tranquo I visited this wondrous
whale, and saw the skull an altar, and the artificial smoke
ascending from where the real jet had issued, I marvelled that
the king should regard a chapel as an object of vertù. He
laughed. But more I marvelled that the priests should swear
that smoky jet of his was genuine. To and fro I paced before
this skeleton — brushed the vines aside — broke through the
ribs — and with a ball of Arsacidean twine, wandered, eddied
long amid its many winding, shaded colonnades and arbors.
But soon my line was out; and following it back, I emerged
from the opening where I entered. I saw no living thing
within; naught was there but bones.

Cutting me a green measuring-rod, I once more dived within
the skeleton. From their arrow-slit in the skull, the priests
perceived me taking the final altitude of the final rib. "How
now!" they shouted; "Dar'st thou measure this our god! That's
for us." "Aye, priests — well, how long do ye make him,
then?" But hereupon a fierce contest rose among them, concerning feet and inches; they cracked each other's sconces with
their yard-sticks — the great skull echoed — and seizing that
lucky chance, I quickly concluded my own admeasurements.

Two interpretations, not conflicting, of this scene may be
suggested, both in keeping with Melville's satiric turn of
mind and with his habit of speaking on two or three levels

[122] "Observations of Africa by John Leo," etc., in *Hakluytus Posthumus
or Purchas his Pilgrimes* (Glasgow, 1905–1907), V, 369–70. Melville possibly
knew Purchas's version of Pory's translation of Leo's work, but the version
in *Moby-Dick* was probably drawn from the 1705 edition of *Harriss's Voyages*,
I, 316–38.

of communication at once. The first paragraph suggests that Melville was ironic about the elegant, costly churches which are treated as architectural wonders rather than as places of worship. Entering such a building Ishmael finds that "naught was there but bones." The question which the intruder, or the seeker of truth, asks the priests is not given to him, but instead the priests fall to buffets with each other as to whose measurement is the right one. Could this possibly be Melville's satire of religious disagreement, a theme which he had treated to good effect in *Mardi* but which he has now given a cetological setting?

The second paragraph suggests more than religious satire, perhaps. Ishmael is seeking the measurements of the whale just as Melville is attempting to give precise information to his readers on the same subject. But when each goes to the authorities — the priest for Ishmael, the scientists for Melville — each gets no answer and so makes hasty measurements for himself. In other words, does not Melville say, "I have now reached the place in *Moby-Dick* where if I am to be complete, I must present the 'interior structural details' of the Sperm Whale. But since I have never studied this question closely I must perforce speak from vague memory. The scientists will question me. When I ask them for the facts they will not give me them in agreement, so that I must hastily make my own measurements and then withdraw before they attack me." The chief of the zoologists thus satirized seems to be the ever-reliable Thomas Beale. Melville probably had in mind Beale's anxiety to set "at rest the various opinions which have been hazarded upon the number of bones which the skeleton of this kind possesses." Or perhaps the quarreling priests of Moby Dick satirize what Beale called the "pleasant rivalry . . . manifested among the scientific gentlemen of Hull, in showing to me all that they knew respecting the Leviathans of the deep."

Though cautioning his readers "that, in this matter, I am not free to utter any fancied measurements I please," Melville's skeletal feet and inches are not those of any fish document I have been able to find. And as for the three whale skeletons which anyone interested might examine, Melville mentions, as though he knew all of them, the ones at Hull, Manchester, New Hampshire, and Burton Constable, Yorkshire. The first, at Hull, Melville had never seen; but he read in Beale (and marked it!): "The Museum of Natural History at Hull can boast of several fine skeletons." The second, Melville may have seen when he passed through Manchester on his honeymoon, in 1847. The third he saw in the pages of Thomas Beale's *Natural History,* and it is this one which furnished the factual basis for whatever he has to say about the osteology of the whale.

Melville's first allusion to the Yorkshire whale skeleton is characteristically complex in its accumulation of experience, in its imagery:

> Moreover, at a place in Yorkshire, England, Burton Constable by name, a certain Sir Clifford Constable has in his possession the skeleton of a Sperm Whale, but of moderate size, by no means of the full-grown magnitude of my friend King Tranquo's.

> In both cases, the stranded whales to which these two skeletons belonged, were originally claimed by their proprietors upon similar grounds. King Tranquo seizing his because he wanted it; and Sir Clifford, because he was lord of the seignories of those parts. Sir Clifford's whale has been articulated throughout; so that, like a great chest of drawers, you can open and shut him, in all his bony cavities — spread out his ribs like a gigantic fan — and swing all day upon his lower jaw. Locks are to be put upon some of his trap-doors and shutters; and a footman will show round future visitors with a bunch of keys at his side. Sir Clifford thinks of charging twopence for a peep at the whispering gallery in the spinal column; threepence to hear the echo in the hollow of his cerebellum; and sixpence for the unrivalled view from his forehead.[123]

---

[123] Above Beale's sentence: "This part of the book will likewise contain a short description of the skeleton of the sperm whale preserved at Burton-Constable, which I have been enabled to give through the kind permission of Sir Clifford Constable, Bart. to whom the skeleton belongs," Melville wrote some comment, now erased, with another comment, erased, at the bottom of the same page. Two pages later he wrote another comment on the skeleton, erased, and on the next page underlined "lord of the seigniories of Holderness."

The parody of guidebook language in the last two sentences is of course Melville's recollection of his 1850 visit to Saint Paul's Cathedral, where he paid his pennies for the famous whispering gallery, and for a sixpence saw the "unrivalled view" of London from the top of the great dome. It is a bold and grotesque imagination which correlates a Yorkshire whale skeleton with the majesty of Saint Paul's.

Before passing to precise figures concerning the whale's bones, Melville first lays "before you a particular, plain statement, touching the living bulk of this leviathan," for, indeed, few phenomena are more impressive than the monstrous mass of the full-grown whale. Scoresby, he says, estimates seventy tons for a full-size Greenland whale; Melville therefore estimates the sperm whale's weight at ninety tons: "he would considerably outweigh the combined population of a whole village of one thousand one hundred inhabitants."

Turning to the bones, Melville picks and chooses according to his whim, explaining, "I shall now simply point out what is most interesting in the general bulk of his unobstructed bones." Few as are his facts, they are all drawn from Beale's book, where Melville read the fourteen-page account of Sir Clifford Constable's whale skeleton. Since Sir Clifford's whale had not been a large one, Melville in order better to magnify and boast about the sperm whale, used his Tranquian measurements (i.e. from his imagination), so that his whale skeleton is seventy-two feet long as compared with forty-seven feet seven inches for the Yorkshire one. Allowing for this quite pardonable expansion, we can see that for everything else Melville kept his eye on Beale's fourteen pages, but with a cavalier freedom of translation which would have horrified the exact Beale. "I did not," says Melville, "trouble myself with the odd inches; nor, indeed, should inches at all enter into a congenial admeasurement of the whale." But Melville was careless because Beale was so very careful. An entire chapter of this sort of thing by Beale:

Of the Cervical Vertebrae

These are only two in number, the atlas and dentata: they resemble the human very much in form, except that the second has no odontoid process. The atlas is in width 3 feet 4 inches; in depth, 1 foot 7½ inches; in thickness, 6½ inches. The dentata is in width 2 feet 10½ inches; in height, 1 foot 11½ inches; in thickness, 9½ inches. This bone has a thick, but short spinous process.

— are dreary reading at best; and such facts were far from Melville's interest, who would certainly have agreed with Emerson's observation that "All the facts in natural history taken by themselves, have no value, but are barren, like a single sex." Or possibly with William James's remark: "I find this whole descriptive sort of treatment *tedious* as few things can be tedious, tedious not as really hard things, like physics and chemistry, are tedious, but tedious as the throwing of feathers hour after hour is tedious." Melville was impatient with the measuring-stick philosophy of life which attempted to reduce life and experience to mechanical logic and to the limits of calipers and test tube. Whales and whaling were not to be appreciated or understood merely through a bare catalogue of feet and inches, through descriptive throwing of feathers. Not by handling dead bones could the terror and mystery of whales and whaling, as Melville had known them and imagined them, be conveyed "livingly":

> How vain and foolish, then, thought I, for a timid untravelled man to try to comprehend aright this wondrous whale, by merely poring over his dead attenuated skeleton, stretched in this peaceful wood. No. Only in the heart of quickest perils; only when within the eddyings of his angry flukes; only on the profound unbounded sea, can the fully invested whale be truly and livingly found out.

Life, in other words, may be known only by living.

This is the brief history of Sir Clifford's whale skeleton which so delighted Beale, and thus stirred the satiric imagination of Melville. On the afternoon of Thursday, 28 April, 1825, the body of a sperm whale drifted in with the ebb tide onto the coast of Yorkshire near Holderness. Fortunately for the local scientists the news of this unusual sight was not quickly spread, so that by the time the Reverend Christopher Sykes, "an ardent promoter of science," reached the scene, the natives had not hacked away the flesh. Sykes measured the fish, finding it to be fifty-eight and a half feet from the snout to the division of the tail, and with a fourteen-foot spread of flukes. James Alderson, who recorded the discovery for the local scientific society, was struck by the astonishing difference between the blubbered carcass and the later, bared skeleton, the "unobstructed bones" of Melville. "Nothing," said Alderson, "can be more contrasted than the view of the animal perfect, and its skeleton. The enormous and preposterous mass of matter upon its cheek and jowl bearing no proportion to that of any animal whatever, when compared with the bones of the head." The bones were placed in great pits to macerate during the summer, and in the following season they were articulated by Sir Clifford's steward, Mr. Iveson, and by Mr. Wallis. The find was written up in various periodicals, none of which Melville had seen, but it was given scientific prominence by its description in Beale's classic study of the Sperm Whale. There Melville read:

. . . through the kindness of Mr. Pearsall of Hull, that the skeleton of an adult male sperm whale had been preserved at the seat of Sir Clifford Constable, Bart., at Burton-Constable in Yorkshire, about nine miles north of Hull, I embraced an opportunity which offered itself to visit it, for the purpose of gaining permission of Sir Clifford to inspect this enormous and magnificent specimen of osseous framework which adorns his domain. The whale to which this skeleton belonged was cast on the coast of Yorkshire, at a place called Turnstall, in the Holderness, in 1825, and which was claimed by Sir Clifford, he being lord of the seignories of Holderness. Its skeleton was preserved, and was articulated only about two years since, I believe principally under the superintendence of Mr. Wallis.

One example will suffice of Melville's free use of the bare bones of Beale to living exposition. Describing the various vertebrae, Beale, finally, wrote: "From the fifteenth to the twentieth terminal vertebrae there is a gradual decrease in size, losing also their upper spines, and becoming nearly round in figure. . . . The last bone of the vertebrae is nearly round, and is about 1½ inches in diameter." Reading this, and the many similar paragraphs preceding it, Melville summed them all up in a concluding paragraph, his eye falling on the word "round," which his particularizing pen made into a billiard ball, and to which he added a philosophical reflection:

> There are forty and odd vertebrae in all, which in the skeleton are not locked together. They mostly lie like the great knobbed blocks on a Gothic spire, forming solid courses of heavy masonry. The largest, a middle one, is in width something less than three feet, and in depth more than four. The smallest, where the spine tapers away into the tail, is only two inches in width, and looks something like a white billiard-ball. I was told that there were still smaller ones, but they had been lost by some little cannibal urchins, the priest's children, who had stolen them to play marbles with. Thus we see how that the spine of even the hugest of living things tapers off at last into simple child's play.

Although lacking the powerful discordance of Hamlet's "Thus we see that even a king may make a progress through the guts of a beggar," Melville's closing sentence is not unreminiscent of some of Hamlet's less agitated reflections to the gravediggers.

In "A Bower in the Arsacides" and "Measurement of the Whale's Skeleton" Melville has again followed his technique of treating a subject in two phases in two chapters: one a scene or a small story, fanciful and lively, the other more expository and informative. Discussing the bones of the whale, Melville's imagination has a disciplined wildness. From a beached whale in Yorkshire, from the "old Barbary traveller," Leo Africanus, from a tour by Melville through Saint Paul's Cathedral, from a scientific textbook in Natural History, and, finally, from the inexplicable mind of Herman Melville indulging in a brief moment of play as "monstrous as the gambols of the whales themselves," the reader may now move with his author to the gathering of the storm, the gathering of the threads out of which will be woven the tempestuous conclusion of *Moby-Dick*.

25

"We count the whale immortal"

MELVILLE HAS NOW DISCUSSED the whale in almost every aspect: biological, sociological, phrenological, paleontological, historical, anatomical, and economical. He is almost ready to renew the search for Moby Dick and to start building for his great climax. But one more item was left for consideration. "Does the Whale's Magnitude Diminish? — Will He Perish?" (105) is the final chapter in the great expository section of *Moby-Dick,* here termed the Cetological Center. The questions asked in the title of the chapter are answered on Melville's part by an emphatic "No!" Were whales larger in past ages? Though the ancients spoke of whales of incredible length, Melville tells us that Pliny and Aldrovandus both mention mammoth whales which were pure fancy. Later writers have done the same, he adds, "And Lacépède, the French naturalist, in his elaborate history of whales, in the very beginning of his work (page 3), sets down the Right Whale at one hundred metres, three hundred and twenty-eight feet." Melville — who has taken the Lacépède reference straight from Scoresby, and not from Lacépède himself [124] — will have none of this exaggeration: "No. The whale of to-day is as big as his ancestors in Pliny's time. And if ever I go where Pliny is, I, a whaleman (more than he

[124] Scoresby wrote: "The style of La Cépède is animated and poetical, and his Histoire Naturelle de Cétacées is a most interesting work; but the interest, in many cases, is augmented at the expense of truth. After this assertion, an example or two may be necessary. — One can hardly doubt, says he (page 3), but that Mysticetus may have been seen, at certain times, and in certain seas, 100 metres, that is 328 feet, long." Lacépède saw whales as "les symboles de la puissance éternelle et créatrice," a point of view similar to Melville's. Lacépède has this to say about the special might of the Sperm Whale: "Il y exerce un empire redouté: il ne se contente pas de repousser l'ennemi qui l'attaque, débriser l'obstacle qui l'arrête, d'immoler l'audacieux qui le blesse; il cherche sa proie, il poursuit ses victimes, il provoque au combat; et s'il n'est pas aussi avide de sang et de carnage que plusieurs animaux féroces, s'il n'est pas le tigre de la mer, du moins n'est-il pas l'éléphant de l'Océan?"

was), will make bold to tell him so." One might well construct a "Dialogue with the Dead" in which Melville's conversation with Pliny is imagined! Apparently Melville got the idea of considering the problem of the whale's diminishing proportions from Scoresby's sentence: "Large as the size of the whale certainly is, it has been much over-rated; for such is the avidity which the human mind receives communication of the marvellous . . . Yet I believe that whales now occur of as large dimensions, as at any former period since the commencement of the whale-fishery." Melville accepts the viewpoint of Scoresby in challenging the travelers' tall tales.

The question of the eventual disappearance of the whale through excessive slaughter is the second part of Melville's chapter. Here the *Narrative* of Charles Wilkes suggested the topic to Melville. Wilkes wrote in his last chapter — the one used by Melville in writing "The Chart":

> It will readily be seen that there is ample room for a vast fleet to operate. . . . An opinion has indeed gained ground within a few years that the whales are diminishing in numbers; but this surmise, as far as I have learned from the numerous inquiries, does not appear to be well founded.
>
> They have indeed become wilder, or as some of the whalers express it, "more scary," and, in consequence, not so easy to capture; but if we consider the numbers that continue to be yearly taken, there will, I think, be no reason to suppose that any great decrease has occurred. On an average, it requires fifty whales to fill a ship, and it would therefore take about five thousand whales annually, to supply the quantity of oil that is imported. This would appear but a small proportionate number, if these animals were as prolific as our herds on shore, when it is considered that they have a feeding-ground of twenty millions of square miles.

Taking the hint from Wilkes's words, Melville compared the whale hunt with the buffalo hunt in America and the elephant hunt in Siam, pointing out the differences in circumstances, and stressing the seemingly infinite range which the whales had to roam in as against all land animals. With further considerations, especially that the whales had the inaccessible polar regions to flee to, Melville concludes in a stirring flourish of rhetoric:

> Wherefore, for all these things, we account the whale immortal in his species, however perishable in his individuality. He swam the seas before the continents broke water; he once swam over the site of the Tuileries, and Windsor Castle, and the Kremlin. In Noah's flood he despised Noah's Ark; and if ever the world is to be again flooded, like the Netherlands, to kill off its rats, then the eternal whale will still survive, and rearing upon the topmost crest of the equatorial flood, spout his frothed defiance to the skies.

Considering these words on the whaling level, one must point out that Melville could not anticipate the development of the machine, the perfection of the whaleship so that whaling factories would one day set out to do more damage to the whale population in one month than the entire Nantucket and New Bedford fleet achieved in three seasons; [125] nor the appearance of bomb warfare with bombardiers mistaking innocent whales for submarines. On the other hand, the international agreements which have been made in recent years for the protection of whales may insure Melville's ringing prediction a good chance of remaining true. The concept of man and his institutions as interlopers on this earth, and man not worthy of his place of power, is not a new one; nor, indeed, is it an exhausted one, with all the potentialities for destruction now being devised by suicidal man. And if one wishes to consider the whale symbolically, and the ocean likewise, Melville is right in pointing out that the world-ocean is the element in which the whale has his eternal being. Make of it what you will, Melville's rhythmical celebration of the immortality of the whale is a fitting conclusion to his cetological center.

---

[125] According to *Time*, 3 June, 1946, Britain's whaling fleet of three factory ships, equipped with sonic submarine detectors and radar, returned from its first postwar expedition with little more than half the oil they had hoped to get. Whales, they reported, were not to be caught with the new devices, nor were they any more numerous than before the war. On the side of the whale, Melville would have been pleased at the whale's defeat of man's science, but he would not have cared for the news about their diminishing numbers.

V.

The Narrative Conclusion

WITH SPECULATIONS concerning the immortality of the whale, Melville finished the cetological section of his novel. Now we are ready for the narrative conclusion. Fully prepared through knowledge of the whale and whaling lore, we may participate intelligently and feelingly in the chase for Moby Dick. We also by now acknowledge (or at least are not overly skeptical) that the sperm whale is mighty and terrifying, and we now expect dire consequences when the *Pequod* meets the White Whale. Effectively Melville has blended information with narrative, fact with suggestion and strange omen, to prepare us for the climactic battle between ship and whale.

In fast, jabbing sequence scene succeeds scene in strange, demonic light and spirit and event. Through old Ahab, Melville clears the decks for action, both literally and metaphorically. The ship is stripped and made ready in ways more suitable to the madness of Ahab than to the rational planning of steady, practical Starbuck. The nautical proprieties are violated. We meet strange characters: the carpenter and the blacksmith — and ever Fedallah; and we behold stranger activities: the destruction of the quadrant, the manufacture of an ivory leg for Ahab, the forging of a special harpoon for Moby Dick. We behold with horror the spectacle of Captain Ahab, an Oedipus of Nantucket, pulling down around his own grayed head his doom and his damnation as he fiercely seeks what he believes to be (in Nietzsche's phrase) "the antagonism at the heart of the world."

Queequeg comes down with a mysterious fever, and Ishmael sits by him in attendance: "An awe that cannot be named would steal over you as you sat by the side of this waning savage, and saw as strange things in his face, as any beheld who were bystanders when Zoroaster died. For whatever is truly wondrous, and fearful in man, never yet was put into words or books."

371

Queequeg orders a "dark canoe" to be made for him, and thus he rests in a coffin which the carpenter nails together. But with all preparations made for death, Queequeg inexplicably recovers. His coffin becomes his sea chest and he carves it with strange figures. Later the coffin will be put to even stranger uses.

It would seem that we are now far from "my numerous fish documents" and that Melville's imagination is freely at work, unhampered by literary sources or checks. On the contrary. The retentive mind of Melville has not, like Ahab, abandoned his helps — the works of other men — but instead is still gathering further hints for elaboration. A striking example of new borrowing is traceable in "The Forge" (113), the scene in which Ahab orders old Perth, the blacksmith,[1] to forge a special harpoon for Moby Dick. Melville had handled harpoons, but it may be doubted that he had in 1841–1842 inspected them with an analytical eye, expecting some day to describe them in a book. Consequently, for Perth's making of a harpoon, Melville turned to the much satirized *An Account of the Arctic Regions* by William Scoresby, Jr.

There he read:

> The most important part in the construction of this instrument [the harpoon][2] is the shank: As this part is liable to be forcibly and suddenly extended, twisted and bent, it requires to be made of old horse-shoe nails or *stubs,* which are formed into small rods, and two or three of these added together; so that should a flaw happen to occur in any one of the rods, the strength of the whole might still be depended on. . . . A test sometimes used for trying the sufficiency of a harpoon, is to wind its shank round a bolt of inch iron, in the form of a close spiral, then to unwind it again, and put it into a straight form. If it bears this without injury in the *cold* state, it is considered as excellent.

---

[1] Interestingly, Professor George Arms, in " 'Moby Dick' and 'The Village Blacksmith,' " *Notes and Queries,* 192 (May 3, 1947), 187–188, has suggested that old Perth is possibly a satire of Longfellow's famous blacksmith.

[2] For harpoons and other whaling instruments the standard work is James Temple Brown, *The Whale Fishery and Its Appliances* (Washington: Government Printing Office, 1883).

Melville dramatized Scoresby's sober passage into a scene of Ahabian violence:

> "Look ye here!" jingling the leathern bag, as if it were full of gold coins. "I, too, want a harpoon made; one that a thousand yoke of fiends could not part, Perth; something that will stick in a whale like his own fin-bone. There's the stuff," flinging the pouch upon the anvil. "Look ye, blacksmith, these are the gathered nail-stubbs of the steel shoes of racing horses."
>
> "Horse-shoe stubbs, sir? Why, Captain Ahab, thou hast here, then, the best and stubbornest stuff we blacksmiths ever work."
>
> "I know it, old man; these stubbs will weld together like glue from the melted bones of murderers. Quick! forge me the harpoon. And forge me first, twelve rods for its shank; then wind, and twist, and hammer these twelve together like the yarns and strands of a tow-line. Quick! I'll blow the fire."
>
> When at last the twelve rods were made, Ahab tried them, one by one, by spiralling them, with his own hand, round a long, heavy iron bolt. "A flaw!" rejecting the last one. "Work that over again, Perth."

In transforming Scoresby's exposition into a dramatic episode Melville further adds the ghostlike figure of Fedallah, who gives the scene his fiendish sanction when "bowing over his head towards the fire, [he] seemed invoking some curse or some blessing on the toil. But, as Ahab looked up, he slid aside."

With the rods made, Ahab then directs Perth to make the barbs of the harpoon: "But now for the barbs; thou must make them thyself, man. Here are my razors — the best of steel; here, and make the barbs sharp as the needle-sleet of the Icy Sea." Perth's reluctance to use Ahab's razors for the barbs was his protest against the violation of the ordinary procedure of the whale fishery. Melville knew both from experience and from Scoresby's *An Account of the Arctic Regions* that ordinarily the harpoon's barbs were made out of soft iron so that they might easily be resharpened for repeated use against many whales. Dedicating this harpoon to one whale only, Ahab wished the barb made of the hardest available steel (a practice unknown to Perth) for one attack only.

The steel is tempered in the blood [3] of the three pagans, Tashtego, Queequeg, and Daggoo, to Ahab's delirious dedication, "Ego non baptizo te in nomine patris, sed in nomine diaboli!" [4] Since to Ahab the White Whale stands for the malevolent forces of the universe, he will capture him with an appropriately dedicated weapon — hoist with his own petard, as it were. The irony (such the blindness of Ahab's self-assertiveness) is that Ahab's overwhelming desire to capture Moby Dick is itself, by a profound metaphor, inspired by the powers of darkness. The dedication is completed, but now the harpoon must be attached to its hickory shaft. Again Scoresby came to Melville (and Perth's) aid:

> A harpoon was recently produced in Hull, the design of which was to prevent the loss of a whale, provided the shank of the instrument should happen to break. To effect this, the thick part of the shank immediately adjoining the mouth of the harpoon, was pierced with an oblong hole, in the direction of the plane of the withers. Through this hole a small rope, or a *strand* of whale line, is passed, and both ends secured to the line attached to the other end of the harpoon. Hence, should the shank of the harpoon break, the connection between the line and the part of the harpoon fixed in the whale is still preserved.

And Melville adapted Scoresby's information to his own narrative purpose:

> Now, mustering the spare poles from below, and selecting one of hickory, with the bark still investing it, Ahab fitted the end to the socket of the iron. A coil of new tow-line was then unwound, and some fathoms of it taken to the windlass, and stretched to a great tension. Pressing his foot upon it, till the rope hummed like a harp-string, then eagerly bending over it, and seeing no strandings, Ahab exclaimed, "Good! and now for the seizings."

[3] See Joseph Jones, "Ahab's 'Blood-Quench': Theater or Metallurgy?" *American Literature*, XVIII (March, 1946), [35]–37.

[4] In his study of Melville Charles J. Olson, *Call Me Ishmael* (New York, 1947), has made this scene an important part of his analysis of *Moby-Dick*.

At one extremity the rope was unstranded, and the separate spread yarns were all braided and woven round the socket of the harpoon; the pole was then driven hard up into the socket; from the lower end the rope was traced half-way along the pole's length, and firmly secured so, with inter-twistings of twine. This done, pole, iron, and rope — like the Three Fates — remained inseparable, and Ahab moodily stalked away with the weapon; the sound of his ivory leg, and the sound of the hickory pole, both hollowly ringing along every plank. But ere he entered his cabin, a light, unnatural, half-bantering yet most piteous sound was heard. Oh, Pip, thy wretched laugh, thy idle but unresting eye; all thy strange mummeries not un-meaningly blended with the black tragedy of the melancholy ship, and mocked it!

The difference between Scoresby's passage and Ahab's is not one of fact; it is a matter of the skill with which Melville has introduced Pip, and has sounded a note of forewarning — it is the difference between the V chord and the V^9 chord in the first inversion.

In reading the last chapters of *Moby-Dick*, at times the mind becomes bewildered by the accumulation of effects, the massing of meanings, if one approaches the book sym-bolically as well as literally. Any approach which does not recognize the symbolical richness and multiplicity of *Moby-Dick* is not worth long study. But space is limited and in-sight is bewildered by the multiplicity of meanings. Our at-tention must largely be confined to Melville's use of sources, even in the kaleidoscopic pages with which the great narra-tive closes.

Blindly, inexorably, Ahab moves to his tragic fate. Doom gathers about him like a net. He dreams of hearses, only to be told by Fedallah that he must see two coffins (one of them American) before he dies, and that hemp alone can kill him. Reassured, as was Macbeth when told that he could not be killed by man born of woman, Ahab confi-dently continues to hunt the White Whale. Delusions of grandeur seize him. In a frantic fit he hurls the quadrant to the deck and tramples it "with his live and dead feet" — a symbolical rejection of the aids furnished man by his society, in this case science.[5] Isolated Ahab feels himself able to cope with the sea and with Moby Dick. He needs no scientific instrument to find his way through the waste of waters. Humility is not in him, and the winged words of Father Mapple, we realize, have never reached his spirit. And, naturally, he who rejoices in this tragic rejection of society is Fedallah, for a "sneering triumph" passes over his face.

Fedallah and Ahab share the center of the stage in the next scene, "The Candles" (119). While in the Japan waters, the *Pequod* sails directly into a terrific typhoon, coming, significantly, "from the eastward, the very course Ahab is to run for Moby Dick." The thunder rolls, the lightning flickers dangerously around the ship, but Ahab defiantly refuses permission for the use of the rods whereby the lightning might be grounded to the greater safety of all. And then suddenly a most brilliant sight appears:

> All the yard-arms were tipped with a pallid fire; and touched at each tri-pointed lightning-rod-end with three tapering white flames, each of the three tall masts was silently burning in that sulphurous air, like three gigantic wax tapers before an altar. . . . "The corpusants have mercy on us all!"

The men are struck with superstitious terror; only Ahab and Fedallah refrain from cowering before the spectacle. Sailors of many centuries have been superstitious about the appearance of corposants.

During his South Seas travels Melville had never seen this remarkable electrical phenomenon. Traveling to Liverpool much later, he recorded in his journal, 13 October, 1849:

> About midnight, I rose & went on deck. It was blowing horribly — pitch dark, & raining. The Captain was in the cuddy, & directed my attention "to those fellows" as he called them, — meaning several 'Corposant balls' on the yard arms

---

[5] "Thou canst not tell where one drop of water or one grain of sand will be tomorrow noon; and yet with thy impotence thou insultest the sun! Science! Curse thee, thou vain toy; and cursed be all things that cast man's eyes aloft to that heaven, whose livid vividness but scorches him, as these old eyes are even now scorched with thy light."

& mast heads. They were the first I had ever seen, & resembled large, dim stars in the sky.

Undoubtedly Melville registered this scene for use; soon it turned out, in his next novel now in preparation within his mind: *Moby-Dick*.[6]

Melville had read the famous storm scene in *Two Years Before the Mast* in which corposants spectacularly appear. But other reading may have contributed to Melville's great scene. Among his favorite authors was Samuel Purchas, whose *Hakluyt Posthumous or Purchas His Pilgrimes* records the second voyage of John Davis with Sir Edward Michelborne, Knight, to the East Indies. In May, 1605, they were off the Cape of Good Hope when a storm blew up:

> In the extremities of our storme appeared to us in the night, upon our Topmast head, a flame about the bignesse of a great Candle; which the Portugals call Corpo Sancto, holding it a most divine token, that when it appeareth the worst is past. As thanked be God, we had better weather after it. Some thinke it to be a spirit: others write that it is an exhalation of moyst vapours, that are ingendred by foule and tempestuous weather. Some affirme that the Ship is fortunate where it lighteth, and that shee shall not perish. It appeared unto us two nights together, after which time we had a faire wind and good weather.

Purchas also includes Fotherby's voyage to Greenland, where is recorded as happening in December, 1614: "This night the Master and others saw a light upon the Forebonnet, which the Saylers call a Corpo Sant: it appeared like the flame of a Candle, and (as Sea-men observe) it always presageth an ensuing storme."

Melville was equally familiar with Hakluyt's *The Principal Navigations Voyages Traffiques & Discoveries of the English Nation*, the great classic of English travel. There he probably read "The Voyage of Robert Thomas Marchant into Nova Hispania in the yeere 1555," where is told:

6 Sumner W. D. Scott, "Some Implications of the Typhoon Scenes in *Moby Dick*," *American Literature*, XXI (March, 1940), 91–98, suggests that the typhoon scene is related to the rest of the book, saying that the conflict which has been going on between Starbuck and Ahab is resolved in the victory of Ahab during the storm.

I do remember that in the great and boysterous storm of this foule weather, in the night, there came upon the toppe of our maine yarde and main maste, a certain little light, much like unto the light of a little candle, which the Spaniards called the Cuerpo santo, and said it was S. Elmo, whom they take to bee the advocate of Sailors. At the which sight the Spaniards fell downe upon their knees and worshipped it, praying God and S. Elmo to cease the torment, and save them from the perill that they were in, promising him that at their coming on land, they would repaire unto his Chappell, and there cause Masses to be saide, and other ceremonies to be done. The friers cast reliques into the sea, to cause the sea to be still, and likewise said Gospels, with other crossings and ceremonies upon the sea to make the storme to cease: which (as they said) did much good to weaken the furie of the storme. But I could not perceive it, nor gave no credite to it, till it pleased God to send us the remedie and delivered us from the rage of the same, His Name be praised therefore. This light continued aboard our ship about three houres, flying from maste to maste, and from top to top: and sometime it would be in two or three places at once. I informed my selfe of learned men afterward what that light should be, and they said, that it was but a congelation of the winde and vapours of the Sea congealed with the extremitie of the weather, which flying in the winde, many times doeth chance to hit on the masts and shrowds of the ships that are at sea in foule weather. And in trueth I do take it to be so: for that I have seen the like in other ships at sea, and in sundry ships at once. By this men may see how the Papists are given to beleeve and worship such vaine things and toyes, as God, to whom all honour doth appertaine, and in their neede and necessities do let call upon the living God, who is the giver of all good things.

These accounts suggest that the corposants were symbols of good rather than evil fortune. To Ahab they come as a good omen; to the readers they are evil. Melville may have learned of their interpretation as bad-luck signs by reading in Robert Burton's *Anatomy of Melancholy* ("atheistical Burton" Melville called him):

Fiery Spirits or Devils are such as commonly work by blazing stars, firedrakes, or *ignes fatui* . . . which never appear,

saith *Cardan*, but they signify some mischief or other to come
unto men; though some again will have them to pretend good,
and victory to that side they come towards in sea-fights; *St.
Elmo's* fires they commonly call them, and they do likely appear after a sea storm.

This from Burton may have suggested to Melville the use
of the corposants as an *ambiguous* symbol.

But whether Melville's source was Dana, Purchas, Hakluyt, Burton, and / or his own recent experience aboard the
Southampton is a relatively unimportant matter, once established. What is to be noted is the amazing use which Melville made of the corposant scene, a use no less amazing than
Shakespeare's Ariel, the fiery corposant who dazed and dazzled
the sailors in the *Tempest*. "The Candles" reinforces Melville's presentation of the theme of self-reliance. Ahab's as-
sertive individualism has been underscored reiteratively
throughout *Moby-Dick*; but, except for the scene in which,
with mad ferocity, Ahab darts the harpoon at Moby Dick,
nowhere else does Ahab assert the inconsiderate rights of
his own egoism more categorically than in "The Candles."

To make his point, Melville incorporates material from
Zoroastrian doctrine as gleaned by him from the pages of
Pierre Bayle's *Dictionary* [7] (which had already served him
so well in his chapter on Jonah). In Zoroastrian religion, one
worshiped the God through his symbol, fire. But Ahab defies
the fire of the "candles" to assert his own Godhood against
that of God's emblem:

> "Oh! thou clear spirit of clear fire, whom on these seas I
> as Persian once did worship, till in the sacramental act so
> burned by thee, that to this hour I bear the scar; I now know
> thee, thou clear spirit, and I know that thy right worship is

[7] Bayle's article on Zoroaster was printed in *The Phenix* (New York,
1835), a strange little volume of esoteric lore, published by William Gowan,
a bookseller patronized by Melville, but Melville had, of course, the volumes
of Bayle at hand to consult firsthand, and also to consult the footnotes, not
included in *The Phenix*. It is doubtful that Melville had seen Anquetil du
Perron's three-volume French translation of the *Zend-Avesta* (Paris, 1771),
or that he knew about John Wilson's *The Parsi Religion: as Contained in the
Zand-Avasta* (Bombay, 1843). He may have known the various references
to Zoroastrianism in Gibbon.

defiance. To neither love nor reverence wilt thou be kind; and e'en for hate thou canst but kill; and all are killed. No fearless fool now fronts thee. I own thy speechless, placeless power; but to the last gasp of my earthquake life will dispute its unconditional, unintegral mastery in me. In the midst of the personified impersonal, a personality stands here. Though but a point at best; whenceso'er I came; whereso'er I go; yet while I earthly live, the queenly personality lives in me, and feels her royal rights. But war is pain, and hate is woe. Come in thy lowest form of love, and I will kneel and kiss thee; but at thy highest, come as mere supernal power; and though thou launchest navies of full-freighted worlds, there's that in here that still remains indifferent. Oh, thou clear spirit, of thy fire thou madest me, and like a true child of fire, I breathe it back to thee."

Magnificent as the assertion of the sacredness of the individual personality may be, it may also be misguided. As William James wrote:

After all, what accounts do the nethermost bounds of the universe owe to me? By what insatiate conceit and lust of intellectual discipline do I arrogate the right to know their secrets, and from my philosophic throne to play the only airs they shall march to, as if I were the Lord's anointed? Is not my knowing them at all a gift and not a right?

Had this been Ahab's view, *Moby-Dick* would have required a different, a more peaceful, ending. In Ahab spiritual blindness and heroism are blended for the creation of catastrophe. "The greatest act of faith," Justice Holmes once wrote, "is when a man decides that he is not God." [8]

The ominous events pile up. The magnetic needle of the compass is affected by the electrical storm — a warning to the hell-bound crew. Egotistically confident that he is able,

---

[8] In a note in his forthcoming edition of *Pierre*, Henry Murray cites a passage from Book 20 of Goethe's *Autobiography, Truth and Poetry* (a copy of which Melville bought in London in December 1849) in which Goethe discusses the demonic element found in some men: "a tremendous energy seems to be seated in them, and they exercise a wonderful power over all creatures." Reading the full passage one must conclude with Murray that it may have assisted Melville in his conception of Ahab. And in *Pierre*, Melville quoted Goethe's *"Nemo contra Deum nisi Deus ipse,"* which might well serve as an epigraph for "The Candles."

unaided, to sail life's seas, Ahab repairs the needle. The log is heaved overboard, but it snaps and sinks into the sea. Nothing daunted, Ahab boasts: "I crush the quadrant, the thunder turns the needles, and now mad sea parts the log-line. But Ahab can mend all. Haul in here, Tahitian; reel up, Manxman. And look ye, let the carpenter make another log, and mend thou the line. See to it." Never was the egotistic frenzy more vividly pictured. It is terrifying to the crew as well as to the reader. When Ahab moves away the Manxman mutters to himself, "There he goes now; to him nothing's happened; but to me, the skewer seems loosening out of the middle of the world" — a remarkably poetic statement of what is happening to the world of the *Pequod,* and what will happen to any world centered on uncontrolled aggression. (The Germany of Hitler bears testimony to this point.) The Manxman's words anticipate William Butler Yeats's lines three quarters of a century later:

> Things fall apart; the centre cannot hold;
> Mere anarchy is loosed upon the world,
> The blood-dimmed tide is loosed, and everywhere
> The ceremony of innocence is drowned.[9]

Omen follows omen. On her way to the Equator, where they expect to meet Moby Dick, the *Pequod's* men hear a weird, unearthly sound:

> At last, when the ship drew near to the outskirts, as it were, of the Equatorial fishing-ground, and in the deep darkness that goes before the dawn, was sailing by a cluster of rocky islets; the watch — then headed by Flask — was startled by a cry so plaintively wild and unearthly — like half-articulated wailings of the ghosts of all Herod's murdered Innocents — that one and all, they started from their reveries, and for the space of some moments stood, or sat, or leaned all transfixedly listening, like the carved Roman slave, while that wild cry remained within hearing. The Christian or civilized part of the crew said it was mermaids, and shuddered; but the pagan har-

9 From "The Second Coming," from *Collected Poems 1933,* by W. B. Yeats, copyright, 1933, by The Macmillan Company, and used with the permission of Mrs. W. B. Yeats, The Macmillan Company, Macmillan and Company, Ltd., and The Macmillan Company of Canada, Ltd.

pooneers remained unappalled. Yet the grey Manxman —
the oldest mariner of all — declared that the wild thrilling
sounds that were heard, were the voices of newly drowned
men in the sea.

It is Ahab who gives a rational explanation of the event
when it is told him the next morning by Flask:

> Those rocky islands the ship had passed were the resort
> of great numbers of seals, and some young seals that had lost
> their dams, or some dams that had lost their cubs, must have
> risen nigh the ship and kept company with her, crying and
> sobbing with their human sort of wail. But this only the
> more affected some of them, because most mariners cherish
> a very superstitious feeling about seals, arising not only from
> their peculiar tones when in distress, but also from the human
> look of their round heads and semi-intelligent faces, seen peer-
> ingly uprising from the water alongside. In the sea, under
> certain circumstances, seals have more than once been mis-
> taken for men.

This peculiar event, deftly inserted to prepare us for the
Pequod's doom, was inspired by Captain James Colnett's
account of his voyage to the South Seas, in the following
paragraph:

> When we were in Latitude 24°, a very singular circumstance
> happened, which as it spread some alarm among my people,
> and awakened their superstitious apprehensions, I shall beg
> leave to mention. About eight o'clock in the evening an ani-
> mal rose along-side the ship, and uttered such shrieks and
> tones of lamentation so like those produced by the female
> human voice, when expressing the deepest distress, as to oc-
> casion no small degree of alarm among those who first heard
> it. These cries continued for upwards of three hours, and
> seemed to encrease as the ship sailed from it: I conjectured
> it to be a female seal that had lost its cub, or a cub that had
> lost its dam; but I never heard any noise whatever that ap-
> proached so near those sounds which proceed from the organs
> of utterance in the human species. The crew considered this
> as another evil omen, and the difficulties of our situation were
> sufficient, without the additional inconvenience of those ac-
> cidental events, to cause any temporary depression of those

spirits which were so necessary to meet the distresses we might be obliged to encounter.

It will be seen at a glance that the episode in Colnett became the ominous incident of *Moby-Dick*. But Melville did more than take; he transformed Colnett's journalistic account into an episode of symbolic suggestiveness. The delusive cry is but a minor incident, but it foreshadows the greater delusion soon to be perceived: the hopelessness of capturing the White Whale. Ahab and the men are again warned, and again they will not listen.[10]

Immediately after this dissonant episode, the first tragedy strikes the world of the *Pequod*. The first man sent specially into the lookout to watch for Moby Dick falls, by a strange fatality, into the sea. The life-buoy cask hanging on the back of the ship for such an emergency, is thrown overboard to help the sailor, but both man and cask sink leadenly into the watery depths. This, the crew agree, is the fulfillment of the seal-shriek omen; now they may jettison their superstitious fears:

> Indeed, in some sort, they were not grieved at this event, at least as a portent; for they regarded it, not as a foreshadowing of evil in the future, but as the fulfillment of an evil already presaged. They declared that now they knew the reason of those wild shrieks they had heard the night before.

Delusion is contagious. The perverse spiritual blindness of Ahab has infected his men.

To replace the life buoy which sank, the carpenter seals Queequeg's coffin, and it is hung on the stern of the *Pequod* to serve in need. The *Pequod* has a brief gam with the *Delight*, a whaleship about to bury five men destroyed by Moby Dick. As one of the corpses drops from the deck of the *Delight* into the ocean, the splash strikes the side of the *Pequod* — a baptism for death (although Melville does not explicitly say so). And as the *Delight* sails away, her men jeer at the coffin suspended on the stern. But neither news nor baptism nor jeers swerves Ahab from his fixed purpose.

10 The reader familiar with Robert Frost's "The Demiurge's Laugh" will find an interesting contemporary handling of a somewhat similar episode.

With the baptism of death, the *Pequod* is prepared to meet the White Whale. Before the tremendous chase begins, there is a brief moment of quiet, one chapter of intermission. "The Symphony" (132) gathers into focus the themes and developments of the entire novel. It is Ahab's recognition, too late, of his fatal impulse, of the starvation that has been his because of his separation from his fellows, from the land. D. H. Lawrence described "The Symphony" as "the Gethsemane of Ahab, before the last fight: the Gethsemane of the human soul seeking the last self-conquest, the last attainment of extended consciousness — infinite consciousness." It is Ahab's appalled recognition that you can't go home again. Fittingly the scene takes place on deck, by night, as Ahab talks with Starbuck, his spiritual opposite — Starbuck the Christian, a man who accepts reasonable limitation; Starbuck the symbol of the social, normal life with wife and family and daily work. Ahab surveys his "forty years on the pitiless sea," to ask "how the richer or better is Ahab now?" And with felicitous symbolism he refers to himself as "Adam, staggering beneath the piled centuries since paradise." Yeats's lines might be applied to Ahab:

> He had much industry at setting out,
> Much boisterous courage, before loneliness
> Had driven him half-crazed;
> For meditations upon unknown thought
> Make human intercourse grow less and less.[11]

In his despair and bewilderment, Ahab senses, recognizes that he is doom-driven, but the "cruel, remorseless emperor" who commands him is his own conscience having been weakened by his surrender to evil whim.[12] Coleridge describes the sort of situation we meet in Ahab:

[11] From "All Souls' Night," from *Collected Poems 1933*, by W. B. Yeats, copyright, 1933, by The Macmillan Company, and used with the permission of Mrs. W. B. Yeats, The Macmillan Company, Macmillan and Company, Ltd., and The Macmillan Company of Canada, Ltd.

[12] The reader is urged to study carefully Ahab's long speech — although spoken to Starbuck (keeper of the Captain's conscience), it is virtually a soliloquy — and to think about the symbolical opposition of forces and concepts in the entire scene. Full elucidation has still to be written on this chapter by a poet-critic.

When once the mind, in despite of the remonstrating conscience, has abandoned its free power to a haunting impulse or idea, then whatever tends to give depth and vividness to this idea or indefinite imagination, increases its despotism, and in the same proportion renders the reason and free will ineffectual. . . . Hence the evil consequences of sin in such cases, instead of retracting or deterring the sinner, goad him on to his destruction.

The quiet reflections in "The Mat-Maker" have become turbulent and tragic in moving from Ishmael and Queequeg to Ahab and Starbuck. Ahab's great speech is that of a desperate and doomed man, betrayed by his blind, irrational urge to capture Moby Dick. His plight, Starbuck's, and mankind's, is described in the close of Arthur Koestler's *Thieves in the Night*:

We shall be betrayed because something in us asks to be betrayed. There is this urge in us for the return to earth and normality; and there is that other urge to continue the hunt for a lost Paradise which is not in space. This is our predicament; but it is not a question of race. It is the human predicament carried to its extreme.

In "The Symphony" is stated,[13] full orchestra, Ahab's isolation and exile from the secure land, from the world of the homely and familiar; Ahab's weariness, and his doomed pursuit of the avenging dream, leagued with the devilish delusion, Fedallah. Here, however, is his rational, perceptive moment, before the storm within him and outside breaks and the great symphony swirls to its crashing climax. For in the very next chapter, Moby Dick is sighted at last, and the fatal, unforgettable, three-day chase is begun. This speech of Ahab's is a strange equivalent to Macbeth's fifth act reflections about the futility of his quest for power; and to Ham-

---

13 The universality of Melville's vision is seen when one recalls the woe of Oedipus, in words which Ahab paraphrases:

Great God! to me
There is no joy in city nor in tower
Nor temple, from all whom, in this mine hour,
I that was chief. . . .
I have made me separate for ever.

let's cry of despair: "Thou wouldst not think/ How ill all's here about my heart."

The death of Ahab comes with appropriate dramatic suddenness, in exact fulfillment of Fedallah's strange prophecy that only hemp could kill him. Ahab having fleshed the harpoon in Moby Dick's side, the whale swims rapidly away:

> . . . with igniting velocity the line ran through the groove; — ran foul. Ahab stooped to clear it; he did clear it; but the flying turn caught him round the neck, and voicelessly as Turkish mutes bowstring their victim, he was shot out of the boat, ere the crew knew he was gone. Next instant, the heavy eye-splice in the rope's final end flew out of the stark-empty tub, knocked down an oarsman, and smiting the sea, disappeared in its depths.

The episode is possibly completely "original" with Herman Melville; but having seen his method of transforming materials from the fish documents, we might consider it possible that he has altered the following episode, described in Bennett's *A Whaling Voyage Round the Globe*:

> The ship Seringapatam, while cruising in Timor Straits, in the season of 1836, lost a man under the following circumstances. A boat, occupied in killing a whale, received a severe blow from the flukes of the animal, which passed so close to a boy pulling the after-oar as to graze his breast slightly; while the man at the tub-oar was either cast out of the boat by the same contact or carried away by the harpoon-line. His body was found entangled in the line, when the latter was hauled into the boat, but life was extinct. It was noticed at the time, that the concussion the boat received from the whale had cast some coils of line over the shoulders of the deceased, and it is probable that he was hurled from the boat when the whale again took the line; but his disappearance was so instantaneous that, in the confusion of the moment, neither his absence nor the events connected with it were immediately noticed by his companions.[14]

---

[14] In William Scoresby's *Journal of a Voyage to the Northern Whale-Fishery* (Edinburgh, 1823), pp. 123–125, is the story of one of Scoresby's men, who, upon reaching over to replace the taut line back on its stem, is dragged overboard when the bight of the line catches his arm. Much is made of the incredible speed with which it happened. The man's body was not recovered. Melville drew this book from the New York Society Library.

But whether or not Bennett's words suggested to Melville the method for killing his hero, we see now that in the careful exposition of such chapters as "The Line," Melville was not only divulging information but was also preparing us for what was to come.

The attack of Moby Dick upon the ship is also from a literary source, as I have earlier indicated. Melville has made free use of Owen Chase's description of the attack of the sperm whale upon the *Essex,* in which the ship was so effectively stove in that she had to be abandoned. In *Moby-Dick* Melville quoted, in a footnote, a long passage from Chase's pamphlet, italicizing the words which spoke of the malevolent and malignant mind, deliberately destroying the *Essex.* Such detail as the sharks snapping at the oars of the boat crew is also to be found in the Chase *Narrative.*

Melville's marvelous closing pages were not written through pure unconscious inspiration; they came from a mind actively at work in out-of-the-way books, eagerly seeking suggestions ripe for development. Most startling, perhaps, of all the findings of that searching mind, is a passage from Bennett's *A Whaling Voyage* which almost certainly served as the core of the closing episode of the *Pequod's* career: the episode of Tashtego and the sea-hawk. In the back part of his second volume — not, be it noted, among the cetacean notes which Melville mainly used — Bennett included many pages of ornithological description. Among the details important for the classification and description of the frigate bird, or sea hawk (*Pelicanus Aquila*) Bennett wrote:

. . . sometimes the bird may be seen balanced in mid-air, its wings spread but apparently motionless, its long forked tail expanding and closing with a quick alternate action, and its head turned inquisitively from side to side to inspect the ocean beneath; sometimes it wheels rapidly, or darts to the surface of the water in pursuit of prey; and at others, soars to so great a height that it is lost to vision, or becomes a mere speck in the sky — an elevation of flight which is alone sufficient to distinguish this from all other sea-birds.

They apparently take a delight in soaring over the masthead of a ship, from which they usually tear away the pieces of coloured cloth fixed in the vane. One individual, thus occupied over the Tuscan, was taken by hand by the man at the mast-head. The look-out at the time was kept by a landsman, remarkably tall and slender, and his mess-mates would never believe but that poor bird, accustomed to the figure of a sailor, had mistaken him for a spare spar, and thus fallen a victim to want of discernment.

Melville had already used Bennett's first paragraph in the sea hawk which seized Ahab's hat and flew away into the heights out of vision. The second paragraph, however, suffered a true sea-change into something rich and strange as Melville developed the "coloured cloth" to the red whaling signal at the mast, and "the man at the mast-head" became Tashtego:

> But as the last whelmings intermixingly poured themselves over the sunken head of the Indian at the mainmast, leaving a few inches of the erect spar yet visible, together with long streaming yards of the flag, which calmly undulated, with ironical coincidings, over the destroying billows they almost touched; — at that instant, a red arm and a hammer hovered backwardly uplifted in the open air, in the act of nailing the flag faster and yet faster to the subsiding spar. A sky-hawk that tauntingly had followed the main--truck downwards from its natural home among the stars, pecking at the flag, and incommoding Tashtego there, this bird now chanced to intercept its broad fluttering wing between the hammer and the wood; and simultaneously feeling that ethereal thrill, the submerged savage beneath, in his death-gasp, kept his hammer frozen there; and so the bird of heaven, with archangelic shrieks, and his imperial beak thrust upwards, and his whole captive form folded in the flag of Ahab, went down with his ship, which, like Satan, would not sink to hell till she had dragged a living part of heaven along with her, and helmeted herself with it.
>
> Now small fowls flew screaming over the yet yawning gulf; a sullen white surf beat against its steep sides; then all collapsed and the great shroud of the sea rolled on as it rolled five thousand years ago.

It is not merely a transformation in style, a dramatization of a commonplace anecdote that makes Melville's vortex scene so very great. It is that the details adapted from Bennett have taken on symbolical significance, to be seen by each intelligent reader as he wills. One symbolism may be missed because it has its significance in a fact familiar to whalemen. When the fish had been struck, the men on the ship would signal the men in the boats to return by means of a red flag flown at the top of the main-truck. So that here, the *Pequod* which itself has been struck, and not the whale, is signaling its return home, to its eternal home in Hell. The damned ship drags the sea hawk, symbol of heaven, with her.

Melville's vortex scene is perhaps his masterpiece of style. Sound and sense come together as only in the best poetry. The swirling polysyllables parallel the spin of the *Pequod* in the vortex; the long streaming clauses rise and fall with the swell of the ocean waves themselves, stirring the sensibilities of the reader to the breaking point as he mounts to the measureless crush and crash of the climax. And then, with a dramatic shift, the style becomes simple, sharp, the beat regular and clear in the short paragraph with which the scene closes. It is as though the great orchestra has suddenly stopped — save for the percussion, which beats pianissimo the concluding measures. The monosyllables of the closing words are as the falling of clods on the coffin of the *Pequod*.

D. H. Lawrence did not overpraise the great scene when he wrote:

> So ends one of the strangest and most wonderful books in the world, closing up its mystery and its tortured symbolism. It is an epic of the sea such as no man has equalled. . . . it is a great book, the greatest book of the sea ever written. It moves one in the soul.
> The terrible fatality.

"The drama's done. Why then here does any one step forth? — Because one did survive the wreck." With Ishmael the novel began; with Ishmael the novel closes. For most profoundly, *Moby-Dick* is Ishmael's book as much as it is Ahab's. Ishmael survives, you may say, because someone had to live to tell the story — an explanation which is not only vulgar but which also does not explain, since Melville could have writ-

ten from another point of view, in the third person. Ishmael survives because he was not entirely of the *Pequod,* either literally or symbolically. When Moby Dick struck the *Pequod,* Ishmael was some distance from the ship. By the time that he was pulled into the vortex it had subsided into a harmless pool. Afloat in the sea, he was saved by the coffin life buoy which suddenly, as though released by a spring, shot from the center of the circle and floated by his side. Thus even in his dying, Queequeg saved his friend's body as his companionship had saved his spirit. "Buoyed up by that coffin, for almost one whole day and night, I floated on a soft and dirge-like main. The unharming sharks, they glided by as if with padlocks on their mouths; the savage sea-hawks sailed with sheathed beaks." [15] On the second day Ishmael was rescued by the *Rachel* "in her retracing search after her missing children." [16]

With this epilogue of Ishmael's rescue, the great spiritual theme of *Moby-Dick* is rounded off. Ishmael had started for the South Seas in a state bordering on suicide, alone and angered at life. Ishmael learned the law of aloneness and the law of companionship, the psychological duality. But Ishmael has also learned the law of acceptance, to accept what Fate has in store for him, not to fight it in the manner of Ahab. And now, afloat with his coffin, he has achieved spiritual rebirth, symbolically pictured. The "Epilogue"

[15] Thomas Ollive Mabbott, "A Source for the Conclusion of Melville's Moby Dick," *Notes and Queries,* CLXXXI (26 July, 1941), 47–48, points out that in Southey's *Commonplace Book* in an extract "A Coffin Used as a Boat," ascribed to Mandelsoe, is the story of a Dutch prisoner who attempted an escape over water by using a disinterred coffin. It is a possible but not a proved source.

[16] Probably the *Rachel* and her search was suggested to Melville's amplifying imagination by a short section from *Ribs and Trucks:* "or lost in the haze of the horizon, and overtaken by night, with the accompaniment of an anxious gun from the guardian ship, which frets and worries and tacks about, with every symptom of motherly anxiety. The ensuing display of lanterns, as twilight thickens; then their gradual extinction when the recovered boat is swung up to its place alongside, with some congratulations and no little scolding, on the part of the tired ship-keepers." The latter part of this passage may also have been of use in writing "The First Lowering," but it is easy to see how Melville would take the tacking ship in its motherly anxiety and combine it with his knowledge of the Biblical Rachel, and produce the results in *Moby-Dick.*

deals with the metaphysics of resurrection. Ishmael has, in Keats's phrase, experienced a "dying into life." "Entbehren sollst du! sollst entbehren." It is the law of maturation; rejected, it is Ahab's heroic but futile and destructive struggle; ignored it is Flask's and Stubb's stupidity; accepted it is Ishmael's survival. Symbolically, it exemplifies the paradox of Christian doctrine (and of other religions) that a man must lose his life to save it. Or as Emerson put it: "The man who renounces himself, comes to himself." *Moby-Dick* has returned at last to the memorable message of Father Mapple.

THE END

Index